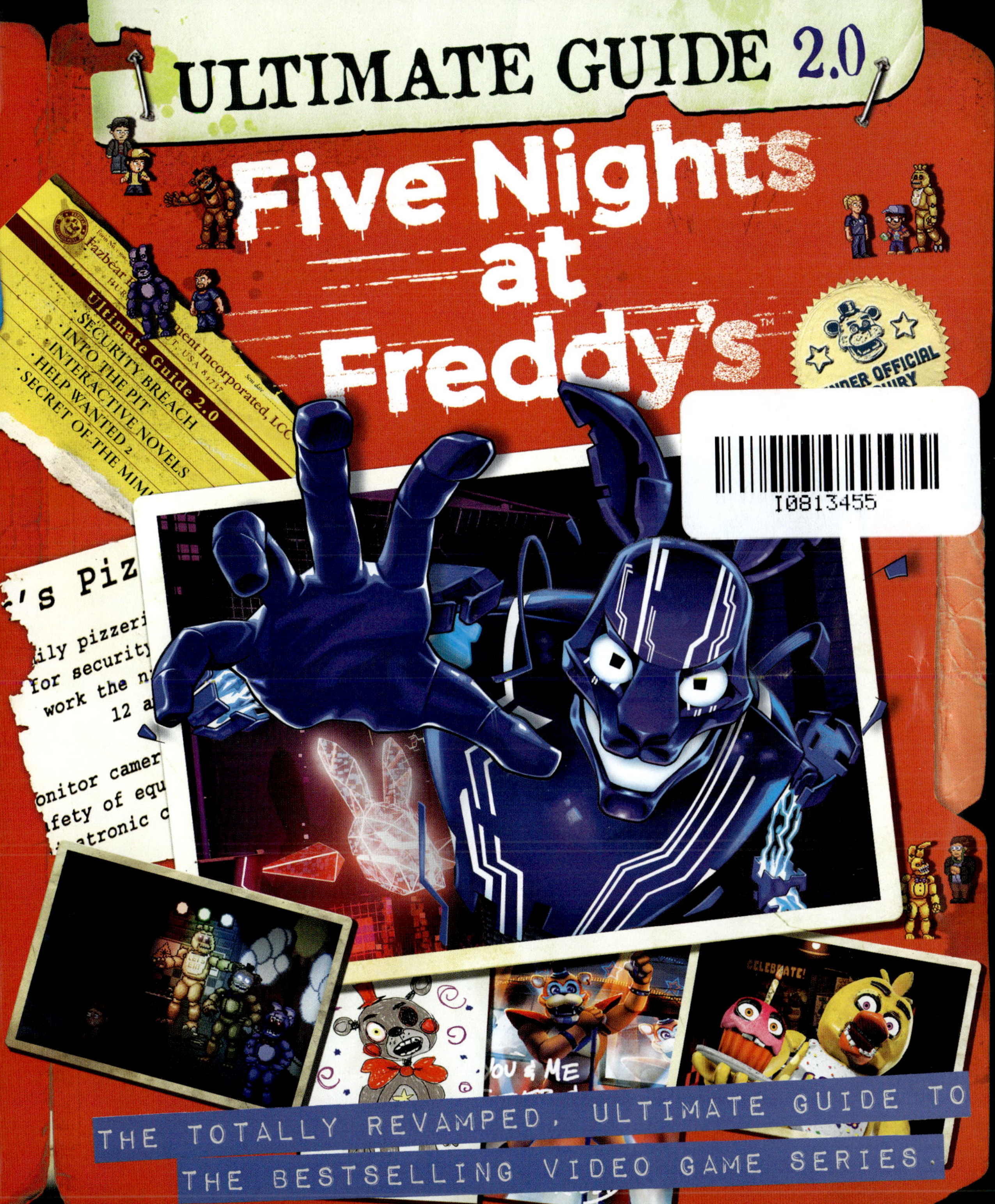
ULTIMATE GUIDE 2.0
Five Nights at Freddy's™
UNDER OFFICIAL
I0813455
Fazbear
Ultimate Guide 2.0
· SECURITY BREACH
· INTO THE PIT
· INTERACTIVE NOVELS
· HELP WANTED 2
· SECRET OF THE MIMI
's Piz
ily pizzeri
for security
work the n
12 a
onitor camer
afety of equ
atronic c
CELEBRATE!
YOU & ME
THE TOTALLY REVAMPED, ULTIMATE GUIDE TO
THE BESTSELLING VIDEO GAME SERIES.

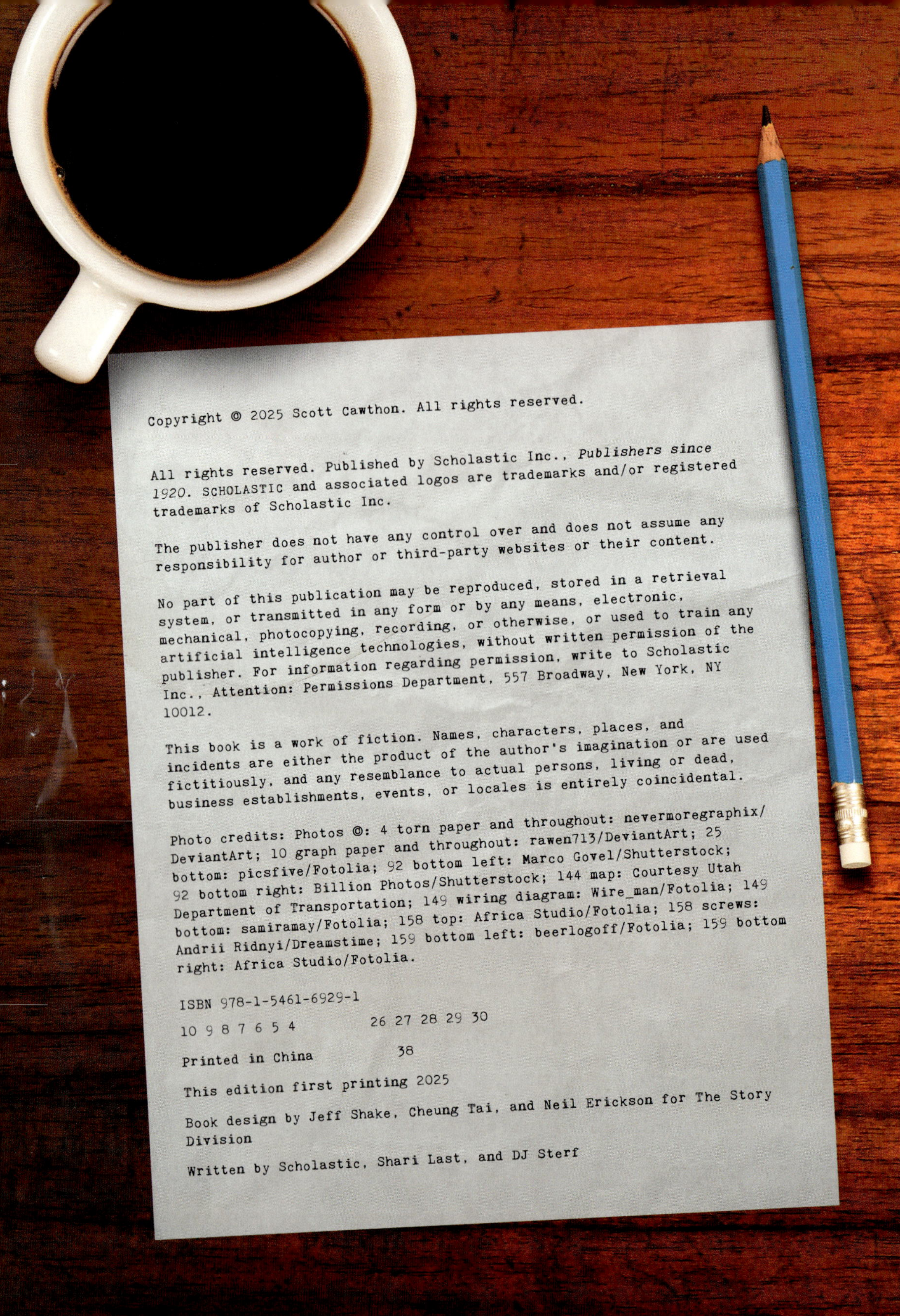

Photo credits: Photos ©: 4 torn paper and throughout: nevermoregraphix/DeviantArt; 10 graph paper and throughout: rawen713/DeviantArt; 25 bottom: picsfive/Fotolia; 92 bottom left: Marco Govel/Shutterstock; 92 bottom right: Billion Photos/Shutterstock; 144 map: Courtesy Utah Department of Transportation; 149 wiring diagram: Wire_man/Fotolia; 149 bottom: samiramay/Fotolia; 158 top: Africa Studio/Fotolia; 158 screws: Andrii Ridnyi/Dreamstime; 159 bottom left: beerlogoff/Fotolia; 159 bottom right: Africa Studio/Fotolia.

ISBN 978-1-5461-6929-1

10 9 8 7 6 5 4 26 27 28 29 30

Printed in China 38

This edition first printing 2025

Book design by Jeff Shake, Cheung Tai, and Neil Erickson for The Story Division

Written by Scholastic, Shari Last, and DJ Sterf

Table of Contents

Chapter 1

Five Nights at Freddy's

It's the game that launched a million screams.

Five Nights at Freddy's (*FNAF*) is a point-and-click horror survival game that was founded on a simple enough premise: Last one week working as a night guard in a pizzeria populated by homicidal animatronics. But what evolved from this concept quickly consumed gamers the world over.

Fast-forward a bit and (thanks in part to *FNAF*'s startling jump-scares) hilarious/terrifying Let's Plays dominated video-sharing sites, fueling the public's curiosity and resulting in billions of views. Still, gamers soon realized there was more to *FNAF* than just deadly animatronics.

Lurking in the darkened corners of Freddy Fazbear's Pizza are the threads of a disturbing mystery. This mystery—hidden throughout the game in posters that change, hallucinations, and even the mysterious fifth animatronic—has kept fans playing and replaying that first game since it was released in August of 2014.

So, what's all the hype about? We're glad you asked.

The Freddy Scoop

The game begins with a "Help Wanted" ad for Freddy Fazbear's Pizza. You'll be working as a security guard on the midnight to 6:00 a.m. shift. The pay is pretty bad at just $120 a week ($4 an hour), but we'll get to that later.

You occupy a stationary position in the office. You can turn to the right or left to see two sets of buttons. One button in each set shuts a door; the other turns on a light outside the door. You can also pull up a monitor to check the security cameras.

Once you land in the office, the phone starts ringing.

Things We Learn From Phone Guy:

1. Phone Guy apparently worked in the same office, but he's on his last week. If you die (dun dun duuuuuuun!), "a missing persons report will be filed within ninety days—or as soon as property and premises have been thoroughly cleaned and bleached and the carpets have been replaced." Yep. That sounds like a completely normal thing to say.
2. "If I were forced to sing those same stupid songs for twenty years, and I never got a bath . . ." Why haven't these animatronics been cleaned? Wait—how does one clean an animatronic?
3. The animatronics' servos lock up if they get turned off for too long. The animatronics used to be allowed to walk around during the day, but that was before "The Bite of '87." Apparently someone had a daytime run-in with an animatronic and lost his or her frontal lobe, but survived.
4. Since the animatronics will see you as a metal endoskeleton without its costume on,* they'll try to stuff you into a Freddy Fazbear suit. Yikes. So let's avoid that death.
5. You should only close the doors "if absolutely necessary." As Phone Guy says, "Gotta conserve power."

* Phone Guy's endoskeleton explanation doesn't add up. Bonnie often enters the Backstage, sees the costumeless endoskeleton sitting on the table, and never tries to put a costume on it.

Gameplay and Strategy

With your accessories like the light and fan running by default, the minimum power usage is 1 block of power at any time. Closing each door takes one block of power usage. Checking the cameras uses one block of power. Using either hall light uses one block of power, but the lights will automatically shut off when you go into the cameras. You start each night with 99.9% power. A deduction of Ø.1% of your power is done PER block of power being used, per second. There is also power leakage starting on Night Ø2, which gets worse until it peaks on Night Ø5.

You CAN MAKE FIVE POWER BARS APPEAR BY CLOSING BOTH DOORS, TURNING ON A LIGHT, AND FLIPPING OPEN THE SECURITY CAMERAS QUICKLY. BUT THE FIFTH BAR ONLY APPEARS FOR A SPLIT SECOND SINCE YOU CAN'T HAVE THE LIGHT ON AND SECURITY CAMERAS OPEN AT THE SAME TIME.

BWANANANANANANA MATH MAN!

Night	Leakage Frequency	Total Amount of Power Leakage per Night
Ø2	Every 6 sec	8.9%
Ø3	Every 5 sec	10.7%
Ø4	Every 4 sec	13.4%
Ø5+	Every 3 sec	17.8%

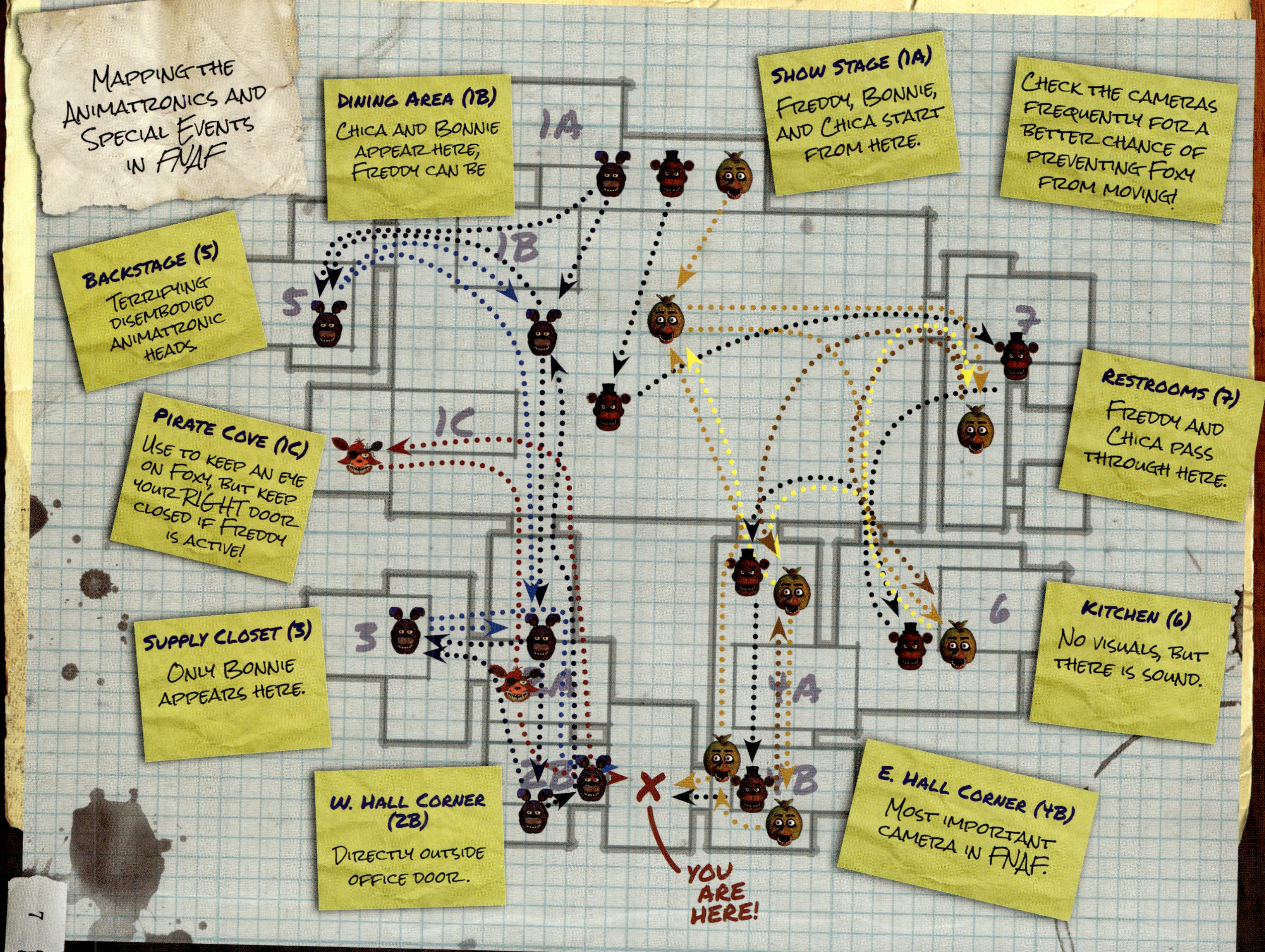
Mapping the Animatronics and Special Events in FNAF
Dining Area (1B)
Chica and Bonnie appear here, Freddy can be
Show Stage (1A)
Freddy, Bonnie, and Chica start from here.
Check the cameras frequently for a better chance of preventing Foxy from moving!
Backstage (5)
Terrifying disembodied animatronic heads.
Pirate Cove (1C)
Use to keep an eye on Foxy, but keep your RIGHT door closed if Freddy is active!
Restrooms (7)
Freddy and Chica pass through here.
Supply Closet (3)
Only Bonnie appears here.
Kitchen (6)
No visuals, but there is sound.
W. Hall Corner (2B)
Directly outside office door.
E. Hall Corner (4B)
Most important camera in FNAF.
You are here!
1A
1B
1C
2A
2B
3
4A
4B
5
6
7

Night	AI Levels for Each Animatronic			
	Freddy	Bonnie	Chica	Foxy
01	0	0 → 1 → 2 → 3	0 → 1 → 2	0 → 1 → 2
02	0	3 → 4 → 5 → 6	1 → 2 → 3	1 → 2 → 3
03	1	0 → 1 → 2 → 3	5 → 6 → 7	2 → 3 → 4
04	1 or 2 (random 50/50)	2 → 3 → 4 → 5	4 → 5 → 6	6 → 7 → 8
05	3	5 → 6 → 7 → 8	7 → 8 → 9	5 → 6 → 7
06	4	10 → 11 → 12 → 13	12 → 13 → 14	6 → 7 → 8

BLACK: 12:00 A.M. AI UPDATE GREEN: 2:00 A.M. AI UPDATE
BLUE: 3:00 A.M. AI UPDATE RED: 4:00 A.M. AI UPDATE

For each animatronic, there are checks at regular time intervals to see if the animatronic will move or not. The AI level plays into the likelihood of the animatronic moving. Every movement check involves a random number drawn between 1 and 2Ø: if the AI level is greater than or equal to the number drawn, the animatronic will move.

AI increases for everyone during the night, except for Freddy—his AI remains constant. But, even if you start a night with all Øs (like Night Ø1), by 2:ØØ a.m., Bonnie can move. Just because an animatronic is off to start, that doesn't mean it won't turn on at a later point in the night!

Animatronic Movement Check Intervals			
Bonnie	Chica	Foxy	Freddy
4.97 seconds	4.98 seconds	5.01 seconds*	3.02 seconds

* Foxy's advancement is also affected by how recently you checked the camera, with leniency randomly determined between 0.83 to 17.5 seconds.

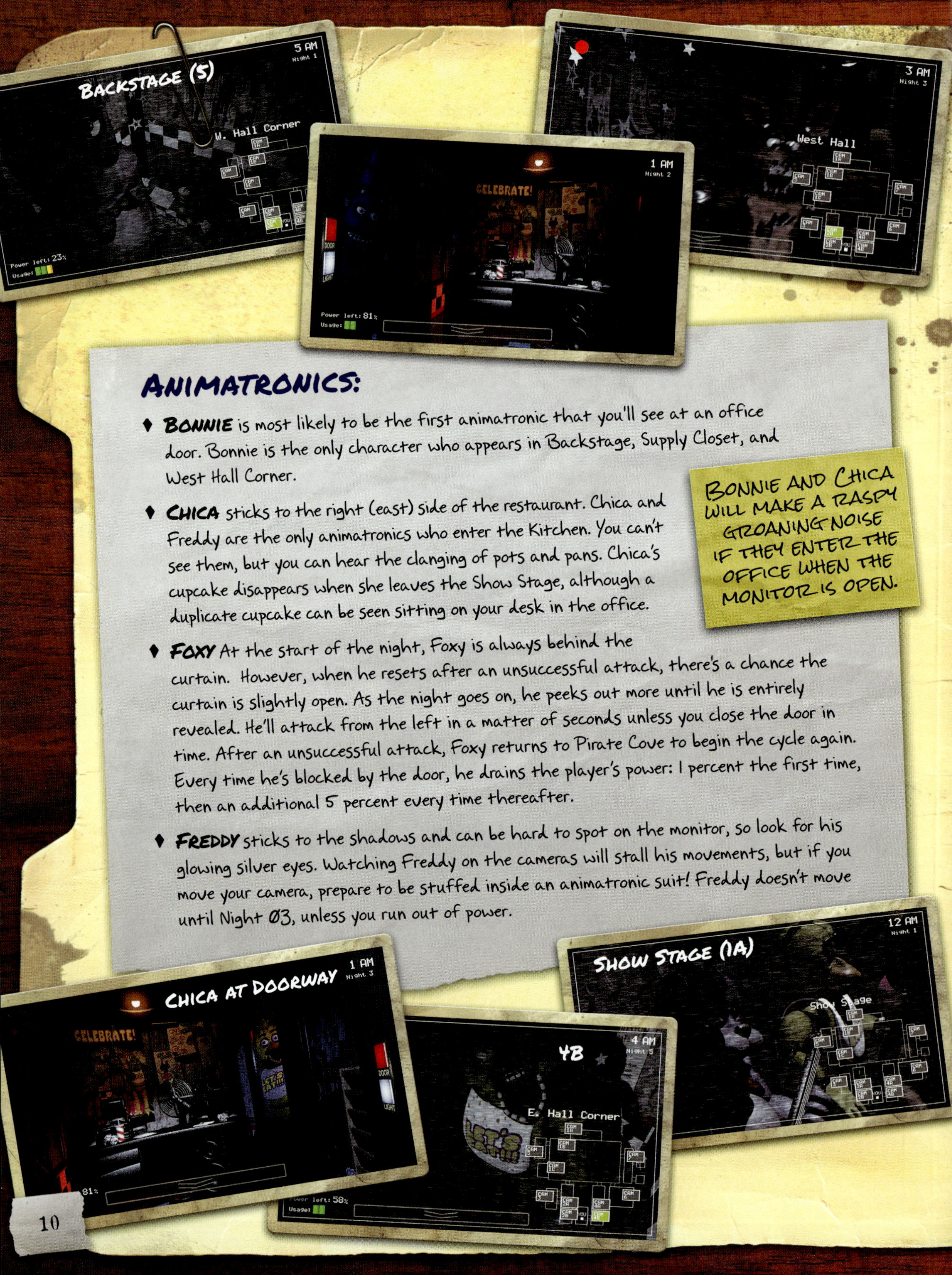

ANIMATRONICS:

- **BONNIE** is most likely to be the first animatronic that you'll see at an office door. Bonnie is the only character who appears in Backstage, Supply Closet, and West Hall Corner.
- **CHICA** sticks to the right (east) side of the restaurant. Chica and Freddy are the only animatronics who enter the Kitchen. You can't see them, but you can hear the clanging of pots and pans. Chica's cupcake disappears when she leaves the Show Stage, although a duplicate cupcake can be seen sitting on your desk in the office.
- **FOXY** At the start of the night, Foxy is always behind the curtain. However, when he resets after an unsuccessful attack, there's a chance the curtain is slightly open. As the night goes on, he peeks out more until he is entirely revealed. He'll attack from the left in a matter of seconds unless you close the door in time. After an unsuccessful attack, Foxy returns to Pirate Cove to begin the cycle again. Every time he's blocked by the door, he drains the player's power: 1 percent the first time, then an additional 5 percent every time thereafter.
- **FREDDY** sticks to the shadows and can be hard to spot on the monitor, so look for his glowing silver eyes. Watching Freddy on the cameras will stall his movements, but if you move your camera, prepare to be stuffed inside an animatronic suit! Freddy doesn't move until Night Ø3, unless you run out of power.

BONNIE AND CHICA WILL MAKE A RASPY GROANING NOISE IF THEY ENTER THE OFFICE WHEN THE MONITOR IS OPEN.

Codes, Glitches, and Secrets

- Hold down C, D, and + to skip a night.
- Click on the poster in the office to honk Freddy's nose.
- Try changing the date on your computer to October 31 and booting up the game.

Going on a Bear Hunt

In the West Hall Corner (camera 2B) is a poster of Freddy, which has a very small chance of changing. The poster becomes a close-up of Freddy's face, but his fur is golden, and there aren't any eyes in the mask. Once the poster changes, drop the monitor and an empty animatronic suit, "Golden Freddy," will appear in the office, alongside flashes of IT'S ME. Seeing him will cause the game to crash, but you can avoid this by bringing up the monitor again quickly.

You can also trigger Golden Freddy by inputting 1/9/8/7 on the custom night. You won't see the scene of the empty animatronic suit in the office, though.

- **Show Stage (1A):** This secret screen can only be found in the game files.
- **W. Hall Corner (2B):** Poster changes to an image of Freddy ripping his head apart.
- **Backstage (5):** All the parts in Backstage turn toward the camera, including the endoskeleton.

Lore and Theories

LOCAL NEWS

Local pizzeria said to close by year's end.

After a long struggle to stay in business after the tragedy that took place there many years ago, Freddy Fazbear's Pizza has announced that it will close by year's end.
Despite a year-long search for a buyer, companies seem unwilling to be associated with the company.
"These characters will live on. In the hearts of kids- these characters will live on." - CEO

FAN THEORIES: THE MISSING CHILDREN

If you really want to dig into the story of the game, keep an eye on the E. Hall Corner, where the Rules for Safety will change to a series of newspaper clippings that reveal the horrific secrets lurking at the heart of the game:

- Kids Vanish at Local Pizzeria—Bodies Not Found
- Five Children Now Reported Missing. Suspect Convicted.
- Local Pizzeria Threatened with Shutdown over Sanitation.
- Local Pizzeria Said to Close by Year's End.

allowed to walk
ut then there was the B
I-It's amazing that the human
vithout the frontal lobe,

ing your safety, the only
u as a night watchman here,
fact that these characters,
pen to see you after hours
recognize you as a person.
likely see you as a metal
without its costume on. Now
ainst the rules here at
ar's Pizza, they'll probably
lly stuff you inside
bear suit. Um, now, that
ad if the suits themselves
with crossbeams, wires, and
ces, especially around the
you could imagine how
head forcefully pressed inside

MISSING CHILDREN

Kids vanish at local pizzeria - bodies not found

Two local children were reportedly lured into a back room during the late hours of operation at Freddy Fazbear's Pizza on the night of June 26th. While video surveillance identified the man responsible and led to his capture the following morning, the children themselves were never found and are presumed dead.
Police think that the suspect dressed as a company mascot to earn the children's trust.

LOCAL NEWS

Local pizzeria threatened with shutdown over sanitation.

Local pizzeria Freddy Fazbear's Pizza has been threatened again with shutdown by the health department over reports of foul odor coming from the much-loved animal mascots.
Police were contacted when parents reportedly noticed what appeared to be blood and mucus around the eyes and mouths of the mascots. One parent likened them to "reanimated carcasses."

one of those ... se a bit of
Uh, the only parts
y see the light of
eyeballs and teeth
ront of the mask,
you these things
y, first day should

Five children were apparently lured to a back room by someone who wore a mascot costume to gain the kids' trust. A suspect was arrested and charged, but the bodies of the children were never found and they were presumed dead. Shortly thereafter, customers complained of odors and reported seeing blood and mucus around the eyes and mouths of the animatronics, implying that the bodies of the children were stuffed inside Freddy and his friends. This matches Phone Guy's words from Night Ø1—if you were to be stuffed inside a suit, "the only parts of you that would likely see the light of day again would be your eyeballs and teeth, when they pop out the front of the mask."

One thing seems certain—the animatronics themselves have been possessed by the spirits of the dead children, looking for revenge.

Another rare screen in E. Hall (4A) shows the posters replaced with images of crying children.

One Tragedy of Many?

In the years since the original game, it's been established that the Freddy Fazbear's Pizza where *FNAF* takes place is just one of many franchise locations, and its horrific murders were far from an outlier. Fans have instead directed their efforts toward identifying why this location was special, and when its murders may have occurred in the timeline.

MISSING CHILDREN

Five children now reported missing. Suspect convicted.

Five children are now linked to the incident at Freddy Fazbear's Pizza, where a man dressed as a cartoon mascot lured them into a back room. While the suspect has been charged, the bodies themselves were never found.
Freddy Fazbear's Pizza has been fighting an uphill battle ever since to convince families to return to the pizzeria. "It's a tragedy."

Fan Theories: Lingering Questions

The Bite of '87

Phone Guy mentioned "The Bite of '87," in which someone was attacked by an animatronic and lost their frontal lobe. This event is why the animatronics' movements are restricted during the day. But questions still remain around which animatronic committed the bite, whether an employee or a child was bitten, and what connection (if any) this bite has to the events of *FNAF4*.

Why Is Foxy Out of Order?

FNAF is the first time we meet Foxy, and while Pirate Cove may be "Out of Order," it's clear that Foxy, well, *isn't*. Other games and stories depict Foxy in various states of repair or disrepair for fans to speculate over. Some point to *Help Wanted*, where you ultimately repair him—while dodging his sharp hook and jerky movements—as evidence that Foxy is definitely unsafe for kids. Still others look to the *Foxy Go! Go! Go!* minigame in *FNAF2* (see page 31). Was an OUT OF ORDER sign and a functional animatronic the perfect way to lure kids to an isolated area? Or was Foxy decommissioned because, per the gameplay around Withered Foxy in *FNAF2*, he isn't fooled by a person in an animatronic suit?

IT'S ME

Another mystery that's kept the fandom talking. In *FNAF* it appears in various hallucinations on the Pirate Cove OUT OF ORDER sign, the East Hall walls, with Golden Freddy's appearance, and in-game flashes as early as Night 01. To make it even more confusing, it seems to be used by different characters . . .

- Teaser images for *FNAF4* ask, "Was it me?" implying that the phrase could be tied to one of the animatronic bites.
- *The Curse of Dreadbear* features an Easter egg that turns the whole prize screen purple, complete with a banner that says, "IT'S ME."
- In *The Silver Eyes* novel, "IT'S ME" is connected to the souls of the missing children inside the animatronics, when the ghost of Michael tells Carlton it is him inside the animatronic.
- In *The Week Before*, "IT'S ME" is used multiple times, possibly shedding new light on its meaning.

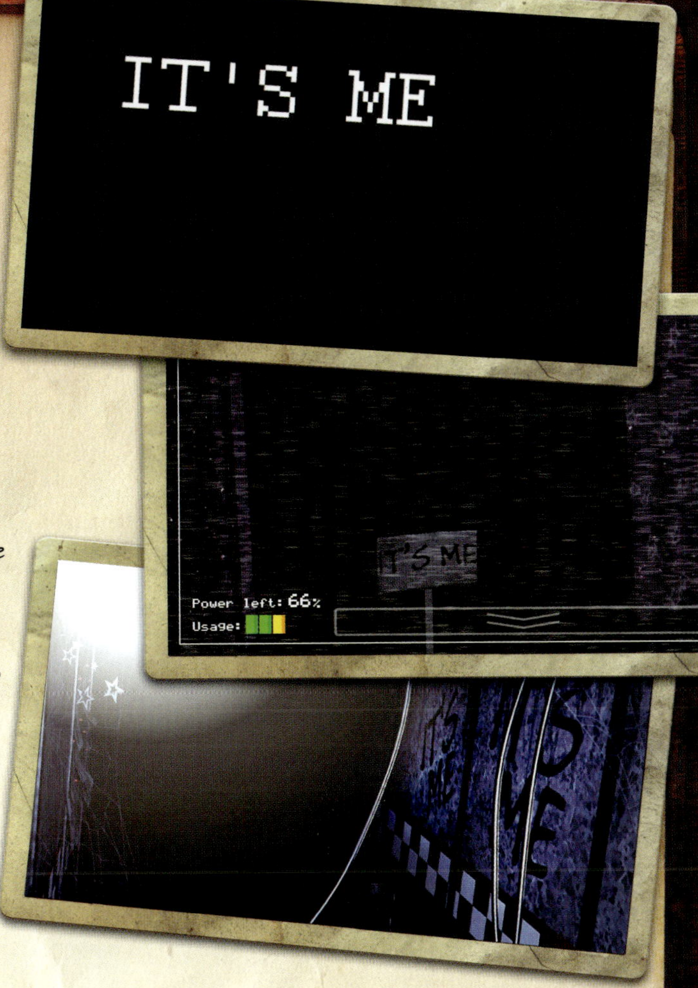

DURING THE FADE TRANSITION SCREENS, HIT ALT+F4 TO SKIP THOSE TRANSITIONS AND SAVE A FEW FRAMES. BUT BE CAREFUL! IF YOUR TIMING ISN'T RIGHT, YOU'LL JUST CLOSE THE GAME.

MIKE SCHMIDT

When you receive your paycheck at the close of Night 05, you'll learn that your name is Mike Schmidt. Many have speculated that Mike isn't just some security guard off the street. In *FNAF*, playing through to Night 07 gets Mike fired for tampering with the animatronics' AI (referring to custom night), which could imply that Mike has knowledge of the animatronics. Fans have also pointed out that he shares a first name with Mike from *FNAF4* (who seems to be "Michael Afton"), and "Mike," the owner of the Survival Logbook.

Chapter 2

Five Nights at Freddy's 2

The terror continues in *Five Nights at Freddy's 2* (*FNAF2*), a game that pushed many players to the limit in terms of . . . multitasking? Yes, there is a *lot* here to manage, and that's putting it mildly. Eleven animatronics roam the floor, looking to kill you—not to mention the other four animatronics that are apparently just there to populate your nightmares. Plus there's a frighteningly long list of to-dos: Keep the music box wound, keep the vents clear, strobe that flashlight in Foxy's direction . . . More animatronics now have a set of unique instructions (similar to Foxy from *FNAF*), so there are plenty of details to juggle.

Also new to *FNAF2* are the "death minigames" that are triggered with jump-scares. Each minigame has a creepiness factor off the charts and has spawned a flurry of theories about the rapidly expanding mystery at the heart of Freddy Fazbear's Pizza.

The game is also chock-full of new revelations from Phone Guy, like the two *additional* Freddy's locations, one of which he calls "Fredbear's Family Diner," the seeming origins of the franchise. But we're getting ahead of ourselves. Let's start with Night Ø1.

The Freddy Scoop

HELP WANTED

Grand Re-Opening!!!

Vintage pizzeria given new life!

Come be a part of the new face of Freddy Fazbear's Pizza!

What could go wrong?

$100.50 a week!
To apply call:
1-555-FAZ-FAZBEAR

We Meet Again . . . Phone Guy

Sounds like Phone Guy is still alive, so this game likely takes place before the events of the last one. That, or Phone Guy is immortal. Once again, you're working as a security guard on the midnight to 6:00 a.m. shift for Freddy Fazbear's Pizza, but the layout of the place is completely different. . . and there are no doors. Because why would a security office need doors?

Uh, hello? Hello,
welcome to your n
and improved Fred
I'm here to talk
things you can e
first week here
down this new an

Uh, now, I want
may have heard
know. Uh, some
negative impres
that old restau
for quite a wh
you, Fazbear E
to family fun
They've spent
new animatron
advanced mobi
walk around d
neat? -clears
they're all t
database, so
mile away. H
to guard you.

Uh, now that being said, no m
without its... kinks. Uh... you're only

Here's What Phone Guy Reveals:

1. Something very bad happened at the "old location," so Fazbear Entertainment spent a lot of money on their new animatronics, including facial recognition systems that interface with criminal databases.
2. The animatronics weren't programmed with a proper "night mode," so they wander around looking for people. As a temporary solution, a music box has been placed in the Prize Corner. Its music should keep *one* of the animatronics at bay.
3. You've been supplied with an empty Freddy Fazbear head to wear as a mask. When you wear it, any animatronic that comes into the office will see you, think you're one of them, and wander back out again.
4. This Freddy head won't work on Foxy, unfortunately, but shining your flashlight on him should make him go away.
5. The building lights will never run out of power, but the flashlight will.
6. Old animatronics are sitting creepily in the back room, but they're now used for spare parts. (These *look* like the animatronics from *FNAF*, but they're not exactly the same. Check the animatronics inventory for specifics.)

As we've come to expect from *FNAF*, things tend to unravel quickly. On Night 04, we learn the restaurant is being investigated and may need to close temporarily, as someone seems to have tampered with the animatronics' facial recognition systems. On Night 05, the restaurant is put on lockdown, with no one allowed in or out—especially prior employees.

END-OF-NIGHT HALLUCINATIONS

When you first boot up the game, as well as at the end of Nights 02, 03, and 04, you'll experience a nightmare. In it, you're wearing the Freddy Fazbear head and can only see a peek of what looks like the empty dining area from *FNAF*.

The first time, you'll see Bonnie and Chica on either side of you and hear unseen children laughing. The sequence will exit out, and code saying "err" will appear in the upper left corner of the screen. Night 02 features a repeat of this nightmare, but now Bonnie and Chica are looking at you. On Night 03, Bonnie and Chica appear angrier than before, and Golden Freddy stands right in front of you. The fourth and final time, Golden Freddy has disappeared, but Bonnie and Chica remain. The Puppet blocks your view no matter which way you look.

When the game "crashes" on Nights 02 through 04, a different code appears in the upper left corner of the screen: "it's me."

NIGHT 06

After completing Night 05, Jeremy Fitzgerald (i.e. you) receives a paycheck for $100.50. This amount probably would have felt more significant in 1987. In any case, making it this far brings up a menu option for a sixth night. Phone Guy will tell you that the restaurant is being closed down after one final event scheduled for tomorrow—a birthday party.

Your reward for making it through an extra night? An overtime paycheck for a measly $20.10.

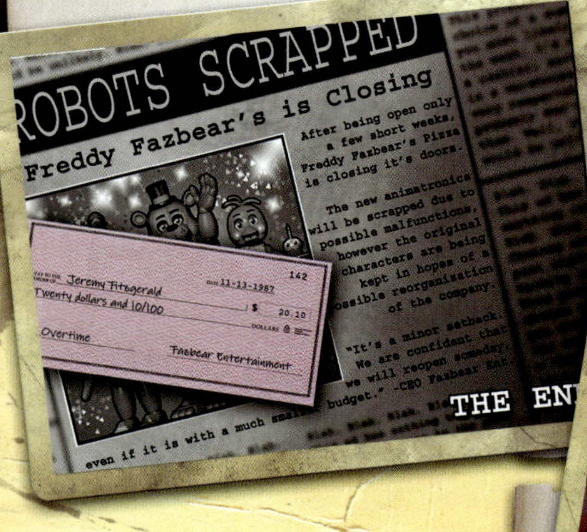
ROBOTS SCRAPPED

Freddy Fazbear's is Closing

After being open only a few short weeks, Freddy Fazbear's Pizza is closing it's doors.

The new animatronics will be scrapped due to possible malfunctions, however the original characters are being kept in hopes of a possible reorganization of the company.

"It's a minor setback. We are confident that we will reopen someday, even if it is with a much smaller budget." -CEO Fazbear Ent.

Custom Night

As in the first game, surviving the first six nights unlocks a custom night that allows you to change the AI settings of each animatronic. New this time around is a series of ten preset difficulties. For nine of them, beating the night unlocks a collectible toy for the office desk; beating the 10/20 mode earns you a star.

So, aside from some desk swag, what reward do you get for surviving a custom night? Nothing more than a termination notice, made out to—who the heck is Fritz Smith? Looks like Jeremy *did* get switched over to the day shift after Night 06.

Interestingly, they fire Fritz for the same reasons they fire Mike from *FNAF*: "Odor" and "Tampering with animatronics."

Game Mode	Freddy	Bonnie	Chica	Foxy	BB	Toy Freddy	Toy Bonnie	Toy Chica	Mangle	Golden Freddy
20/20/20/20	20	20	20	20	0	0	0	0	0	0
New & Shiny	0	0	0	0	10	10	10	10	10	0
Double Trouble	0	20	0	5	0	0	20	0	0	0
Night of Misfits	0	0	0	0	20	0	0	0	20	10
Foxy Foxy	0	0	0	20	0	0	0	0	20	0
Ladies Night	0	0	20	0	0	0	0	20	20	0
Freddy's Circus	20	0	0	10	10	20	0	0	0	10
Cupcake Challenge	5	5	5	5	5	5	5	5	5	5
Fazbear Fever	10	10	10	10	10	10	10	10	10	10
Golden Freddy	20	20	20	20	20	20	20	20	20	20

Character AI Settings

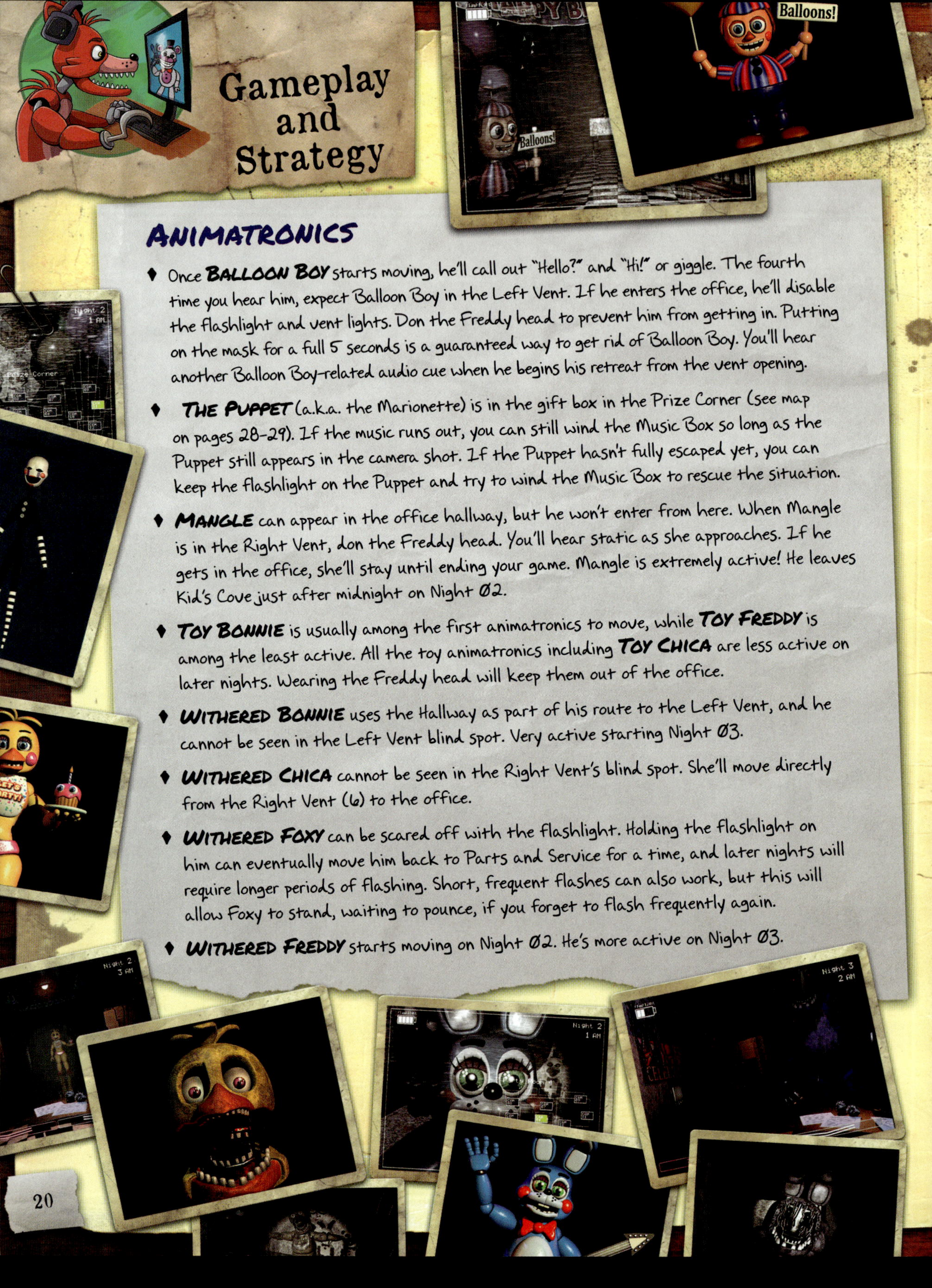

Gameplay and Strategy

Animatronics

- Once **BALLOON BOY** starts moving, he'll call out "Hello?" and "Hi!" or giggle. The fourth time you hear him, expect Balloon Boy in the Left Vent. If he enters the office, he'll disable the flashlight and vent lights. Don the Freddy head to prevent him from getting in. Putting on the mask for a full 5 seconds is a guaranteed way to get rid of Balloon Boy. You'll hear another Balloon Boy-related audio cue when he begins his retreat from the vent opening.
- **THE PUPPET** (a.k.a. the Marionette) is in the gift box in the Prize Corner (see map on pages 28–29). If the music runs out, you can still wind the Music Box so long as the Puppet still appears in the camera shot. If the Puppet hasn't fully escaped yet, you can keep the flashlight on the Puppet and try to wind the Music Box to rescue the situation.
- **MANGLE** can appear in the office hallway, but he won't enter from here. When Mangle is in the Right Vent, don the Freddy head. You'll hear static as she approaches. If he gets in the office, she'll stay until ending your game. Mangle is extremely active! He leaves Kid's Cove just after midnight on Night Ø2.
- **TOY BONNIE** is usually among the first animatronics to move, while **TOY FREDDY** is among the least active. All the toy animatronics including **TOY CHICA** are less active on later nights. Wearing the Freddy head will keep them out of the office.
- **WITHERED BONNIE** uses the Hallway as part of his route to the Left Vent, and he cannot be seen in the Left Vent blind spot. Very active starting Night Ø3.
- **WITHERED CHICA** cannot be seen in the Right Vent's blind spot. She'll move directly from the Right Vent (6) to the office.
- **WITHERED FOXY** can be scared off with the flashlight. Holding the flashlight on him can eventually move him back to Parts and Service for a time, and later nights will require longer periods of flashing. Short, frequent flashes can also work, but this will allow Foxy to stand, waiting to pounce, if you forget to flash frequently again.
- **WITHERED FREDDY** starts moving on Night Ø2. He's more active on Night Ø3.

Secret Animatronics

Golden Freddy

Unlike *FNAF*, nothing specific triggers Golden Freddy. He is active on Night Ø6 and in the custom night—randomly appearing in the office hallway as a ghostly head, or in the office itself as a crumpled animatronic suit. Quickly equip the Freddy mask to prevent Golden Freddy's attack.

RWQFSFASXC and Shadow Freddy

A shadow version of Freddy occasionally appears in the Parts and Service Room. An animatronic known as RWQFSFASXC, or Shadow Bonnie, can occasionally be seen standing on the left side of the office. Looking at RWQFSFASXC for too long will cause your game to crash. Every time you drop your monitor, you have a very rare chance of getting RWQFSFASXC. Flashing your flashlight before the 4-second mark is your key to success here.

Endoskeleton

A bare endoskeleton can be seen in the Prize Corner and Left Vent, though it never attacks the player. There are some interesting fan theories about which animatronic this endoskeleton belongs to.

JJ

An animatronic like Balloon Boy (but with pink eyes) is sometimes staring at you from under your desk. JJ doesn't appear elsewhere in the game and cannot kill you.

Super-Advanced Game Mechanics and Quirks

Night	Freddy	Bonnie	Chica	Foxy	BB	Toy Freddy
01	0	0	0	0	0	0 → 2
02	0	0	0	0 → 1	0 → 3	0 → 2
03	0 → 2	1 → 3	1 → 2	2 → 3	1	0
04	0 → 3	1 → 4	0 → 4	7	3	0
05	2 → 5	2 → 5	2 → 5	5 → 7	5	5 → 1
06	5 → 10	5 → 10	5 → 10	10 → 15	5 → 9	0 → 5

BLACK: 12:00 A.M. AI RED: 1:00 A.M. AI GREEN: 2:00 A.M. AI BLUE: 3:00 A.M. AI

NIGHT 02 RARITY: GOLDEN FREDDY HAS A 1 IN 1,000 CHANCE OF HAVING HIS AI SET TO 1 ON NIGHT 02 AT 1:00 A.M. THE USUAL CONDITION TO NEGATE THIS BACK TO 0 IS NOT ACTIVE, AND 1:00 A.M. HAPPENS AFTER THAT POINT. SO THERE'S A VERY SMALL CHANCE OF GOLDEN FREDDY HAVING AI = 1 ON NIGHT 02 STARTING AT 2:00 A.M.

NIGHT 06: AT THE START OF NIGHT 06, GOLDEN FREDDY HAS A 10% CHANCE OF HAVING AI = 1 INSTEAD OF AI = 0. AT 2:00 A.M. ON NIGHT 06, HIS AI IS SET TO 3, WHICH GIVES YOU A MUCH GREATER CHANCE OF SEEING HIM ON CAMERA FLIPS.

NIGHT 07 (CUSTOM NIGHT)

AI Caps

There are AI level caps that will max out before 20 on the custom night. In many cases, the caps were likely put in place to add variability to the movement patterns of most of the animatronics, as AI = 20 would force a movement success every time a movement check is done. Even if you set the cap to 20, the AIs will max out their caps as follows:

Withered Foxy (i.e., Foxy) caps at AI = 17.

Puppet's AI is forced at AI = 15 on Night 07, so you can't set Puppet's AI in the Custom Night menu.

Mangle, Balloon Boy, Toy Freddy, Toy Bonnie, and Toy Chica cap at AI = 15.

Withered Bonnie, Withered Freddy, and Withered Chica cap at AI = 15.

Golden Freddy caps at AI = 10.

Toy Bonnie	Toy Chica	Mangle	Golden Freddy	Puppet
0 → 2 → 3	0 → 2	0	0	1
0 → 3	0 → 2	0 → 3	0 → 0.1%@1	5
0 → 1	0	0	0	8
0 → 1	0	5	0	9
2	2	1 → 10	0	10
0 → 5	0 → 5	3 → 10	10%@1 → 3	15

Paper Pals

There is a 1% chance of having the possibility of Paper Buddy appearing on Night 07.

- There's a chance of one of the Paper Pals entering the office as a prop on the wall behind the fan.
- There may be some extra static effect if Paper Buddy is in your office, but it doesn't seem to affect the other animatronics' dynamics.

Music Box Emptying

- On Night 07 (AI level 15), the Music Box winds down from full to empty in 16 2/3 seconds.
- If your Music Box is empty, there's a check every second to see whether or not the Puppet will advance, based on AI/20 odds.
- On Night 07, when AI is forced at 15, every second there's a 75% chance that an empty Music Box will cause the Puppet to advance another stage out of the Music Box. On Stage 3, the Puppet is now loose and approaching your office.
- If you're on CAM 11 and flashing your flashlight at the Puppet, you can thwart this check.
- If your Music Box is empty and you tap the "Wind Music Box" button/area, it gives you an instant 2 1/2 seconds of charge. You should wind this up for longer than just a tap, but the game at least tries to help you out in this instance.

Mouse-Down Advantage (PC)

- On the PC version, if you have your mouse down, you just have to hover over the "Wind Music Box" button/area and it will work. This will give you a few frames of extra winding bonus as the Music Box winds up.
- So for most strategies that don't rely on CAM stalling, try clicking the "GO" button to start the custom night and then holding down your mouse from then on for the entire run.

TOY BONNIE

- There is randomness to whether Toy Bonnie will cooperate or not. There is also a chance of his walk-across animation playing out in full.
- The current strategy that various players and strategy crews have used effectively for dealing with Toy Bonnie is to click on various cameras that prevent certain animatronics from advancing.
- Toy Bonnie is stubborn—if he's at your vent opening, whether or not he responds to your mask being on is random. This can ruin your run, if Toy Bonnie decides not to walk across while you have your mask on.
- In theory, there is no limit to how many "rejections" of walking across that Toy Bonnie can do, so there is a chance Toy Bonnie may decide to never leave.
- With no other threats, every Ø.5 seconds, Toy Bonnie has a 5Ø% chance of walking across, if you have your Freddy Mask on.
- With other threats present, every 1 second, Toy Bonnie has a 33.33% chance of walking across if you have your Freddy Mask on.
- On average (but not always), he takes about 3 seconds to start the walk-across animation, but the full animation takes 5 seconds. This is harsh because the Music Box will run down faster on later nights, and especially on Night Ø7.

NIGHT 01: YOU HAVE 100 FRAMES AT 60 FRAMES PER SECOND TO PUT ON YOUR MASK (1 2/3 SECONDS)

NIGHT 02: 80 FRAMES (1 1/3 SECONDS)

NIGHT 03: 60 FRAMES (1 SECOND)

NIGHT 04: 55 FRAMES (11/12 SECOND)

NIGHTS 05 AND 06: 50 FRAMES (5/6 SECOND)

NIGHT 07: 45 FRAMES (3/4 SECOND)

Desk Animatronics

Desk Animatronics appear at your desk for an attack and include Withered Freddy, Withered Bonnie, Withered Chica, and Toy Freddy (yes, Toy Freddy).

At every 10-second juncture in the night, if you are winding the Music Box on CAM 11 and a Desk Animatronic is an immediate threat, your camera will be forcibly pulled down, and you will have to react.

Reacting to Desk Animatronics

There is greater leniency on earlier nights as you get used to the game. But even if you have super low AI on the custom night, you have to have very fast reaction times with the mask.

Withered Foxy

- Even at AI = 0, and with the Ladies Night preset, Foxy will appear and be a threat during the night.
- Withered Foxy operates like a thermometer—if you don't flash him with the flashlight, his anger builds up, but when you do flash him, his anger goes down.
- If you don't load up Foxy with flashes from your flashlight, at every 10-second juncture there will be a check to determine whether or not Foxy will attack.
- You can force Foxy back to Parts and Service for awhile, but you have to load up enough time flashing him with the flashlight.
- Later nights will take more flash time to force him out of the hallway and back to Parts and Service.
- Realistically, a quick flash right before the 10-second marks will keep Foxy in the Hallway staring at you, but he won't be angry enough to jump at you if you sync your cycles with the various movement checks going on.
- On Night 07, if you sit with your flashlight on Foxy for 11 2/3 seconds straight, Foxy should retreat on the next movement check, but your Music Box will basically be dead. On earlier nights you have to flash Foxy less to cause this retreat.

Because the Flashlight has a Battery Meter, you can't infinitely flash Foxy.

Foxy can return after going back to Parts and Service. Foxy can be very harsh in how often he appears and how much attention he requires.

Vent Animatronics

The other Vent Animatronics are BB, Toy Chica, and Mangle. Wearing a mask for 5 consecutive seconds guarantees these three will leave. Every second you have the mask on, there's a 10% chance that the animatronic will leave. Taking the mask off will reset the counter to 0, so you have to be decisive here!

BB

- When BB is at the vent opening, you will always hear the "HI!" sound effect, but this sound effect can also be a random effect as he leaves.
- On the approach, "HI!" is your time to check the left vent opening.
- BB stealing your batteries will usually end in a jump-scare from Foxy, unless you're right at the 6:00 a.m. mark. You can still win, but on a later night, and especially on a 10/20 run, this has to be right at the end of the night for this to be a possible win.

Toy Chica

- Toy Chica used to have a walk-across animation, but in the final game the animation was removed. Chica responds to the Freddy Mask being on.

Mangle

- The sound cues of Mangle are very helpful. No visual cue is needed to determine whether Mangle has left or not!

The "Blackout Phase"

- This is when a Desk Animatronic or Toy Bonnie causes the power surge effect.
- Lasts 300 frames at 60 frames per second, which comes to a total of 5 seconds.
- If an animatronic is attacking your desk and you have your mask on during this phase, it is often the case that any vent animatronic present will also leave, since you will have your mask on for 5 consecutive seconds.

Version 1.0 Mask + Flashlight Combo

In Version 1.0 of the game you could have your Mask on at the same time as your flashlight with a little bit of a glitch. This is now disallowed, but there are some ways to glitch the Mask/camera dynamics if you're really getting silly.

Rare Screens

Eyeless Animatronics: Withered Freddy, Toy Bonnie, and Withered Foxy each have a 1 in 1,000 chance of appearing in various scenarios:

- Withered Freddy after losing a night
- Toy Bonnie at Start of the Night
- Withered Foxy at Start of the Game

You can use CD+ to finish any night instantly, but unlike in *FNAF1*, you have to position your mouse pointer over Toy Freddy's nose on the CELEBRATE poster on the left office wall for this to work.

Cycles:

Every hour is 70 seconds long in newer ClickTeam builds. Each Night is 420 seconds in total, and every 10 seconds you have the following:

- Minor cycle at every 5 seconds
- Major cycle at every 10 seconds

This means there are 84 minor cycles, and 42 major cycles, through the night.

Right Vent Camp Principle

If you handle the Right Vent animatronics, you usually won't have to check your Left Vent much, if at all. So, some strategies allow you to focus on the right side instead of going left, then middle, then right. Always flash Foxy when you can!

"Flash your light at him from time to time" —Notion from Phone Guy

Technically, you can tap the flashlight and then stall out Foxy for a little bit, if you're flashing him right before a major movement check. However, you will likely do better on most nights by holding down the flashlight for a bit longer than a few taps, so that you decrease Foxy's "anger" meter a substantial amount.

Mapping Paths of the Withered Animatronics

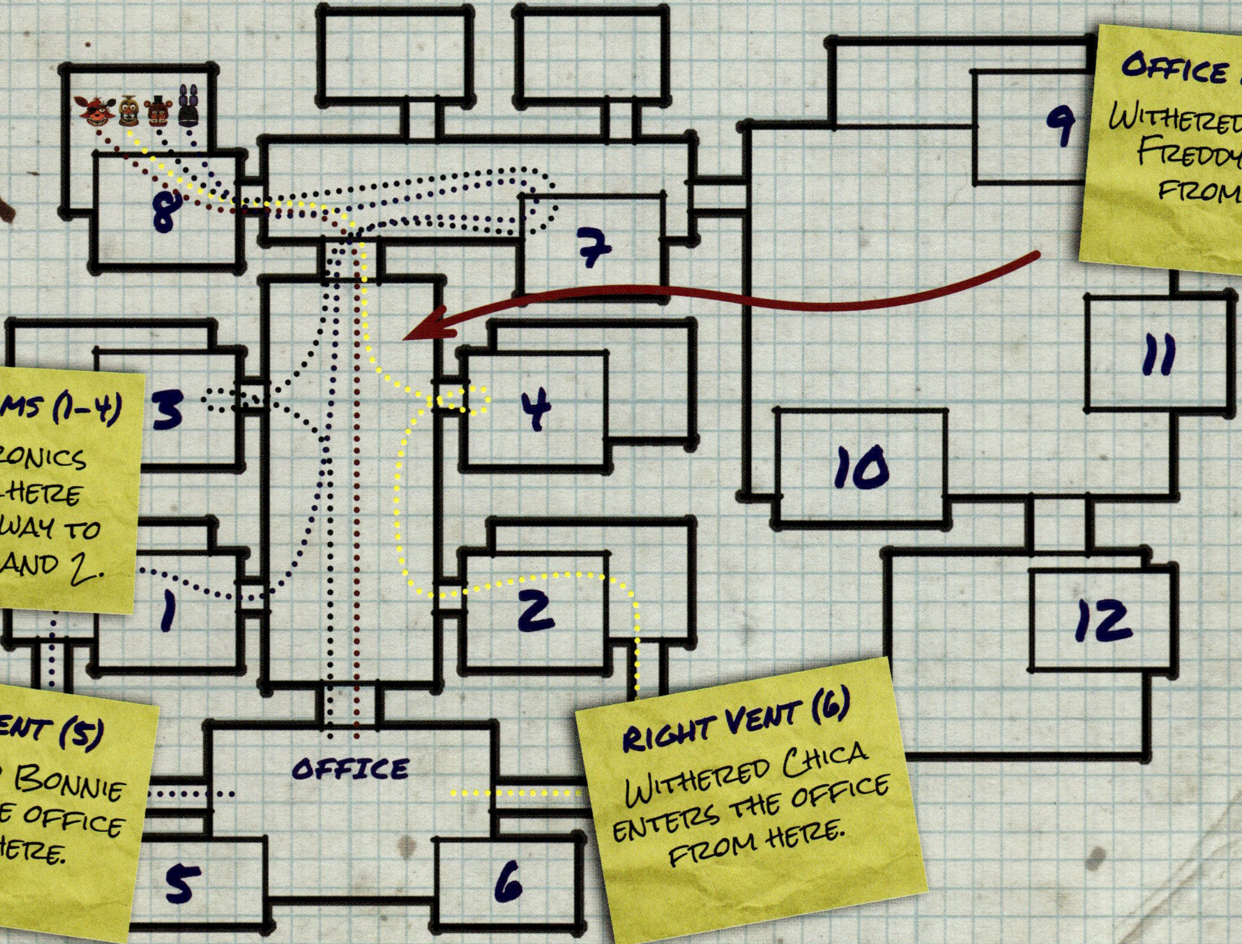

Office Hallway
Withered Foxy and Freddy attack from here.

Party Rooms (1–4)
Animatronics appear here on their way to vents in 1 and 2.

Left Vent (5)
Withered Bonnie enters the office from here.

Right Vent (6)
Withered Chica enters the office from here.

8
7
9
3
4
11
10
1
2
12
Office
5
6

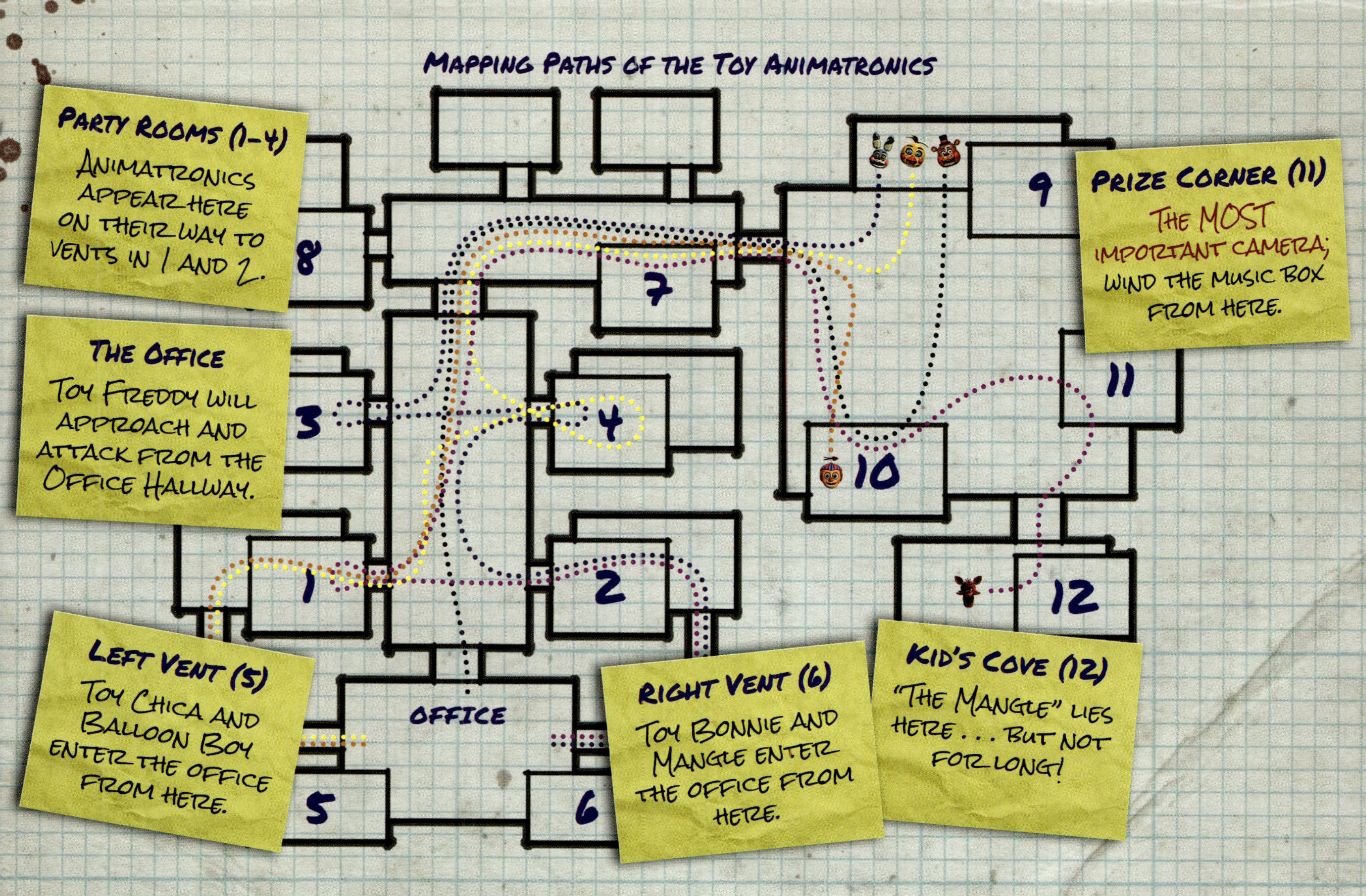

Mapping Paths of the Toy Animatronics
Party Rooms (1–4)
Animatronics appear here on their way to vents in 1 and 2.
The Office
Toy Freddy will approach and attack from the Office Hallway.
Left Vent (5)
Toy Chica and Balloon Boy enter the office from here.
Right Vent (6)
Toy Bonnie and Mangle enter the office from here.
Kid's Cove (12)
"The Mangle" lies here . . . but not for long!
Prize Corner (11)
The MOST important camera; wind the music box from here.
Office
1
2
3
4
5
6
7
8
9
10
11
12

Codes, Glitches, and Secrets

Almost everything about this game is different, but one thing stayed the same: Click on the poster in the office to honk Freddy's nose.

FNAF·2 RETRO ARCADE

Death minigame: SAVETHEM

Dying in *FNAF2* might trigger one of several minigames rendered in 8-bit graphics. These are perhaps the most talked-about element of the game because they're so different from anything we've seen before. The first minigame is known as SAVETHEM (the phrase spelled by the letters you will hear being called out). Using the keyboard for movement (W = up, A = left, S = down, D = right), you, as Freddy, follow the Puppet through a map of the restaurant until reaching the Prize Corner. You'll pass slumped-over children and pools of blood along the way.

On rare occasions, "Purple Guy" will end the minigame early. If Purple Guy appears, a scrap of text will appear in the lower left corner following the game crash: "you can't."

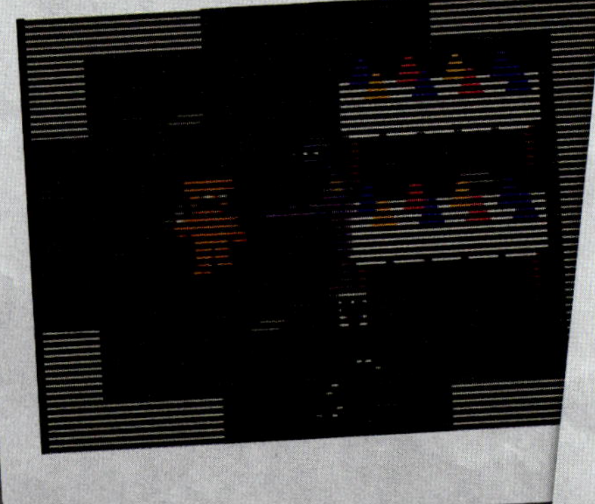

FNAF·2 RETRO ARCADE

Death minigame: Take Cake to the Children

This post-death minigame has Freddy taking cake to six children (with another child visible outside the room). Walking into the room changes the kids' color to green—if you turn them all green at once, you lose control of Freddy. Neglecting the kids changes their color to red. Midway through the game, a car pulls up outside. The aforementioned Purple Guy exits and kills the crying child, who turns gray. The letters being called out are "S-A-V-E-H-I-M" . . . but you can't. In fact, you move slower and slower until all of the children turn red. The minigame ends with a jump-scare courtesy of the Puppet.

It's important to note that Freddy looks slightly different in this minigame than he does in SAVETHEM. The minigame map here is also the smallest. These discrepancies have an important bearing on some fan theories.

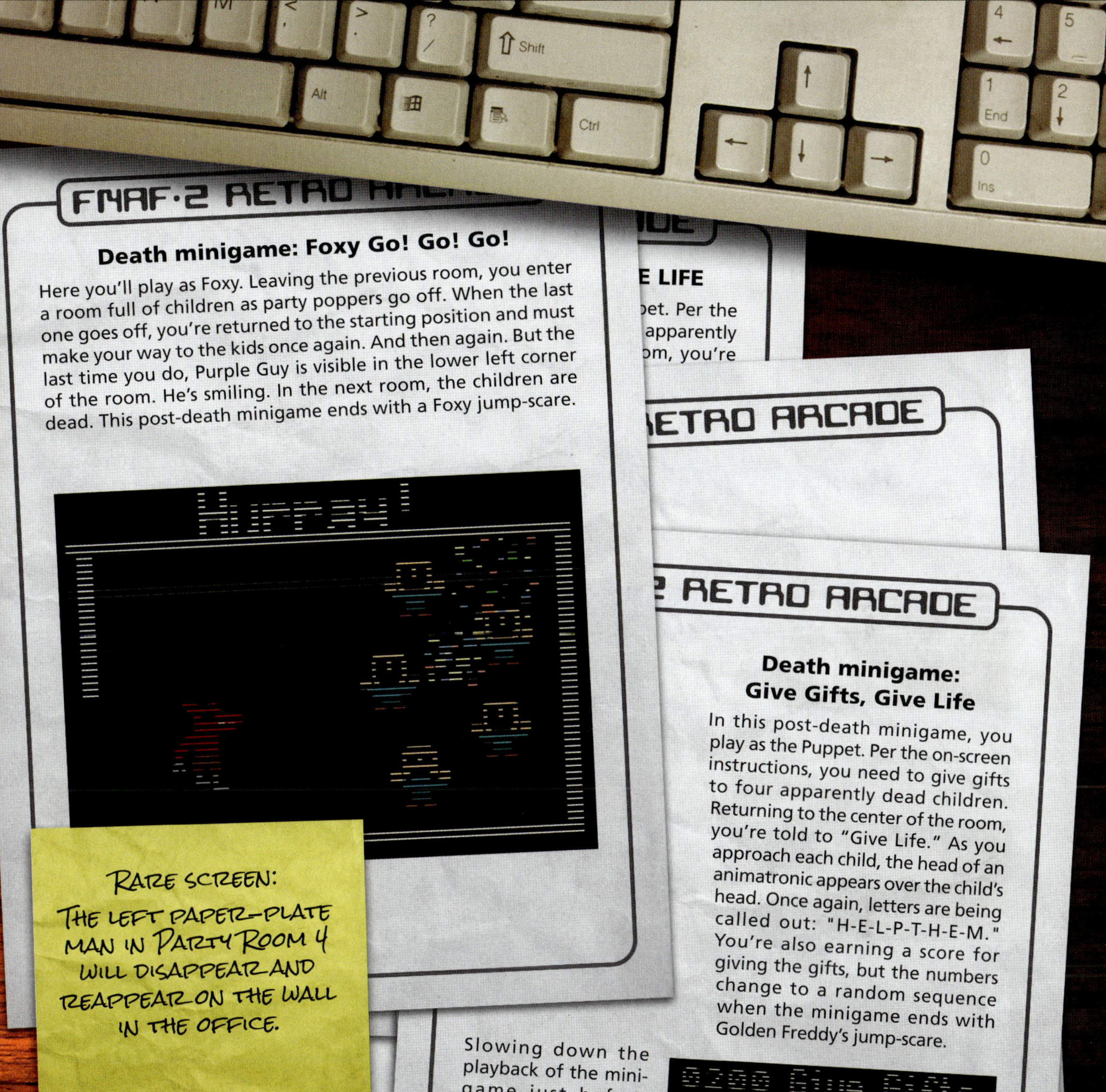

Death minigame: Foxy Go! Go! Go!

Here you'll play as Foxy. Leaving the previous room, you enter a room full of children as party poppers go off. When the last one goes off, you're returned to the starting position and must make your way to the kids once again. And then again. But the last time you do, Purple Guy is visible in the lower left corner of the room. He's smiling. In the next room, the children are dead. This post-death minigame ends with a Foxy jump-scare.

RARE SCREEN: THE LEFT PAPER-PLATE MAN IN PARTY ROOM 4 WILL DISAPPEAR AND REAPPEAR ON THE WALL IN THE OFFICE.

Death minigame: Give Gifts, Give Life

In this post-death minigame, you play as the Puppet. Per the on-screen instructions, you need to give gifts to four apparently dead children. Returning to the center of the room, you're told to "Give Life." As you approach each child, the head of an animatronic appears over the child's head. Once again, letters are being called out: "H-E-L-P-T-H-E-M." You're also earning a score for giving the gifts, but the numbers change to a random sequence when the minigame ends with Golden Freddy's jump-scare.

Slowing down the playback of the minigame just before the jump-scare reveals a fifth child in the center of the room. Golden Freddy's jump-scare originates from the child, perhaps implying that the Puppet placed a fifth animatronic head (Golden Freddy's) on this child.

Lore and Theories

Fan Theories: The Minigames Reveal Multiple Killings

A prominent strain of theory maintains that each of the four minigames in *FNAF2* reveals a different set of murders.

Fan Theories: Freddy Franchises

Phone Guy tells us on Night 01 that a previous location was left to rot after something terrible happened there, and then later, on Night 05, we learn there was an original restaurant called "Fredbear's Family Diner," which was apparently franchised out to create the other locations. This was reiterated in *The Silver Eyes* novel, in which Charlie tracked down the old diner, and it was revealed that a single child had gone missing there. *Pizzeria Simulator* picks up that thread with the "HRY223" secret audio file, and the closing sequence of the game.

SAVETHEM is believed to be in the *FNAF2* restaurant—the minigame map is similar to the camera map. There are five dead children here as well. Purple Guy also looks different; he's now wearing something gold on his chest and holding something in his hand.

Foxy Go! Go! Go! has a completely different map, which now has two rooms (Pirate Cove and a Party Room). The game reveals that five children are murdered.

is believed to take place at Fredbear's Family Diner, since the map consists of only one room and a street (denoting a smaller location) and the playable Freddy looks different from the Freddy in SAVETHEM (meaning an older version of Freddy). Theorists assert the game shows Purple Guy's first murder. This seems to be confirmed after *Pizzeria Simulator* showed this child to be the daughter of Cassette Man (Cassette Man is believed to be Henry Emily, the inventor of the animatronics). This child later possessed the Puppet.

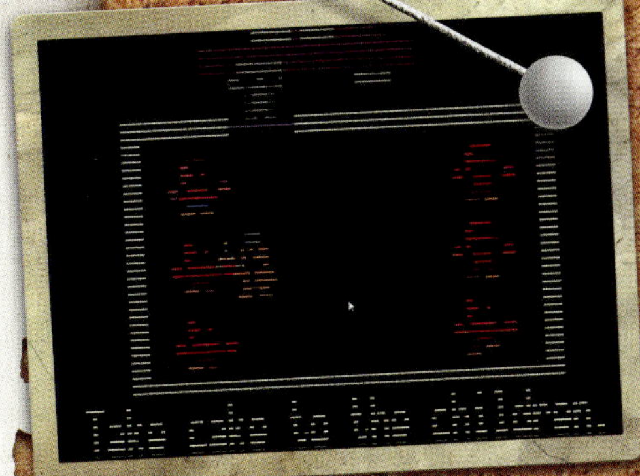

Give Gifts, Give Life shows five dead children as well as the Puppet, but at a seemingly different location (it's one room, but the room's dimensions are different from Take Cake).

ON A FINAL, DISTURBING NOTE, THE MODELS FOR THE DEAD CHILDREN ARE DIFFERENT FROM GAME TO GAME, SUPPORTING THEORISTS' CLAIMS THAT THERE COULD BE FOUR UNIQUE SETS OF VICTIMS.

Strategy Specifics and Evolution of Strategy for 10/20 Mode:

First Iteration: CAM 11 Strategy

Keep your camera on CAM 11 at all times. After you click once, hold the mouse button down since you just have to hover over the "Wind Music Box" area on CAM 11. Wind about 7 ticks each time you go into CAM 11, and if Toy Bonnie has just moved across your view, maybe even go up to 8 ticks (be fast with your mouse!).

Put on your mask every time you go back to the Office view. Check Left Vent—Flash Hallway (Foxy)—Check Right Vent, and respond accordingly with the Mask. Cross your fingers that Toy Bonnie doesn't take forever to start his animation across. Rinse and repeat, but know that multiple Toy Bonnie appearances, and being too fast with the Mask takeoff with Vent Animatronics, can end a night very easily.

Second Iteration: Right Vent Camp Strategy

For this strategy, mainly ignore the Left Vent Animatronics, and focus especially on Toy Bonnie. Let the Desk Animatronics pull down the camera whenever possible, and use your Mask whenever you're being attacked. Wait about 3/4 second to take off the Mask after the Blackout Phase. Be sure to flash Foxy when possible. If there are no Desk Animatronics, go back to the First Iteration (CAM 11) strategy.

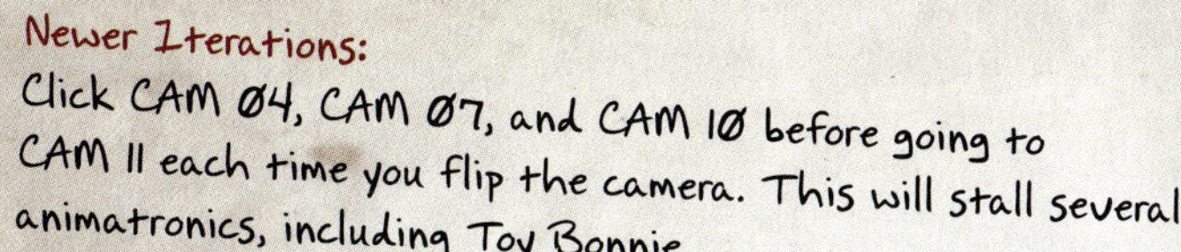

Newer Iterations:

Click CAM Ø4, CAM Ø7, and CAM 1Ø before going to CAM 11 each time you flip the camera. This will stall several animatronics, including Toy Bonnie.

Wind the Music Box

These "Minus" strategies use the CAM stalling dynamic to stall multiple animatronics, making the Office Phase much easier to handle, especially if you've prevented Toy Bonnie entirely.

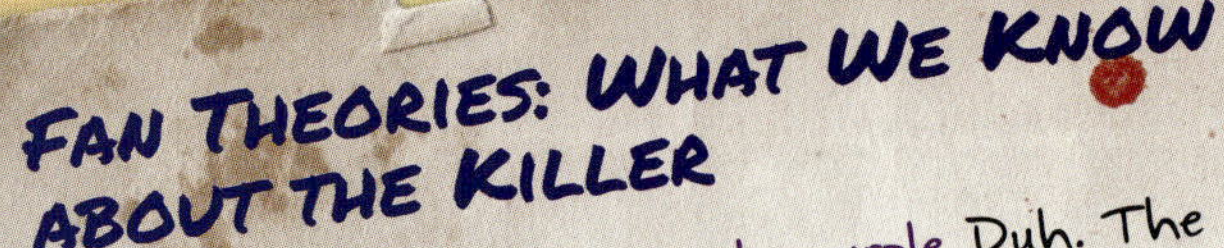

Fan Theories: What We Know About the Killer

- He's associated with the color purple. Duh. The real question is: What does the purple coloring mean? This could be part of his uniform, or something else.
- He might be a security guard. In SAVETHEM, Purple Guy has a golden object pinned to his chest. This has led many to believe that he's a security guard and the object is a badge.
- He may know how to work the animatronics. In Night 04, you're instructed not to make eye contact with the animatronics, as "someone may have tampered with their facial recognition systems." All signs point to Purple Guy as the culprit. After all, if he's in the criminal database, he would need to disable their facial recognition to sneak into Freddy's.
- He was likely an employee of Freddy's. Phone Guy on Night 05 warns: "The building is on lockdown, uh, no one is allowed in or out, you know, especially concerning any . . . previous employees." Though it's never explicitly stated, why would Phone Guy give this warning if the wrongdoing wasn't committed by an employee?

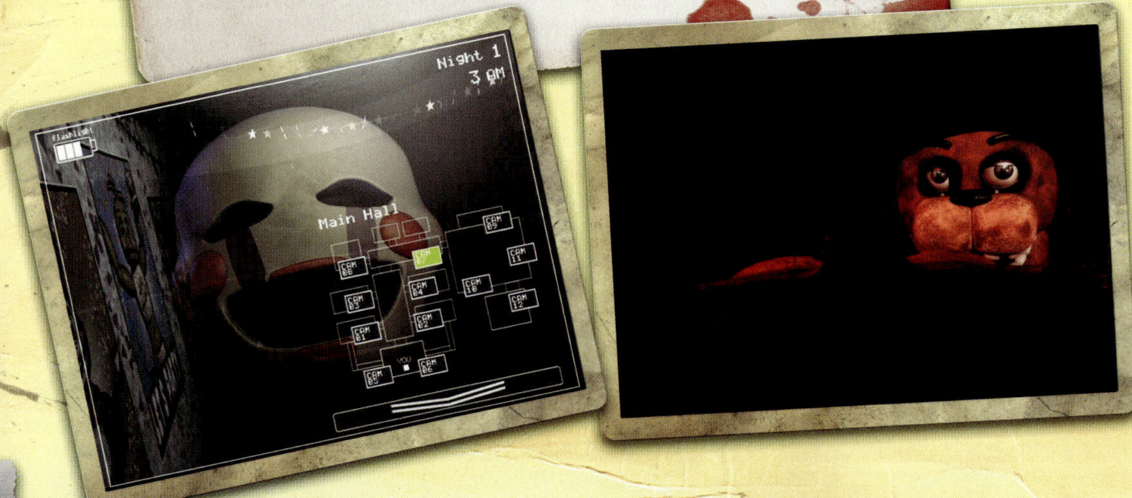

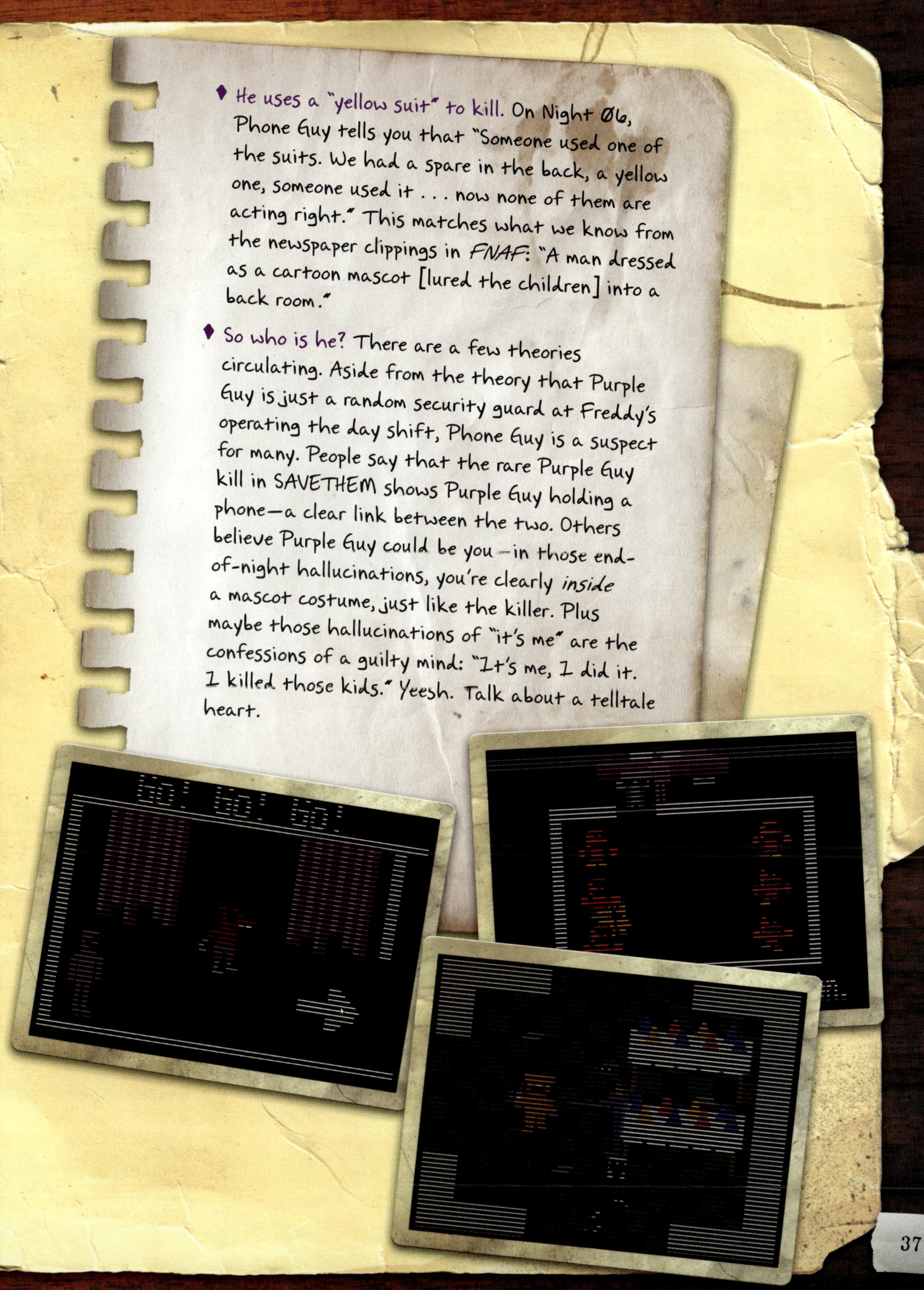

- **He uses a "yellow suit" to kill.** On Night Ø6, Phone Guy tells you that "Someone used one of the suits. We had a spare in the back, a yellow one, someone used it . . . now none of them are acting right." This matches what we know from the newspaper clippings in *FNAF*: "A man dressed as a cartoon mascot [lured the children] into a back room."
- **So who is he?** There are a few theories circulating. Aside from the theory that Purple Guy is just a random security guard at Freddy's operating the day shift, Phone Guy is a suspect for many. People say that the rare Purple Guy kill in SAVETHEM shows Purple Guy holding a phone—a clear link between the two. Others believe Purple Guy could be you—in those end-of-night hallucinations, you're clearly *inside* a mascot costume, just like the killer. Plus maybe those hallucinations of "it's me" are the confessions of a guilty mind: "It's me, I did it. I killed those kids." Yeesh. Talk about a telltale heart.

Chapter 3

Five Nights at Freddy's 3

If you thought it was impossible for *FNAF* to take a darker turn, allow us to introduce you to *Five Nights at Freddy's 3* (*FNAF3*). Set thirty years after the horrific events that took place at Freddy Fazbear's Pizza (though which *specific* events is up for debate), this game operates on two disturbing levels.

In the present, you're working at a horror attraction built around the mythos of the infamous murders. Only one animatronic is real, but the "phantoms" (read: hallucinations) of other animatronics also appear every now and again to mess with you. A perpetually failing network of ventilation, audio, and cameras adds to the torment, and needs constant attention.

In a series of six minigames, you're working to gain closure for the souls of the five children who were murdered at the hands of Purple Guy many years ago. The minigames are difficult to access, must be completed in the correct order, and, even after you do successfully complete them, your current night gets reset. It can be a frustrating process, but one that's ultimately satisfying.

It's the dawn of a new era for *FNAF*, and—since Old Phone Guy is most likely dead—that means a new Phone Guy. It's been thirty years since the last Freddy Fazbear's Pizza shut down, and a company is trying to capitalize on the restaurant's gruesome past by launching "Fazbear's Fright: The Horror Attraction." The attraction opens next week, so they have to make sure everything works and NOTHING CATCHES ON FIRE. (Always important.) After talking to the original designer of the building, the company finds a boarded-up room inside the restaurant that they're planning to investigate. On Night 02, New Phone Guy reveals they've obtained a real animatronic—Springtrap—which they're using for the attraction. It's loose inside the building, but don't worry . . . it'll find you.

Things We Learn From Old Phone Guy's Training Cassettes:

In addition to the Springtrap animatronic, New Phone Guy also found some old training tapes, recorded by—you guessed it—Old Phone Guy!

Springlock Suits

- At one point, Freddy's had two "springlock" suits that doubled as animatronics and mascot costumes.
- To wear the suits as a costume, you use a hand crank to "recoil and compress the animatronic parts around the sides of the suit." Springlocks must be fastened tight in order to keep the animatronic parts compressed, leaving room for a human occupant. The slightest pressure or moisture can cause the springlocks to trip, releasing the machinery and crushing the person inside the suit.
- When the springlock suits are in animatronic mode, they're pre-set to walk toward any sound they hear.
- On Night 04, Old Phone Guy informs you of an incident at the restaurant's sister location involving multiple springlock failures, at which point the company deemed the suits unsafe and retired them.

Safe Rooms

Also gleaned from Old Phone Guy's audio is the existence of "safe rooms" within each restaurant.

- There is a designated safe room in every Freddy's location. This room is not included in the digital map programmed into the animatronics, or in the building's security blueprints. This room is "hidden to customers, invisible to animatronics, and is always off camera," meaning there are no security cameras in these rooms.
- On Night 04, Phone Guy reminds employees, "Under no circumstance should a customer ever be taken into this room and away from the show area."
- On Night 06, it's announced that the room is being sealed, and that employees should never talk to anyone else of its existence. No one is allowed to enter the room to collect their belongings, either.

Night End Minigames

At the end of each night, a minigame begins with you in control of an animatronic (Freddy, Bonnie, Chica, Foxy). The goal is to follow Shadow Freddy through the restaurant toward the safe room. After you try to enter the safe room, expect to be dismembered by Purple Guy . . . ending the minigame and the night.

Although you will always need to "die" to continue to the next night, you are still able to wander a short distance. Heading to the left is the Parts and Service Room; among the parts, there appears to be a human skull. If you continue down past the Pirate Cove area into a hallway, you'll find hints for unlocking the minigames required to access the "good" ending.

SEE PAGES 48–51 FOR MINIGAME HINTS.

follow me.

follow me.

follow me.

follow me.

NIGHT 05 END MINIGAME

On Night 05, you control a crying child during the post-night minigame. Go toward the safe room as before, and you'll see dismembered animatronics along the way. You're now able to enter the safe room where the animatronics could not go before. Once inside, you'll notice four crying children blocking Purple Guy from leaving the room. Eventually, he dons what appears to be the empty springlock suit; sure enough, it soon malfunctions and crushes him.

If you play the game straight through, after the Night 05 end minigame, you'll see an image of broken animatronic heads, each with a lit eye. Faded text in the background reads "Bad ending."

NIGHTMARE MODE!

As with the two prior games, a more difficult night is unlocked after the fifth, called simply (and most appropriately) "Nightmare." On this night, the ventilation system fails a lot more quickly than it normally does, so get ready for a challenge! But, if you flip your camera quickly and frequently, you never have to reset Ventilation, and Springtrap won't attack unless he goes through a vent directly to the office.

If you beat the game's Nightmare mode, regardless of how you played the minigames, you'll see a newspaper informing you that the attraction has burned to the ground due to faulty wiring. But . . . is that Springtrap watching from the background in the article's picture? Maybe this isn't the end of the Freddy's saga after all.

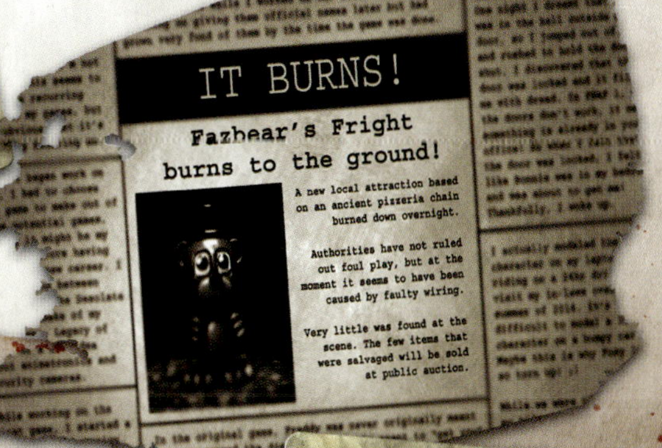

IT BURNS!

Fazbear's Fright burns to the ground!

A new local attraction based on an ancient pizzeria chain burned down overnight.

Authorities have not ruled out foul play, but at the moment it seems to have been caused by faulty wiring.

Very little was found at the scene. The few items that were salvaged will be sold at public auction.

THE BLURRED TEXT AROUND THE ARTICLE CONTAINS DEVELOPMENT STORIES FROM GAME CREATOR SCOTT CAWTHON.

Gameplay and Strategy

Revenge of the Math

Not counting failure due to a phantom animatronic, you have a certain number of audio uses before the system goes down. Your number of uses changes each night.

	Night 01	Night 02	Night 03	Night 04	Night 05
Audio Uses	unlimited	10	4	3	2

The camera system will go down more rarely than the other systems. This mainly results from overuse. The ventilation system most frequently fails due to phantom animatronics. Similar to the audio, the other two systems fail more frequently as the week progresses.

Note that it takes between 6 to 8 seconds each to restart the cameras, audio, or ventilation. It takes between 12 to 14 seconds to reboot them all at once. If two or more systems go down, we recommend rebooting everything.

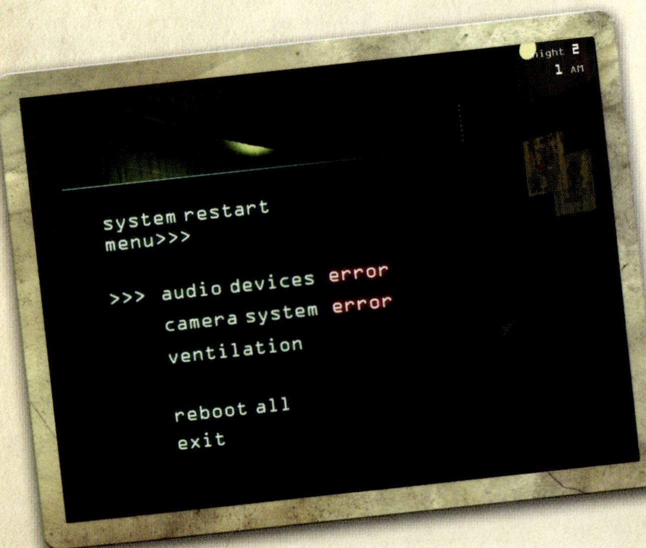

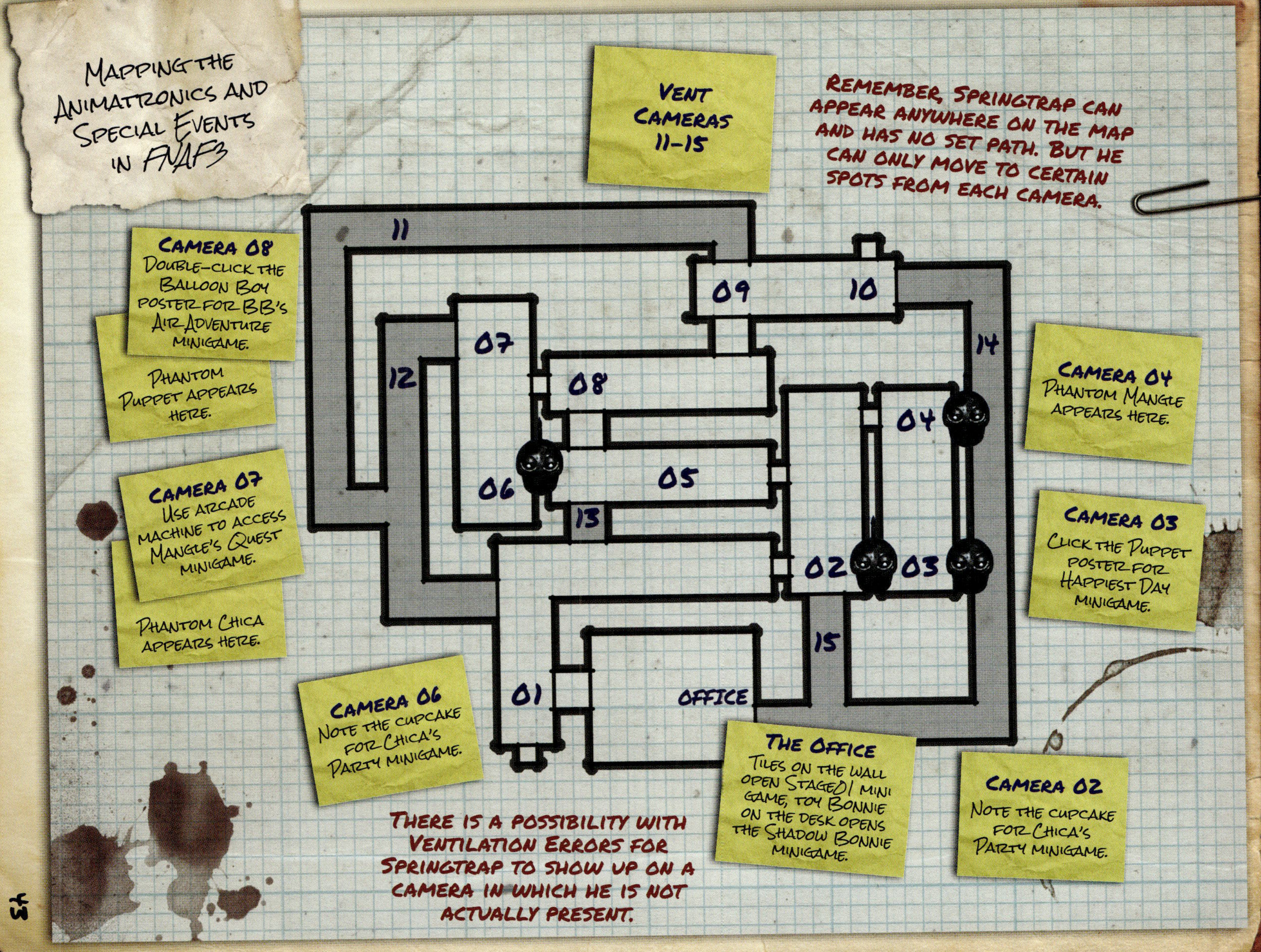

Mapping the Animatronics and Special Events in FNAF3
Vent Cameras 11–15
Remember, Springtrap can appear anywhere on the map and has no set path. But he can only move to certain spots from each camera.
Camera 08 Double-click the Balloon Boy poster for BB's Air Adventure minigame.
Phantom Puppet appears here.
Camera 07 Use arcade machine to access Mangle's Quest minigame.
Phantom Chica appears here.
Camera 06 Note the cupcake for Chica's Party minigame.
Camera 04 Phantom Mangle appears here.
Camera 03 Click the Puppet poster for Happiest Day minigame.
Camera 02 Note the cupcake for Chica's Party minigame.
The Office Tiles on the wall open Stage01 mini game, toy Bonnie on the desk opens the Shadow Bonnie minigame.
There is a possibility with Ventilation Errors for Springtrap to show up on a camera in which he is not actually present.
11
09
10
07
12
08
14
04
06
05
13
02
03
15
01
Office

SPRINGTRAP

Springtrap is the only real animatronic in this game, and the only one who can kill you. He has no set starting position and can move through every room and the vents.

You can use the audio device to lure Springtrap to adjacent rooms, but it won't work if he's more than one room away. Springtrap only moves to rooms adjacent to his last position or connected to it by an air vent. If Springtrap enters a room with an adjoining vent, it's best to seal it off by double-clicking on that camera.

When Springtrap approaches the office, he'll slink past the window.

PHANTOM ANIMATRONICS

In addition to Springtrap, there are animatronic hallucinations to deal with. All of them will cause systems to malfunction unless you take quick action, and, suspiciously, all the animatronics appear burned.

TRAPPING SPRINGTRAP

If Springtrap doesn't hop through vents too much, you can bounce him between CAM 09 and CAM 10. However, CAM 09 and CAM 10 are both connected to dangerous vents. CAM 10 connects with the vent leading directly to the office (CAM 14), and CAM 09 connects to CAM 11, which leads down just before CAM 01. Either one is a point of no return for Springtrap in the standalone game. Keep in mind that you can only shut one of these cameras at a time. If you leave to reset anything via the Maintenance Panel (for example, Audio), Springtrap can move quickly enough through either one of those vents, so whichever one is open becomes an immense danger. If he gets closer, use the audio to get Springtrap into the CAM 05 room, then close off the vent. You can trap him in there for a while using the audio and keeping the vents closed.

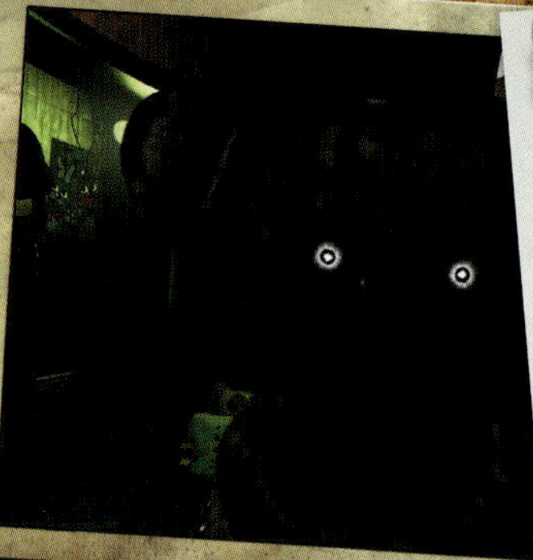

PHANTOM FREDDY

crosses the hallway window before appearing inside the office. Avoid a jump-scare by watching the cameras or maintenance panel until he passes.

DISABLE VENTILATION

PHANTOM BALLOON BOY

can appear in any camera except vents.

PHANTOM CHICA
appears on CAM Ø7 in the arcade machine monitor.

DISABLE CAMERA & VENTILATION

PHANTOM FOXY
randomly appears in the office. Pull up the cameras to avoid his jump-scare.

DISABLE AUDIO

PHANTOM MANGLE
appears on CAM Ø4, hanging from the ceiling and screeching. She will then appear in the office behind the window unless you lower the monitor or switch cameras as soon as he appears.

DISABLE AUDIO & VENTILATION

PHANTOM PUPPET
appears on CAM Ø8. Switch to another camera fast or it will appear in the office and block you from using the maintenance panel and monitor for a prolonged period of time.

GLITCH ZONE
You can edit the save file while the game is open and access all the way down to Night -999,999,999. The attack formula is pretty odd, so it's rare that Springtrap will attack on a negative night, but it is still possible.

Continue Game Glitch

In *FNAF1*, *FNAF2*, and *FNAF3*, you can also glitch-click on "Continue Game," if your save file has a value above the normal night range, and if you're lucky, you can access unintended nights (Night 08, 09, 1987, etc.), by clicking on "Continue Game" at just the right time. You have to be very precise after scrolling your mouse fast across multiple Menu options.

CAM 07 and CAM 12

These two cameras connect and are away from any other vents, so they are padded enough to allow you some leeway if you go to reset your cameras. With this strategy, many people favor moving Springtrap to CAM 06 and CAM 07 (note that CAM 05 leads to the vent in CAM 13, which is dangerous, BUT if you can catch Springtrap going through CAM 13 quickly enough, you can pull him back to CAM 02 with an Audio Lure).

With this strategy, it's best to keep Springtrap in CAM 07, and preventively shut CAM 12 to avoid a point of no return.

Keep a free Audio Lure when possible, in case you find Springtrap sneaking over to CAM 05!

It's best not to use CAM 08 at all, if possible. The Puppet's attack takes up way too much time, and you have to reset Ventilation afterward, which makes it hard to recover if you're late in the game and not at the start of the night.

Forcing Phantom Freddy

Phantom Freddy will stop appearing after he startles you once, on any given night. So, if you force Phantom Freddy to attack by staring at him in the office (no panels open or open/closing), you can reset after his 1:00 a.m. appearance and startle, and then not have to worry about him at 3:00 a.m. and 5:00 a.m.

Note that with the "Fast Nights" cheat, Phantom Freddy will appear at 2:00 a.m.

Springtrap Staredown

Usually, the Forced Phantom Freddy strategy will help with a late-game staredown. So, if you go to your Maintenance Panel with Springtrap at the door, there's a good chance (especially on later nights), that he will attack while you're in the panel and trying to reset something.

But you will have some time where you can stare him down. He won't attack if you're staring at him with the monitors down and without a ventilation error.

However, if you're blacked out, you're basically done. Without the "Fast Nights" cheat, it's usually successful to stare down Springtrap either after Phantom Freddy has crossed entirely, or a little bit into 5:00 a.m. with Phantom Freddy already forced earlier in the night.

Camera Wafting

You can technically waft your camera with very few frames in-camera and hold off Springtrap's attacks indefinitely, if you don't break rhythm. Camera wafting also has to be done frequently enough to prevent Phantom Freddy from startling you if you're too inactive without flipping the Camera Panel.

CAM 02 Strategy

For this strategy, try to force Springtrap over to CAM 02. Close the vent in CAM 15 to prevent an instant death. If you see Springtrap in front of you, use an Audio Lure immediately in CAM 02 to bring him back to CAM 02.

If Springtrap runs across your view at 4:00 a.m., there's a good chance that you can still win with a staredown.

If it's 5:00 a.m. and he starts to run across, do a Ventilation Reset and then get out of the cameras when possible for a staredown. Phantom Freddy will complicate this, unless you've already forced him to startle you.

Path to the Good Ending

To view the game's "good" ending, players must complete minigames in a specific order. Hints appeared throughout the night-end minigames on the walls of a room one left and three down from the Show Stage room.

FNAF·3 RETRO ARCADE

Minigame: BB's Air Adventure

The hint for *BB's Air Adventure* was "BBdblclick"—double-click on the Balloon Boy poster visible on CAM 08. Control Balloon Boy with the keyboard (A=left, D=right, W=jump) and collect all the balloons. Instead of exiting the game, jump onto the platform above the exit and then jump toward the left wall.

Passing through this barrier will send you to a pixelated gray screen with terrifying dead Balloon Boys. Move to the right and you'll find a new playfield containing a rainbow-colored balloon. Jump through the left wall to reenter the minigame and collect the final balloon. This will restart your night in the main game.

FNAF·3 RETRO ARCADE

Minigame: Mangle's Quest

This game must be accessed on Night 02; its hint was a series of squares that correspond to button presses. On CAM 07, click the arcade machine's buttons in this order: top left, bottom left, top right, bottom right.

Collect all of Mangle's parts without running into a child. Instead of exiting the game, jump through the secret opening above the exit. You'll enter a pixelated red screen with a large, crying version of what looks like the Puppet. Move to the left to enter a new section of the game. Jump onto each balloon platform and a cake will appear at the end of the path. Collect it to reset your night.

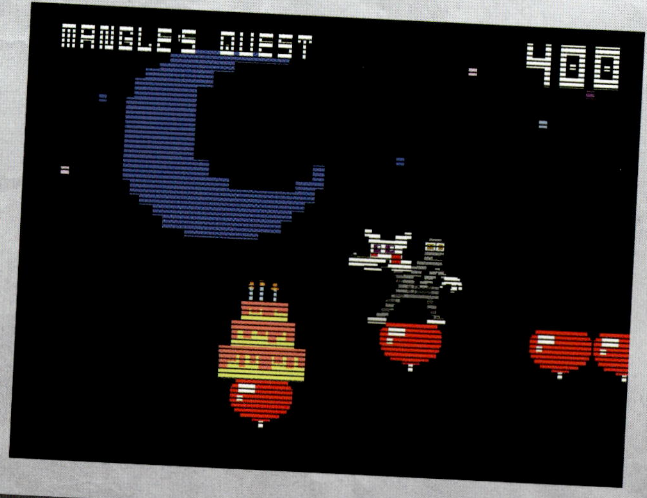

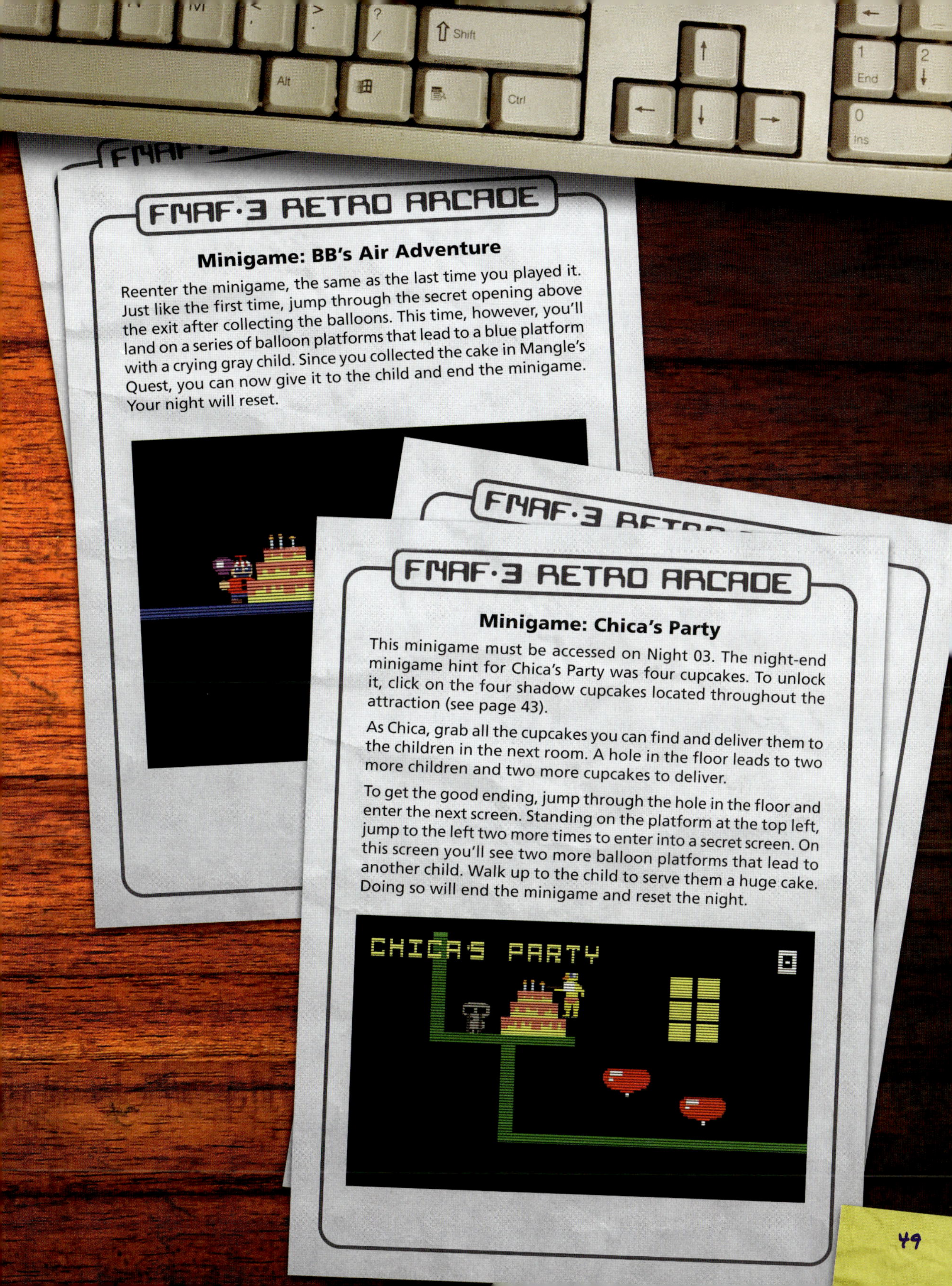

FNAF·3 RETRO ARCADE

Minigame: BB's Air Adventure

Reenter the minigame, the same as the last time you played it. Just like the first time, jump through the secret opening above the exit after collecting the balloons. This time, however, you'll land on a series of balloon platforms that lead to a blue platform with a crying gray child. Since you collected the cake in Mangle's Quest, you can now give it to the child and end the minigame. Your night will reset.

FNAF·3 RETRO ARCADE

Minigame: Chica's Party

This minigame must be accessed on Night 03. The night-end minigame hint for Chica's Party was four cupcakes. To unlock it, click on the four shadow cupcakes located throughout the attraction (see page 43).

As Chica, grab all the cupcakes you can find and deliver them to the children in the next room. A hole in the floor leads to two more children and two more cupcakes to deliver.

To get the good ending, jump through the hole in the floor and enter the next screen. Standing on the platform at the top left, jump to the left two more times to enter into a secret screen. On this screen you'll see two more balloon platforms that lead to another child. Walk up to the child to serve them a huge cake. Doing so will end the minigame and reset the night.

FNAF·3 RETRO ARCADE

Minigame: "Stage 01"

This minigame must be accessed on Night 04. The hint for Stage 01 was a numerical code: 395248. The code corresponds to wall tiles in the office, left of the desk, arranged in a 3 x 3 grid. Click on each tile as you would dial numbers on a phone.

In this minigame, players control Golden Freddy while entertaining children with Spring Bonnie. Jump toward the children to glitch through the wall on the left side of the room. As you fall, you'll see that same stage room, twice, until you hit the ground. There are actually nine playing fields arranged in a 3 x 3 grid. All of them are the same except for the top right (3) and middle right (6)—Room 6 only has two children. Follow the path in the map below to get to Room 3 and deliver cake to the lone crying child.

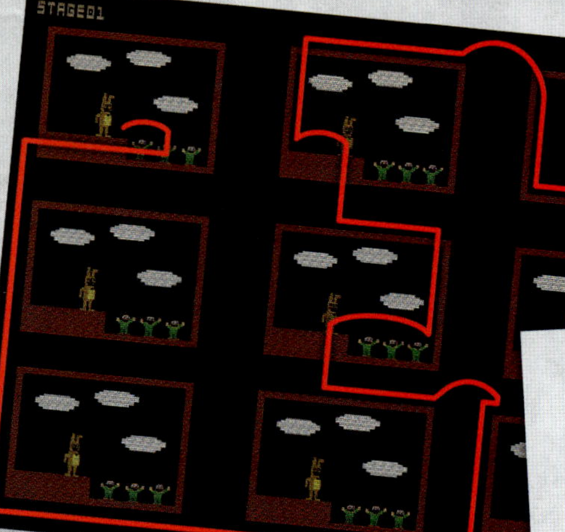

Freddy's Fun Fact

This number backward, 842593, as a hexadecimal number, is a familiar shade of purple. 395248 is also shown in *FNAF Ruin*. This could be an employee ID number or a serial number—maybe one day we'll find out.

FNAF·3 RETRO ARCADE

Minigame: Shadow Bonnie

The hint for this minigame appeared as a shadow version of Bonnie. To access it, double-click on the shadowed Toy Bonnie figurine on the right side of the office desk on Night 05.

This minigame is a mash-up of all the others. Pressing "S" phases the character from one game setting into a new purple room, and pressing "S" again phases the character into the previously played minigames.

There's a child at the bottom-left corner of the purple room, but outside the walls. To reach them, press "S" until you land in BB's Air Adventure. Jump to the upper left platform and into the wall, passing through it and falling to the ground. Walk to the center of the screen and press "S" to phase back to the purple room. You are now outside the walls and can approach the child to give them cake.

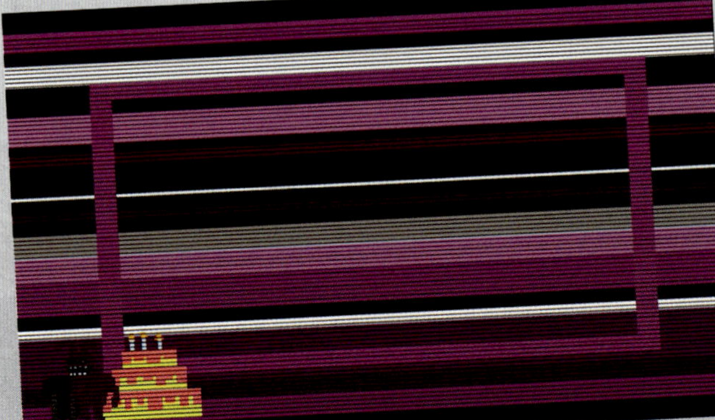

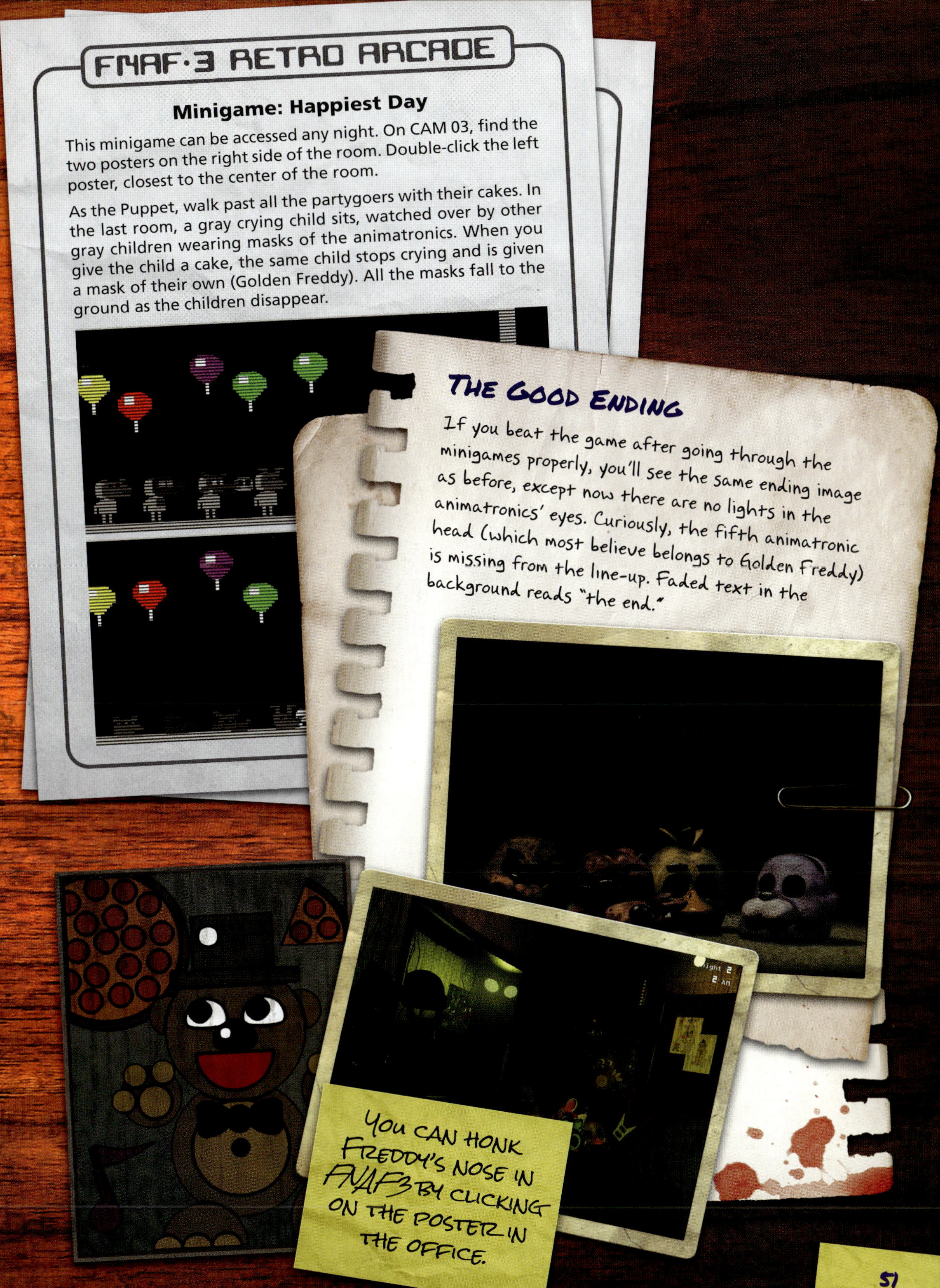

FNAF·3 RETRO ARCADE

Minigame: Happiest Day

This minigame can be accessed any night. On CAM 03, find the two posters on the right side of the room. Double-click the left poster, closest to the center of the room.

As the Puppet, walk past all the partygoers with their cakes. In the last room, a gray crying child sits, watched over by other gray children wearing masks of the animatronics. When you give the child a cake, the same child stops crying and is given a mask of their own (Golden Freddy). All the masks fall to the ground as the children disappear.

The Good Ending

If you beat the game after going through the minigames properly, you'll see the same ending image as before, except now there are no lights in the animatronics' eyes. Curiously, the fifth animatronic head (which most believe belongs to Golden Freddy) is missing from the line-up. Faded text in the background reads "the end."

You can honk Freddy's nose in *FNAF3* by clicking on the poster in the office.

Codes, Glitches, and Secrets

Extras Option

There is no custom night in *FNAF3*. However, beating Night Ø5 opens up an Extras option in the main menu. From here, players can view the animatronics' jump-scares, play the minigames (as long as the good ending was unlocked), and enable some fun cheats. You can speed up time, equip a Springtrap "radar" (to help you find him more easily), and even increase Springtrap's aggression level. (We'll pass on that last one.)

EXTRA
ANIMATRONICS
MINIGAMES
JUMPSCARES
CHEATS
EXIT
FAST NIGHTS
RADAR
AGGRESSIVE
NO ERRORS

Rare Springtrap Images

There are three rare Springtrap images that can appear randomly before the menu screen. All three show that there is someone *inside* the Springtrap suit. Someone long dead.

Rare Screens

Don't miss these rare screens from *FNAF3*!

Camera 04

The Bonnie poster will change to a pink cupcake or a golden cupcake.

Camera 02

Retro Freddy poster changes to Spring Bonnie—is he winking at us?

The Office

Crumpled Freddy suit sometimes appears in the corner of the office.

The Office

Two paper plate characters appear on the walls of the office.

Camera 10

Retro Freddy poster changes to Spring Bonnie.

WHO ARE THE SHADOW ANIMATRONICS?

Though introduced in *FNAF2*, Shadow Bonnie and Shadow Freddy don't really take center stage until *FNAF3*. Shadow Freddy plays a crucial role in the night-end minigames, while Shadow Bonnie has his own role to play in the good-ending minigames. Just who are these characters, and what are their intentions?

FORMER EMPLOYEES? One theory maintains that Shadow Freddy and Shadow Bonnie are the ghosts of the Freddy's employees who were killed by the springlock suits. On Night 04, Phone Guy mentions "multiple, simultaneous springlock failures" at Freddy's sister location. Theorists believe this explains why the shadow animatronics help the dead children—as the ghosts of employees, they feel guilty about not being able to stop the murders.

LINK TO THE KILLER? Interestingly enough, the shadow animatronics take on a purple coloring, which is heavily associated with William Afton. Shadow Bonnie also appears in *Special Delivery*, when a player collects too much negative Remnant. Remnant has featured heavily in Afton's plans. But does Shadow Bonnie appear there as an antagonist . . . or as a warning?

WHAT WE KNOW FOR SURE:

- Shadow animatronics existed prior to the events of *FNAF2*, based on their appearance in that game.
- They don't seem to have a physical form. Unlike the physical animatronics, Shadow Freddy can enter the safe room in *FNAF3* and goes unnoticed by Purple Guy. In the minigames, Shadow Bonnie's figure seems to dissipate and re-form often. He is also able to travel to different minigames, something none of the other minigame animatronics can do.

WHAT WE WONDER ABOUT:

- Do they help the children as it seems? In the night-end minigames, Shadow Freddy tries to lead you to the killer, who's hiding out in the safe room. In his minigame, Shadow Bonnie gives cake to one of the children.

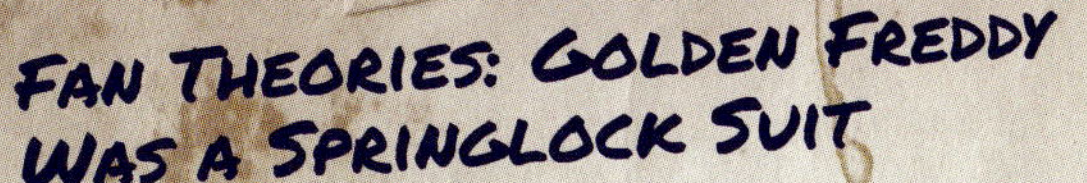

Fan Theories: Golden Freddy Was a Springlock Suit

There's been a lot of speculation about Golden Freddy—where he came from, why he seemingly can't move, and why he appears and disappears randomly. One theory says that *FNAF3* provides us with the answer: Golden Freddy is a springlock suit.

Theorists point to the crumpled sitting position of Golden Freddy, and how it matches the sitting position of the empty Springtrap suit in the night-end minigame on Night Ø5. Fans also believe this could answer why Golden Freddy appears and disappears like a hallucination—the springlock suits were retired (and presumably destroyed) long ago. All that would remain is a ghost of the animatronic.

This point seems more solid considering the unique Fredbear encounter in *Ultimate Custom Night*. The animatronic can only be seen by setting Golden Freddy to one and all other animatronics to zero, then giving Golden Freddy a Death Coin when he appears. Could this allude to Golden Freddy's origins as a Fredbear springlock suit?

Still, others reject this idea on the basis that Golden Freddy has four-fingered hands, which would be awkward for a human occupant. Springtrap has five fingers. And, if you adjust the color for the scene using color correction, it turns out that crumpled suit may actually be Shadow Freddy. The greenish hue of the room affects what the suit actually looks like.

Chapter 4

Five Nights at Freddy's 4

Five Nights at Freddy's 4 (*FNAF4*) marks a huge next step for the series. Gone are the Security Office, the stationary playable character, and the . . . well, the paycheck wasn't worth much to begin with. But for all this change, *FNAF4* kept the elements players like best: 8-bit minigames at the end of each night, perhaps the most nightmare-inducing animatronics of any game to date, and mysterious Easter eggs that have become the hallmark of the series.

That said, this game is *punishing*. It forces you to crank up the volume in order to hear a variety of subtly distinct sounds. Failing to respond correctly to those sounds results in an eardrum-shattering jump-scare that will likely send you (and possibly your keyboard) flying.

Beyond the gameplay, there's a lot to be gleaned here in terms of lore, and *FNAF4* kicked off one of the most intense fan-theory debates in the series' history—The Bite of '87 vs. The Bite of '83—as well as the million simultaneous cries of "What's in the box?"

Let's dig into some of these questions and more.

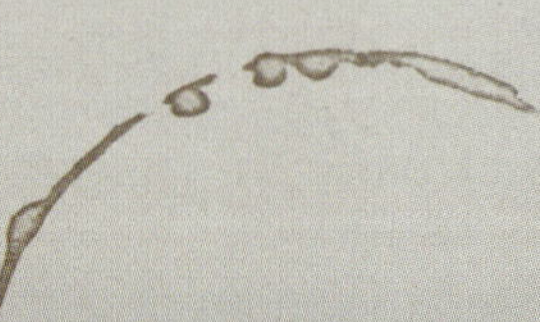

The Freddy Scoop

FNAF4 begins with a screen that announces "5 days until the party" followed by an 8-bit image of a little yellow Freddy wearing a purple hat. His name is Fredbear, and he reveals that you've been locked in your room.

The screen dissolves, and you'll see yourself as a crying (but alive) child in a bedroom with plush toys. The aforementioned Fredbear is a stuffed animal on your bed whose creepy eyes follow your every movement . . .

Using the keyboard (W = up, A = left, S = down, D = right), make your way toward the (locked) bedroom door. You won't be able to open it, but that's okay. The screen dissolves—tomorrow is another day.

After the minigame, you'll find yourself launched into the primary gameplay. You're playing as a child, trying to ward off nightmare versions of the animatronics who are attacking you in your bedroom.

Like the other games, you need to survive from midnight until 6:00 a.m. by checking your closet, the hallways outside your room, and your bed, where the nightmare animatronics lurk. Before each night begins, you'll also have the chance to skip two hours by playing a minigame with Plushtrap. If Challenges or Cheats are active, this will skip 1 hour.

YOUR ALARM CLOCK WILL FLASH A RANDOM SERIES OF NUMBERS AT THE END OF EACH NIGHT BEFORE HITTING 6:00 A.M.

FNAF·4 RETRO ARCADE

Night 01 End minigame

Four days until the party. Your bedroom door is now unlocked. Fredbear tells you that someone is hiding, and he won't stop until you find him. Exit your room to explore the house. Heading back and to the left, you'll end up in a living room with a TV. Walk to the TV to be jump-scared by your older brother and end the minigame.

NOTE THE DISMEMBERED MANGLE TOY ON THE FLOOR.

Night 02 End minigame

Three days until the party. Tonight you're at a Freddy's restaurant, but someone has left without you. The game urges you to run toward the exit. If you go left, the game prompts you with "No! Don't you remember what you saw?" A man in a Fredbear suit blocks the exit to your right. The game urges, "Find someone who will help! You know what will happen if he catches you!" On the next screen, you're told to run past a silhouetted Freddy and Spring Bonnie (does that look like Shadow Bonnie and Shadow Freddy?), but walking forward ends the minigame.

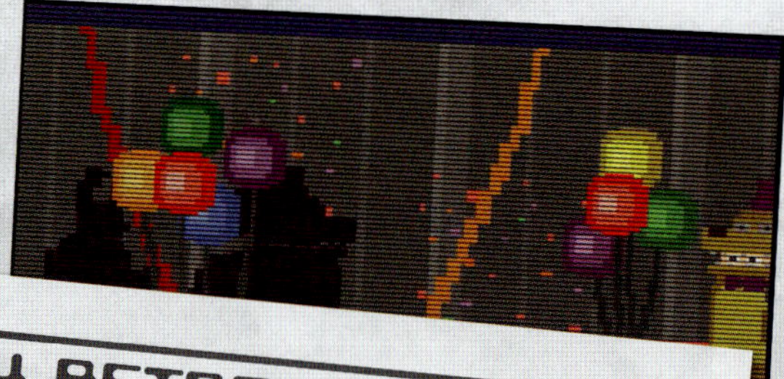

FNAF·4 RETRO ARCADE

Night 03 End minigame

Two days until the party. You're back at the pizzeria, but this time you can escape. On the way home, talk to the kids you see—one reveals that the upcoming party is for you. At home, head to your bedroom to be jump-scared and end the minigame.

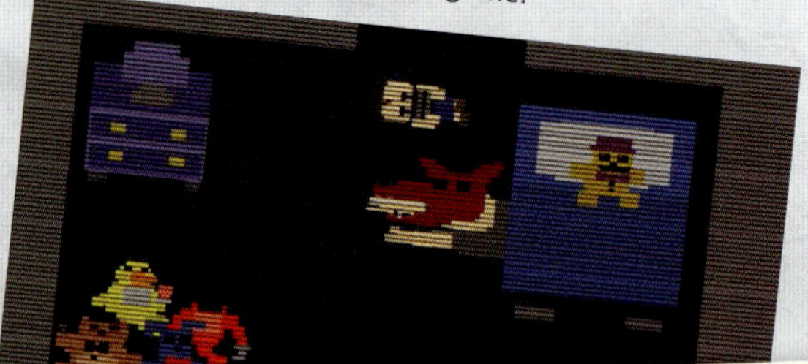

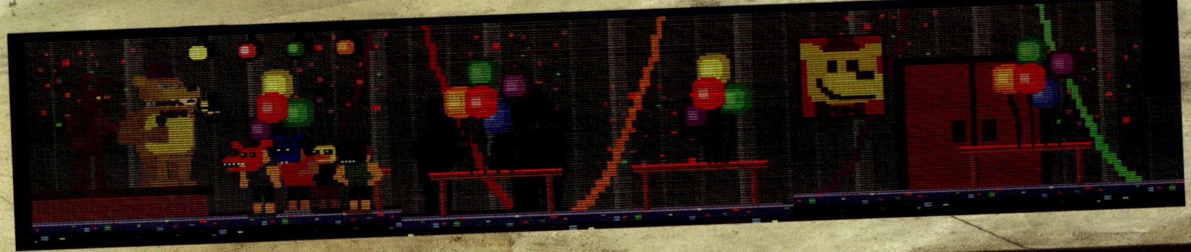

FNAF·4 RETRO ARCADE

Night 04 End minigame

One day until the party. You're locked in the spare parts/ maintenance room of the pizzeria. Unable to escape, you once again end up crying on the floor, begging to be let out, until the minigame ends.

FNAF·4 RETRO ARCADE

Night 05 End minigame

Zero days until the party. Tonight you're back at the pizzeria with no control—you just have to watch. Your brother and his friends (all wearing animatronic masks) tease you with the Fredbear animatronic. Your head ends up in Fredbear's mouth, followed by a sickening crunch as the animatronic bites down.

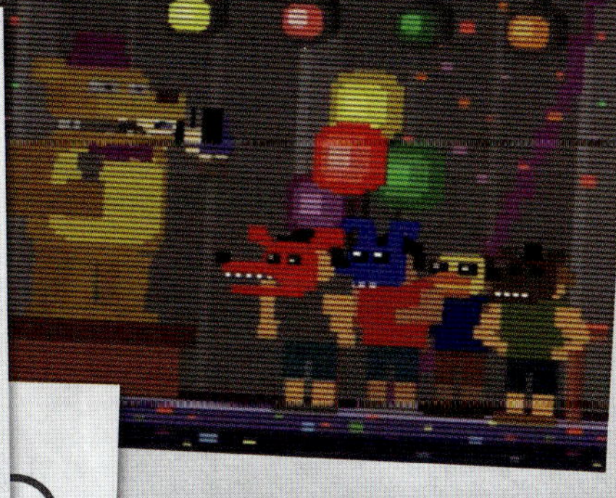

FNAF·4 RETRO ARCADE

Night 06 End minigame

Sitting with the plush Fredbear, someone tells you they're sorry. They tell you that you're broken, but that the speaker will put you back together. You can hear the sound of a heart monitor flatlining.

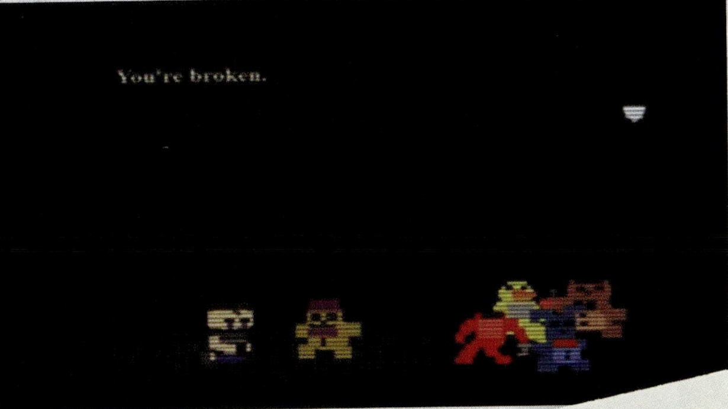

NIGHT 07 END MINIGAME

Beating Night 07 brings up an image of a locked box. You can click the locks to rattle them, but they won't open. The text reads, "Perhaps some things are best left forgotten, for now."

Gameplay and Strategy

Sounds

Like we said, this game is punishing on sound—you need to learn how to tune your ear to hear *everything*. Here's a list of what to listen for.

Sounds You Should Disregard:

- Dog barking
- Clock chimes
  (Good luck. Those chimes are *loud*.)
- Distorted radio

Sounds to Listen For:

- Breathing: Before you turn on your flashlight at the doorway, be sure to listen for breathing, as it means an animatronic is outside your room. If you hear it, shut the door and don't open it until you hear . . .
- Footsteps on gravel: This means an animatronic is walking away from or toward your room.
- Deep, slow-motion laugh: Nightmare Fredbear/Nightmare has entered your room.
- Metallic-sounding giggles: Freddles are accumulating on the bed behind you. Did you know? The Freddles sound effect was a stock sound effect from pigs being slaughtered. Creepy, right?
- Dishes clanking: Chica is in the Kitchen . . . for now.
- Pitter-patter running, followed by a creak: Nightmare Foxy has entered your closet.

Sound is oriented to where you are in the room, so if you hear a sound from your left, you should check the left door. This includes when you're at the door and can hear breathing, laughing, or other sounds.

And of Course, Listen Carefully for the Sweetest Sound of All:

The alarm clock hitting 6:00 a.m.

Hours are exactly sixty seconds long, making each night last exactly six minutes.

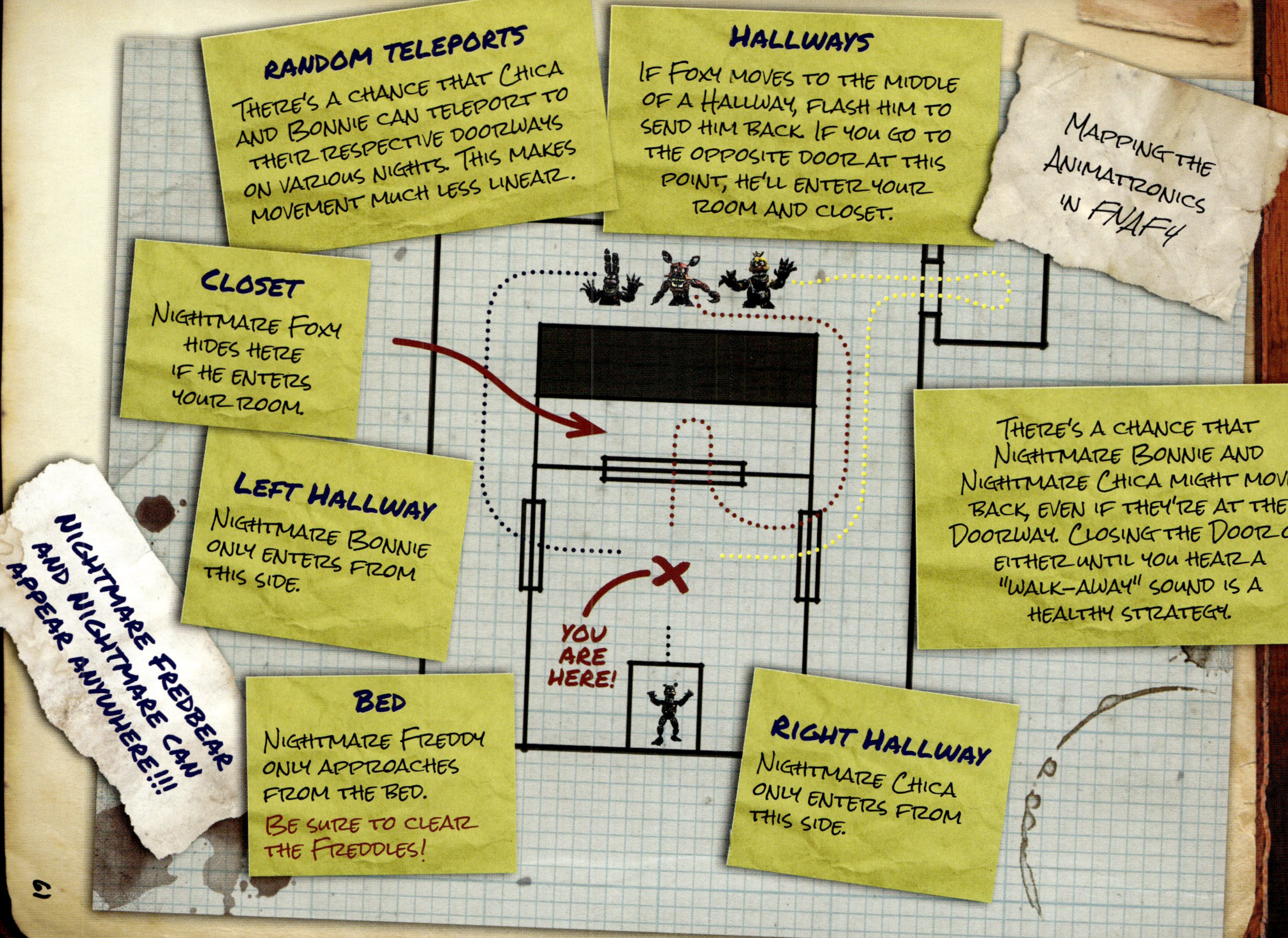
Mapping the Animatronics in FNAF4
Random Teleports
There's a chance that Chica and Bonnie can teleport to their respective doorways on various nights. This makes movement much less linear.
Hallways
If Foxy moves to the middle of a Hallway, flash him to send him back. If you go to the opposite door at this point, he'll enter your room and closet.
Closet
Nightmare Foxy hides here if he enters your room.
There's a chance that Nightmare Bonnie and Nightmare Chica might move back, even if they're at the Doorway. Closing the Door on either until you hear a "walk-away" sound is a healthy strategy.
Left Hallway
Nightmare Bonnie only enters from this side.
You are here!
Nightmare Fredbear and Nightmare can appear anywhere!!!
Bed
Nightmare Freddy only approaches from the bed.
Be sure to clear the Freddles!
Right Hallway
Nightmare Chica only enters from this side.

ANIMATRONICS

- **FREDDLES** appear on the bed, but flee when you shine the flashlight on them. The more Freddles there are, the longer it takes to clear them. **NIGHTMARE FREDDY** will attack if you do not check the bed often enough.

IF YOUR FLASHLIGHT FLICKERS, IT MEANS YOUR FREDDLE COUNT IS INCREASING.

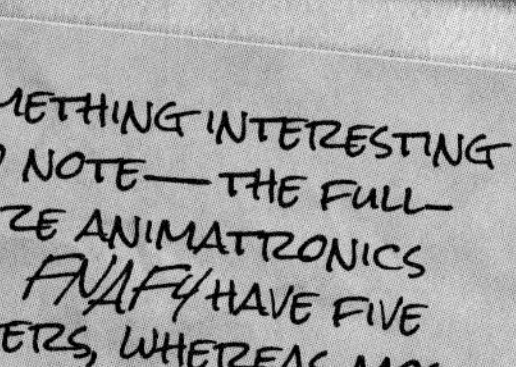

- **NIGHTMARE BONNIE** attacks from the left hallway or the center of the bedroom. Nightmare Bonnie is very active on the first few nights; check the left hallway often to avoid a jump-scare.

- **NIGHTMARE CHICA** is very active on the first few nights, and attacks players from the right hallway. While she does not enter the bedroom, her **CUPCAKE** does, and its jump-scare is just as bad.

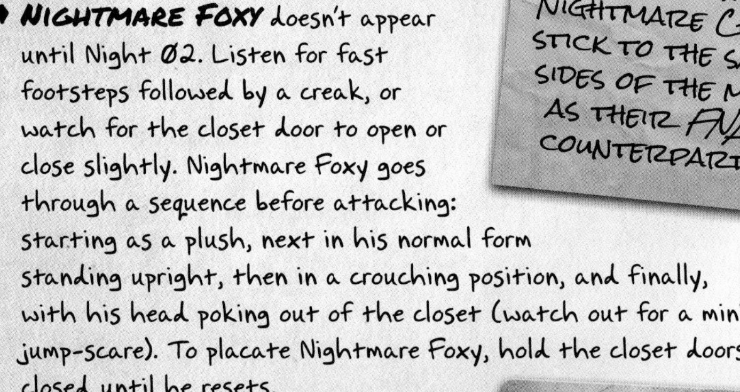

SOMETHING INTERESTING TO NOTE—THE FULL-SIZE ANIMATRONICS IN *FNAF4* HAVE FIVE FINGERS, WHEREAS MOST OF THE PREVIOUS GAMES' ANIMATRONICS (EXCEPT SPRINGTRAP) HAVE FOUR.

NIGHTMARE BONNIE AND NIGHTMARE CHICA STICK TO THE SAME SIDES OF THE MAP AS THEIR *FNAF* COUNTERPARTS.

- **NIGHTMARE FOXY** doesn't appear until Night 02. Listen for fast footsteps followed by a creak, or watch for the closet door to open or close slightly. Nightmare Foxy goes through a sequence before attacking: starting as a plush, next in his normal form standing upright, then in a crouching position, and finally, with his head poking out of the closet (watch out for a mini jump-scare). To placate Nightmare Foxy, hold the closet doors closed until he resets.

- **NIGHTMARE FREDBEAR** shows up at the start of Night 05 and on Night 06 at 4:00 a.m., and can attack from anywhere. When he's around, however, none of the others will be. Audio clues are your friend: If you hear laughter followed by footsteps, check the hallway.

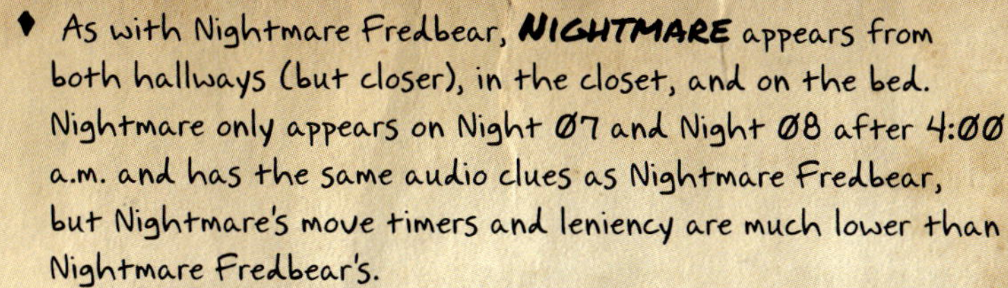

- As with Nightmare Fredbear, **NIGHTMARE** appears from both hallways (but closer), in the closet, and on the bed. Nightmare only appears on Night 07 and Night 08 after 4:00 a.m. and has the same audio clues as Nightmare Fredbear, but Nightmare's move timers and leniency are much lower than Nightmare Fredbear's.

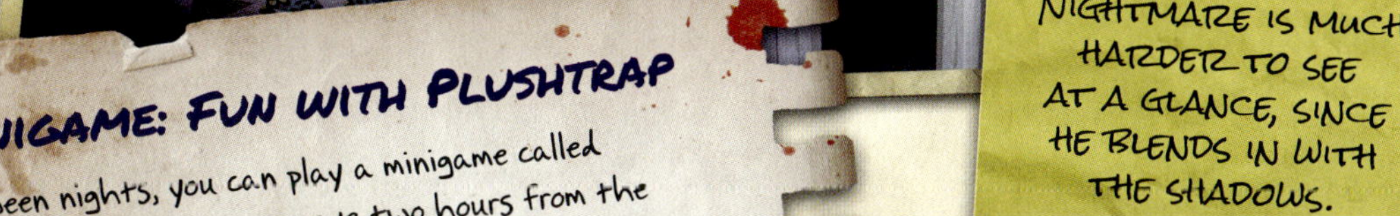

NIGHTMARE IS MUCH HARDER TO SEE AT A GLANCE, SINCE HE BLENDS IN WITH THE SHADOWS.

MINIGAME: FUN WITH PLUSHTRAP

Between nights, you can play a minigame called *Fun with Plushtrap* to remove two hours from the clock (game starts at 2:00 a.m.). Your goal is to get Plushtrap to land on an X on the floor of the darkened hallway. When you flick the flashlight on, Plushtrap will either go limp or hide in an adjacent room. If you don't check on him enough, Plushtrap will jump-scare you; check on him too often and he won't make it to the X within the time limit. To win, wait until you hear two main scurrying noises (running footsteps). Then, when you hear the next walking sound, flash your flashlight.

- **NIGHTMARE FREDBEAR AND NIGHTMARE** will run down either hallway. Leniency on Nightmare Fredbear is higher than Nightmare on reaction time. Sometimes, going to the opposite side and letting them teleport to the Bed or Closet (random) is a good strategy to reset each one's pathing. Laughs from these two can be completely random. They don't necessarily indicate a teleport to the Bed or Closet.

Codes, Glitches, and Secrets

Extras Menu

Beating Night 05 unlocks the Extras menu, allowing players to view animatronics, a "Making of . . ." gallery progression, jump-scares, minigames, Nightmare mode, and cheats. Some of these options remain locked until players complete Night 06.

Cheats include a map of the house with a "radar" of the animatronics, faster nights (thirty seconds instead of sixty seconds each), and a danger indicator near the hallway doors.

Night 08

Though there is no "custom night" in *FNAF4*, there is still a way to play 20/20/20/20. Enter the new Extras menu and type "20202020" to access this final challenge. All the animatronics are set to their maximum difficulty level, and Nightmare does appear after 4:00 a.m.

Rare Screens

Don't miss these rare screens in *FNAF4*, which point to a darker plot twist. Turning around to clear Freddles from the bed, you may get one of these three rare screens, which show a pill bottle, an IV, and a vase of flowers on your bedside table.

Night-End Minigame Easter Eggs

Night 02: When you're urged to run past a silhouetted Freddy and Spring Bonnie, turn back to the right first to get a glimpse of Purple Guy helping someone into the Spring Bonnie suit. This is our only glimpse of Purple Guy in *FNAF4*.

Night 03: The girl with pigtails along your walk home reveals that the animatronics "come to life at night" and that "if you die, they hide your body and never tell anyone." On the previous screen, a kid holds a Spring Bonnie plush.

Night 03: Click on the TV in the living room to watch the *Fredbear & Friends* TV show. Notice the copyright date: 1983.

Halloween Edition

The FNAF4 Halloween update replaces Nightmare with Nightmarionne, Nightmare Foxy with Nightmare Mangle, and both Nightmare Bonnie and Nightmare Chica with their own jack-o'-lantern versions.

The update also alters the night-end minigames to fit the Halloween theme (check out the Halloween decor in the house and at Freddy's).

Explore the Extras menu for terrifying new challenges including Blind Mode, Mad Freddy, Insta-Foxy, and All Nightmare.

Try clicking the nose of the plush Freddy on the bed.

NIGHTMARE FOXY AND NIGHTMARE MANGLE DEFENSE:

Flashing the hallway where Foxy ends up can force him to move back to his starting spot. Foxy will enter the room and closet if he is in the mid-hallway and you go to the opposite door from where Foxy remains.

You have to keep track of the running footsteps and the Stereo side of where the footsteps end, as well as the louder version of it, to determine when Foxy is ready to enter the room—louder footsteps on one side mean that Foxy is waiting to enter if you go to the opposite door.

Foxy technically bypasses the nearest spot to the door on either side, but you can still see Foxy when you flash the flashlight if he is at the closest spot in the hallway that he reaches before being able to enter the room.

Using the flashlight on the hallway with Foxy in a threatening spot forces Foxy to the back of the hallway, where he can move sides and/or advance to the middle of his current hallway.

Sometimes Bonnie and Chica are greater threats to deal with, so a good plan is to try to keep Foxy away until 3:00 a.m. or later.

NIGHTMARE BONNIE AND NIGHTMARE CHICA

- Using the flashlight when these two are at the nearest spot in their hallways will cause a jump-scare.
- If the door is closed when they're at the nearest spot at a movement check, each will retreat to the back of the Hallway.
- Flashing the hallway multiple times can be a plus, as long as Bonnie and Chica aren't there.

If you do 15 consecutive seconds of Bed Viewing, Foxy will jump-scare you, even on Night 01 (Foxy technically isn't supposed to be active until Night 02).

One Pretty Big Issue: No Preloaded Lit Areas

FNAF4 doesn't use optimized image compression, and preloading isn't done on a lot of the hallway and bed "flashed" images. So, it's a good idea to start the night by holding down your flashlight until the "flashed" version of each area loads. If you don't do this, Nighmare is likely to jump-scare you on Nights 07 and 08. There's more leniency with Nightmare Fredbear, but it's not a good idea to hope that your images will load in before you're attacked . . .

A Funny Exploit

You can technically win Nights 01–06 without closing the doors, and relying on movement and flashlight mechanics.

AI Levels Per Night

Night 03 puts Bonnie a bit more in the background, which allows you to learn the dynamics of the other animatronics better as Chica is much more active, and Freddy starts to move, too.

The Bite of '83

It's now widely accepted among fans that *FNAF4* doesn't show the infamous Bite of '87, but instead a different Bite of '83. The evidence?

- **Fredbear & Friends:** In the Night 03 minigame, the TV plays a show with a 1983 copyright date.
- **Responsibility:** The Bite of '87 forced management to introduce new rules for the animatronics.
- **Frontal Lobe:** The Bite of '87 resulted in the loss of the victim's frontal lobe. The frontal lobe deals with coordination, memory, planning, reasoning/discernment, and the like.
- **Secret Cameras:** In the Private Room of *Sister Location*, a remote control is held by the Fredbear plush that we see in the *FNAF4* night-end minigames. A secret keypad on the wall has the passcode "1983"; the keypad brings up a security camera feed . . . of the *FNAF4* house.
- **Cameo:** The *Curse of Dreadbear* seemingly takes place during "Fall Fest '83." The *FNAF4* house appears on a hill in the distance.

Fan Theories: What's Up with Fredbear?

It seems clear someone is spying on the bite victim, between the creepy way the Fredbear plush follows him around in the *FNAF4* night-end minigames and the *FNAF4* camera feed in *Sister Location*'s Private Room. Why though? Could it be because of what the child saw at the pizzeria? Or because the keeper of the cameras knows how dangerous the animatronics are?

At the end of the game, the Fredbear plush does give you a clue as to the bite victim's fate:

> "You're broken . . . I'm still here. I will put you back together."

Some interesting theories:

- Based on a similar wording in *Sister Location*, could this mean whoever is spying wants to put the bite victim's soul into an animatronic?
- The "putting you back together" notion is also a central theme in *FNAF World*.
- Is this line coming from one of the creators of the animatronics, either Henry or William Afton?
- Could the bite victim ultimately possess Golden Freddy, whom many fans believe to be an old Fredbear springlock suit?

Chapter 5

Five Nights at Freddy's: Sister Location

If you thought *FNAF4* was a departure, allow us to introduce you to *Five Nights at Freddy's: Sister Location*, the game that took the series in a completely different direction. For the first time in *FNAF*, you're out of the one-room setup and allowed (mostly) free rein of the building. Added to your night-guard duties are various maintenance tasks, including repairing the animatronics, which you somehow have to do *without* getting murdered by them.

The series continues to get darker with the introduction of Ennard (try explaining this character to your grandma) as well as a number of mysterious Easter eggs that have launched a whole new string of theories. This game also features a full cast of voice characters in the animatronics who are—not surprisingly—pretty talkative. With the added dialogue comes some quirky humor, a refreshing light in this deep and winding saga.

But perhaps the biggest change for the series is the absence of, well, Freddy's. *Sister Location* is set at Circus Baby's Entertainment and Rental—an apparent warehouse of animatronics. The animatronics live here, but they're rented out for parties.

There's a lot to unpack, so let's get started.

Exotic Butters

As you boot up the game, you'll overhear a conversation. An unnamed man questions a "Mr. Afton" on some of his animatronic design choices, but you never hear the end of the conversation.

Similar flashback audio plays before each night, but this time you'll hear a little girl—Mr. Afton's daughter—talking. She begs her father to play with Circus Baby, at one point asking, "Didn't you make her just for me?" At the end of Night 05, you'll hear an ominous line implying the girl may have been killed by the animatronic. "Don't tell Daddy that I'm here . . . I don't know why he won't let me come see you . . . Where did the other children go?"

Welcome to Circus Baby's Pizza World!

The game begins in an elevator, where you meet the Handyman's Robotics and Unit Repair System Model 5 (aka HandUnit). Your first task is to enter your name in the system, but it autocorrects to "Eggs Benedict." When you get to the bottom, head toward the caution tape to crawl through the vent.

As you crawl, HandUnit explains that Freddy Fazbear's Pizza was a huge success until it was closed down, at which point there was room for a "new contender in children's entertainment." The animatronics here are rented out for parties; your job is to keep them working.

Night 01

Follow HandUnit's directions to administer a "controlled shock" to Ballora and Funtime Foxy, summoning them to their stages. Once they appear, crawl through the vent to the Circus Gallery Control Module (aka Circus Control) to summon Circus Baby. She won't appear.

NIGHT 02

On your elevator ride, select a new voice for HandUnit. Whatever button you press, it autocorrects to "angsty teen."

In the Primary Control Module, follow HandUnit's instructions. Trying to summon Funtime Foxy and Ballora to the stage will cause a glitch, restoring HandUnit's default voice. Head through the vents to summon Circus Baby. This time, however, as you try to "motivate" Circus Baby, there's a power malfunction. HandUnit reboots the system, which also takes down the security doors, vent locks, and oxygen!

Circus Baby tells you to hide in a space under the desk that a previous guard created. After hiding there, pull on the metal sheet to close off the space, and keep it closed when Bidybabs start tugging on it.

After the Bidybabs retreat, Circus Baby tells you not to listen to HandUnit's instructions about Ballora. Seconds later, HandUnit returns—you'll need to restart the system manually in the Breaker Room. As you cross Ballora Gallery, ignore HandUnit's urging to speed up. Ballora is triggered by sound, so advance across the gallery slowly and stop if Ballora's music gets louder.

In the Breaker Room, click and hold the buttons on the left side of the map to restore power to each area. Listen for Funtime Freddy's approach and play audio to distract him. Once the breakers are back on, your shift is over. If you can avoid Ballora as you go through Ballora Gallery, you'll reach the Breaker Room door.

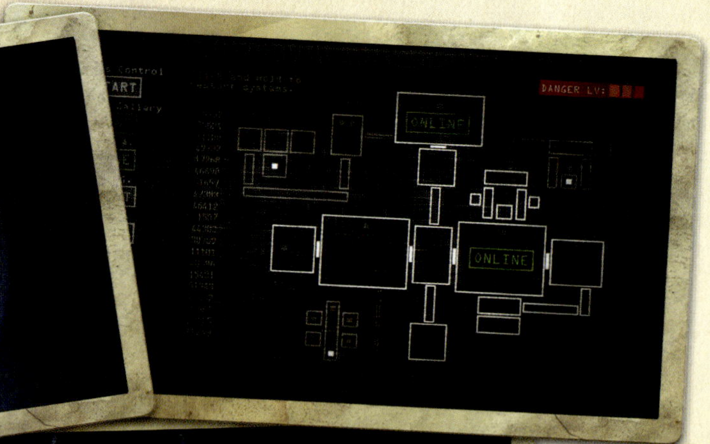

NIGHT 03

Your elevator trip includes a musical selection: "Casual Bongos." Tonight you're performing maintenance work on Funtime Freddy. You may not be qualified to do this, but that's okay!

At the control center, check on Ballora and Funtime Foxy. Ballora is on the stage in pieces. Funtime Foxy isn't there, but HandUnit doesn't notice. HandUnit tells you not to visit Circus Baby. Proceed into the right vent.

To perform maintenance on Freddy, you'll have to make it past Funtime Auditorium . . . and Funtime Foxy. Her auditorium is dark, but you can use the flash beacon as needed. Funtime Foxy is motion-activated, so be patient and move in short bursts, flashing your light periodically. If you see him, stop and wait until she moves away.

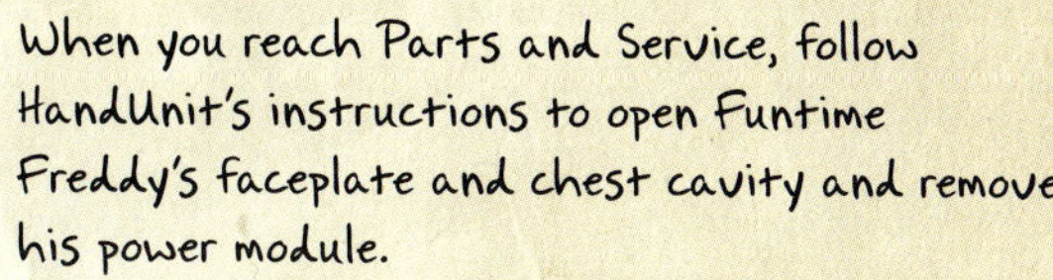

When you reach Parts and Service, follow HandUnit's instructions to open Funtime Freddy's faceplate and chest cavity and remove his power module.

Now you must collect the secondary power module on the Bon-Bon puppet. Bon-Bon hides from your flashlight, so wait for him to appear at the edge of the light. When Bon-Bon's chest is visible, click on the button below his bow tie to complete the repair.

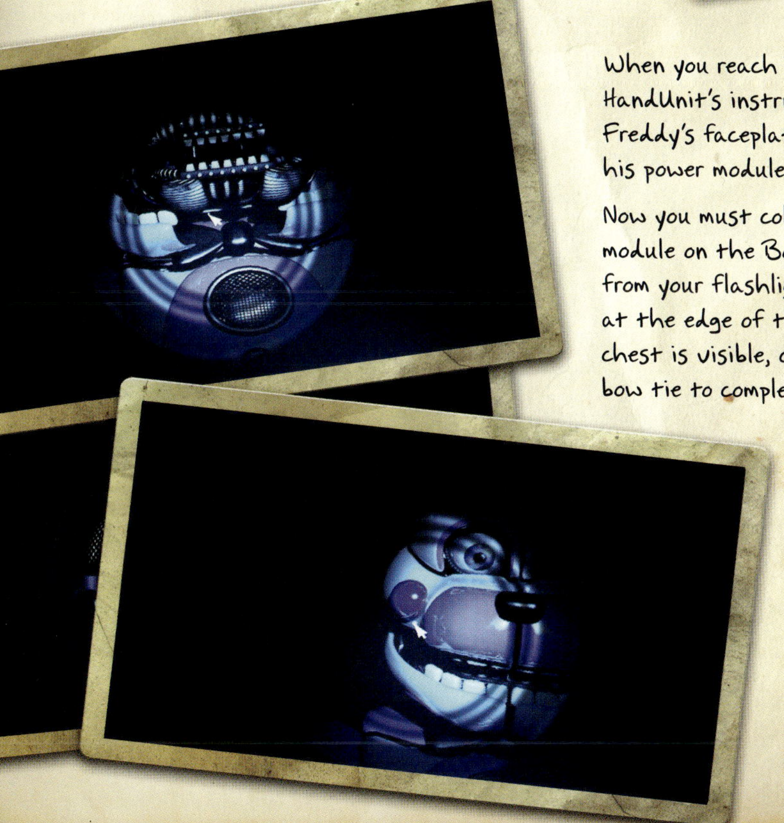

Exit through Funtime Auditorium, but don't worry about moving slowly—it's impossible to avoid triggering Funtime Foxy's jump-scare, which ends the night.

NIGHT 04

When you awake, you're inside a springlock suit, compliments of Circus Baby. You watch as two technicians bring Ballora into the Scooping Room, where the "Scooper" machine rips Ballora's endoskeleton out of her body. After the techs leave, Circus Baby opens the springlock suit's faceplates so the company can find you on the security cameras. You'll have to survive in the meantime.

There are ten springlocks—five on each side—and they turn red when they're about to trip. Click and hold the springlocks to keep them wound. You have to be very fast and very precise with your mouse movement so you have enough time winding. If you aren't precise, you won't have enough time to wind the springlocks to prevent a jump-scare. On a PC, you can hold down your mouse button and hover over the springlocks instead of clicking them individually each time. Beware the Minireenas closing in. Shaking them off causes the springlocks to unwind faster, but you'll need to do so to avoid a jump-scare. You can't avoid the Minireenas climbing into the suit, but shake off the ones crawling up the sides before they exit the top of the screen. Try to minimize the number of times you shake the suit, because it will affect the springlocks.

NIGHT 05

To celebrate the end of your first week, the company is sending a gift basket of . . . Exotic Butters. HandUnit reveals that there are still two technicians on site. When you check on Funtime Foxy and Ballora, you'll find the techs—hanging from the show stage.

Pass through the empty Funtime Auditorium to enter Parts and Service and perform maintenance on Circus Baby. There Circus Baby tells you she's broken and they want to scoop her, but that won't solve the problem. She asks you to save the good parts of her so the bad will be destroyed.

Following her instructions, pull up Baby's hidden keypad and enter the code quickly and correctly. Failing to input the code results in an endoskeleton jump-scare. Open the hatch on her arm, take the green card, and press the button "Conveyor Belt."

REAL ENDING

Follow Circus Baby's directions to reach the Scooping Room. HandUnit quickly reveals that you've entered a restricted area—you're on the wrong side of the Scooper.

Unfortunately, this was all part of Circus Baby's plan. As she explains, "If we looked like you, then we would have somewhere to go." You'll catch a glimpse of a new animatronic in the window—Ennard—an amalgam of the animatronics you've met. You'll find yourself powerless to prevent Ennard from "scooping" your insides out and replacing your skeleton with itself. Now Ennard can use your body to escape into the world. As the credits roll, brightening up the image shows the text "REAL ENDING" in the lower left corner.

THE IMMORTAL AND THE RESTLESS

At the end of each night, you watch a soap opera called *The Immortal and the Restless,* which features a vampire named Vlad arguing with his mistress, Clara, about child support, the paternity of their precocious baby, etc. It's pretty obvious Vlad is the father . . . and that he and Clara are a bad match. Clara burns down his house, threatens to sell her ring, and more, but they ultimately reconcile. What could these soap operas mean?

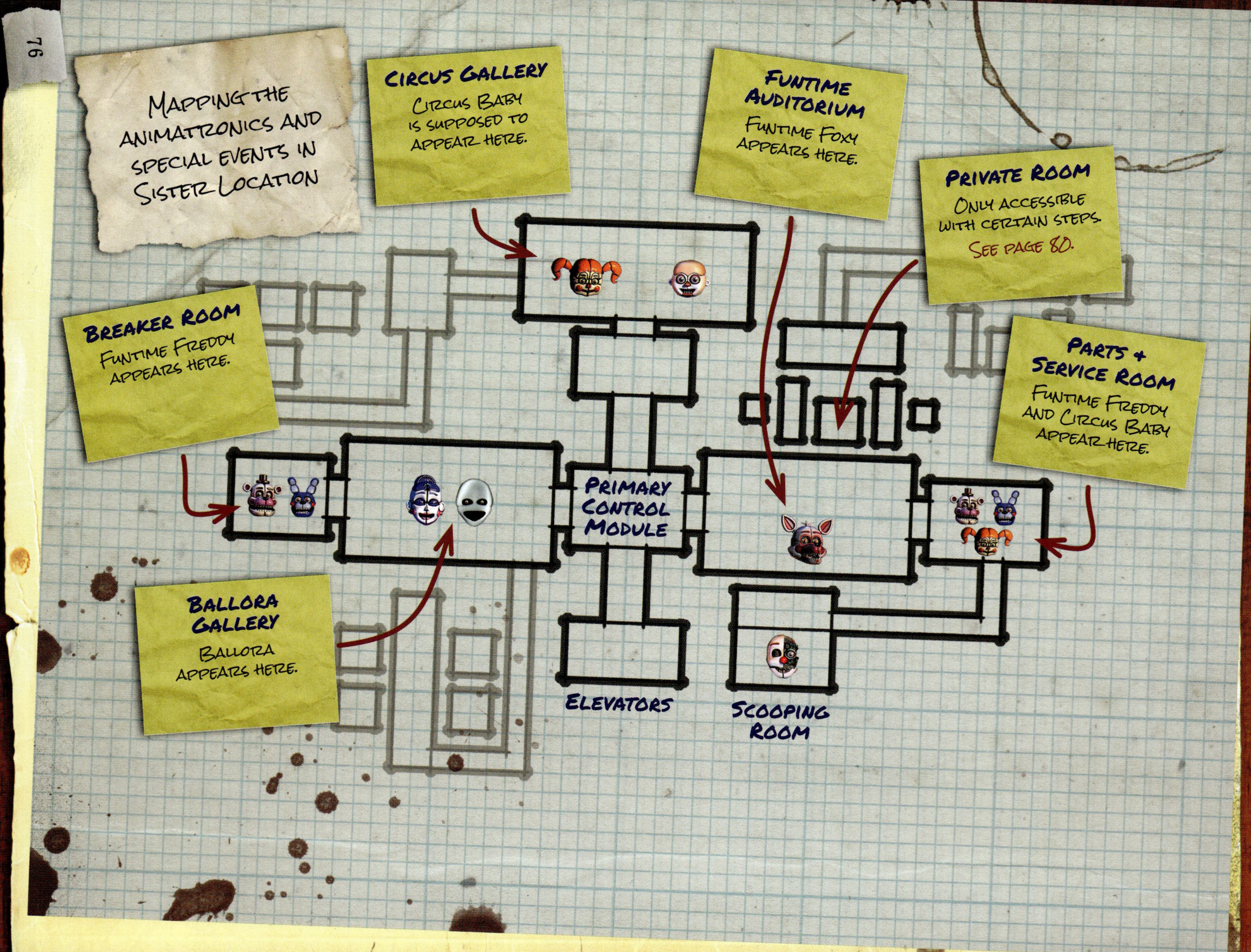

Mapping the animatronics and special events in Sister Location
Circus Gallery
Circus Baby is supposed to appear here.
Funtime Auditorium
Funtime Foxy appears here.
Private Room
Only accessible with certain steps.
See page 80.
Breaker Room
Funtime Freddy appears here.
Parts & Service Room
Funtime Freddy and Circus Baby appear here.
Primary Control Module
Ballora Gallery
Ballora appears here.
Elevators
Scooping Room

Codes, Glitches, and Secrets

BLUEPRINTS

Blueprints for Circus Baby, Funtime Freddy, Ballora, and Funtime Foxy can rarely be found on the game load screen. Their design choices seem meant to lure children in to be kidnapped, and are no doubt what the technicians were referencing in the prologue.

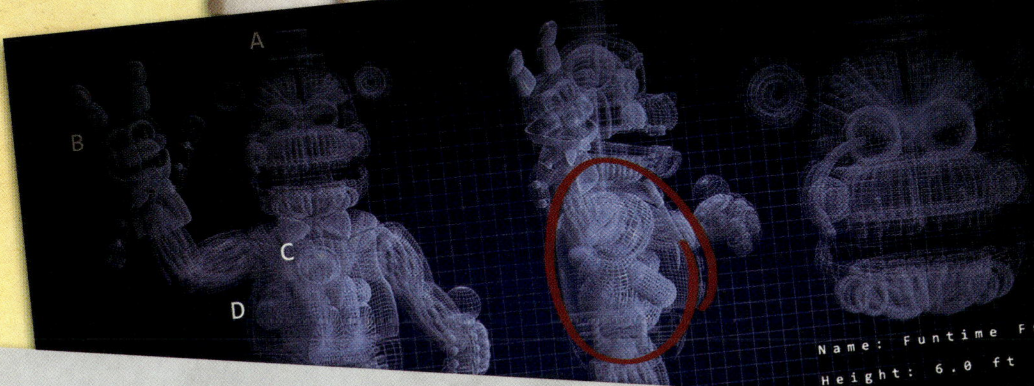

ROAD TO THE SECRET ENDING!

On Night Ø3, before heading to Funtime Auditorium, go to the Circus Gallery Control Room and enter the crawl space under the desk. Circus Baby will tell you about the first and only night she was onstage. Part of her programming requires her to count children. As soon as there was only one child left in the room with her, she lost control of herself. Her stomach opened and made an ice-cream cone. Then she pulled the unfortunate little girl inside herself. Baby is still haunted by her screams.

IS THAT A KID IN FREDDY'S STORAGE TANK?

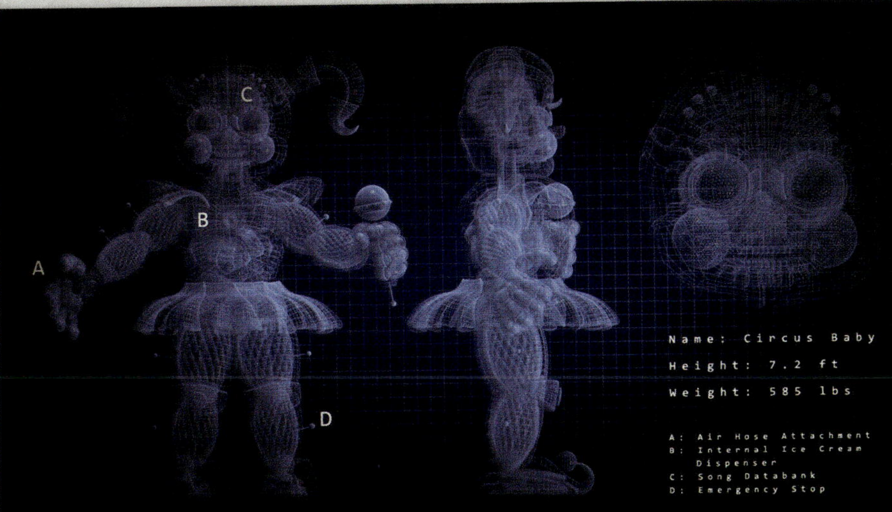

FNAF·SL RETRO ARCADE

Circus Baby minigame

The Circus Baby minigame may appear after a jump-scare. In order to unlock the secret ending, you need to fully complete this minigame. Playing as Circus Baby, you must collect food and give it to children within a limited amount of time. Each kid needs to be fed two cupcakes, unless you hit them with a green cupcake. Their color will change from green to red when they've had their fill.

Collectible Food:

- **Pink Cupcake:** Single throw cupcakes
- **Blue Cupcake:** Triple throw; can feed kids lined up vertically
- **Green Cupcake:** Single throw; can fully feed multiple kids lined up horizontally
- **Ice-Cream Cone:** Unlocks secret child

Jump to grab the pink cupcakes, and throw two at the first child and then another two at the next child. Continue right into the next area, but do *NOT* target the kids on the lower level! Instead, jump up and throw another two cupcakes each at the kids on the platforms.

From the upper-right platform, jump right into the next screen to leap over a blue cupcake and land on a middle island. Proceed right to the next area, and throw your last two pink cupcakes right as you jump to the first platform.

Return left to grab the blue cupcake, then head right again. Jump to the middle platform and throw twice to hit all three kids lined up vertically at the same time. Continue to the right, but do not grab the green cupcake. Hop onto the left edge of the platform to jump over it. In the next area, jump and throw twice to hit the three kids arranged vertically.

Now return left to collect the green cupcake. Continue left until you reach the area where you ignored the two unfed kids. Throw a green cupcake at them. Quickly return to the right, jumping all of the gaps. In the area where you hit the last set of three kids arranged vertically, there is a gap at the far end. Jump it, and immediately throw a cupcake to hit the kids in the next room! Continue to the right, jumping gaps and throwing cupcakes as necessary.

At the end of the screen, take the ice-cream cone but *don't* exit to the GOAL. Instead, run all the way back to the left. You'll reach the end with only seconds to spare, but as long as the timer doesn't expire, a girl will come out for the ice cream. Circus Baby grabs her with a terrible scream.

TO ACCESS THE GAME QUICKLY, GO TO THE EXTRAS MENU AND MOVE YOUR MOUSE TO THE LOWER LEFT CORNER. CLICK ON THE ICON OF CIRCUS BABY WHEN IT APPEARS.

Gameplay and Strategy

Private Room

After completing the Circus Baby minigame, you can disobey Baby's directions on Night 05. Move right in Funtime Auditorium to find the Private Room. HandUnit will inform you that you're not allowed to leave until 6:00 a.m. Sound familiar?

Your task is to survive the night against Ennard in a manner similar to *FNAF*. Listen carefully for sound clues to determine Ennard's whereabouts and use the monitor and doors sparingly. Survive the night and you'll be treated to a final installment of *The Immortal and the Restless*—complete with your Exotic Butters gift basket—but you're not alone. Ennard has followed you.

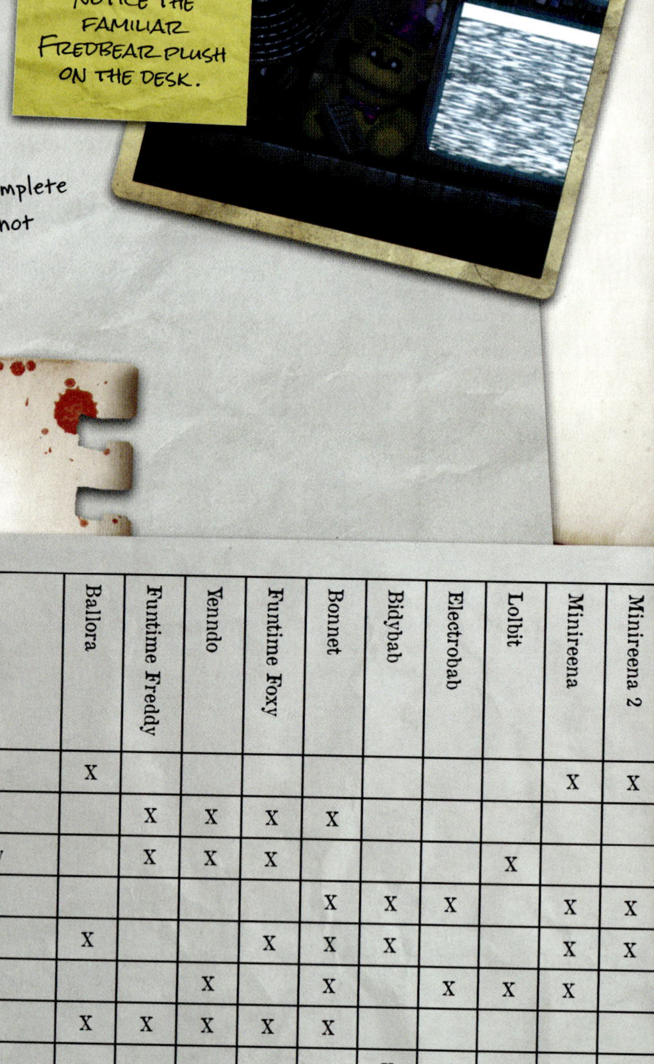

Enter 1-9-8-3 on the keypad to bring up *FNAFY* camera feeds on the desk monitors!

Notice the familiar Fredbear plush on the desk.

Custom Night

Defeating Ennard unlocks a series of custom nights with preset AI difficulties. You must defeat each on V. Hard to access bonus cut scenes.

	Ballora	Funtime Freddy	Yenndo	Funtime Foxy	Bonnet	Bidybab	Electrobab	Lolbit	Minireena	Minireena 2
Angry Ballet	X								X	X
Freddy & Co.		X	X	X	X					
Funtime Frenzy		X	X	X				X		
Dolls, Attack!					X	X	X		X	X
Girls' Night	X			X	X	X			X	X
Weirdos			X		X		X	X	X	
Top Shelf	X	X	X	X	X					
Bottom Shelf						X	X	X	X	X
Cupcake Challenge	X	X		X	X		X	X	X	
Golden Freddy	X	X	X	X	X	X	X	X	X	X

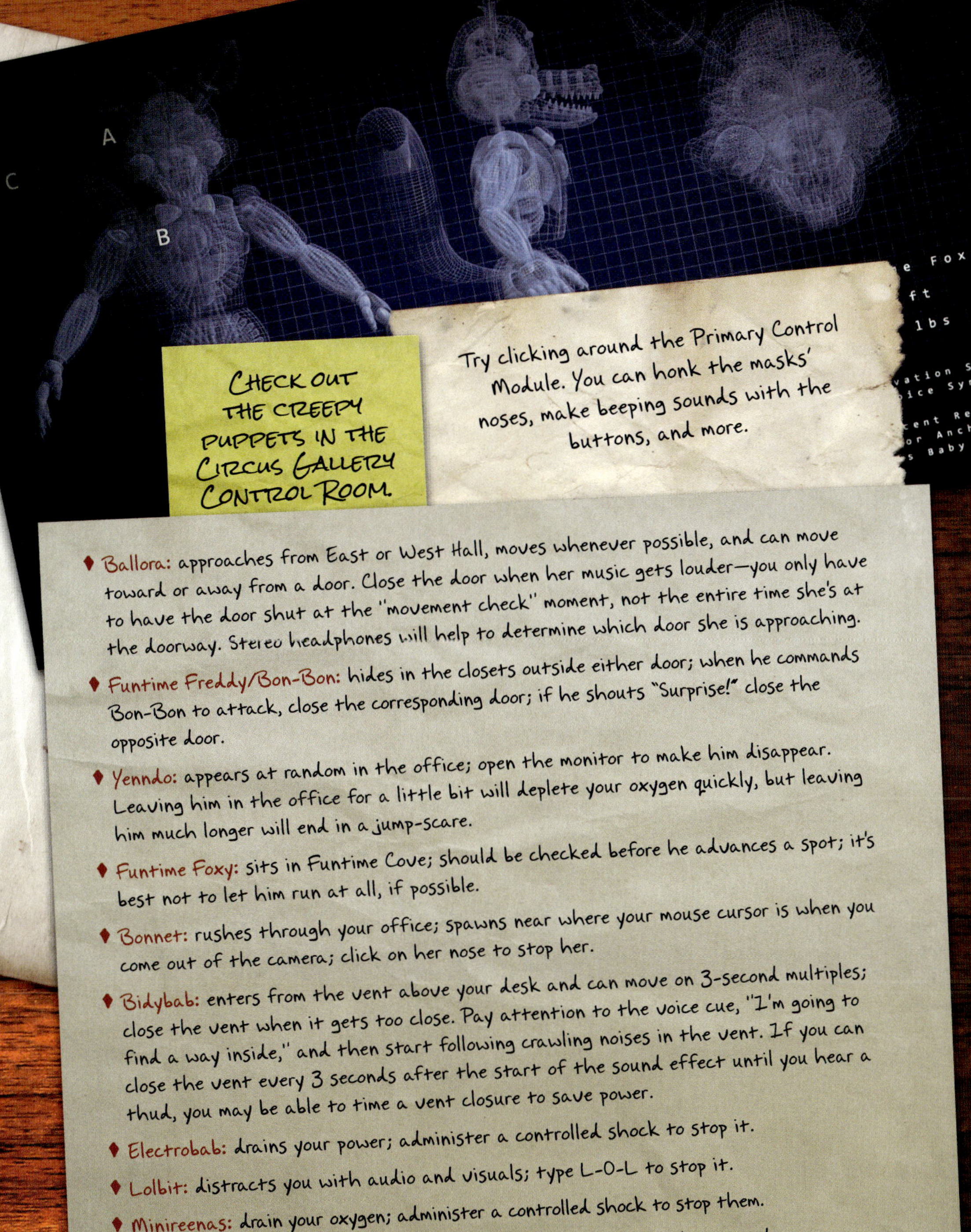

CHECK OUT THE CREEPY PUPPETS IN THE CIRCUS GALLERY CONTROL ROOM.

Try clicking around the Primary Control Module. You can honk the masks' noses, make beeping sounds with the buttons, and more.

- **Ballora:** approaches from East or West Hall, moves whenever possible, and can move toward or away from a door. Close the door when her music gets louder—you only have to have the door shut at the "movement check" moment, not the entire time she's at the doorway. Stereo headphones will help to determine which door she is approaching.
- **Funtime Freddy/Bon-Bon:** hides in the closets outside either door; when he commands Bon-Bon to attack, close the corresponding door; if he shouts "Surprise!" close the opposite door.
- **Yenndo:** appears at random in the office; open the monitor to make him disappear. Leaving him in the office for a little bit will deplete your oxygen quickly, but leaving him much longer will end in a jump-scare.
- **Funtime Foxy:** sits in Funtime Cove; should be checked before he advances a spot; it's best not to let him run at all, if possible.
- **Bonnet:** rushes through your office; spawns near where your mouse cursor is when you come out of the camera; click on her nose to stop her.
- **Bidybab:** enters from the vent above your desk and can move on 3-second multiples; close the vent when it gets too close. Pay attention to the voice cue, "I'm going to find a way inside," and then start following crawling noises in the vent. If you can close the vent every 3 seconds after the start of the sound effect until you hear a thud, you may be able to time a vent closure to save power.
- **Electrobab:** drains your power; administer a controlled shock to stop it.
- **Lolbit:** distracts you with audio and visuals; type L-O-L to stop it.
- **Minireenas:** drain your oxygen; administer a controlled shock to stop them.
- **Minireenas 2:** randomly appear over your line of sight; cannot be stopped.

NOTE THAT NONE OF THE CUSTOM NIGHT GAMEPLAY IS CONSIDERED CANON. (SORRY TO THE LOLBIT FANS.)

ON NIGHT 05, THE ENNARD MASK IN THE PRIMARY CONTROL MODULE IS MISSING, THOUGH IT WILL SOMETIMES CHANGE TO A LOLBIT MASK.

- If you think you've got the skills, give this minimalist camera route a try:
  - CAM 07 for Funtime Foxy—flip regularly to be safe
  - CAM 07 check for Funtime Foxy again
  - CAM 04 for Electrobab + Shock him, then back to CAM 07 for Funtime Foxy
  - CAM 07 check for Funtime Foxy
  - CAM 03 for Electrobab + Shock him, then back to CAM 07 for Funtime Foxy

- Flip twice on the regular when coming out of the cameras, or until Yenndo is removed.
- Handle Bonnet's nose while keeping an eye on Lolbit appearances to get ready to type L-O-L.
- Keep track of Funtime Freddy and his cues.
- Listen for Bidybab's noises.
- Add in Minireena checks if you want a much brighter experience with oxygen!

Fun Fact: The S.C.U.P. has its name shown in Freddy Fazbear's Pizzeria Simulator in a blueprint!

Audio Skipping

You can technically use Ctrl+S and then Ctrl+S again to skip entire audio sequences, which is helpful for speedrunning. But, if you don't hit the keys cleanly, you can get out-of-phase and have no audio for awhile.

Ennard Room / Private Room Strategy

- You need the keycard to play this Strategy. Get it from the "return route" on the Circus Baby/Ice Cream minigame.
- Go Forward and Right (W+D) as you go down the unlit Funtime Auditorium.
- Make sure you're using stereo headphones and are in Stereo mode if playing on a PC.
- The entire night is 9 minutes long, which means every hour is 90 seconds long.
- Note that Baby speaking and other sound effects can sometimes stop the audio cue for Ennard's movement . . . It's possible that Ennard can move silently.
- CAM 01, CAM 02, and CAM 05 are the only cameras you really need to check (doors and vent) in the Private Room.

Ennard's Movements

Ennard doesn't move until 40 seconds into the night—don't bother with camera usage or door manipulation until you reach this point.

- Ennard will move every 8 seconds until 3:00 a.m.
- Ennard will move every 6 seconds when it's 3:00 a.m.
- Ennard will move every 3 seconds when it's 4:00 a.m.
- Ennard will move every 2 seconds when it's 5:00 a.m. (until it hits 6:00 a.m.).

Get used to Ennard's movement noises. The Vent noises, for example, are characteristic compared to a hallway movement.

Ennard's retreat noise is also characteristic, often like a faucet sound.

Conserve power where possible—don't keep doors shut that don't have to be shut.

Running out of power vs. Ennard moving every 2 seconds in the last hour is really rough, so just don't run out of power.

Note: the power scaling on the Private Room won't leave you a ton of power remaining.

Final Cut Scenes

After defeating each of the first nine custom nights, you'll watch one of seven 8-bit cut scenes. Ennard (who now occupies your body) is going through the world like normal, only your body is decaying. Ennard's endoskeleton eventually leaves in search of a fresher body, but strangely, your body comes back to life.

Defeating the Golden Freddy custom night on Very Hard unlocks something even more earth-shattering: this message from Michael.

"Father, it's me, Michael. I did it. I found it—it was right where you said it would be. They were all there. They didn't recognize me at first, but then they thought I was you. And I found her. I put her back together, just like you asked me to. She's free now. But something is wrong with me. I should be dead, but I'm not. I've been living in shadows. There is only one thing left for me to do now. I'm going to come find you. I'm going to come find you."

Lore and Theories

MICHAEL . . . AFTON?

The second secret ending of *Sister Location* was quite a doozy, confirming that William Afton's son, Michael, is out there, possibly helping his father. Since then, many theories have popped up about Michael's role in the *FNAF* universe.

One strain of theories posits that Michael is the player character across *FNAF*, *FNAF2*, *FNAF3*, and *Sister Location*.

- **Aliases:** Fans use the fact Michael goes by "Mike" in *Sister Location* to link him to the guard "Mike Schmidt" from *FNAF*. The names on the paychecks in *FNAF2* (Jeremy, Fritz) interestingly match the first names of some of the murder victims we see on the gravestones screen from *Pizzeria Simulator*.
- **Pink Slips:** The player character is repeatedly fired for tampering with the animatronics—which, aside from alluding to the custom night and knowledge of animatronics, could point to turning off their facial recognition or collecting Remnant. Another reason cited in *FNAF2* is "odor"—which could link to Michael's decomposing body.

Fan Theories: A Family Affair

Many theorists insist that *Sister Location* proves that *FNAF* is truly a "family affair." Some theorists purport that *FNAF4* introduces us to the family of William Afton, and *Sister Location* shows us where they end up.

The Younger Son: The Bite Victim

William Afton seems to have been watching the bite victim in *FNAF4*, between the camera feeds in the Private Room and parts of the Breaker Room map matching up with the layout of the *FNAF4* house. Plush Fredbear's line at the close of *FNAF4* says, "I will put you back together." Sound familiar?

It's the same thing Michael Afton says during the last custom night cut scene in *Sister Location*: "I put her back together, just like you asked me to." Could this mean that the younger son was also put back together in a similar manner, and is possessing an animatronic?

The Older Son: Michael Afton, AKA, You

This theory seems confirmed by the game. In the final cut scene, you call William Afton "father," and state your name—"Michael." (Remember how we saw "Mike" taped to the keypad in the elevator?) Strangely, in the 8-bit Ennard cut scene, when you come back to life, it's Circus Baby's voice—your sister's voice—that seems to bring you back.

The Daughter: Elizabeth Afton, aka Circus Baby

At the end of each night in *Sister Location*, we overhear a girl pleading with her father to let her play with Circus Baby. On the final night, she is left alone with Circus Baby, and we know from Circus Baby's dialogue on Night Ø2 how that ended. Further proof comes from Circus Baby's eye color, which changes in her minigame to match that of the little girl. From the novel series and *Pizzeria Simulator*, we get seeming confirmation that Circus Baby is indeed Afton's daughter, Elizabeth.

Further proof for this theory seemed to come from *Pizzeria Simulator*, where the rare screen of Lefty in the back alleyway shows an interesting poster.

Chapter 6

Freddy Fazbear's Pizzeria Simulator

CONGRATULATIONS! You, yes, you, have been chosen as the newest franchise owner of a Fazbear Entertainment restaurant! The sixth game in the Five Nights at Freddy's series, *Freddy Fazbear's Pizzeria Simulator*, puts you in the driver's seat of your very own restaurant. Choose the decor, the games, the entertainment; the possibilities are endless!

But it's not all fun and games. Split into three parts, the gameplay consists first of restaurant management, where you buy and place animatronics, games, and decor. The next stage is office maintenance, where hardcore *FNAF* fans are sure to shine. Your goal seems innocent enough: complete the tasks assigned to you in your dark office. But depending on your choices, you could find yourself fighting for your life against a horde of vicious animatronics, including some, er, not-so-friendly faces. The final part of your day is salvaging, where you must sort through and test old animatronics that were found outside your door.

Pizzeria Simulator shocked and delighted fans with its new concept, allowing for near-infinite possibilities and a variety of different endings. Though first appearing as a fun and funny new take on the mythos of *FNAF*, the game quickly takes a dark turn. With creepy minigames that both answer old questions and open up new ones, and a "good" ending that seemingly wraps up some of the many mysteries of the franchise, *Pizzeria Simulator* is sure to keep you on your toes . . . and keep you up at night.

The Freddy Scoop

Before the 8-bit minigame starts, choose toppings for your own pizza. If you choose a specific vegetable-only set (Onions, Mushroom, Olives, Peppers), you'll start with an extra $200! After your toppings selection, dive into the minigame, where Freddy has to deliver pizzas to hungry customers. As the levels increase, a Shadow Freddy will appear and try to block you from delivering the pizzas. As you continue to get past him, the game suddenly glitches, causing multiple shadow Freddys to appear until the screen cuts to black.

When the screen flickers back to life, you'll see Scrap Baby, a broken-down version of Circus Baby. Look down to find a piece of paper and a tape recorder. The tape recorder plays and the Cassette Man asks you to document the responses of the animatronic based on various aural stimuli. Two noises play and seemingly nothing happens, so you can check "No," "Yes," or "Maybe" in each box. On the third test, the pitch of a creepy song rises and rises until the screen cuts to a training video.

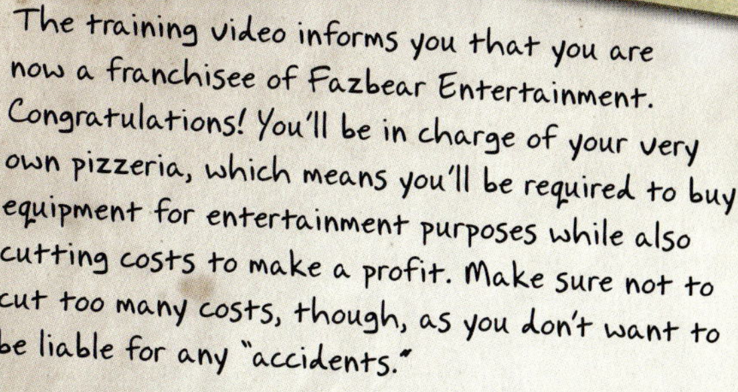

The training video informs you that you are now a franchisee of Fazbear Entertainment. Congratulations! You'll be in charge of your very own pizzeria, which means you'll be required to buy equipment for entertainment purposes while also cutting costs to make a profit. Make sure not to cut too many costs, though, as you don't want to be liable for any "accidents."

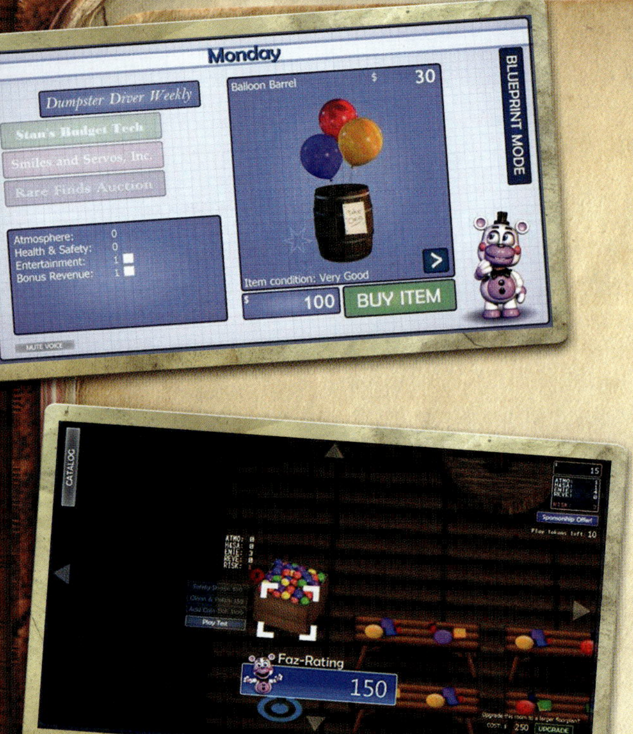

DAY 1: MONDAY

On the Restaurant Management screen, you can buy equipment for your restaurant. After buying the franchise license, you have $100 left, which means only items from "Dumpster Diver Weekly" are affordable (unless you've gone with a vegetarian pizza in the first minigame). As you buy more expensive items, better categories become available. Each item has a value for Atmosphere, Health & Sanitation, Entertainment, Bonus Revenue, and Liability. Placing a Sanitation Station down immediately will help you get some endings, like Certificate of Mediocrity, more reliably.

When you're done buying, move to Blueprint Mode to place equipment in your restaurant. There's a blinking "Sponsorship Offer" in the top-right corner, which gives you extra money. Testing the games also nets bonus revenue. But keep in mind that the Sponsorship Offers you take will result in ads, which can complicate things with Volume when you're in a pinch and may have animatronics lurking . . .

When you're done, click "Finished!" in the bottom-right corner to move to the next phase: the office. Here you must do all the tasks on the computer terminal. Click on a task to start it. Your tasks don't cost money to complete, but you can spend money to upgrade your equipment to make it quieter or more efficient.

Tutorial Unit warns that your terminal and ventilation system are loud, so disable them if the noise draws unwanted attention. Be careful about keeping the ventilation system off, though, as the room will heat up.

You can keep track of what's going on in the vents to your left and right by checking a motion detector, deploying an audio decoy, or using a secondary ventilation system. If all else fails, shine your flashlight into the vent to scare off any visitors.

HONK THE NOSE ON THE HELPY DOLL ON TOP OF YOUR TERMINAL.

After finishing your tasks, log off. The Tutorial Unit congratulates you on a job well done, but reminds you that you must get through the full week in order to prove yourself. There's a big party this Saturday, and if you are successful, you'll be rewarded.

The final phase of the day is salvaging. You're brought back to the dimly lit desk, a piece of paper and a recorder in front of you. Only this time you're facing Molten Freddy, a broken-down Funtime Freddy.

Cassette Man tells you to inspect the animatronics found by the back door. No one knows why they're there, but they can be used for spare parts. You can either salvage them for extra money or throw them away. If the animatronic attacks, you can shock it. If you shock it more than three times, you will irreparably damage the hardware and its value will decrease.

Fail this phase and you will receive a jump-scare and a notification: you lost the salvage, and now something is loose in your pizzeria.

Make it through all five stimuli, shocking each time the animatronic moves, and you will receive money. If you're salvaging for high-level efficiency and don't want to risk losing money, the optimal thing to do is shock the animatronic when it looks very aware and ready to attack. As the screen cuts to black, a distorted voice is heard saying, "Thanks for letting me join the party. I'll try not to disappoint." The animatronic is still loose in your pizzeria.

The day ends with a summary screen totaling the amount of money you made from your restaurant for that day. Great job!

Summary

New Visitors		20
Returning Visitors		0
Turned Away		0
Total Visitors		20
Food Revenue	$	183
Bonus Revenue	$	0
Salvage Revenue	$	0
Total Revenue	$	183
New Lawsuits		

GREAT JOB!

DAY 2: TUESDAY

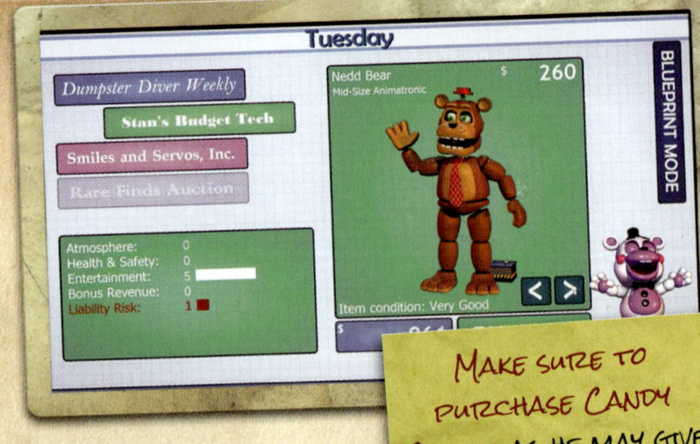

Welcome back! On the Restaurant Management screen, you can buy better equipment with yesterday's profits. Watch the liability ratings on the items, particularly if it says something undesirable might be hiding inside.

MAKE SURE TO PURCHASE CANDY CADET, AS HE MAY GIVE YOU A SURPRISE! (SEE PAGE 107.)

On the Blueprint screen, you can now modify what you've bought by adding coin slots for bonus revenue, cleaning and polishing the item for extra atmosphere, or adding safety straps to reduce risk. There's another sponsorship offer as well.

Once finished, you're brought back to your office. If you salvaged an animatronic or purchased a high-liability animatronic, it will come for you through the vents. Complete your tasks quickly while monitoring the vents.

You can pause a task or shut down your terminal completely if you need to check the vents. The animatronics are attracted to sound, so use an audio decoy to distract them. Beware of sponsorships, as your tasks can be interrupted by a loud advertisement on your terminal if you took one. Be sure to monitor the temperature, too, though the fans and vents can be pretty loud.

If the temperature hits 120 degrees, you'll pass out and be sent back to the Main Menu.

After completing your tasks, you're brought to the Salvage screen again, where you can choose to salvage Scraptrap or throw him away. If you salvage successfully, Scraptrap can be heard saying, "What a deceptive calling. I knew it was a lie the moment I heard it, obviously. But it is intriguing nonetheless . . ."

The Tutorial Unit reminds you, "Don't forget: Saturday, you want them to all be in one place!"

Day 3: Wednesday

Halfway there! You're once more brought to the Restaurant Management and Blueprint screens. Note that you can upgrade the size of your restaurant to accommodate more items, or take another sponsorship to earn more cash.

BUY AND TEST THE ARCADE GAMES MIDNIGHT MOTORIST AND FRUITY MAZE FOR A SPECIAL SURPRISE! (SEE PAGES 98, 100, 102, 104, 108, 109.)

Now back to the office! If you attempted to salvage both animatronics, you'll notice things have gotten a little harder. Complete your tasks without dying and you're brought to the Salvage screen, where you can choose to salvage Scrap Baby, whom you saw at the beginning of the game. If you salvage successfully, you can hear her say, "You don't really know who your employer is . . . do you?" as the screen cuts to black.

Depending on what you bought and the liability issues associated with the equipment, you might find yourself presented with several lawsuits on the Summary screen that you can choose to either fight or settle.

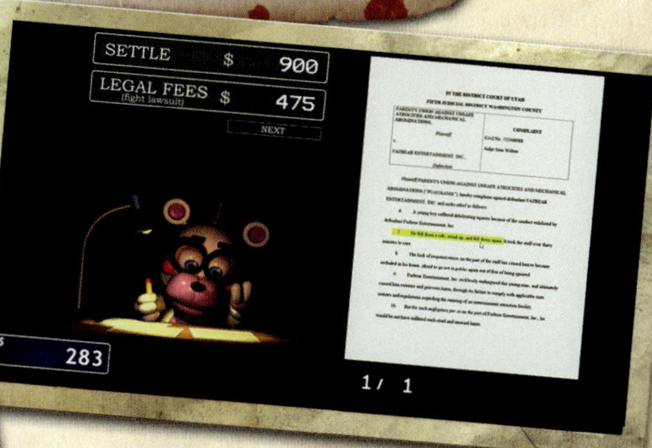

DAY 4: THURSDAY

Another day, another dollar! You're brought back to the Management screen, where you can continue to buy equipment and change the blueprint of your restaurant, upgrading as you see fit. The office will get even more difficult if you salvaged Scrap Baby.

IF YOU'RE ABLE TO MAKE ENOUGH MONEY THROUGH SALVAGING, SPONSORSHIPS, AND BONUS REVENUE FROM TESTING YOUR PRODUCTS, PURCHASE THE SECURITY PUPPET FOR A SURPRISE! (SEE PAGES 98, 103, 104, 106, 394.)

On tonight's Salvage screen, you're presented with Lefty. If you purchased him from the store, you'll be presented with a sign of a winking smiley face that says, "No one is here. I'm already inside." You know the drill: if you choose to salvage him, tase Lefty every time he moves, but not more than three times or you'll reduce his value.

DAY 5: FRIDAY

Keep on keeping on. Buy all the new things! Blueprint those things! Be careful in your office. Lucky you—no salvages today!

DAY 6: SATURDAY

Go about your business filling your restaurant with all the goodies your money can buy. Move along to the office and stay alive through your tasks.

REAL ENDING

After you complete your tasks for the night, the screen goes dark and you'll hear Scrap Baby's voice: "You played right into our hands . . . You gathered them all together in one place, just like he asked you to. All of those little souls in one place. Just for us. A gift. Now we can do what we were created to do and be complete . . ."

Cassette Man interrupts Scrap Baby, calling her Elizabeth. He explains that all the animatronics carrying trapped souls have been brought here and sealed inside as the restaurant is set on fire. Scrap Baby, Scraptrap, Lefty, and Molten Freddy are shown burning as they try to escape, along with images of the various 8-bit minigames from past *FNAF* games.

Cassette Man further states that the restaurant was made to lure the animatronics inside and destroy them so the souls can be freed. All except for one. "The darkest pit of Hell has opened to swallow you whole, so don't keep the Devil waiting, old friend," he says as Scraptrap burns.

Addressing the player, he goes on to say that he had designated an escape route for you, but has a feeling you don't want to leave. Lastly, Cassette Man talks to his daughter and apologizes for not being able to save her.

As the feed cuts out, you're presented with a new voice-over, congratulating you with a Certificate of Completion.

Gameplay and Strategy

Money Money Money

- Use all ten daily tokens to test out games in the pizzeria. You make bonus revenue if you perform well!
- Different games have different difficulties, require different skills, and will pay out different amount potentials.

The Office

- Monitor the motion sensor and watch out for blips on the screen, indicating an animatronic's location.
- Use the audio decoy to move animatronics away from you. Use the decoy within an animatronic's circular audio range; otherwise, it won't hear the decoy!
- Listen closely to distinguish between the sounds of animatronics entering the hall, entering the vent, and shuffling out of the vent!

Don't Tase Me!

- During salvage, the animatronics only move when you check off their responses. If the animatronic is suddenly sitting upright, shock it!

Animatronics

- **Molten Freddy** is worth $500 and can be salvaged on the first night, unless you buy the Discount Ball Pit on Monday—he'll enter the restaurant by hiding in the ball pit. He doesn't speak or make any sound as he climbs through the vents.

- **Scraptrap** appears on the second night and is worth $1,000. If you purchase the Nedd Bear animatronic on Tuesday, Scraptrap won't appear, implying that he hides inside Nedd Bear during the day. As he approaches you from the vents, he makes a loud clamoring sound and says, "You may not recognize me at first, but I assure you, it's still me."

- **Scrap Baby** can be salvaged on the third night and is worth $2,000. As she approaches in the vents, she can be heard saying, "I heard your call!" and "It feels like . . . my birthday. Did you have a gift for me?"

- **Lefty** can either be bought for $5 with a liability rating of 9, the highest of any piece of equipment, or salvaged on the fourth night for $5,000. Similar to Molten Freddy, he doesn't speak when he is in the vents.

Mapping Animatronics and Tips in Freddy Fazbear's Pizzeria Simulator

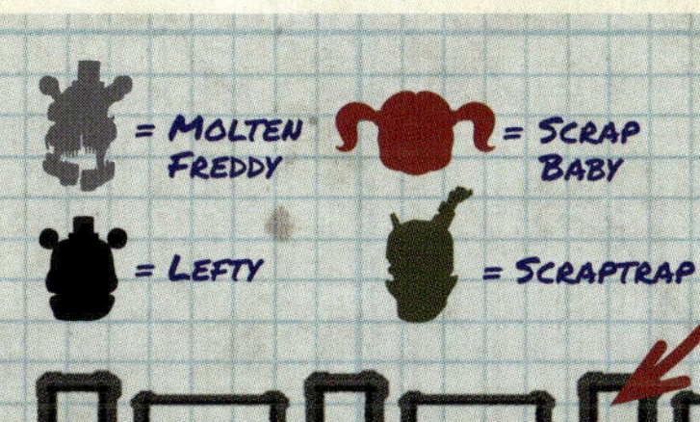

This is the safest place to play an audio cue, as it's the farthest from you.

This big square is the restaurant.

Animatronics can take any path to you!

You are here.

You'll hear audio cues from Scrap Baby and Scraptrap when the animatronics are in these vents.

Additional Certificates

- If you refrain from buying or salvaging anything, you are awarded the **Certificate of Mediocrity** and the "lazy" ending, where you're fired from the restaurant.

- If you run out of money, either by purchasing expensive equipment or incurring lawsuits, you are awarded the **Certificate of Bankruptcy** and fired from the restaurant.

- If you end the game with a risk rating of fifty or higher and win (i.e., don't go bankrupt), you're awarded the **Blacklisted Certificate** and can never work for a Fazbear Entertainment establishment ever again.

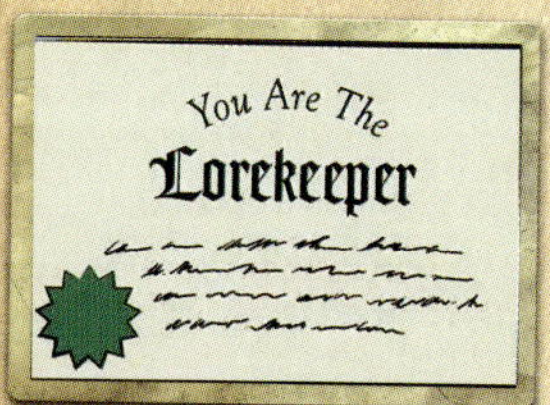

- If you unlock the secrets of Midnight Motorist, Fruity Maze, and Security Puppet, and get the "real ending," you're awarded the **Lorekeeper Certificate** and a secret ending screen after the credits roll.

- Obtain the **Certificate of Insanity** by buying and placing Egg Baby (aka Data Archive) in your restaurant. When you get to the office, turn off the monitor by pressing "Z," then click and hold the power button on the monitor, and press "Z" again. An audio file called "HRY223" plays, and secret blueprints of several animatronics and devices come onto the screen. After listening to the file, you're awarded the certificate and told that no one will believe you.

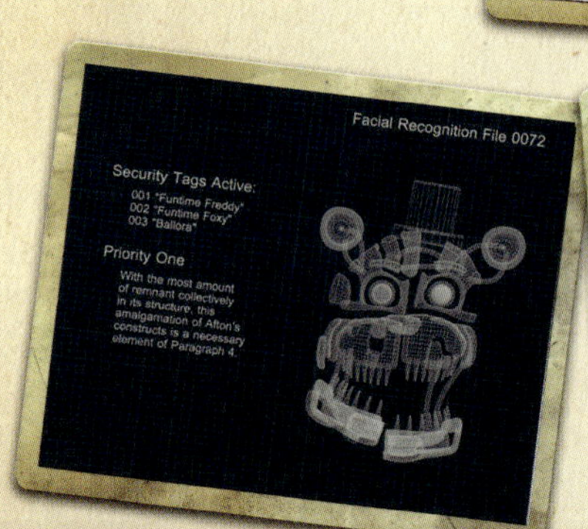

ACHIEVEMENT BADGES

Trash and the Gang

To unlock the **Trash and the Gang** achievement badge, place Bucket Bob on the Star Curtain Stage and the rest of the "trash" animatronics on the Deluxe Concert Stage.
Trash and Gang Achievement: **$1,000** award

Mediocre Melodies

To unlock the **Mediocre Melodies** achievement badge, place Orville Elephant on the Star Curtain Stage and the rest of the cheaper animatronics on the Deluxe Concert Stage.
Mediocre Melodies Achievement: **$10,000** award

Rockstars Assemble

To unlock the **Rockstars Assemble** achievement badge, place Lefty on the Star Curtain Stage and the rest of the Rockstar animatronics on the Deluxe Concert Stage.
Rockstars Assemble Achievement: **$20,000** award

Posh Pizzeria

To unlock the **Posh Pizzeria** achievement badge, place the three most expensive animatronics (El Chip, Funtime Chica, Music Man) on the Deluxe Concert Stage. The award is $0, BUT this award helps you get the Jar of Pickles in the Rare Finds catalog, if you buy everything in the catalog in addition to getting this achievement. Who needs money when you can get the Pickles, right?!

PURCHASE AND PLAY PRIZE KING TO WIN FUNTIME CHICA AT NO ADDITIONAL COST.

FFPS RETRO ARCADE

Midnight Motorist

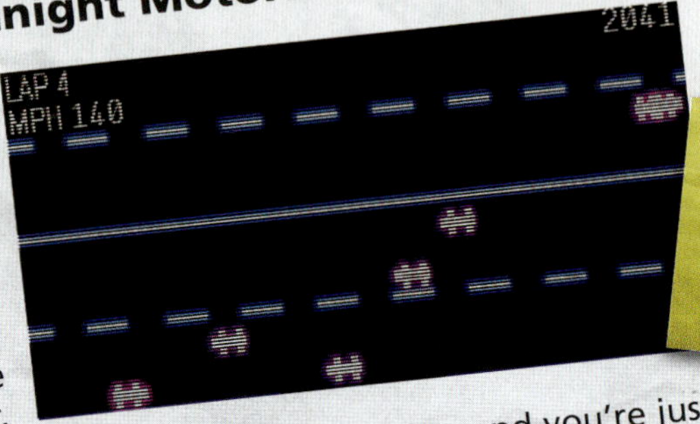

During the fourth lap of *Midnight Motorist*, hit other cars to slow down, then drive across to the bottom lane. Eventually you'll see there is an opening at the bottom of the screen you can enter.

MIDNIGHT MOTORIST IS FINE FOR EARLY-GAME MONEY.

You'll be led to another screen, where it's raining and you're just one purple car driving along a winding road. As you drive to the U-shaped bend in the road, crash your car into the dark clearing in the trees. You can get out (you'll find that your character is yellow, not purple!) and walk to an open spot in the trees. In the upper left corner, there's an unmarked pile of dirt.

Get back in your car and you'll reach a fork in the road where you can either go left or continue straight. If you turn left, you're brought to a parking lot where there's a restaurant called JR's. There's a green man standing outside the restaurant. Park and get out of the car.

As you approach the green man, he says, "Come on, you know you can't be here. Don't make this more difficult than it has to be." Nothing else happens.

THERE IS A BUG WITH THE PRECISION DRIVING PORTIONS. YOU CAN MOVE THE CAR BEYOND THE THRESHOLD FOR EXITING, AND EVENTUALLY DRIVE "INTO" JR'S, AND THEN DRIVE "INTO" THE HOUSE. BECAUSE IT THINKS YOU'RE STILL IN THE CAR, YOU'LL BE INVISIBLE INSTEAD OF HAVING YOUR USUAL YELLOW SPRITE.

FFPS RETRO ARCADE

FFPS RETRO ARCADE

Get back in your car and turn right. Keep driving until you reach a blue house. You can get out of your car and walk around the house. The sound of music fades away and is replaced with the sound of rain. The closer you get to the house, the more it zooms in on your character. Go to the front door and enter the house. The game falls silent. There's a person dressed in gray sitting in a chair in front of a TV. The gray person says, "Leave him alone tonight. He had a rough day."

Go down the hall and knock on the door. You'll shout, "I told you not to close your door." Then, "This is my house. He can't ignore me like that." Then "OPEN THE DOOR," and finally, "I'll find a way in from outside."

Leave the house and walk around to the back. The window is broken and there are two sets of footprints, one human and one animatronic. Your character says: "Ran off to that place again. He'll be sorry when he gets back."

FFPS RETRO ARCADE

Fruity Maze

On the first level, hit a magnet to attract nearby fruits and a purple cape to walk through walls. The cape will allow you to fly over the borders of the maze, but be careful—it will also allow you to fly outside of the map, causing you to lose the minigame. Collect all the fruits before the time runs out to advance to the next level. You'll see a reflection in the screen of a happy blonde girl.

As you start the second level, the music sounds slowed down. This time you're collecting bloodied dogs along with fruits. Now when the screen flashes, the little girl is frowning.

As you start the third and final round, you're collecting dead dogs, flowers, and white boxes. You leave behind bloody footprints as you walk. The music is slowed down even more and you'll find you can't use the Speed/Lightning power-up. As the screen flashes, you'll see the girl crying with Springtrap lurking behind her.

Suddenly, a car horn starts honking. Time ended! The game disappears and the text on the screen reads, "He's not really dead . . . ," "He is over here," and "Follow me . . ." as the screen starts flickering.

FFPS RETRO ARCADE

Security Puppet

You're brought to a screen with directions to not let your assigned child reach the exit. Your child's code is green. Near the exit there's a large purple-and-white wrapped present. Every now and then the lid lifts up and the Puppet's green eyes peek out. After a couple of rounds pass with no sight of a child with a green armband, the screen cuts to black.

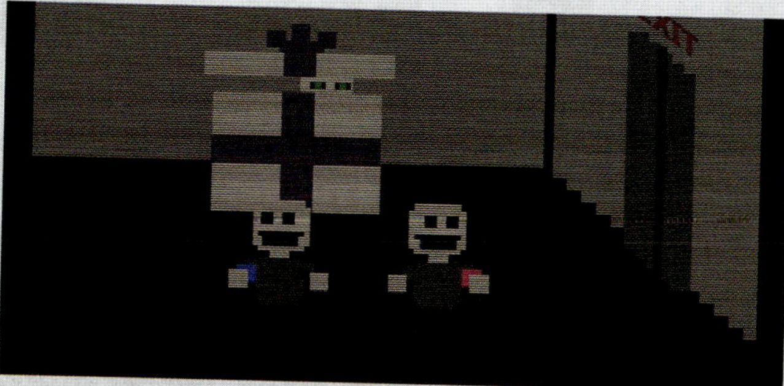

Next, the game opens and a child wearing the green armband is outside in the rain, looking in the window. There's another box on top of the purple one. Suddenly, the Puppet leaps out of the purple box and floats toward the child at the window.

The Puppet exits the building in the rain. The Puppet keeps walking, but then slumps over. Eventually its green eyes die out and it becomes grayer and grayer as it short-circuits. The Puppet drags itself forward. There's a gray child on the ground. The Puppet slumps over and dies holding the child.

Gravestones

If you play the *Midnight Motorist*, *Fruity Maze*, and *Security Puppet* games and receive the Lorekeeper Certificate, you're rewarded with this rare screen after the credits. The names on the graves are Gabriel, Fritz, Susie, and Jeremy—whom fans believe to be the victims of the original killings. One of the graves is hidden from view. The last grave is on the hill in the background. Some fans believe that the distant grave is Charlie, or Charlotte, implying that Henry's daughter is still watching over the children. The hidden grave is also believed to be Golden Freddy's. To uncover the secret of the hidden grave, check out the *Survival Logbook*.

PICKLES ARE THE ONLY ITEM WITH A HAPPINESS RATING, BUT THEY'RE SOLD OUT FOR THE ENTIRE GAME. TO UNLOCK THEM, YOU ONLY HAVE TO GET THE FOUR MAIN BADGE ACHIEVEMENTS—WHICH INCLUDES THE POSH PIZZERIA BADGE. AFTER THAT, THE PICKLES ARE PURCHASABLE FOR $15!

Rare Screens

Besides the Gravestones screen, the Spring Bonnie/Little Blonde Girl Fruity Maze screen, and the "I'm already inside" salvaging screen, there are four rare screens showing the animatronics waiting to be salvaged in the alleyway.

Molten Freddy is seen here, resembling Ennard from *Sister Location*. You can spot a yellow-orange eye from Funtime Foxy, a magenta eye from Bon-Bon, a blue eye from Funtime Freddy, and a purple eye from Ballora. Molten Freddy's blueprint, which accompanies the HRY223 audio, also confirms that the animatronics fused together to create this new one.

Scrap Baby is seen with four posters on the wall behind her. One is of a clown laughing, two appear to be contracts, and another looks like Twisted Wolf from *The Twisted Ones* novel.

Scraptrap's rare screen shows four posters behind him, including two posters of contract pages. The other two posters depict a Halloween "Spook-Fest" and a building with gargoyle lions flanking a set of stairs (One Night at the Opera). Some fans have connected the Spook-Fest to either *FNAF3*'s Fazbear Fright attraction or the "Fall Fest '83" seen in *The Curse of Dreadbear*. The poster of the building bears some interesting, if possibly coincidental, resemblance to Heracles Hospital from the short story "The Man in Room 1280."

On Lefty's rare screen, you can spot a thin-striped appendage—reminiscent of the Puppet—poking out of his arm. A poster to the right depicts a puppet as well. Some fans suggest the poster behind Lefty represents William Afton and his children. William would be the elderly ventriloquist; Michael, the talking dummy who resembles the old man; Elizabeth, believed to possess Circus Baby, is the clown; and the bear with the razor-sharp teeth is the third Afton child, considered by many to be the bite victim from *FNAF4*. Interestingly, *The Curse of Dreadbear*'s Prize Room has some posters that share similarities with some of these posters out in the alley of FFPS.

So . . . What Does It All Mean?

Pizzeria Simulator revealed a lot of lore, and seemingly closed the book on one chapter of the franchise. There's a lot of evidence to support that . . .

- Henry Is Cassette Man: Henry is known from the novel series as Afton's old business partner, and the inventor of the animatronics. He calls Afton "old friend" and the animatronics "small souls trapped in prisons of my own making." The secret audio file is also labeled "HRY223," which fans have speculated means "Henry 2023."
- Connections to Past Games: "2023" could imply that *Pizzeria Simulator* follows *FNAF3*, which takes place thirty years after *FNAF*. The HRY223 audio file also seems to confirm that William Afton was collecting Remnant from the possessed animatronics:
    - "He lured them all back, back to a familiar place, back with familiar traits. He brought them all together . . . He set some kind of trap, I don't know what it was, but he led them there, again. He overpowered them, again. And he robbed them of the only thing that they had, again."
- Henry's Daughter, the First Victim, the Puppet: Cassette Man insists he must "heal this wound, a wound first inflicted on me, but then one that I let bleed out to cause all this." The events of the Security Puppet minigame, coupled with the *Take Cake to the Children* minigame from *FNAF2*, seem to confirm this. While Charlotte waited outside in the rain, she was murdered by Afton, and her body was thrown in the alleyway. The Security Puppet tried to save her, but short-circuited while holding her, allowing her spirit to merge with the Puppet.
- The Puppet Is Inside Lefty: The final HRY223 blueprint also reveals that Lefty is an acronym: "Lure Encapsulate Fuse Transport & Extract" (L.E.F.T.E). This animatronic seems designed to trap and placate the Puppet, so it can't interfere with Cassette Man's plan.
- Remnant: From the HRY223 blueprints, you learn that the Scooper from *Sister Location* infuses things with soul energy, or "Remnant." Remnant can be destroyed by overheating, thus the fire. Remnant is featured heavily in *The Fourth Closet* novel, the *Special Delivery* game, and the stingers of the Fazbear Frights short story series.

Balloon Barrel Glitch

There's a huge money glitch with the Balloon Barrel that can make any run extremely easy. Buy the Balloon Barrel and go to your Floor Plan. Click on a slot where you could place it, but don't actually place it on your floor. Click the "Catalog" button and rush over to place the Balloon Barrel on that slot. If your Bonus Revenue is -1 after your Office Phase on your totals screen, you've succeeded. Your Bonus Revenue will be . . . excessive.

Candy Cadet

If you spend a token on Candy Cadet, there's a chance he may reveal a secret story to you. These stories seem connected to Remnant and possibly the HRY223 audio—the idea of luring five things together and combining them.

- The first story is about a young woman who is sealed in a small room and given five keys. Each key opens the door to a child, but she can save only one. She melts the keys into one, hoping to save all five. Unfortunately, the key now opens none of the doors and all the children die.
- The second story is about a boy who owns a hungry snake. One day he finds five kittens and keeps them in a shoebox. Each night for five nights, the snake sneaks out of its cage and eats a kitten. Filled with regret, the boy cuts open the snake and sews together the remains of the five kittens, putting them back in the shoebox.
- The last story is about a kind man who adopts five orphans to protect them from the world. While the man is away, a criminal breaks into his home and kills the children. The man can afford only one coffin, so he stitches the children together to form one body. That night, there is a knock at the door . . .

Fan Theories: The Arcade Minigames

These arcade machines can be purchased in the Restaurant Management Catalog.

Fruity Maze

In *Fruity Maze*, you're shown flashes of a blonde girl smiling as she collects fruits. In the next levels, she gradually gets sadder as she collects dead and dying dogs. Some fans theorize that this girl is one of the original kidnapping victims—"Susie"—whose name appears on one of the gravestones at the end of the game. *The Fourth Closet* novel supports this theory—one of the original missing kids, Susie, talks about how Spring Bonnie helped her find her dog. Susie's story is further explored in the "Coming Home" Fazbear Frights short story.

Another popular theory posits that Mangle from *FNAF2* is the girl's dog. Fans believe the girl's dog died and she was lured away by William Afton to watch him reanimate it as an animatronic. Fans point to the fact that the dog in the game is missing an eye, like Mangle, and that Mangle is unlike other animatronics in that he doesn't speak, only makes garbled radio noises.

Midnight Motorist

Midnight Motorist surprised fans by revealing that the driver of the purple car was yellow instead of the much-anticipated Purple Guy. Since then, a flurry of conversation has arisen around his identity.

- Some have theorized that the yellow guy is still William Afton (Springtrap is yellow, after all) and that the gray person watching TV in the house is his son Michael. The runaway son is believed to be the bite victim, who was stolen by the animatronic, as there were two sets of footprints—one human and one animatronic—leading away from the broken window.
- Another interesting theory posits that the yellow man isn't Afton at all, but the father of one of the kidnapping victims. The animatronic footprints were made by Afton, wearing the Springtrap suit, who broke into the house and stole the child from his bed.
- Other theories have also popped up around the secret grave in the clearing, with many fans linking it to the twisted animatronics from *The Twisted Ones* novel, who would bury themselves to hide during the day.

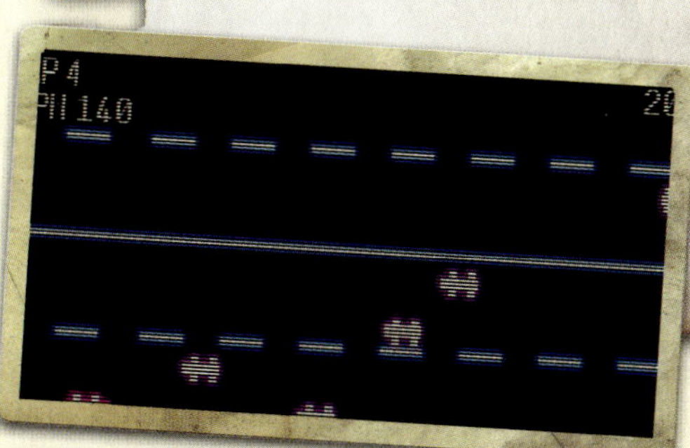

Chapter 7

ULTIMATE CUSTOM NIGHT

You asked for it, you got it! *Ultimate Custom Night* is the seventh and arguably most difficult of the *FNAF* games to date.

You're once again stuck in an office with murderous animatronics, but this time, there are more than fifty of them roaming the building . . . and they each have their own way of attacking, distracting, and annoying you! Lucky for you, you can set their difficulty from zero to twenty and decide whom you want to fight, or have a go at one of sixteen themed challenges. As you rack up points, you unlock cutscenes and lore, possibly relating to who you are and what you're doing.

From your office you need to keep an eye on doors, vents, and air hoses that allow those pesky animatronics to get in. You also need to monitor the heater, air-conditioning, music box, and power generator, as well as the camera, ventilation, and air duct systems. (You know, for those animatronics that are heat or sound sensitive.)

But don't worry, you'll learn on your feet. At least you get a Freddy mask and a flashlight! Don't forget to set those laser traps in the vents, purchase items from the Prize Counter, and watch those Pirate Cove curtains closely, all while collecting Faz-Coins.

Like we said: you asked for it.

Gameplay begins with the character screen, where you have the option to set fifty animatronics to difficulty levels ranging from zero to twenty. On the sidebar you have the option to set them all to zero, five, ten, or twenty, or to add one individually. You can also see how many points you would receive for a perfect score based on the difficulty of the animatronics. The game will record your highest score and, when in 50/20 mode, your best time. When you've made your selections, press "Go!"

HONK THE NOSE OF THE LITTLE FREDDY FAZBEAR ON YOUR DESK.

You're greeted by the Controls screen, which will help you react quickly to the various animatronics. Press "Go!" when you're ready to be brought to your office. There are doors on your left and right, along with a vent in front of you and to your right. There are also two duct hoses coming down from the ceiling. Your job is to fight off the animatronics, which differ in number and difficulty based on your character settings. This means the gameplay will change for every setting but the controls remain the same.

Gameplay and Strategy

YOUR BASIC SCREEN shows you the number of Faz-Coins you have in the top left corner, your power usage and percentage along with noise level in the bottom left corner, the time in the top right corner, and the temperature in the bottom right corner.

YOUR POWER INDICATOR appears in the bottom left corner of your screen, showing how much power you have left, and how much power you're using. When on, the Silent Ventilation, Monitor, Power A/C, and Heater use 1 block of power. When closed, the Left Door, Right Door, Top Vent, and Right Vent, use 1 block of power. All of these are equal in power usage, but if you don't keep your usage minimized, you will start running into power issues. You can turn the ventilation off until the temperature reaches eighty, but you will attract heat-sensitive animatronics. Also, don't forget that the ventilation system needs to be reset around every 45 seconds. If it's notably hotter in the room (red blinking temperature), your ventilation reset timer is shortened.

The longer the doors and vents are shut, the more power you lose. While you can't get power back, you can potentially receive a Battery Power-Up (start the round with 102% power) the more often you play (even if you lose), or by clicking on Rockstar Foxy's parrot, which will summon him and offer you one of four boosts, including 1 percent more power. The only way to slow down power consumption is to use the additional power generator, which can be activated by pulling up your monitor and clicking on the "Power Generator" button in the top right of your screen. But be careful—the generator causes a lot of noise, and if you use Power A/C or Heater they will turn off the power generator.

Number of power bars	Average time it takes to drain 1%	Power drained per hour
Idle	10.8 seconds	4.16%
1	3 seconds	15%
2	1.36 seconds	33%
3	0.77 seconds	58.42%
4	0.5 seconds	90%
5	0.35 seconds	128.57%
6	0.25 seconds	180%

THE GAME RECORDS THE FOLLOWING:

- HIGHEST OVERALL SCORE (NON-CHALLENGES)
- COMPLETIONS FOR CHALLENGES
- BEST TIME ON 50/20 MODE

YOUR MONITORING SYSTEM is activated by swiping down on the right white arrow at the bottom of your screen. There you can monitor the camera, ventilation, and duct systems. You can also reset or silence the ventilation, enable the power generator, enable the heater or power the A/C, and turn on the Global Music Box.

THE CAMERA SYSTEM shows eight cameras used to monitor the animatronics.

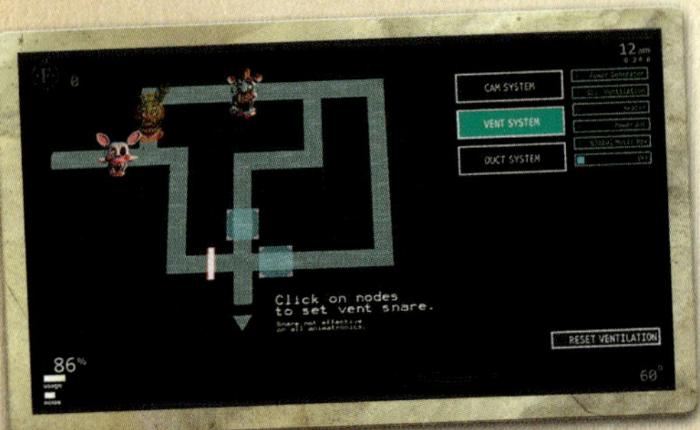

THE VENTILATION SYSTEM shows a small icon of any animatronics that are in the vents. You can deploy vent snares to trap certain animatronics, which will reset the animatronics' pathing on collision.

THE DUCT SYSTEM shows a series of colored caution symbols that correspond to the animatronics in the ducts. You can close only one duct at a time, set an Audio Lure, and/or turn on the heat to push the animatronics back. You can place the Audio Lure strategically to prevent Happy Frog from reaching a vent opening, and this can help attract several others in the ducts.

NOISE LEVEL AND TEMPERATURE go hand in hand. Everything that cools or heats the office causes noise, and everything that stops noise makes the temperature rise, except for Rockstar Foxy's Soundproof boost. The noise can be monitored in the bottom left corner, the temperature in the bottom right. Almost every action makes noise temporarily, including closing the doors.

Collect **FAZ-COINS** by clicking on them as they appear on the cameras (for PC, you only have to mouse over) or by asking Rockstar Foxy. Coins are also awarded as a power-up at the beginning of the game, depending on how often you play and what bonuses you achieve. You can get a randomly awarded 3-Coins Power-Up after each round, and can therefore start a round with three coins if you enable that power-up. Keep track of your coins in the top left corner of your screen.

THE DEATH COIN can be purchased for ten Faz-Coins on CAM 07, but can be used only once per night. It allows you to eliminate certain animatronics without removing points.

THE GLOBAL MUSIC BOX soothes certain animatronics. It doesn't increase your noise level, but it does increase power consumption.

THE FREDDY MASK is enabled by swiping down on the left reddish arrow; this also prevents jump-scares from certain animatronics.

POWER-UPS appear to you after every game played, regardless of performance.

"Frigid" allows you to start playing at a temperature of fifty degrees.

"3 Coins" allows you to start the game with three Faz-Coins.

"Battery" gives you bonus power, allowing you to start a round with 102%.

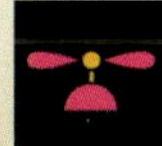

"Dee Dee Repel" prevents Dee Dee and her friends from appearing during the game.

CUTSCENES

THE GAME TRACKS WHAT CUTSCENE YOU'RE ON. AS YOU PROGRESS PER 700 POINTS, IT ADVANCES ONE CUTSCENE AT A TIME. SO, IF YOU RUSH TO 50/20 MODE RIGHT UP FRONT, YOU HAVE A CHANCE OF ONLY SEEING THE FIRST CUTSCENE IF YOU START A FRESH SAVE FILE.

ANIMATRONICS

- **FREDDY** approaches from the left hall, advancing in stages. Watch him on the monitor and shut the door when he reaches the doorway. He moves faster as the building gets warmer; keep him at a cool sixty degrees, or a perfect seventy-two degrees Fahrenheit.

- **BONNIE AND FOXY** are in Pirate Cove.
  - Watch for a figurine on your desk. If the figure is Bonnie, avoid looking at Camera 05 (Pirate Cove). If you do, Bonnie will disable camera visibility for some time, but you can still switch cameras.
  - Try to check CAM 05 if possible. If you don't for a prolonged time, there's a good chance that Foxy breaks apart and slips pieces into your office. Keep ANY parts of Foxy from entering your office for as long as you can. Once he reassembles himself, he'll jump-scare you.

- **CHICA** stays in the Kitchen; you can listen to her on Camera 04. Keep the music box wound for both her and the Puppet. If you stop hearing the noise from the Kitchen, change the music by pressing the button below the Puppet's windup button. If you don't change it, Chica will jump-scare you. You can thwart Chica entirely by having Global Music Box on at every 15-second multiple.

- **GOLDEN FREDDY** appears at random in your office. Stare at him for too long and he'll jump-scare you. Instead, put your monitor or tablet up, or put on the Freddy mask.

- **TOY FREDDY** plays *Five Nights with Mr. Hugs* on Camera 08. In the game, there are three ways into the office and only one door can be closed. Click the cams on Toy Freddy's monitor and close the correct door to block Mr. Hugs. It's a good idea to ensure that Mr. Hugs is blocked at every 5-second multiple, after 10 seconds into the game. If you check on Toy Freddy and see "Game Over" on his screen, that means he lost . . . and he's coming for you.

- **TOY BONNIE** and **WITHERED BONNIE** sneak in through a trapdoor to your right, and both can be cleared by donning the Freddy mask. Toy Bonnie's coming is signaled by a low buzzing sound and flickering lights. Withered Bonnie will similarly cause audio distortions and disrupt your screen.

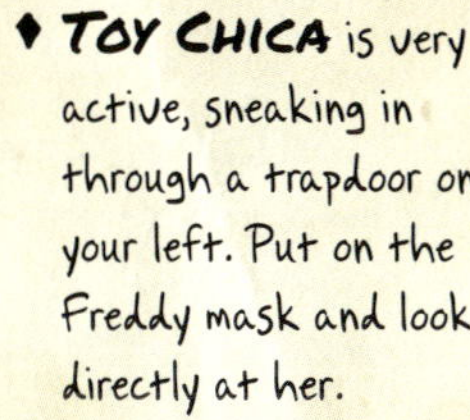

- **TOY CHICA** is very active, sneaking in through a trapdoor on your left. Put on the Freddy mask and look directly at her.

- **WITHERED CHICA** enters through the vents, but can be blocked using the vent snare. She always goes the long route in the vents. If she reaches the office, she'll become stuck, preventing you from closing it. While this also temporarily prevents other animatronics (except Mangle) from entering through the vents, Withered Chica can eventually wiggle free and jump-scare you.

- **MANGLE** climbs through the vents and can be stopped using the vent snare. Once the vent door in your office opens, she'll hang from the ceiling, and cause audio distortions. She will also jump-scare you at random, if you have your monitor up.

- **THE PUPPET** stays in its music box as usual. Make sure the Music Box is wound. You can also use the Global Music Box to charge the music box remotely.

- **BB** and **JJ** will try to sneak in through the side vent. Keep it closed until you hear a thud, indicating he or she is gone. If BB slips in, he'll disable your flashlight. If JJ sneaks in, she'll disable the door controls.

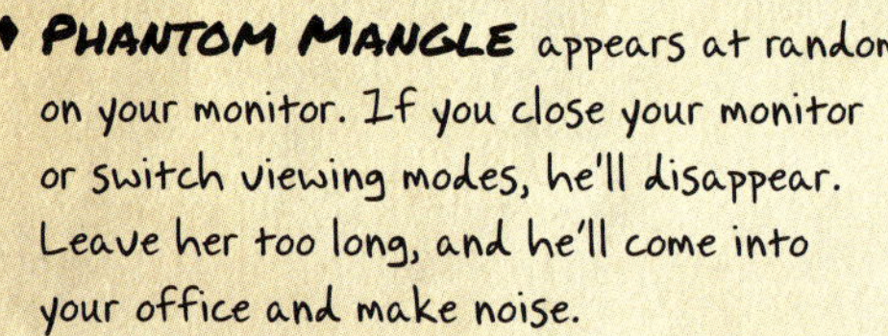

- **SPRINGTRAP** climbs silently through the front vent. Close the vent door on him BEFORE a camera flip. Technically, he won't attack you until you flip your camera.
- **PHANTOM MANGLE** appears at random on your monitor. If you close your monitor or switch viewing modes, he'll disappear. Leave her too long, and he'll come into your office and make noise.
- **PHANTOM FREDDY** materializes at random in your office. Shine your flashlight at him until he's gone or he'll jump-scare you, causing you to black out for a short period. If you get startled by Phantom Freddy and your front vent is open, if there is an animatronic at the vent opening, it will proceed through the vent opening.

- **PHANTOM BB** appears at random on your monitor. Close the monitor or switch viewing modes to avoid a jump-scare and blackout.

50/20 DEATH COIN CONSIDERATIONS

- IF YOU USE A DEATH COIN AND GET RID OF FUNTIME FOXY, THIS WILL ELIMINATE THE NEED TO BE ON CAM 06 AND TO HAVE THE CAMERA UP AT THAT TOP-OF-THE-HOUR MOMENT.
- DEATH COIN THE PUPPET TO MAXIMIZE YOUR POWER (MUSIC BOX USAGE EATS UP A LOT OF POWER).

*NOTE: USING A DEATH COIN DOES NOT SUBTRACT FROM YOUR POINT TOTAL FROM THE START OF THE NIGHT, BUT YOU WILL HAVE TO RESET THE ANIMATRONIC YOU'VE USED THE DEATH COIN ON EACH TIME ON THE MAIN MENU/CHARACTER SELECT SCREEN.

- **FREDDLES** will populate your office at random, while your monitor is up. Shine your flashlight to make them disappear. If too many Freddles accumulate, **Nightmare Freddy** will jump-scare you.

- **NIGHTMARE FREDBEAR** and **NIGHTMARE** can appear as a duo, or independently at random. If you are using a stereo headset on a PC, you can easily tell which one is needing attention. Fredbear appears in the left doorway, Nightmare in the right. Shut the doors as soon as you see their glowing eyes or hear a deep laugh sound cue. Each of them can attack if your monitor is up while they're present, after a grace period based on the AI level.

- **NIGHTMARE BONNIE** and **NIGHTMARE MANGLE** each attack once per night from the right hall, appearing in CAM Ø2. To fend them off, purchase their plush toys on Camera Ø7 with Faz-Coins (the amount varies based on the difficulty). If you keep your camera on CAM Ø2 and don't change it, Nightmare Bonnie, Nightmare Mangle, and Circus Baby will not attack you, even if you don't have a plush.

- As the heat rises in the office, **JACK-O-CHICA** will appear in the right and left doors at the same time. Close the doors before the temperature reaches one hundred degrees Fahrenheit. If you keep the temperature at eighty-nine degrees or lower, Jack-O-Chica won't start to show up at all.

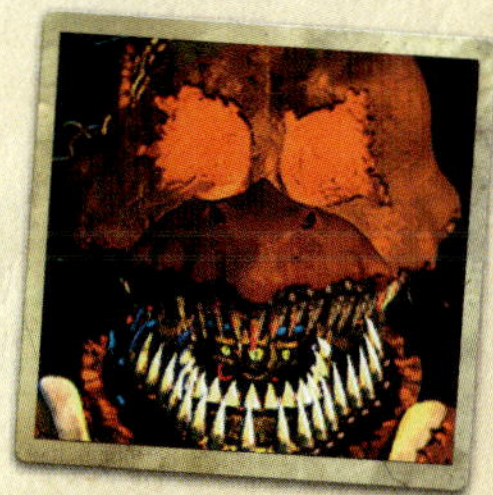

- **NIGHTMARIONNE** appears at random in different areas of the office, and will also be provoked by hovering your mouse over certain hotspots on the screen. Avoid leaving your cursor over him.

- **NIGHTMARE BALLOON BOY** sits slumped over in your office. Do not shine your light on him if he's sitting. If he stands, shine your light on him to return him to the sitting position.

- **CIRCUS BABY** attacks only once per night, from the right hall. Fend her off by purchasing her plush toy on Camera 07, or by keeping your camera on CAM 02 during the threatening time of her appearance there.

- **BALLORA** approaches from the left or right hall, disabling your camera feeds. Listen to her music to determine which side she's approaching from, and close the correct door. Once she causes a "thud" on the respective door, her current approach ends.

- **FUNTIME FOXY** hides behind the curtain in Funtime Cove. The sign outside lists a "showtime" when Funtime Foxy will find you. Watch her as the time approaches and until the time passes. This will buy you a few hours until a new time is listed.

- **ENNARD** approaches from the vents and can be tracked only when in motion. Close the vents when you hear a squeaking noise, BEFORE a camera flip. Ennard will not attack you until you flip your camera.

- **HAPPY FROG, MR. HIPPO**, and **PIGPATCH** use the duct system and hoses to drop into your office. An Audio Lure will keep Happy Frog away, while the heater or Audio Lure can be used to deter Mr. Hippo and Pigpatch, with a high percentage of success.

- **NEDD BEAR** also uses the duct system and hoses, but he's only fooled by the audio decoy half of the time. Use heat to deter him.

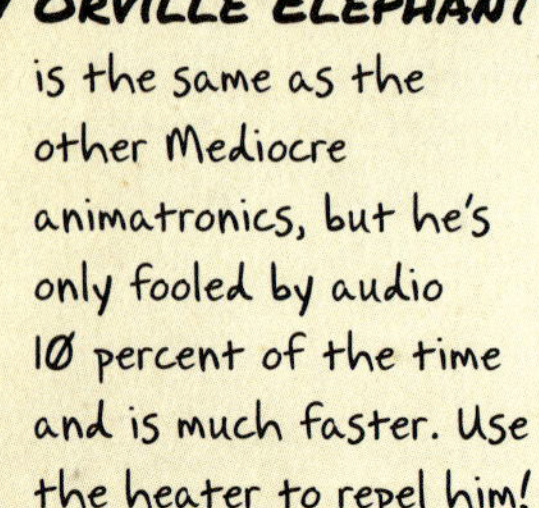

- **ORVILLE ELEPHANT** is the same as the other Mediocre animatronics, but he's only fooled by audio 10 percent of the time and is much faster. Use the heater to repel him!

- **ROCKSTAR FREDDY** remains in the office. When he activates, he'll demand a payment of five Faz-Coins. Turn up the heat for a chance to make him malfunction.

- **ROCKSTAR BONNIE** appears in your office without his guitar. Find and double-click it on the camera system to make him go away.

- **ROCKSTAR CHICA** waits outside the left or right doorway. Double-click the WET FLOOR sign to put it in front of the door and make her leave.

- **ROCKSTAR FOXY'S** parrot will fly across the screen in your office; if you click on it, Rockstar Foxy will appear and either jump-scare you or offer you one of four upgrades: adding 1 percent to your power, resetting the office temperature to sixty degrees Fahrenheit, soundproofing the office, or granting you ten Faz-Coins. The higher the AI for Rockstar Foxy, the greater the chance that you will get jump-scared if you click on his parrot.

- **EL CHIP** periodically interrupts you with advertisements for his restaurant, El Chip's Fiesta Buffet. Click "Skip" or press "Enter" to get rid of them. The higher his difficulty, the more often his ads will appear.

- Make a lot of noise and **MUSIC MAN** becomes active, eventually jump-scaring you. Reducing noise will make him calm down.

- **FUNTIME CHICA** will occasionally appear and pose, accompanied by camera flashes, which will disorient you.

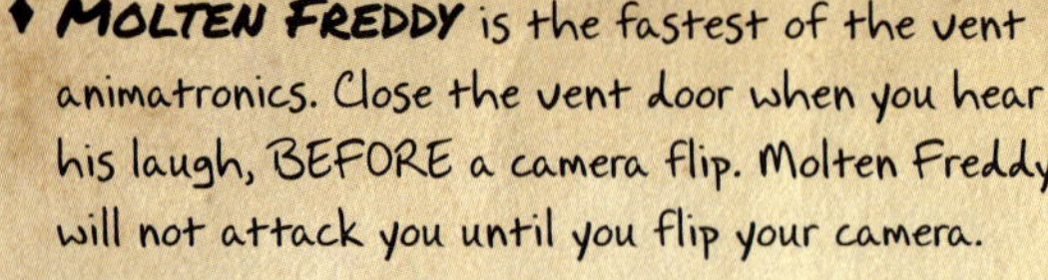

- **MOLTEN FREDDY** is the fastest of the vent animatronics. Close the vent door when you hear his laugh, BEFORE a camera flip. Molten Freddy will not attack you until you flip your camera.

- **SCRAP BABY** appears by the side of your desk, slumped over, once per night. Only shock her if you see her move, as it will drain 1 percent of your power. But, if you don't shock her after she moves, she will jump-scare you the next time you flip your camera.

- **SCRAPTRAP/WILLIAM AFTON** attacks up to once per night, from the right vent. Close the vent if you hear a loud clamoring sound and see flickering lights.

- **LEFTY** stays in the closet on Camera 03. If the office becomes too noisy or too hot, he'll jump-scare you. Soothe him by switching on the Global Music Box, but watch your power supply.

- **PHONE GUY'S** calls make noise. You have a few seconds to mute his call or you have to listen to his entire message.

- **TRASH AND THE GANG** appear in the office at random and create loud noise while blocking your screen. Mr. Can-Do appears on the camera.

- There's a chance that **OLD MAN CONSEQUENCES'S** subscreen will appear in the top-left corner of your screen. Your goal is to press "C" when the fish is on the red dot. If you catch the fish, the screen disappears; otherwise, your camera will be inaccessible for some time. You might be able to use this camera prevention to your advantage—your screen will go dark, but it will prevent any open vents from allowing jump-scares.

- **HELPY** will appear in different spots in different offices. Click on him to avoid being jump-scared with an air horn.

DEE DEE appears at random and adds new animatronics to your game at difficulty levels one through ten. She can either add a character from the Start screen or a special character from her own roster . . .

- **PLUSHTRAP** appears on Camera Ø6, sitting in his chair. Scare him away by staring at him on CAM Ø6 until he bolts out of his chair.

- **RWQFSFASXC** makes your office go dark for 1Ø seconds, once per night.

- **BONNET** walks across the screen at random. Click her nose before she goes off the side of the screen, or you'll be jump-scared.

- **NIGHTMARE CHICA'S** jaws will close slowly around your field of vision until she jump-scares you. Stop her by using the Power A/C.

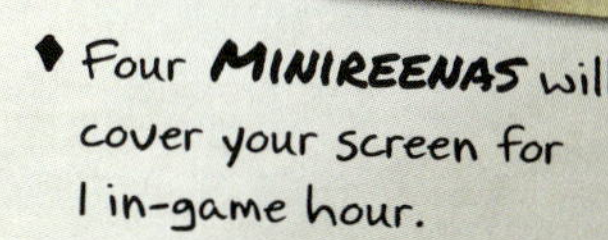

- Four **MINIREENAS** will cover your screen for 1 in-game hour.

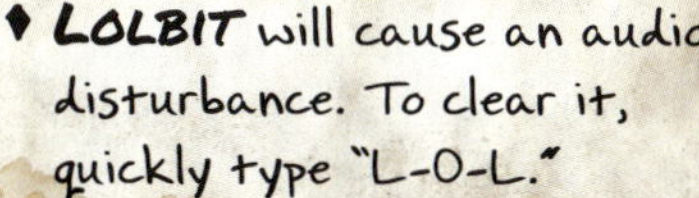

- **LOLBIT** will cause an audio disturbance. To clear it, quickly type "L-O-L."

FREDBEAR can be summoned by setting all animatronics to zero and Golden Freddy to one. If Dee Dee summons another animatronic, you'll need to restart the night. Purchase a Death Coin with ten Faz-Coins, then wait for Golden Freddy to show up. When he does, use the Death Coin on him and you'll be jump-scared by Fredbear.

POINTS AND TROPHIES

Point totals must be accumulated to unlock "Intermissions," office skins, and trophies.

An intermission appears for every 700 points earned. These include Toy Chica: The High School Years, Bear of Vengeance, and a twitching Golden Freddy.

Office skins can also be unlocked, when you reach certain point thresholds. Reach 2,000 points to unlock the *Sister Location*; 5,000 points to unlock the *FNAF3* skin; and 8,000 points to unlock the *FNAF4* skin.

You can also receive three trophies in bronze, silver, and gold if you win against a certain number of animatronics cranked up to 20 difficulty. Bronze is awarded for for 8,000 points, silver for 9,000 points, and gold for beating 50/20 mode (10,600 points).

XOR/Shadow Dee Dee

Sounds to Listen For:

When playing in 50/20 mode, a new animatronic called XOR, or Shadow Dee Dee, will appear, even if Dee Dee Repel is active. She is colorless and eyeless, and arrives accompanied by garbled audio. She eventually calls her entire roster of animatronics, with around 7 seconds between the spawn of each. The order goes: RWQFSFASXC, Plushtrap, Nightmare Chica, Bonnet, Minireenas, and Lolbit. You have to be on CAM 06 to stare/scare away Plushtrap. She can also very rarely appear in normal play.

Death Lines

Most of the animatronics have "death lines" dialogue they speak after killing you.

- Mangle: "He's here and always watching. The one you shouldn't have killed."
- Nightmare: "I am your wickedness made flesh."
- The Puppet: "The others are like animals, but I am very aware."
- Withered Chica: "I was the first. I have seen everything."
- Ballora: "Admit it, you wanted to let me in."

If you're treated to one of Mr. Hippo's extended death lines, don't bother trying to skip through it; just sit back, relax, and let Mr. Hippo have his moment.

Old Man Consequences

If all other characters are set to zero and Old Man Consequences is set to one, catching a fish will result in being sent to Old Man Consequences's pond. Old Man Consequences will say, "Come and sit with me a while," prompting you to press "Enter." When this is done, Old Man Consequences concludes, "Leave the demon to his demons. Rest your own soul. There is nothing else."

Some players have said that by pressing "A" and "D" above the pond, the game will crash. Music can apparently be heard in the background that sounds like robotic screaming.

Mapping the Animatronics in UCN
Springtrap, Withered Chica, Mangle, and Molten Freddy all use the vents.
Vents
Ennard will be visible only when in motion.
Mangle takes a random path, which is unique to him.
Vent Snare can prevent Withered Chica and Mangle from getting to the vent opening. If you let either one go beyond the Vent Snare to the vent opening, make sure the middle/top vent is CLOSED whenever you are in your cameras, or you will let them through.
Ducts
= Happy Frog
= Mr. Hippo
= Orville Elephant
= Pigpatch
= Nedd Bear
All animatronics can come from either duct.

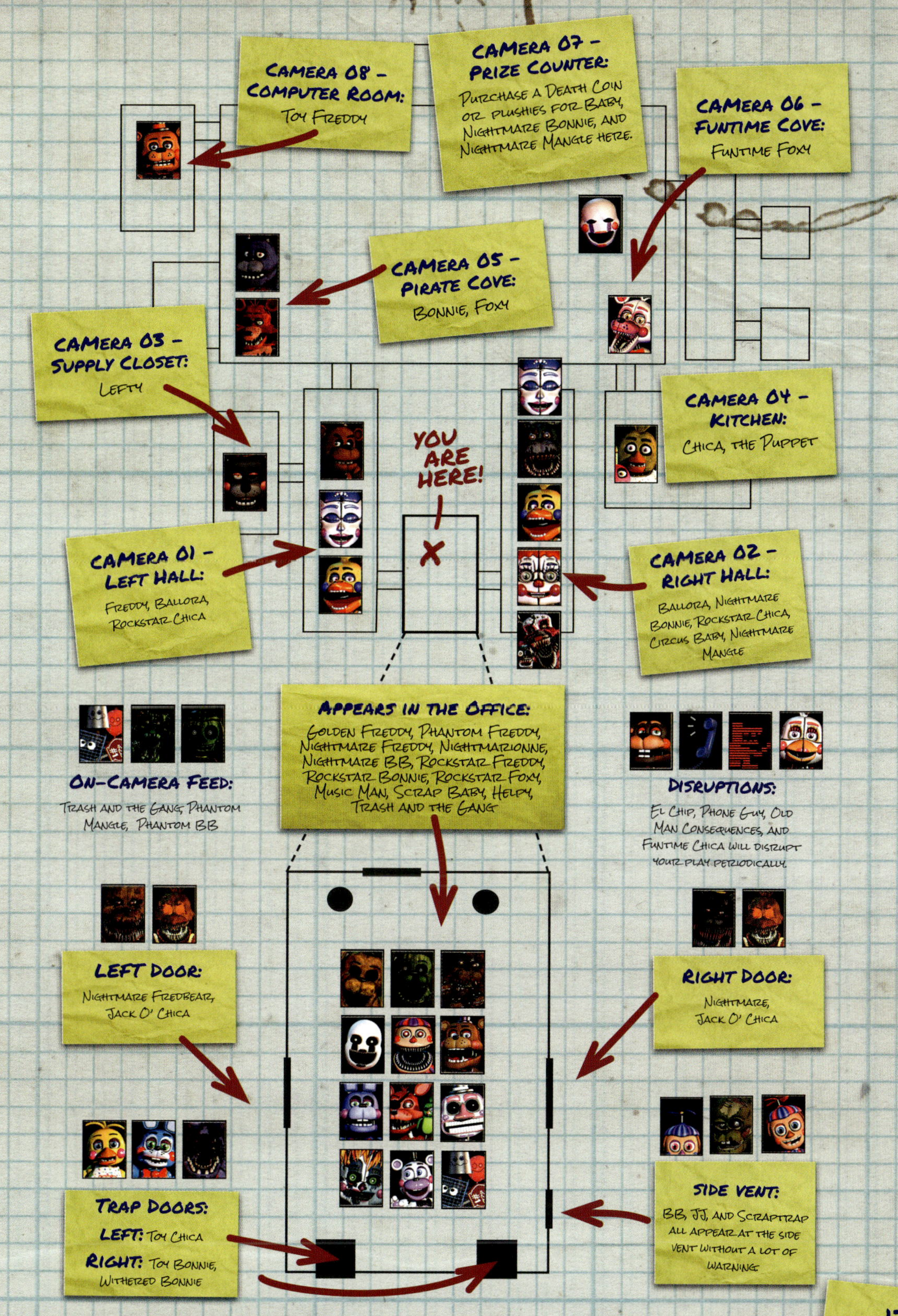

Camera 08 – Computer Room:
Toy Freddy
Camera 07 – Prize Counter:
Purchase a Death Coin or plushies for Baby, Nightmare Bonnie, and Nightmare Mangle here.
Camera 06 – Funtime Cove:
Funtime Foxy
Camera 05 – Pirate Cove:
Bonnie, Foxy
Camera 03 – Supply Closet:
Lefty
Camera 04 – Kitchen:
Chica, the Puppet
You are here!
X
Camera 01 – Left Hall:
Freddy, Ballora, Rockstar Chica
Camera 02 – Right Hall:
Ballora, Nightmare Bonnie, Rockstar Chica, Circus Baby, Nightmare Mangle
Appears in the Office:
Golden Freddy, Phantom Freddy, Nightmare Freddy, Nightmarionne, Nightmare BB, Rockstar Freddy, Rockstar Bonnie, Rockstar Foxy, Music Man, Scrap Baby, Helpy, Trash and the Gang
On-Camera Feed:
Trash and the Gang, Phantom Mangle, Phantom BB
Disruptions:
El Chip, Phone Guy, Old Man Consequences, and Funtime Chica will disrupt your play periodically.
Left Door:
Nightmare Fredbear, Jack O' Chica
Right Door:
Nightmare, Jack O' Chica
Trap Doors:
Left: Toy Chica
Right: Toy Bonnie, Withered Bonnie
Side Vent:
BB, JJ, and Scraptrap all appear at the side vent without a lot of warning

Intermissions:
Toy Chica: The High School Years

The first unlockable intermission portrays Toy Chica as a high school student who obsesses over various "boys" at her school, including Freddy, Toy Bonnie, the Puppet, Funtime Foxy, Pigpatch, and the Twisted Wolf from *The Twisted Ones*. She details in her diary entries how she plans to lure the boys inside and then they'll be hers "forever." Each entry explains, "There is only one thing that could possibly go wrong," before everything resets and Toy Chica has a new target.

In the last cut scene, Toy Chica explains that she's once again brokenhearted, but tomorrow is another day and she knows she'll find another guy for her. As she writes in her diary against a tree, her school bag can be seen behind her filled with body parts of the various "guys" (animatronics) she loved.

Does that locker behind Chica say "Exotic Butters"?!

Intermissions: Bear of Vengeance

This intermission shows various cut scenes portraying Freddy and Foxy as enemies in feudal Japan. Every time Freddy confronts Foxy, he ends up having to perform some sort of household chore for the villain after being defeated in battle. Freddy always vows to seek vengeance the next time.

The title screens are in Japanese, and Freddy's and Foxy's lines are spoken in Japanese; however there are English subtitles. Some fans have noted that the English subtitles don't quite match the spoken Japanese.

Final Intermission: Golden Freddy

After unlocking all the cut scenes from both intermissions, you will be shown Golden Freddy sitting in darkness. He twitches violently as he approaches the screen before fading away into the darkness.

Fan Theories

Who Are You and Where Are You?

Many fans posit that the animatronics' death lines indicate you are playing as William Afton, trapped in Hell. Support for their theory comes from Cassette Man, whom fans believe to be Henry, Afton's old partner, condemning his "old friend" to "burn" at the end of *Pizzeria Simulator*. Some of the animatronics' death lines include the words *burn* and *flame* and *fire*.

Others have pointed to the short story "The Man in Room 1280," which many presume shows that Afton somehow survived the fire in *Pizzeria Simulator*. These theorists believe that Afton is experiencing this while in some kind of coma, as the nurses state that the man has been in the hospital for years.

Golden Freddy

Some fans believe that Golden Freddy's final cut scene, where he twitches and retreats into darkness, means that his spirit has not been put to rest and that he is, or will be, seeking revenge.

The One You Should Not Have Killed (TOYSNHK)

A few different animatronics' death lines use the phrase "the one you should not have killed." Mangle and Withered Chica's death lines suggest this person is a boy, but who exactly is the one you should not have killed? Some fans believe it's Golden Freddy. One of Orville Elephant's death lines says, "He tried to release you, he tried to release us. But I'm not gonna let that happen. I will hold you here, I will keep you here, no matter how many times they burn us." Is the person whom you should not have killed residing in "Hell," haunting and torturing Afton, as some fans suggest?

The Face

Some players have noted that a child's face appears in the game at random intervals. Could this be "the one you should not have killed"?

- **Toy Chica's High School Years**
  Some fans suggest that the different methods laid out by Toy Chica to lure the boys "inside" may be ways that William Afton lured children to him in order to kill them.

- **Bear of Vengeance**
  Fans theorize that the Foxy vs. Freddy drama is actually portraying Freddy as Henry and Foxy as William Afton.

- **Mediocres' Death Lines**
  During the deaths of Happy Frog and her friends, some fans have suggested that a young girl's voice can be heard echoing what the animatronics are saying. Some have even said that the voice resembles that of Scrap Baby from *Pizzeria Simulator*.

- **Nightmare Fredbear's Death Line**
  One of Nightmare Fredbear's death lines says, "Let me put you back together, then take you apart all over again." Some fans believe that this ties into the iconic Fredbear plush quote from *FNAF4*: "I will put you back together." It also ties in with *FNAF World: Update 2*, where the Clock ending relies on you putting the pieces back together.

Chapter 8

HELP WANTED

Seems like a no-brainer, right? Transporting one of the most popular horror games of all time to virtual reality, where fans can fall in love with the terror all over again. But what started out as a fun new way to play *FNAF* quickly morphed into a chilling new chapter for the series.

The setup for *FNAF* games usually involve filling an open position at Fazbear Entertainment—whether you're a night guard, a technician, or even a franchise owner. Here, you're playing a lot of roles: security guard, vent tech, animatronic maintenance . . . but there's another job you hear about: game tester. That's right. *Help Wanted* had a bit of a bumpy road to development, and there might still be some glitches left behind by the game team. But as with every *FNAF* entry, things aren't quite as they appear.

Lurking beneath familiar faces, fun new game modes, and more *FNAF*-themed snacks than you can eat in a lifetime . . . something is festering at the heart of the game. Can you find what it is before it spreads too far? Or is it already too late?

The Freddy Fazbear Virtual Experience

Welcome to *The Freddy Fazbear Virtual Experience*! Fazbear Entertainment has had a rough few decades, thanks in part to some lunatic spreading lies about them through indie video games. But thankfully, the company isn't above laughing at itself, which is the reason for this VR game. At the end of the introduction, the company signs your virtual waiver for you (something-something digital consciousness transference, something-something real-world manifestations of digital characters), and you're good to go.

Looking for Foxy on the menu screen? Turn around.

Main Hub

You land in a new home base of sorts, situated out in what's usually the dining area at Freddy Fazbear's Pizza. Behind you are tables and chairs and the Prize Counter. To your left is Pirate Cove. To your right, in the doorway, a rabbit figure is watching. In front of you is the main show stage as well as a desk, set with several buttons, switches, and monitors.

- **Party Machine:** Throw the switch on your left to enter Nightmare Mode, a more difficult challenge mode of the existing minigames.
- **Go to Gallery:** This button appears after beating the *Pizza Party* minigame. It takes you to a gallery to view the models of the animatronics.
- **Prize Counter:** This button moves you to the Prize Counter.
- **Virtual Menu:** Use this console to select a minigame. As you complete minigames, more are unlocked (up to thirty). There is a secret button on the left side of the console that we'll get to later.
- **Showtime:** This button activates the animatronics show, but it's out of order.
- **Replay Title:** This button replays the Title screen.
- **Token Counter:** To your right, this monitor tracks how many Faz-Tokens you've collected (see page 150).

Prize Counter

Prizes are unlocked by opening a present (similar in style to the Puppet's present) with a hand crank at the end of each minigame. Certain prizes can be worn, some can be eaten, and some you can choke on if you try to eat it three times.

At the Prize Counter, you can collect the prizes you've unlocked. Special prizes become available by collecting the Faz-Tokens hidden throughout the minigames. Use the console on your right to review the prizes and select them. The only prize available at game start is the basketball.

Occasionally, you can earn a jump-scare prize, where Plushtrap will simply jump-scare you upon opening the prize.

Fazbear Entertainment

Where Fantasy and Fun Come to Life

Prize Catalog COLLECT THEM ALL!

Food/Drink

❑ Bonnie Bites

❑ Butter for One

❑ Chica Chug

❑ Disappointment Chips

❑ El Chip's Tortilla Chips

❑ El Chip's Tortilla Chips Bold and Spicy

❑ Exotic Beverage

❑ Fazbar

❑ Foxy Cove Cooler

❑ Freddy Fudgebar

❑ Lemon Chica Bar

❑ Meat Bites

❑ Meat Bites XL

❑ Mixed Nuts

❑ Pirate Plunderbar

❑ Slice of Cake

❑ Stick of Butter

❑ Sodaroni

Plushes

❑ Bonnie

❑ Chica

❑ Foxy

❑ Freddy Fazbear

❑ The Puppet

❑ Toy Bonnie

❑ Toy Chica

❑ TOY FREDDY

❑ NIGHTMARIONNE

❑ CIRCUS BABY

❑ FUNTIME FOXY

❑ FUNTIME FREDDY

❑ SCRAP BABY

ACTION FIGURES (for ages 3 and up)

❑ FREDDY FAZBEAR

❑ ENNARD

❑ MANGLE

❑ TOY FREDDY

❑ TOY BONNIE

❑ TOY CHICA

❑ BALLOON BOY

❑ PUPPET

❑ BONNIE

❑ CHICA

❑ FOXY

❑ NIGHTMARIONNE

❑ CIRCUS BABY

❑ FUNTIME FOXY

❑ FUNTIME FREDDY

❑ NIGHTMARE FREDBEAR

❑ PLUSHTRAP

❑ BON-BON

TOYS (for ages 3 and up)

❑ BALLOON

❑ CUPCAKE

❑ CATERPILLAR

❑ PHONE

❑ ROBOT

UNLOCKABLE WITH FAZ-COINS

❑ BASKETBALL (FREE)

❑ DEAD COCKROACH (5, EDIBLE)

❑ PLASTIC CUP (8)

❑ DESK FAN (10)

❑ ROLLED PAPER (15)

❑ FREDDY MASK (20)

❑ 8-BALL (22)

❑ HELPY (25)

BOBBLEHEADS

❑ BONNIE

❑ CHICA

❑ FREDDY FAZBEAR

Gameplay and Strategy

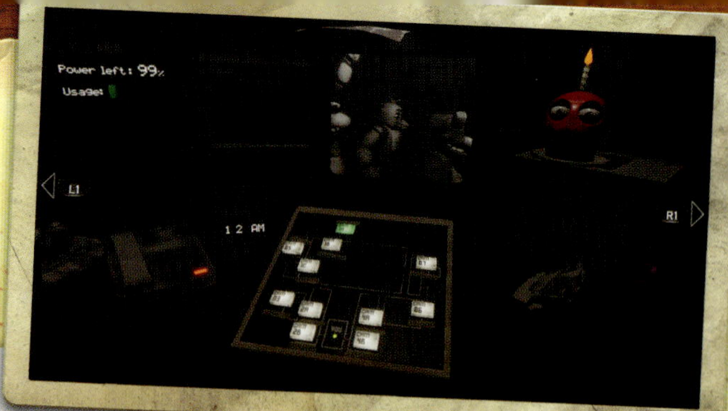

FNAF 1-3

The *FNAF* game modes follow similar rules to their original counterparts, where you need to stay alive until 6:00 a.m. while defending against the animatronics from each game. Check out the Gameplay and Strategy sections on pages 6, 20, 42, 60, 80, and 96 for tips and tricks to these modes. Note that there are a few key differences in *Help Wanted*:

- Only the first four nights are playable in normal mode.
- In *FNAF1* and *FNAF2*, the animatronics are active on Night 01 (no freebies here).
- *FNAF3* gives you a bit of a break. Instead of a pop-up window, you reboot your systems on a terminal to your left. This means you're able to keep watch in the office and view the camera while rebooting systems. You also have more leeway in pulling Springtrap back from the doorway, or even from CAM 01.
- In *Help Wanted*, fans can watch the animatronics walking toward them and are able to peek out into the hallways, look behind them, and interact with more items on the desk.
- The game's original rare screens and secrets do not appear, including Golden Freddy and the *FNAF2* and *FNAF3* minigames.

FNAF1 Foxy's speed is punishing in VR. Keep an eye on Pirate Cove.

NIGHTMARE MODE

Nightmare Modes for *FNAF1*, *FNAF2*, and *FNAF3* each take place on Night Ø5 (and Night Ø6 for *FNAF2*), making Nightmare Mode inherently more difficult. The game also throws a few more curveballs at you.

- *FNAF1*: The screen is now black and white, similar to your security monitor feeds. Your doors and lights are broken, activating randomly.
  - Keep an eye on Freddy, as it will slow him down, and listen for his laugh. He's at the right door by his fifth laugh, and doesn't leave, so keep the door closed.
  - Chica is pretty quiet, but she and Bonnie have similar sound cues: footsteps. Focus on listening for them and closing the doors when you hear them. In VR, you can pick up Mr. Cupcake and throw him into the hallway so that when Chica is approaching you can see the light of the candle being broken by Chica, and thus, you don't have to use the light!
  - Keeping an eye on Freddy and Foxy is tough. Ignore Foxy's camera entirely, and focus on listening for his footsteps in the hall instead.

IN *FNAF1*, THE CUPCAKE ON YOUR DESK APPEARS AS NIGHTMARE CUPCAKE.

- *FNAF2*
  - Night Ø5: The room is dark, like it's under a black light, making it difficult to spot the various animatronics coming at you from the hall, vents, etc. Night Ø5 does not include the withered animatronics, so no need to worry about them.
  - Withered: The room is now almost completely dark, but what you can see is cast in an eerie purple glow. Withered is much more difficult, as it features all animatronics.
- *FNAF3*:
  - This mode seems to be taking place during the fire that we know occurs at Fazbear's Fright at the end of *FNAF3*. The room is now red and you can see flames through the vents. Springtrap moves much faster, so try to trap him early between Cameras Ø9 and 1Ø, and keep rebooting your systems. You can also pull Springtrap over to CAM Ø2, and close the vent at CAM 15 while looking down to avoid being startled by Phantom Freddy for a less risky approach.

DARK ROOMS

PLUSHTRAP

LAND ON THE X

Similar to the night-start minigames from *FNAF4*, the animatronic starts at the end of the hallway. Shining your flashlight causes them to stop in their tracks. Listen for the audio cues and get them to land on the X in front of you before time runs out.

NIGHTMARE BB

NIGHTMARE MODE: NIGHTMARE BB

In Nightmare Mode, you are lower on the ground, and the hallway is filled with balloons.

NIGHTMARE MODE: PLUSHTRAP

In Nightmare Mode, you are lower on the ground, and there are toys obscuring the two nearest rooms.

SURVIVE 'TIL 6:00 A.M.

Similar to clearing Freddles in *FNAF4*, you must shine your flashlight to clear the toys approaching you. The flashlight has limited battery life that recharges over time, so use the flashlight sparingly.

PLUSHBABY

NIGHTMARE MODE: PLUSHBABY

In Nightmare Mode, the room is filled with Circus Baby plushes, and the approaching toys are Scrap Baby plushes.

CROSS THE ROOM

Similar to the Funtime Auditorium level in *Sister Location*, the animatronic in the room with you is motion activated, so the room is dark. Use your Flash Beacon to navigate the darkness. If you see an animatronic in your path, freeze and wait for it to leave. Slow and steady wins.

LOLBIT

NIGHTMARE MODE: FUNTIME FOXY

In Nightmare Mode, the room is filled with Circus Baby, Funtime Freddy, Funtime Foxy animatronics, and other endoskeletons, but Lolbit is the only motion-activated animatronic.

Animatronic Technician Manual

Parts and Service

Hearkening back to your technician tasks in *Sister Location*, your job is to make sure the animatronics are clean, safe, and functioning properly. Follow the instructions exactly if you want to survive.

Bonnie

Bonnie's guitar is out of tune and needs to be recalibrated. To do this, you'll need to access his harmonization module, located in his secondary throat pipe. Start by removing Bonnie's eyes and placing them in the cleaning receptacles. Then press the two buttons on Bonnie's jaw to open his faceplate. Once open, press the blinking button to enter calibration mode. Watch the colors that correspond to the notes to find which note is out of tune, then turn the correctly colored knob on his guitar. Replace Bonnie's eyes, click the buttons on his jaw, and he's good to go.

- **Nightmare Mode:** Bonnie appears under a black light, with a shower of confetti and background music playing. Good luck with that color-coded harmony calibration.

Chica

There have been customer complaints about Chica's acrid smell. Remove all food particles from Chica and put them in the trash bin. Press the two buttons on the side of her head to open her beak. To remove Chica's cockroach infestation, apply the Fazbear Entertainment Restaurant-Grade Chemispray to Chica's exterior by pressing the button under the hanging canister. Avoid inhaling the chemispray, as exposure may result in respiratory problems or skin or eye irritation. Carefully reattach Chica's arm and then her cupcake plate. Reapply the chemispray to

Fazbear Entertainment

clear another round of cockroaches. When the cupcake jumps away, return it to Chica's plate. Be sure to eat a slice of pizza to celebrate your success, or you may have an unhappy animatronic in your face . . .

- **Nightmare Mode:** The room is completely dark, and Chica's cupcake is now its nightmare counterpart. The chemispray is no longer effective, so you must remove the cockroach infestation by hand.

Freddy

It looks like a guest has left a personal item on the star attraction. Grab and remove the child's hat from Freddy's mouth and place it in the lost-and-found bin. Grab Freddy's bow tie and pull outward to open Freddy's chest cavity. Inside, remove the child's watch from the left side of his chest and place it in the lost and found. Remove Freddy's music box, press the red button to reset the safety latch, then remove the child's shoe. Carefully replace Freddy's music box, and then touch Freddy's nose. Your pay will be docked for mishandling of parts.

- **Nightmare Mode:** Freddy is in a dark room, surrounded by high-contrast static screens. Light is coming from his eyes and mouth, and many animatronic parts and toys are strewn about the floor.

Foxy

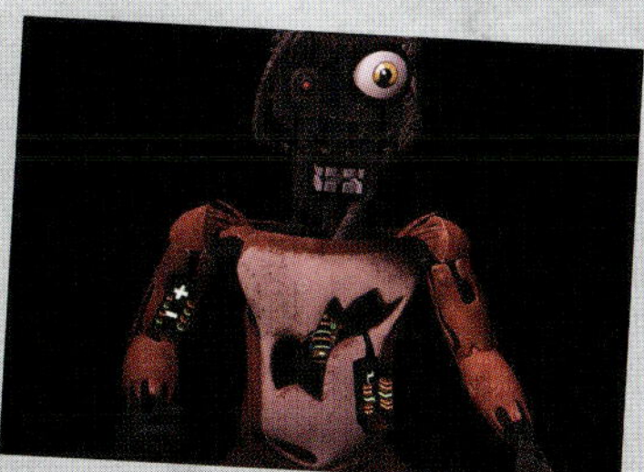

Foxy has been out of commission for quite some time. It's your job to return him to full working condition so that Pirate Cove can be reopened. Begin by placing Foxy's head on his endoskeleton. Doing so prompts a malfunction of his proprietary servo motors. You'll need to place new control fuses in the exposed receptacles, beginning with his legs. Inside the chest, a former employee placed the wrong fuse there. Remove the incorrect fuse and place it in the upper arm. Now insert new fuses for the chest. Finally, place an eye in his right eye socket.

- **Nightmare Mode:** Foxy is completely burned and the workroom is on fire.

Fazbear Entertainment

Vent Technician Certification Program

Vent Repair

Many *FNAF* games feature animatronics that are sensitive to heat, or require activating ventilation systems to keep yourself cool. This mode extends that mission into a series of puzzles in dark, cramped spaces, all in an effort to get the facility to a perfect seventy-two degrees Fahrenheit.

Mangle

Start by pushing the flashing button to hear from Tutorial Unit. You'll then descend to the first set of puzzles. When the service elevator stops, push the second flashing button to open a compartment with a lever. Flip the lever to activate your headlight and scare off Mangle. Listen carefully for Mangle's cues, and shoo him away by turning your headlight on her.

On this level, you must throw four levers to advance. Reach into the second vent that opens and flip the switch on the ceiling. Flip the second lever when it appears on the left side of the vent. Inside the central elevator, find and turn two yellow valves (one above and one below) and a third level will appear. Throw this lever and press the yellow flashing button above you. The final vent will now open. Above the final vent, open the hatch to reveal a blinking light inside the vent that changes colors. You must match the given order on the keypad to your right. Doing so will reveal the final lever. Throw it to complete your task.

- **Nightmare Mode:** A darker level with black-light coloring, and all three vents are open at the same time. Both Mangle and Shadow Mangle are active to attack you.

Ennard

Hit the flashing yellow button to begin. On the first level, as each light turns red, follow the tangled cord from each breaker box to the corresponding button. Hit the buttons in the correct order to open another vent. Solve the same but more complicated puzzle to open a third vent. The third vent has an even more complicated puzzle, and the room is dark, lit only by stray voltage, and Ennard is approaching you. Once solved, Ennard will try to open the doors as you descend to the next level.

In the second level, you must use a small, medium, and finally a large gear to get the machinery up and running. Ennard is present and can attack. Start in the left panel. Grab the small gear and place it in the machinery to access the medium gear. In the middle panel, place the medium gear straight ahead to open a gate on the right side. Now that it's accessible, place the small gear in the top-right side of the machinery, and the medium gear in the top left. This will cause the large gear to drop. Still in the middle panel, replace the medium gear straight ahead to reach the large and small gears. In the right panel, place the large gear on the far left, the small gear one peg below the large gear, and the medium gear on the remaining upper peg. Now the machinery is in working order.

In the boiler room, align the pipes properly to run the gas. There are multiple solutions to these puzzles, but one path is as follows. In the left panel, press buttons 3, 1, 2 in order to open the middle panel. Here, you can press rotate, rotate, 2. In the right panel, press the button to set fire to Ennard.

- **Nightmare Mode:** This mode is similarly dark and cluttered with animatronic parts. The mode is also played upside down; though the puzzles have the same solutions, you may have to take additional steps or think differently to complete them. On the first level, when the second vent opens, Springtrap approaches, limiting your time. After successfully completing the game, Ennard jumps at you, implying that he survived the fire. The elevator crashes.

Night Terrors

This game mode hearkens back to *FNAF4* with some familiar and not-so-familiar faces. As with that game, keep an open ear for audio cues.

Funtime Freddy

Funtime Freddy, Bon-Bon, and Bonnet haunt this game. Funtime Freddy will approach with Bon-Bon from either hall, so be sure to listen at the door before shining your light. Bonnet hides in the dresser drawers and the closet. Shine your flashlight on her or she'll jump-scare you. Note that Bonnet's and Bon-Bon's jump-scares can't harm you.

Nightmarionne

Players will hear "My Grandfather's Clock" (the Puppet's song) playing. Nightmarionne can appear from anywhere—the halls, bed, closet, and a disturbing hole in the ceiling. When it appears at the door, its eyes will be visible in the dark. Shine your flashlight on Nightmarionne's tentacles to repel attacks from the bed, closet, and ceiling. The tentacles are punishing; you may need to hold the door shut against a Nightmarionne attack while removing tentacles from the room.

Circus Baby

In this game, you play from inside the closet, with Circus Baby looking for you. If she sees you, close the door as she runs your way. But be wary: Closing the door for too long will attract attention from the PlushBabies surrounding you. Best to wait until Circus Baby is close to the closet, as the PlushBabies can jump-scare you, even if you're holding the door shut against Circus Baby's attack.

Nightmare Fredbear

As in *FNAF4*, Nightmare Fredbear can attack from all directions. When he's on the bed, shine your flashlight to ward him off. But when he's in the hallways, it's best to look for his red glowing eyes, or use a quick burst of light to scan the area. The flashlight makes Fredbear move faster in the hall. If he's at the hall or closet doors, hold them closed to keep him from getting to you.

Animatronic	Funtime Freddy	Nightmarionne	Circus Baby	Nightmare Fredbear
Length of Nights	3 minutes	3.5 minutes	2 minutes	3 minutes

IT'S EASY TO GET TURNED AROUND AT THE PIZZA PARTY. USE THIS MAP TO MASTER THE MAZE!

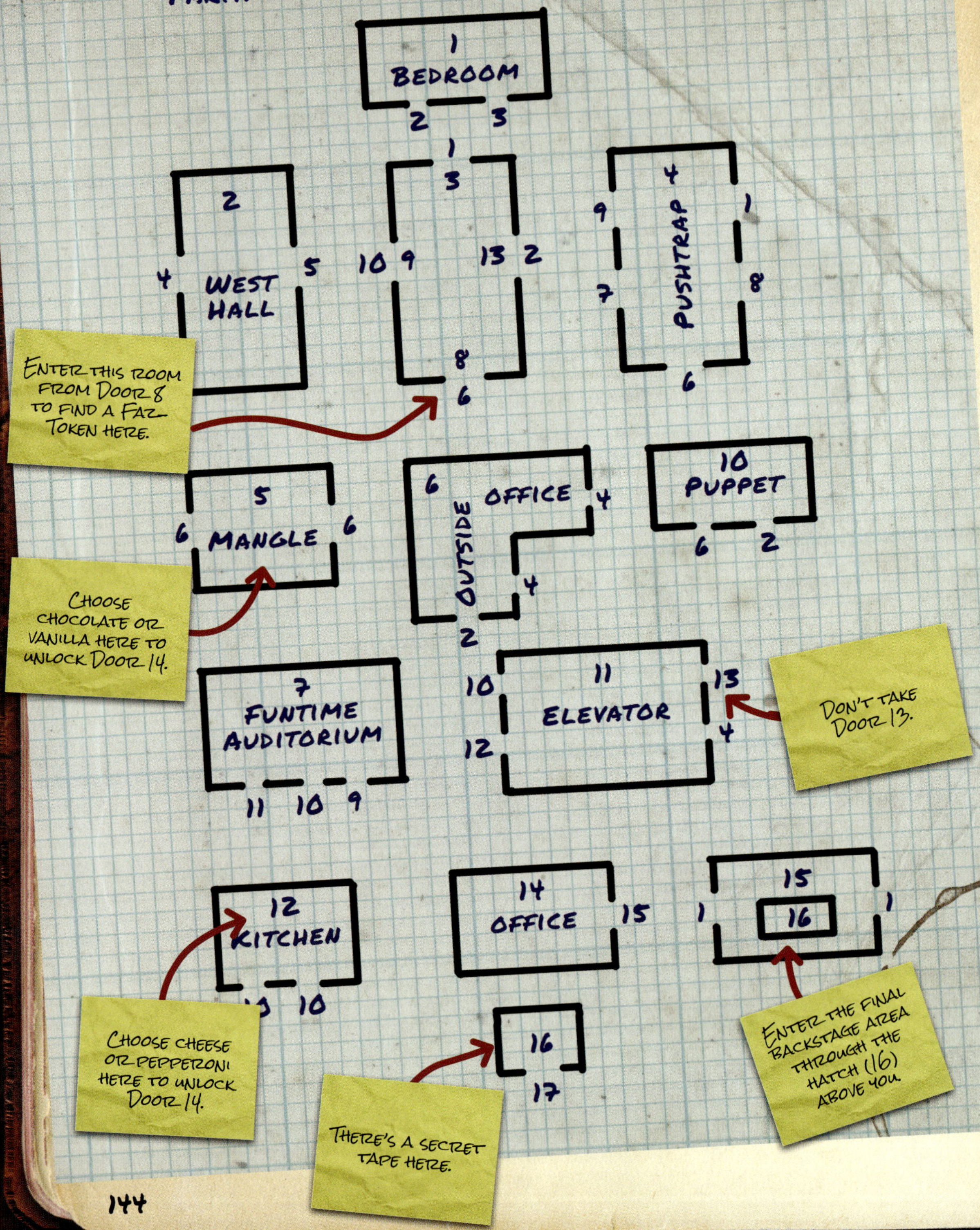

1
BEDROOM
2 3

1
3
10 9 13 2
8
6

2
4 WEST HALL 5

4
9 PUSHTRAP 1
7 8
6

ENTER THIS ROOM FROM DOOR 8 TO FIND A FAZ-TOKEN HERE.

5
6 MANGLE 6

CHOOSE CHOCOLATE OR VANILLA HERE TO UNLOCK DOOR 14.

6 OFFICE 4
OUTSIDE
4
2

10
PUPPET
6 2

7
FUNTIME AUDITORIUM
11 10 9

11
10 ELEVATOR 13
12 4

DON'T TAKE DOOR 13.

12
KITCHEN
10

CHOOSE CHEESE OR PEPPERONI HERE TO UNLOCK DOOR 14.

14
OFFICE 15

15
1 16 1

16
17

THERE'S A SECRET TAPE HERE.

ENTER THE FINAL BACKSTAGE AREA THROUGH THE HATCH (16) ABOVE YOU.

Night Terrors

Nightmare Mode: Pizza Party

This terrifying free-roam game brings you to the first ending of *Help Wanted*. Navigate the surreal black-light maze, which takes you through various locations you've seen throughout the *FNAF* series. Your goal is to reach the Kitchen and Mangle room via Doors 12 and 5, so you can choose the flavors for your cake and pizza. Once you've made your choices, return to the outside office room and take the newly available Door 14. This will lead you through the *FNAF3* office into a new room. Look up and crawl through the hatch to reach backstage, and your pizza party.

The First Ending

The backstage area is filled with cake and presents. Eat as much as you like. Glitchtrap appears, and gestures for you to follow him. Once you do, the screen goes black. You reawaken onstage, presumably stuffed into a Freddy Fazbear suit, performing for an empty pizzeria as Glitchtrap dances in the background. After the credits roll, HandUnit congratulates you.

Congratulations on completing the Freddy Fazbear Virtual Experience. You did an amazing job. You might be wondering if you missed anything, or if there's anything left to see. So just take my word for it: You didn't miss anything, and there's nothing left to see. We're looking forward to a fresh start with you, now that we've had a good laugh at these tall tales, and now that you realize that Fazbear Entertainment is a safe, family-friendly brand with no skeletons in our closet. So good-bye for now, and we'll see you on the toy aisle. Bye-bye. Bye-bye. Bye-Bye. Buh-bye. Take care now.

Codes, Glitches, and Secrets

The Gallery

Once you complete the Pizza Party level, a new button appears on your desk: "Go to Gallery." Here, you can take your time looking at the models for the game's animatronics.

The Secret Tapes

There are two other endings for *Help Wanted*. To get them, you'll need to obtain the secret tapes hidden throughout the game.

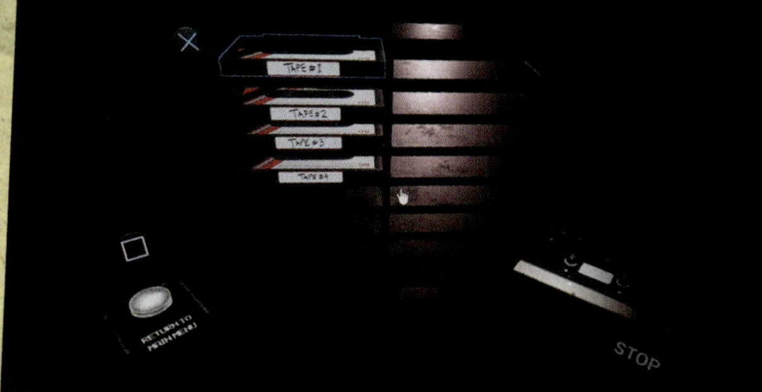

The Tape Player

To listen to the tapes, head to the Prize Counter. Throw a basketball at the tape player (to the right of the Chica plush) to obtain it. When you return to the main hub, activate the Party Machine and a glitching purple tape player will be sitting on top of your Faz-Token counter. Click it to enter the secret room and listen to the tapes.

INVENTORY LOG

Item No.	Description	Location
1	The tapes were created to warn about a malicious code in the game files that the game team is unable to understand or contain.	Intro Sequence, left rail, just before waiver appears
2	The malicious code manifests as a character, and it was watching what Tape Girl was doing.	Prize Counter, under the Disappointment Chips
3	Tape Girl overheard a conversation between her manager and someone else. There's a lawsuit and the project is on the line. It seems to involve Jeremy, who warned that something was wrong.	Prize Counter, inside the left gumball machine
4	Describes the guillotine paper slicer in the supply room, and how Jeremy used to do design work, which is how he knew it was there.	*FNAF1*, right side of the desk
5	The client came to the office and emptied things out, including some old game hardware that the team had scanned into the game files. That was when the anomaly began.	*FNAF3*, desktop behind the maintenance panel
6	Talks about that morning, and how Tape Girl saw Jeremy in the testing room, with the supply room lit brightly.	Dark Rooms, PlushBaby, right of the alarm clock
7	Jeremy had nightmares. The company told Tape Girl to leave him alone, like they knew he'd need to be replaced soon.	Dark Rooms, Funtime Foxy, left wall
8	The company started making a case to fire Jeremy, but Tape Girl believes this was more because of something he'd seen, like they needed to discredit him.	Parts and Service, Chica, refuse bin
9	A seeming continuation of Tape 6, Tape Girl finding Jeremy and thinking that ink had spilled everywhere.	Parts and Service, Freddy, under Freddy's right leg
10	Tape Girl takes over Jeremy's work. Another studio is buying Fazbear Entertainment out and will finish the game. She's trying to isolate the anomaly so the next person who tests it can destroy it.	Parts and Service, Foxy, floor left of Foxy
11	The anomaly seems to have attached itself to these logs; Tape Girl resolves to destroy them.	Vent Repair, Mangle, under the right pipes
12	Tape Girl is unable to delete them, but she has another idea.	Vent Repair, Ennard Nightmare Mode, Nightmare Fredbear's mouth, middle panel, descending between the intro and first puzzle level
13	Tape Girl discovers some old files showing that Fazbear Entertainment was working with the "rogue indie developer" to make light of the past and rebrand the company.	Night Terrors, Circus Baby, on the shelf behind you
14	Tape Girl ran a fragmentation program on the logs, hoping to render the anomaly harmless. It also destroyed her warnings.	Night Terrors, Nightmare Fredbear, behind toy telephone
15	Tape Girl seems to change her tune here—she tells you not to reassemble the logs, as doing so will reassemble the anomaly.	Night Terrors, Nightmare Mode Pizza Party, Backstage beside the pizza box
16	Tape Girl now tells you to let the anomaly try to leave the game through you, then use the emergency disconnect switch by the main stage to cause a hard restart and kill it.	Gallery, inside the cabinet under the monitor

Merge Ending

To obtain the merge ending, don't follow the instructions on Tape 16. At some point when you load into the main hub area, Glitchtrap will approach you. When he does, your view will slowly darken to purple and your screen will glitch, implying that the merge was successful and Glitchtrap can escape into the real world. You're then led to a Game Over screen.

Trapped Ending

To view the trapped ending, follow the instructions on Tape 16. When Glitchtrap is in front of you, hit the "Showtime" button. Wait for Glitchtrap's eyes to turn red. Within about 3 seconds, before his body starts turning purple, hit the secret button on the side of the monitor. Your screen will fade to black, and then you'll be taken to a metal door covered in handprints and scratch marks. Interact with the lock, and a panel slides back. On the other side of the door, Glitchtrap shushes you and walks away.

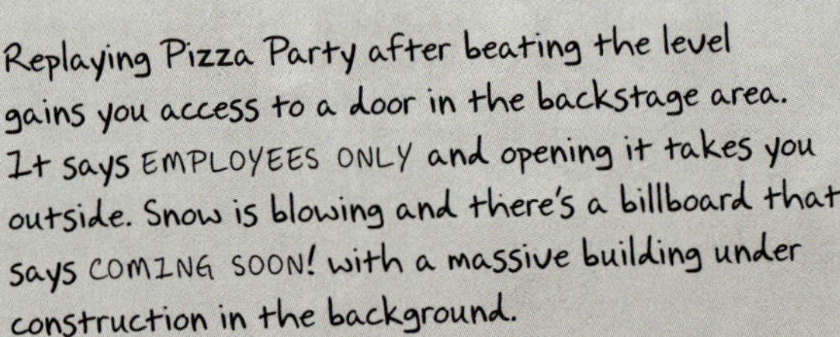

Replaying Pizza Party after beating the level gains you access to a door in the backstage area. It says EMPLOYEES ONLY and opening it takes you outside. Snow is blowing and there's a billboard that says COMING SOON! with a massive building under construction in the background.

Princess Quest

In the mobile port of *Help Wanted*, the secret tapes are replaced with a minigame called *Princess Quest*. To gain access to the game, you must zoom in on a glitching object at the Prize Counter (this occurs occasionally). The screen will fade to black and reopen on the main hub, where *Princess Quest* is now shown on the right monitor.

The game plays like a classic dungeon crawler, and you need to light torches scattered throughout the ten rooms while avoiding the various Glitchtrap enemies. The game ends with the princess unlocking a door covered in purple overgrowth. At the end of the room is a distorted purple bunny monster, and dialogue appears on the screen, but it doesn't look to be written in a language we can understand. Some sleuthing from fans revealed that the text in the dialogue box is "I ALWAYS COME BACK." The distorted voice lines heard here say, "I always come back. Let me out."

This door appears to be locked.

MANY FANS BELIEVE THE SIX TORCHES IN THE GRAVEYARD ARE SYMBOLIC OF THE MISSING CHILDREN.

Room	1	2	3	4	5	6	7	8 (Graveyard)	9	10
Torches to light	0	2	5	0	7	0	0	5 (1 does not produce flame)	1	1 (cannot be lit)
Enemies	0	0	7	5	5	0	7	0	0	1
Hearts	1	0	0	0	0	0	1	1	0	0
Keys	0	0	0	1	0	0	0	0	1	0

FAZ-TOKENS

Gold Faz-Tokens appear throughout the game, and collecting them can net you some interesting secrets as well as let you unlock hidden prizes at the Prize Counter. Nab all thirty and a basket of Exotic Butters will appear on the Prize Counter. Empty out the basket and press the red button at the bottom to activate the TV—the TV has shown different things throughout various patches, including the final room of the Pizza Party level and a tease for *The Curse of Dreadbear.*

Fazbear Entertainment

Item No.	Game Mode/Area	Location
1	Prize Counter	On the counter in front of the monitor
2	*FNAF1*	In the bottom-left desk drawer
3	*FNAF1*	Under the cupcake on the right monitor
4	*FNAF1*	At 3:00 a.m., reach inside the right monitor
5	*FNAF2*	Between the camera monitor and buttons
6	*FNAF2*	Put on the Freddy mask. Coin will appear on the desk.
7	*FNAF2*	Allow the music box to unwind. As the Puppet approaches, a coin appears in front of the telephone.
8	*FNAF3*	Left of the camera monitor
9	*FNAF3*	Tiles above the vent monitor form a number pad; dial 395248
10	*FNAF3*	During a ventilation error, check the vent on the right
11	Dark Rooms, Nightmare BB	Shine the flashlight at the ceiling fan, a coin will drop
12	Parts & Service, Bonnie	Beside the right eye cleaner
13	Parts & Service, Bonnie	Under the Bonnie plush on the left
14	Parts & Service, Bonnie	Strum Bonnie's guitar three times, then a coin appears on the left workbench
15	Parts & Service, Chica	In the trash can on the right

Item No.	Game Mode/Area	Location
16	Parts & Service, Chica	Behind the soda can on the left
17	Parts & Service, Chica	After completing the game, feed Chica pizza. A coin appears on the left.
18	Parts & Service, Freddy	Behind Freddy's left ear
19	Parts & Service, Freddy	Under a music box on the lower left workbench
20	Parts & Service, Foxy	Under the gears atop the right workbench
21	Parts & Service, Foxy	Wear Foxy's head, and it appears on the left workbench
22	Vent Repair, Mangle	Behind the second panel, between the gears and wall
23	Vent Repair, Ennard	Second set of puzzles, in the gear respawn box
24	Vent Repair, Nightmare Mode, Ennard	As the elevator travels between the intro and first set of puzzles, watch the right wall. There's a coin in Bonnet's eye.
25	Night Terrors, Circus Baby	Right side of the closet, on a wooden box
26	Night Terrors, Circus Baby	Left side of the closet, behind the centermost PlushBaby
27	Night Terrors, Circus Baby	Left side of the closet, on the left side of the box that the centermost PlushBaby is on
28	Night Terrors, Nightmare Mode, Pizza Party	Hallway outside the *FNAF3* office, on the floor of the vent to your left
29	Night Terrors, Nightmare Mode, Pizza Party	From Plushtrap's hallway, take the top-left door (8 on the map); a token will appear atop the present to your right
30	Gallery	In the top drawer of left table

Easter Eggs

Helpy

Main Hub:
Helpy appears to the left of the virtual menu, acting as a hint for the trapped ending, pointing to both the secret button on the side of the monitor and the Party Machine switch.

FNAF2:
Nightmare Mode, Withered: Helpy will rarely appear behind you, to your left.

Coffee

FNAF3:
Rarely, Coffee from Scott's previous game *The Desolate Hope* will appear on the desk.

Prize Counter:
Rarely, Coffee will appear on the floor behind the Prize Counter.

They're Watching

Parts & Service:
The animatronics' eyes follow you.

FNAF1:
If you look away from the cupcake, its eyes will be focused on you when you next see it.

Death Screen:
Nightmare Cupcake sometimes appears atop the monitor instead of the normal cupcake.

Sister Location

Night Terrors: Circus Baby:

A Bidybab will sometimes appear beside the flashlight on the floor.

Dark Rooms: Plushtrap:

There's a rare chance that a Minireena will be peeking in from the far left room.

Endo

FNAF2:

Endo 02 will rarely make an appearance, looming over the right side of your desk.

Vent Repair: Ennard:

Endo 02 can rarely be seen peering up at you from the grate below.

Vent Repair: Mangle

A new animatronic, Nightmare Endo, can be found in this mode.

You can honk Freddy's nose on the Menu screen.

SHOWTIME

Avid fans found a few interesting tidbits by digging through *Help Wanted*'s game files. The "Showtime" button remains one of the most talked-about unused features of the game. If you move forward far enough, you can see Freddy, Bonnie, and Chica through the main stage curtain. Animations for the animatronics in the songs are present in the game files, as well as a placeholder recording of the Freddy Fazbear's Pizza theme song.

ls, Fazbear Entertainment
r the one, the only,

a good time? I know I am!

umber

he singer
bear, but

a cotton
listen to

Freddy

s

reat!

BIRD WHO LIKES TO

for a hand! He hangs

you've met all the members of the band!

All: WOO-HOO!! Freddy Fazbear's Pizza, the fun just can't be beat! Freddy Fazbear's Pizza! It's time for us to eat!

Advertiser 1: For the next hour, add meat to any kids' pizza for just a dollar!

Advertiser 2: And if your parents really love you, they'll buy you a thirty-two ounce Freddy Fountain drink!

Advertiser 3: And don't forget: All the popular kids sign up for our mailing list.

All: And get free stuff on their birthday!

Advertiser 1: Freddy Fazbear's Pizza!

All: Where fantasy meets fun! Freddy Fazbear! Freddy Fazbear! Freddy Fazbear Pizza! Freddy Fazbear! Freddy Fazbear! Freddy Fazbear Pizza! Freddy Fazbear! Freddy Fazbear! Freddy Fazbear Pizza!

Achievements

I Scream. You Scream . . . : Get jump-scared.

Now I Will Tell You a Story: Eat a piece of candy.

Pop Goes the Weasel . . . : Get a jump-scare prize! (Get jump-scared while opening a prize.)

Your Special Day!: Activate the Party Machine.

Showtime!: Re-create the main stage show. (You can do this by placing action figures of Freddy, Bonnie, and Chica on the Prize Counter.)

Let's Eat!: Consume all possible edibles in the game. (Eat all food prizes plus the edible cockroach.)

Play!: Complete the Prize Counter.

Numismatist: Find all tokens.

Celebrate!: Unlock all achievements.

Let's Party!: Find a hidden token.

Exotic Butters: Finish the game. (Complete the *Pizza Party* minigame.)

Stay Put!: That is why you don't leave the office. (In *FNAF1*, step outside the office to prompt a jump-scare.)

Rock!: Strum Bonnie's guitar. (In Parts and Service: Bonnie, reach out and strum his guitar.)

Pest Control: Pull 25 roaches off Chica. (In Parts and Service: Chica, manually pick 25 cockroaches off Chica.)

Choking Hazard: For ages 3 and up. (Eat an action figure.)

TAPE GIRL

Many theories have popped up around the girl who made the secret tapes scattered throughout *Help Wanted*. The tapes seem to confirm that:

- Tape Girl was a QA tester for the original game development team. She had a manager, Dale, and a coworker, Jeremy, who tested the game before her.
- The client (assumed to be Fazbear Entertainment) gave the development team old circuit boards to scan, some of which had code on them to use for the game. After it was downloaded, an anomaly began to appear.
- Jeremy complained of nightmares and had seen something in the game that disturbed him. The company was putting together a case of minor offenses to use as evidence to either fire or discredit him.
- Something terrible happened to Jeremy, something that seemingly resulted in a lawsuit, and may be why Fazbear Entertainment handed off development to another company.
- Tape Girl discovered that Fazbear Entertainment was actually *working with* the indie game developer that they claimed to want to discredit. It was all an elaborate cover-up and rebrand scheme.
- Tape Girl was given three days to finish up Jeremy's work before the game development was taken over by a new studio. She decided to try to isolate and delete the anomaly, which she described as a character who watched her while she worked.
- She later discovered that the anomaly had attached itself to her audio logs. She tried to destroy the logs, but was unsuccessful. She ultimately ran a fragmentation program on the files to break them up, rendering the anomaly harmless. She urged whoever was listening not to reassemble the tapes, as doing so will reassemble the anomaly.

Friend or Foe?

Fans have turned a spotlight on Tapes 1 and 15, since Tape Girl seems to introduce herself in both tapes, but gives contradicting directions (find the tapes vs. don't). This, coupled with the secret merge ending and the note on the waiver about "digital consciousness transference," seems to imply that Tape Girl herself may be corrupted by the Glitchtrap anomaly.

142

DATE 11-12-1987

PAY TO THE ORDER OF Jeremy Fitzgerald $ 100.50

One hundred dollars and 50/100 DOLLARS

MEMO Welcome to the family! Fazbear Entertainment

And Who's Jeremy?

Theorists were quick to probe Jeremy's relation to the other two Jeremys in the *FNAF* canon: Jeremy Fitzgerald, the night guard from *FNAF2*, and the missing child confirmed on the tombstone in *Pizzeria Simulator*. The community seems to have reached the conclusion that the duplicate name is just a coincidence.

The Indie Games

At the start of *Help Wanted*, HandUnit explains that an indie game developer created games that were loosely based on real events. Fazbear Entertainment insists that they're currently suing him for the damage he did to their name, but this is later shown to be a lie. In Tape 13, Tape Girl says "They lied to us . . . Fazbear Entertainment hired the game developer. Those indie games were designed to conceal and make light of what happened. This isn't just an attempt to rebrand. It's an elaborate cover-up. A campaign to discredit everything."

Mystery solved, but one question still remains: Which games is she referring to? Theorists have a few ideas . . .

- All *FNAF* Games Up to Now: While this theory was popular upon the release of *Help Wanted*, most fans have since discredited it.
- The 8-bit Minigames: *FNAF 2–4* and *Sister Location* feature a variety of 8-bit minigames that seemingly tell the truth about the horrific murders at the various *FNAF* locations. These games could certainly fit the bill.
- *FNAF World*: *FNAF World* has been ruled as existing outside of *FNAF*'s canon, but that doesn't necessarily mean the game as a game isn't canonical.

Is Scott Cawthon canon? Scott is confirmed to portray the indie developer referenced in the opening, but Scott himself is not canon.

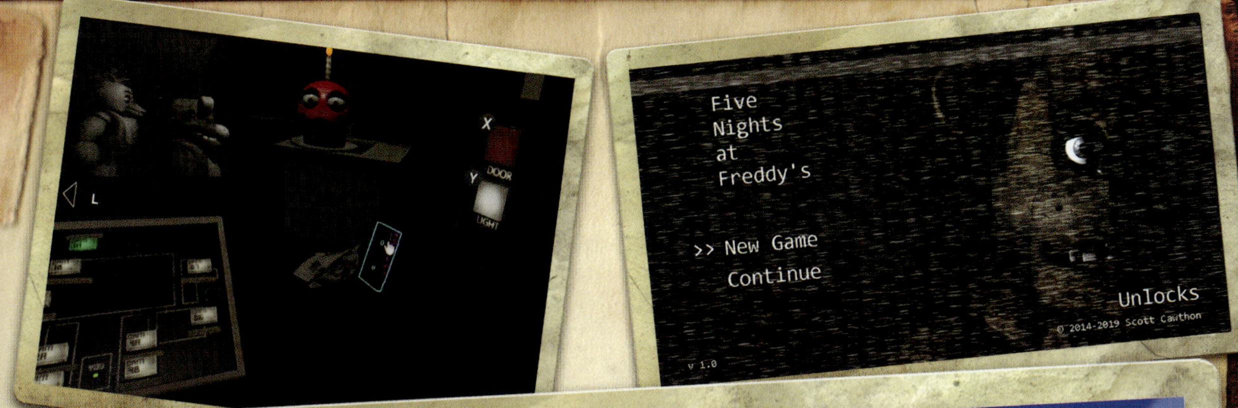
X
Y
DOOR
LIGHT
L
Five
Nights
at
Freddy's
>> New Game
Continue
Unlocks
© 2014-2019 Scott Cawthon
v 1.0

FNAF WORLD

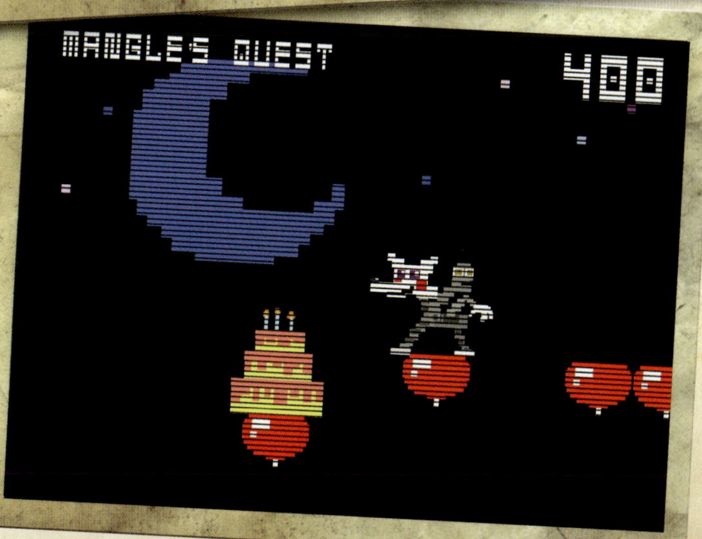
MANGLES QUEST
400

Chapter 9

The Curse of Dreadbear

Five Nights at Freddy's is no stranger to Halloween-themed DLC. All the way back in *FNAF*, Halloween decorations went up in the office like clockwork every October 31. This trend continued through future games, including a particularly robust DLC for *FNAF4*, which featured new animatronics. But *The Curse of Dreadbear* takes the meaning of DLC to a different level.

Far from a re-skin, this expansion throws in three entirely new game modes: Afraid of the Dark, Spooky Mansion, and Danger! Keep Out!, for a total of ten new games. The games, Easter eggs, and new ending have the potential to change the course of future *FNAF* games, with huge implications for lore. And if you're not into the lore, well, Foxy's Pirate Adventure should keep you chasing a twisting road to that high score.

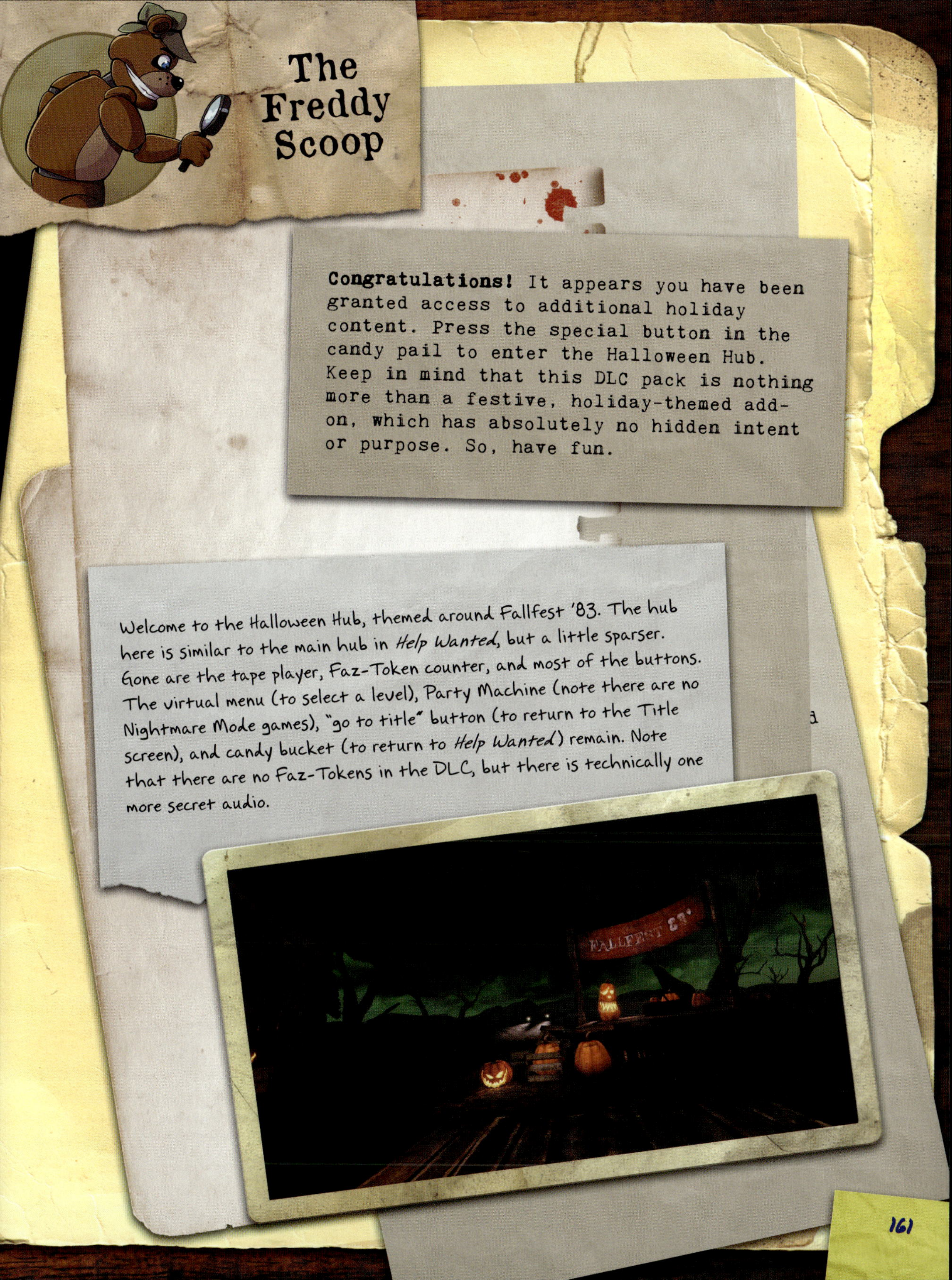

Congratulations! It appears you have been granted access to additional holiday content. Press the special button in the candy pail to enter the Halloween Hub. Keep in mind that this DLC pack is nothing more than a festive, holiday-themed add-on, which has absolutely no hidden intent or purpose. So, have fun.

Welcome to the Halloween Hub, themed around Fallfest '83. The hub here is similar to the main hub in *Help Wanted*, but a little sparser. Gone are the tape player, Faz-Token counter, and most of the buttons. The virtual menu (to select a level), Party Machine (note there are no Nightmare Mode games), "go to title" button (to return to the Title screen), and candy bucket (to return to *Help Wanted*) remain. Note that there are no Faz-Tokens in the DLC, but there is technically one more secret audio.

Prizes

It's not Halloween without treats—check out the new Halloween-themed prizes!

Fazbear Entertainment

Where Fantasy and Fun Come to Life

Prize Catalog COLLECT THEM ALL!

Treats

☐ Bite Late Night

☐ Crudlet

☐ Gobblinz'

☐ Katz Black Licorice

☐ Lavender Dollop

☐ Sloppy

☐ Squirmy

☐ Third Eye

☐ Chewy Treat

☐ Devilish Delight

☐ Eat N' Cry

☐ Fazzies

☐ Moon Drop

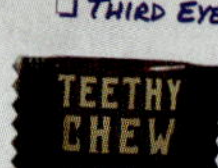

☐ Teethy Chew

☐ Buccaneer Bounty

☐ Chica of the Sea

Action Figures (for ages 3 and up)

☐ Dreadbear

☐ Grimm Foxy

☐ Jack-O-Bonnie

☐ Jack-O-Chica

☐ Nightmare Bonnie

☐ Nightmare Chica

☐ Nightmare Foxy

☐ Nightmare Freddy

☐ Withered Bonnie

☐ Withered Chica

☐ Withered Foxy

☐ Withered Freddy

Masks

☐ Balloon Boy

☐ Bonnie

☐ Chica

☐ Foxy

☐ Freddy

☐ Mangle

Misc.

☐ Cupcake Candy Pail

Jack-O'-Lanterns

☐ Bonnie

☐ Chica

☐ Foxy

☐ Freddy

Gameplay and Strategy

Afraid of the Dark: Plushkin Patch

Plushkins are one of the three *Curse of Dreadbear* animatronics new to *FNAF*. They appear to be PlushBabies who wear the masks of other characters (specifically Balloon Boy, Chica, Foxy, and Freddy).

This game mode is similar to PlushBaby's Dark Rooms from *Help Wanted*. Only, instead of a long, narrow hall, you're situated in a wide-open pumpkin patch. The different dimensions of the screen mean there's more square footage to scan. You'll need to scan vertically, too, since PlushBabies can hide in the trees as well as behind pumpkins. If you see one, shine your flashlight to clear it, but be careful as your battery life is limited. You need to survive until 6:ØØ a.m.

Afraid of the Dark: Pirate Ride

Welcome aboard Cap'n Foxy's Pirate Adventure! Ye can help me with this here adventure by shootin' the targets with that there hand cannon. Do yer best, or I'll send ye to Davy Jones's Locker. For yer safety, keep yer hands inside the ride at all times, or you'll end up like me. Hahahahahaha!

That's right—it's a classic dark ride featuring Cap'n Foxy on a pirate adventure. Your mission is to shoot the color-coded targets around the ride to earn the high score. Hit all the targets in a room and you activate a bonus round to double your score.

During a normal run, the highest-possible score is 3,425 (First Mate). After earning different rankings, four different Helpy cutouts will appear throughout the ride. Shooting him so he points left will take the cart on a different track, to behind-the-scenes areas where high-point values can be found . . . along with Jack-O-Bonnie and Jack-O-Chica.

- Backroom: Hit Helpy in Ride Start. Exits to Underwater.
- The Office: Hit Helpy in Kraken Attack! Exits to Outside.
- Kitchen: Hit Helpy in Underwater. Exits to Set Sail.
- Boiler Room: Hit Helpy in Outside. Exits to Ride Start.

The highest-possible score is 11,150, but the highest the display on your hand cannon can show is 9,975. When you hit 10,000 points, your score display will loop around to 0 again.

Though you can take a route that hits all four Helpys, the highest-scoring path doesn't require it: Ride Start (0) → Set Sail (850) → The Storm (450) → Kraken Attack! (500, hit Helpy) → The Office (2,400) → Outside (0, you reenter the track after the target has passed) → Underwater (850, hit Helpy) → Kitchen (2,500) → Set Sail (850) → The Storm (450) → Kraken Attack! (500) → Fight the Kraken (700) → Outside (100, hit Helpy) → Boiler Room (1,000) → End

Rooms	Blue (25)	Green (50)	Yellow (75)	Pink (100)	Total/Bonus
Ride Start	1 (no points)	1 (no points)	1 (no points)	1 (no points)	0
Set Sail	4	2	3	0	425/850
The Storm	5	2	0	0	225/450
Kraken Attack!	6	2	0	0	250/500
Fight the Kraken	2	3	2	0	350/700
Outside	0	0	1	0	75
Underwater	4	5	1	0	425/850
Backroom	0	0	0	14	1,400
The Office	0	0	0	24	2,400
Kitchen	0	2	0	24	2,500
Boiler Room	0	0	0	10	1,000

At the end of your ride, your score nets you a new title:

- Bilge Rat: 0+
- Scallywag: 1,000+
- Buccaneer: 2,000+
- First Mate: 3,000+
- Captain: 7,000+
- Admiral: 8,325+

SCORING UNDER 1,000 OR 10,000–10,975 WILL EARN YOU A FOXY JUMP-SCARE.

Afraid of the Dark: Corn Maze

In what is perhaps the most frightening game of the lot, you're dropped in the center of a maze of wooden fences. There are four color-coded gates (red, blue, yellow, green) at the north, east, south, and west sides of the maze. The catch? You'll need the correct key to open the gate. The keys spawn at random in different locations, so you'll need to navigate the maze differently with each playthrough, which is tricky with the animatronic on your tail. There are some general rules for key locations though:

- Red Spider Key spawns near the yellow gate.
- Blue Book Key spawns near the green gate.
- Yellow Pumpkin Key spawns near the red gate.
- Green Tombstone Key spawns near the blue gate.

As you collect keys, an icon for each is added to your flashlight.

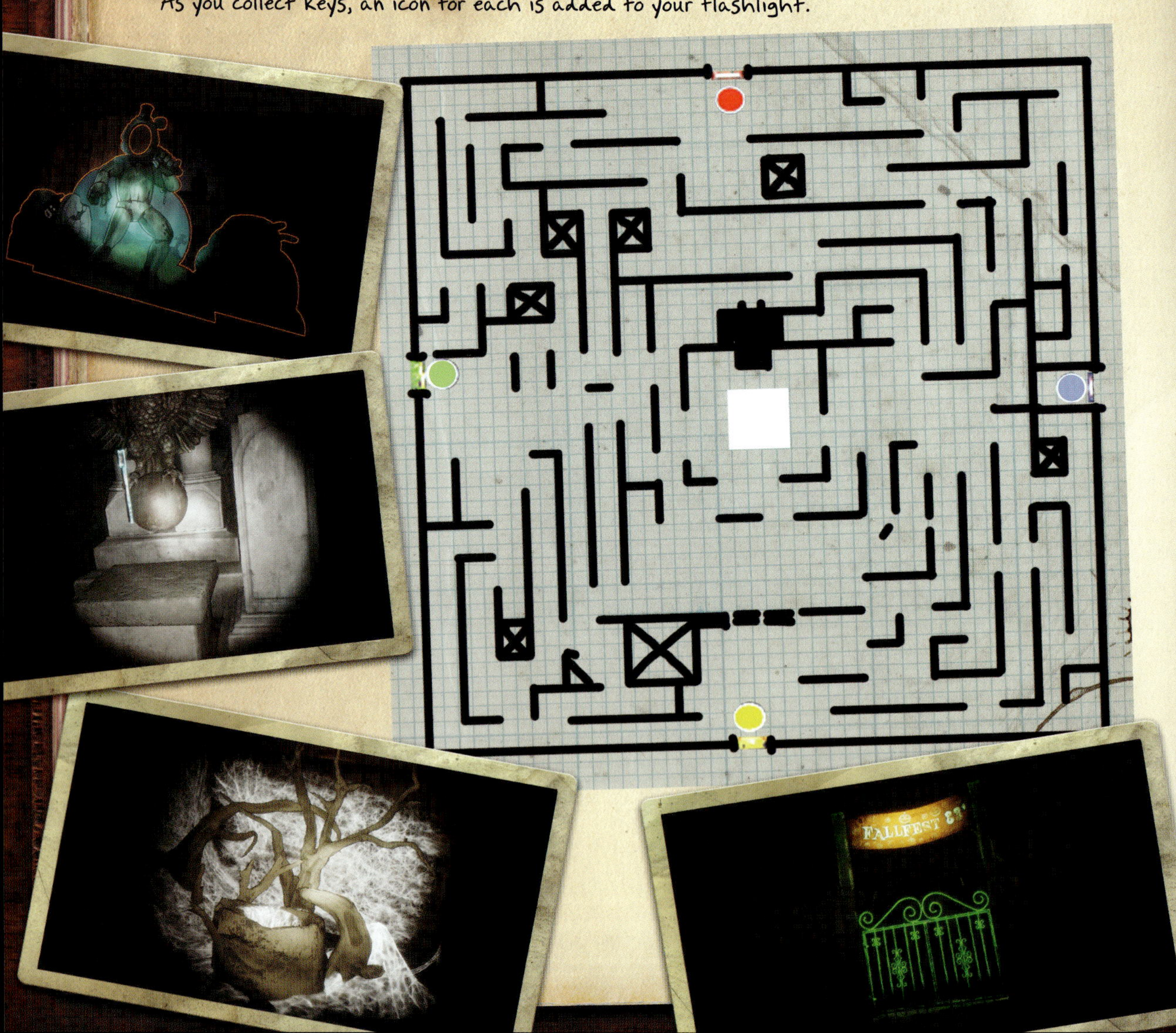

If you get turned around, a good shortcut to reorient yourself is to look for some of the taller objects, like the windmill, which appears by the red gate, or the water tower, which appears by the yellow gate.

Grimm Foxy

Meet another terrifying new addition to the *FNAF* canon: Grimm Foxy. Grimm Foxy is on fire, and he has a large scythe in place of the usual hook. He chases you, and can only be avoided by hiding behind one of the many painted cutouts in the maze. Listen closely for his singing when he draws near, and never be far from a cutout. When in doubt, reset Grimm Foxy by letting him see you and then hiding. This will buy you about fifteen seconds of exploration time, and becomes more necessary as the maze goes on and Foxy is more active.

The Fifth Exit

After collecting all four keys, a fifth, the purple key, becomes available. You have the option of leaving via one of the gates that matches the key you collected (to win a prize), or you can collect the purple key and continue on to the secret ending.

To use the purple key, return to the center of the maze and use it to unlock the cellar doors.

Inside the cellar is a secret prize room, but the prize here has already been opened: a white rabbit mask sits inside. Put it on to finish the game and return to the Title screen.

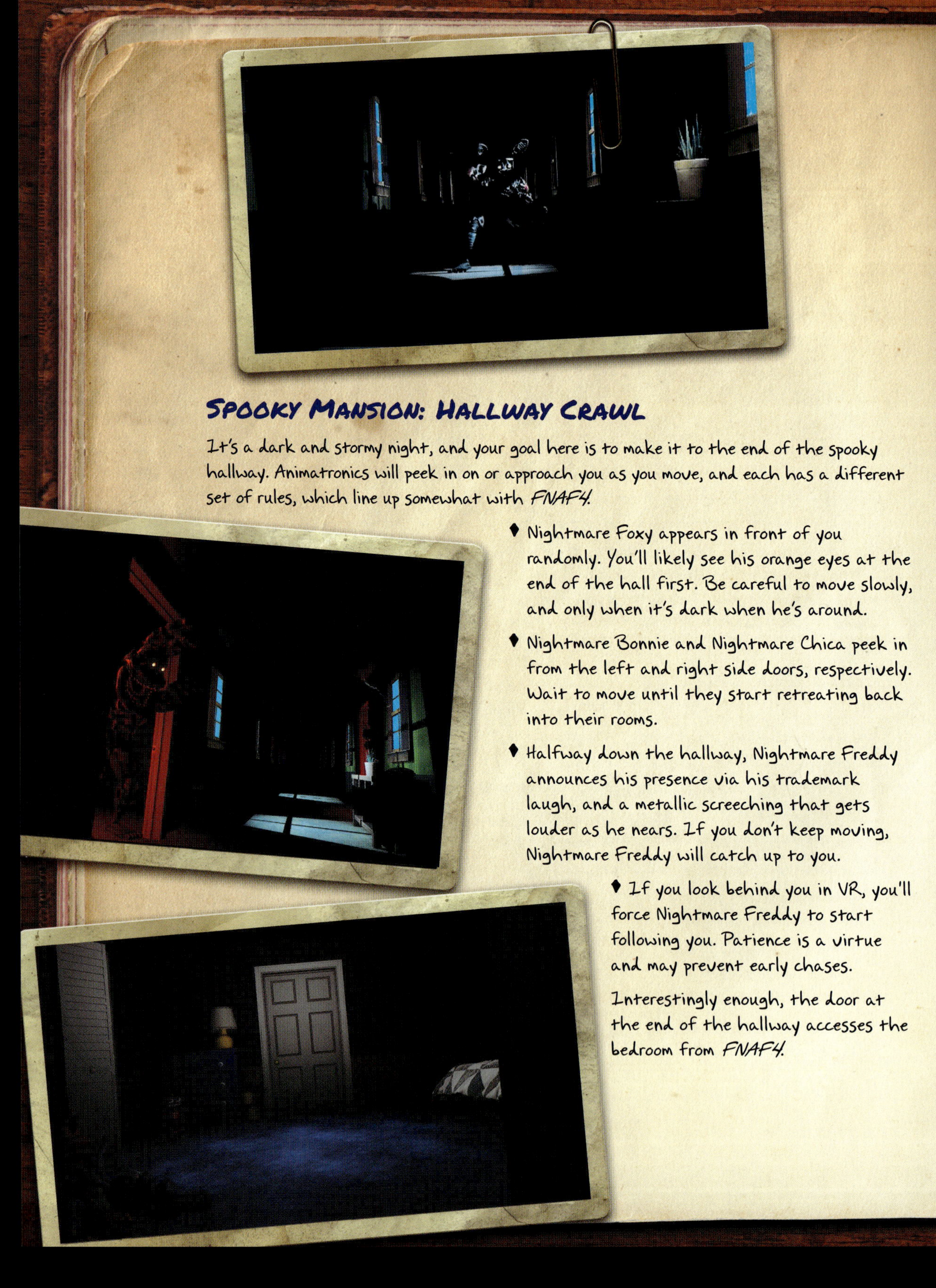

Spooky Mansion: Hallway Crawl

It's a dark and stormy night, and your goal here is to make it to the end of the spooky hallway. Animatronics will peek in on or approach you as you move, and each has a different set of rules, which line up somewhat with *FNAF4*.

- Nightmare Foxy appears in front of you randomly. You'll likely see his orange eyes at the end of the hall first. Be careful to move slowly, and only when it's dark when he's around.
- Nightmare Bonnie and Nightmare Chica peek in from the left and right side doors, respectively. Wait to move until they start retreating back into their rooms.
- Halfway down the hallway, Nightmare Freddy announces his presence via his trademark laugh, and a metallic screeching that gets louder as he nears. If you don't keep moving, Nightmare Freddy will catch up to you.
- If you look behind you in VR, you'll force Nightmare Freddy to start following you. Patience is a virtue and may prevent early chases.

Interestingly enough, the door at the end of the hallway accesses the bedroom from *FNAF4*.

Spooky Mansion: Build-A-Mangle

Welcome to the Fazbear Entertainment Fulfillment Center. Today, we are assembling animatronic performers. Each animatronic unit will bring joy to the children at one of our many Freddy Fazbear locations. Just place the necessary components in the assembly chute, conveniently located at the front of your workstation. Each work order is unique, so gather only the components as shown on the quad monitor array. Use the high-voltage shock buttons to gently remove any unwanted critters that stumbled onto the assembly line. Now let's get to work.

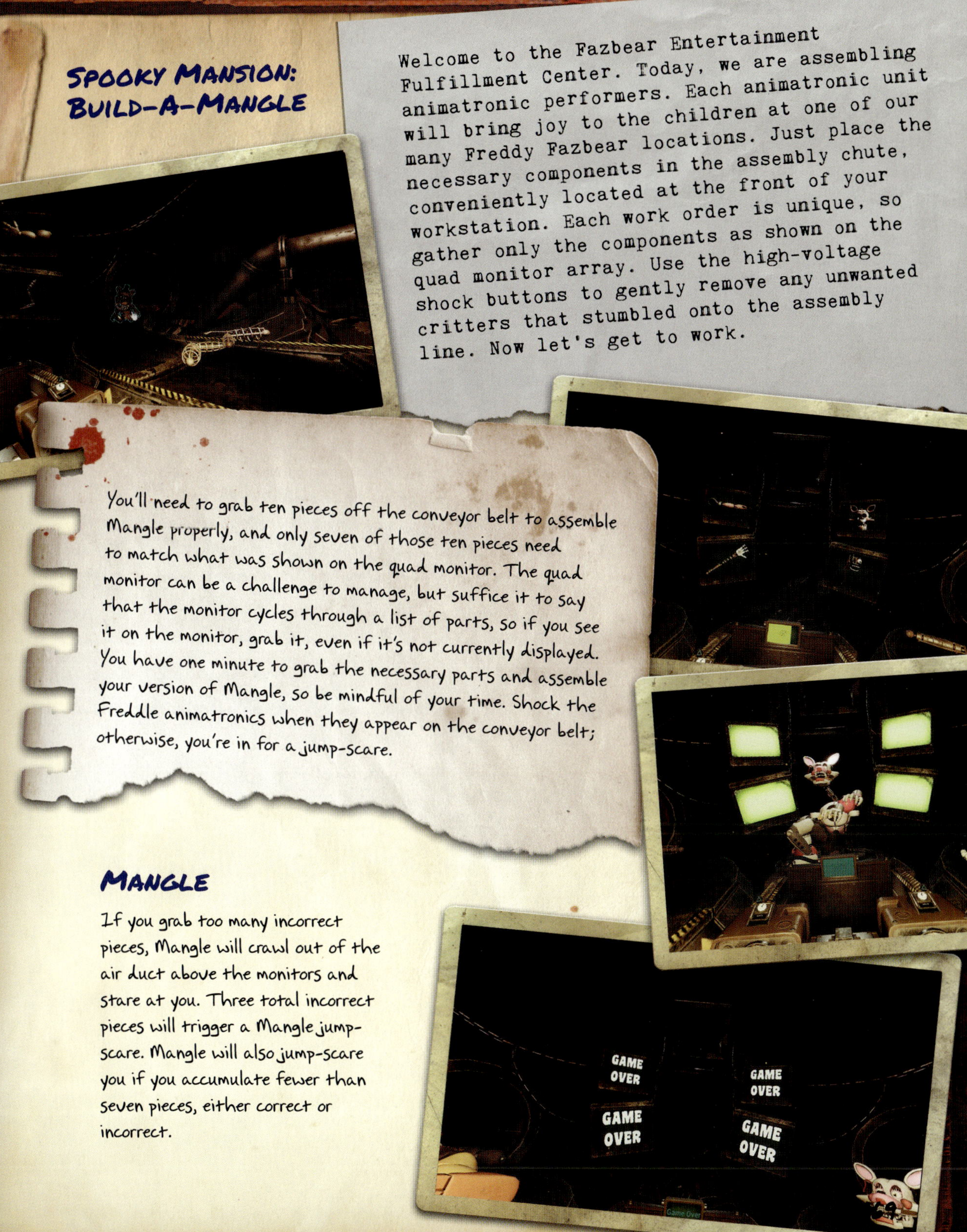

You'll need to grab ten pieces off the conveyor belt to assemble Mangle properly, and only seven of those ten pieces need to match what was shown on the quad monitor. The quad monitor can be a challenge to manage, but suffice it to say that the monitor cycles through a list of parts, so if you see it on the monitor, grab it, even if it's not currently displayed. You have one minute to grab the necessary parts and assemble your version of Mangle, so be mindful of your time. Shock the Freddle animatronics when they appear on the conveyor belt; otherwise, you're in for a jump-scare.

Mangle

If you grab too many incorrect pieces, Mangle will crawl out of the air duct above the monitors and stare at you. Three total incorrect pieces will trigger a Mangle jump-scare. Mangle will also jump-scare you if you accumulate fewer than seven pieces, either correct or incorrect.

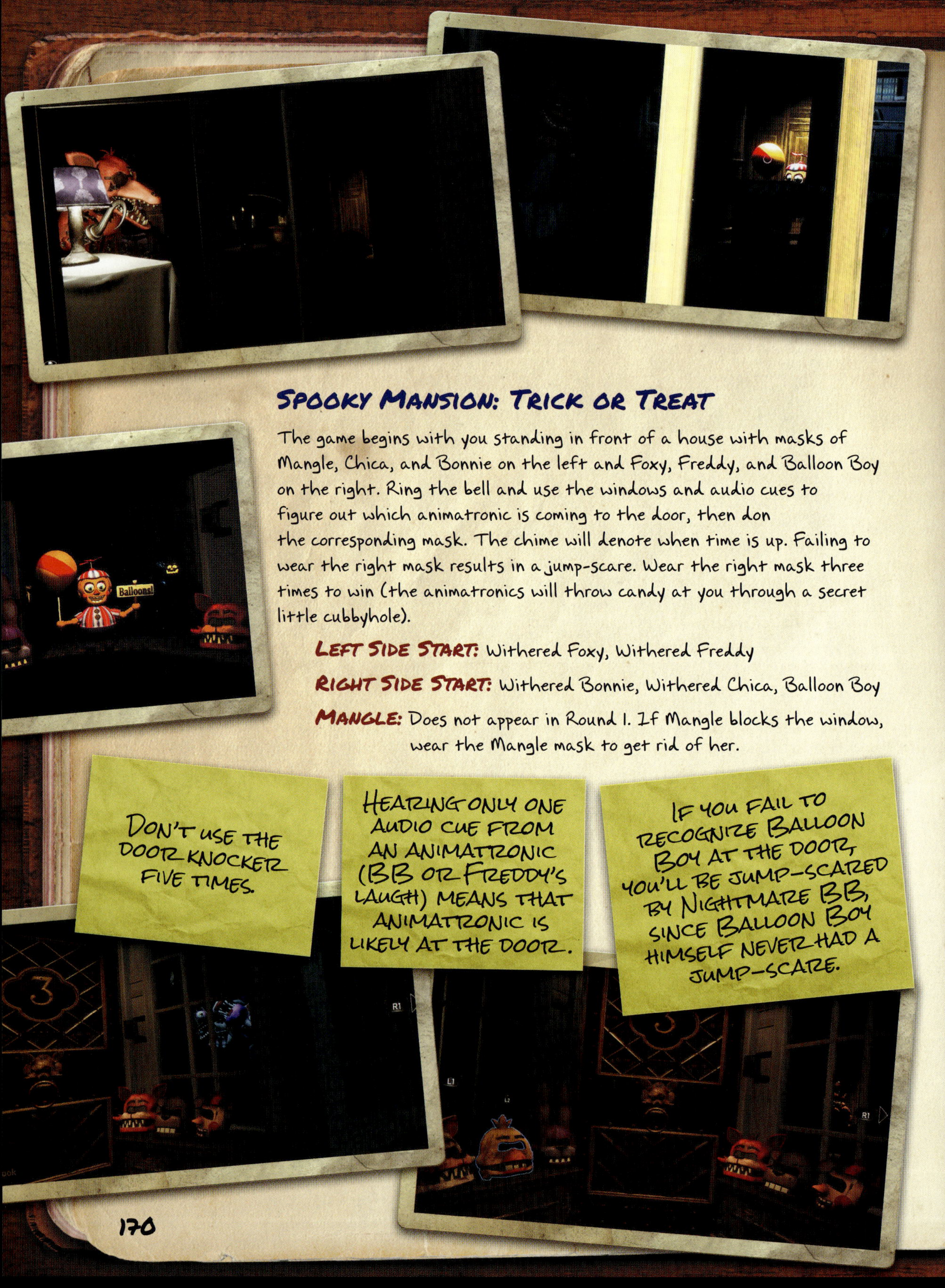

SPOOKY MANSION: TRICK OR TREAT

The game begins with you standing in front of a house with masks of Mangle, Chica, and Bonnie on the left and Foxy, Freddy, and Balloon Boy on the right. Ring the bell and use the windows and audio cues to figure out which animatronic is coming to the door, then don the corresponding mask. The chime will denote when time is up. Failing to wear the right mask results in a jump-scare. Wear the right mask three times to win (the animatronics will throw candy at you through a secret little cubbyhole).

LEFT SIDE START: Withered Foxy, Withered Freddy

RIGHT SIDE START: Withered Bonnie, Withered Chica, Balloon Boy

MANGLE: Does not appear in Round 1. If Mangle blocks the window, wear the Mangle mask to get rid of her.

DON'T USE THE DOOR KNOCKER FIVE TIMES.

HEARING ONLY ONE AUDIO CUE FROM AN ANIMATRONIC (BB OR FREDDY'S LAUGH) MEANS THAT ANIMATRONIC IS LIKELY AT THE DOOR.

IF YOU FAIL TO RECOGNIZE BALLOON BOY AT THE DOOR, YOU'LL BE JUMP-SCARED BY NIGHTMARE BB, SINCE BALLOON BOY HIMSELF NEVER HAD A JUMP-SCARE.

SPOOKY MANSION: DREADBEAR

Welcome back to Research and Development. Today, we are using science to pervert the mysteries of life and reanimate the inanimate.

Begin by turning the left crank to lower the final new animatronic of the DLC, Dreadbear, into place. Once properly positioned, give him a controlled shock with the switch on your forward right.

Today, you'll be working on Dreadbear's control module (his brain). Start by coloring the ten sections of his brain to match the blueprint on the left monitor. Under the blueprint, you'll see a scale with a yellow charge number and a red goal number. Use the red diode to increase the charge or the blue diode to decrease the charge until the yellow number matches the red number. Now place the white diode in the brain to view the neural feedback loop. Use the button on the top left of the console to show the goal in red, then manipulate the three dials to match the neural wavelengths with the goal. When finished, place the brain in Dreadbear's head.

As time goes on, you'll lose power, so be sure to move quickly and efficiently. You can use the controlled shock switch to reset the power, but note that shocking Dreadbear five times (this includes the initial shock) will result in a jump-scare.

DANGER! KEEP OUT!

NIGHT 01

You're in the office from *FNAF*, tasked with staying alive until 6:00 a.m., but instead of doors, the doorways on your left and right sides are boarded up. You can still access the camera system, and the lights on the left and right that can be used to fend off the animatronics. You also have lights on the cameras themselves that can be used to push the animatronics back. In this mode, the lights function more as flashbulbs, similar to the Funtime Foxy level in *Sister Location*.

Power Supply: The camera system doesn't drain your power, but each flash performed drains your power by 20 percent. After using five flashes, you'll need to reset the power system, which takes about 8 seconds.

Night 01 only features Jack-O-Bonnie and Jack-O-Chica, who approach from left and right, respectively. If they make it to the boards, flash them, or they will break the boards down until they reach you. Best advice: stay on top of your power supply. After flashing both animatronics, reset your power. You don't want to be under attack and unable to use your only defense.

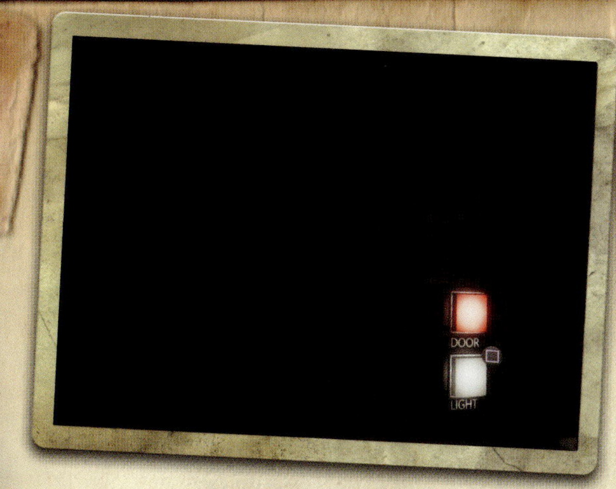

NIGHT 02

Same rules apply as Night Ø1, only now Grimm Foxy has been added to the mix in Pirate Cove. You can use the light button on the cameras to reset his usual cycle, though it's recommended to wait until he's fully in view before flashing him. The animatronics also seem to move faster on this night.

NIGHT 03

Dreadbear appears starting on this night, moving slowly toward you. He cannot be stopped, only slowed using the flash. Keeping track of where he is and stopping him as much as possible, as early as possible, is usually a winning strategy. If you hear a lightbulb shatter, that's your cue that Dreadbear is in the East Hall, and you don't have much longer before his attack. Keep track of him as well as the other animatronics, which are now more aggressive.

Codes, Glitches, and Secrets

Easter Eggs

FNAFY House

The *FNAF4* house sits on the hill ahead of you. This is especially clear when the sky loads in red (it can also load as green, orange, or purple).

Halloween Hub

Party Machine

Turn on the Party Machine, and press the secret button on the left side of the monitor. Look behind you at the car on the hill; its headlights are now purple. If you look in the distance on the hill with the *FNAF4* house, you can see Glitchtrap dancing.

Fallfest '83

If this DLC takes place in 1983, does it have something to tell us about the Bite of '83?

PRIZE ROOM
If a clown poster appears, you can honk its nose.
Rarely, Dreadbear will rise from the lake and walk behind you, into the barn.
FOXY'S SHIP
Foxy's pirate ship sometimes appears on the lake, but it will eventually be dragged under by a kraken.

Prize Screen

Rarely, three clown posters will spawn in the Prize Room. Hit each poster with a dart and the room will turn purple, as though under a black light. The banner's text changes to "IT'S ME."

Danger! Keep Out!: Night 03

Rarely, if you pick up the phone and hold it up, a dial tone will play. The textures on all the objects in the room will then go static, with certain objects (ones with lighting effects) turning purple. The monitor will then say "Scanning for glitches," and "No glitches found" after completing its scan. You'll then be taken to the Title screen.

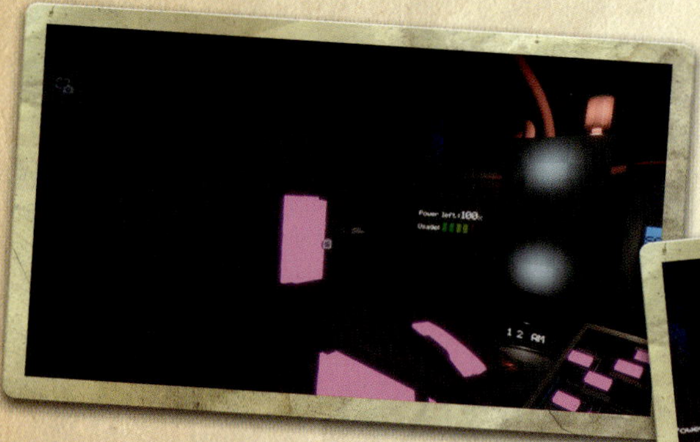

Game Over Screen

A green-and-purple glitching grave, which appears to have a similar texture as the secret tapes and Glitchtrap plush from *Help Wanted*, appears under Dreadbear's hand. The monitor on the table will sometimes say, "Report glitches before they spread" or "Purging system . . ."

Reluctant Follower

After locating the original sixteen secret tapes in *Help Wanted* and completing the fifth exit in the Corn Maze level of *Dreadbear*, fans can unlock a secret final audio. To listen, head back to the Prize Counter in *Help Wanted*. The white rabbit mask you obtained in Corn Maze will be sitting there. Take it back with you to the main hub, and wear it while holding the Glitchtrap plush you obtained to hear the audio.

Yes, I hear you. I know . . . No. There's no miscommunication. I understand. Yes, I have it. I made it myself. I think you would like it . . . No, no one suspects anything. Don't worry, I'll be ready, and I won't let you down. It will be fun.

The Reluctant Follower

- The Mask: The secrets revealed in the Corn Maze level were certainly unnerving. Fans were quick to point out that Tape Girl talked about a Halloween mask on Tape 9, and that there seemed to be another voice looming in the background of that tape.
- The Audio: The secret audio is certainly disturbing, with this character seemingly taking orders from someone and forming some sort of secret plan. When put together, many fans believe that the Reluctant Follower is Tape Girl, under the influence of the Glitchtrap code.
- The Grave: Could the glitching grave on the hill belong to the Reluctant Follower? Or could this be a reference to Afton himself? Interestingly enough, the glitching tombstone is surrounded by seven other tombstones, as opposed to the usual six.

FALLFEST '83

References to 1983 aren't usually dropped into *FNAF* games at random. Most fans accept that the events of *FNAF4* take place in 1983, and this game did have quite a few *FNAF4* references:

- Hallway Crawl takes place in the *FNAF4* house.
- Some of the masks in Trick or Treat look to be the real versions of the masks worn by the bullies in the *FNAF4* night-end minigames.
- The *FNAF4* house appears on the hill in front of the monitor, and there's a Glitchtrap Easter egg that shows him dancing beside the house.

Certain fans have drawn a connection between *FNAF4*'s "I will put you back together" and the theming around Dreadbear. The idea of taking something inanimate, something dead, and giving it new life through an animatronic rang more than a few bells for theorists. We've seen some definite mad-scientist moments from William Afton, particularly in *The Fourth Closet*. But whether this is just an interesting idea, or a spooky tale that could be dropping a hint, remains to be seen. Food for thought: in an earlier patch of the game, it wasn't Glitchtrap on the hill with the *FNAF4* house . . . it was Dreadbear.

Chapter 10

SPECIAL DELIVERY

Five Nights at Freddy's AR
SPECIAL DELIVERY

The VR format of *Help Wanted* and *Curse of Dreadbear* allowed players to insert themselves into the terrifying world of *FNAF*, but with the success of the game, an interesting question arose. What if fans could insert *FNAF* into the real world?

Special Delivery aimed to answer this question with a horrifying new premise and a massive expansion of game lore. You play as a user of Fazbear Funtime Service, in which animatronics are sent to your home at random or by other players. But something is wrong—far from delivering a gift or performing, these animatronics arrive with more sinister aims. Fending off enemies nets you components to build animatronics of your own to send after your friends or to go salvaging for more parts. But as with any *FNAF* game, things aren't as they appear.

Fazbear Entertainment outsourced the Fazbear Funtime Service to an independent company. Through leaked and glitching emails, it's clear the company is having some problems with a virus . . . and with a troubled employee named "Ness."

Fazbear Funtime Service

The game begins with an advertisement for Fazbear Entertainment's new Fazbear Funtime Service, a subscription that sends animatronics to your home to deliver gifts. Although the service seems harmless at first, a series of rapid-fire messages reveal some kinks in the system.

The first pop-up subscribes you for the eternal package, meaning an endless stream of animatronics. The company then appears to override and reboot the system. The system seems to right itself, but it is then followed by a stream of glitches. The first encourages you to deploy your animatronic to salvage for parts. The second encourages you to collect Remnant, glowing orbs of light that longtime fans of the series may recognize.

"You'll never be alone again! It's guaranteed with our exclusive animatronics, you'll always have someone watching your back! They'll provide you with hours of fun fun fun, entertainment, and companionship! You can't hide from a future of fun! Our special delivery will make you jump with excitement. Subscribe today! Don't miss this opportunity! And remember, we're always watching over you."

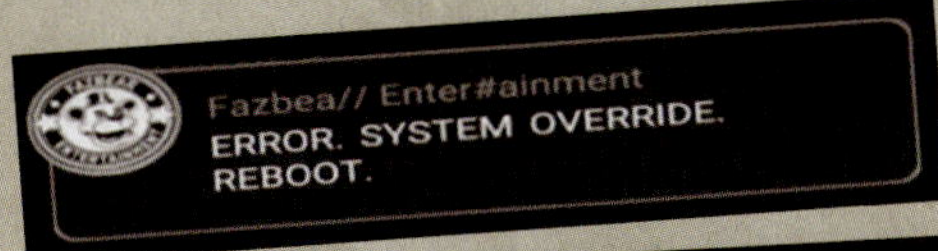

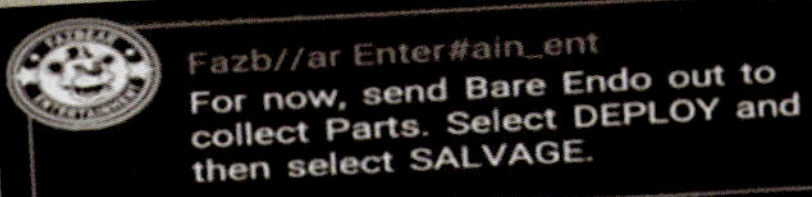

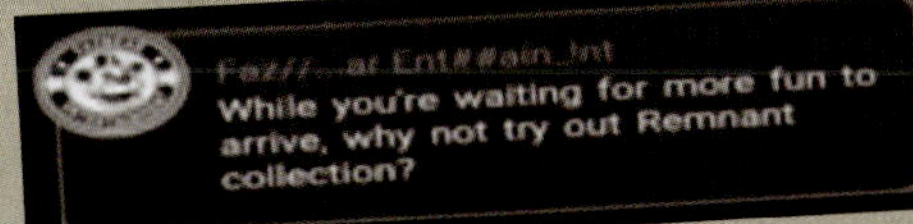

Gameplay and Strategy

Map

On the map, icons with question marks will appear. Clicking on them prompts an event—you could receive an item, be invited to collect Remnant, or encounter an animatronic. Each animatronic has a perception and aggression rating to help you judge the difficulty of the encounter. Once an encounter is clicked, you must engage in the encounter or use Faz-Coins to purchase a jammer to escape.

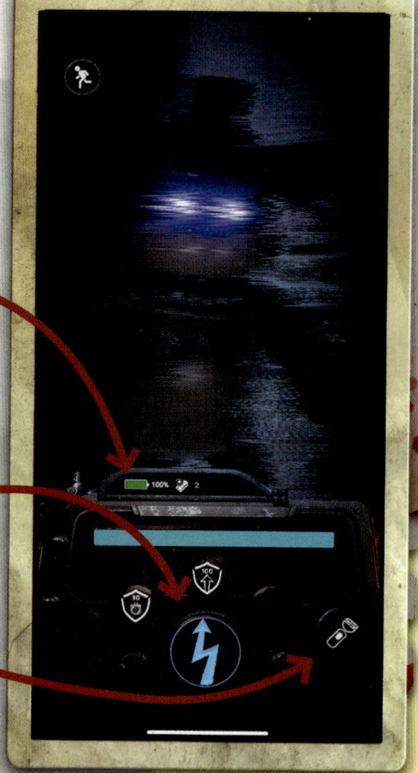

Controls

Fortunately, Fazbear Entertainment hasn't left you totally defenseless. Enter the Diagnostic and Repair Multitool 2.Ø.

- **Battery Power:** At left, it shows how much power you have for your shocker and flashlight. Battery is very important, and it needs time to recharge. To the right you'll see your spare batteries, which can be used if you run out of power.
- **Controlled Shock:** Center, use it to subdue an animatronic when it's de-cloaked. Each shock has a short cooldown time and costs 1Ø percent of your battery. If you have less than 1Ø percent battery overall, the controlled shock becomes unusable.
- **Flashlight:** At right, the flashlight can make static more visible, but leaving it on drains a lot of battery. In fact, it costs 3 percent power just turning it on. If you can, it's best to avoid using it too often.
- **Buffs:** Before beginning an encounter, you can load buffs such as shield buff, attack boost, and more to help you in facing particularly tough animatronics.

Surviving an Encounter

- **Cloaking:** In general, animatronics arrive cloaked in patented Animstealth technology and will not be visible.
- **Static:** When static appears on your screen, it can help you locate the animatronic. You can use your flashlight to find static if necessary. Once you see it, the animatronic will either leave, charge, or go haywire. Certain characters' static might appear differently (Freddy Frostbear's static appears as frost).
- **Interference:** Heavy static can sometimes appear to distract you. Shake your phone to dispel it.
- **Sound:** Footsteps and voice lines often accompany an animatronic's approach. Turn in the direction of the sound to help you spot the animatronic sooner.
- **Rushing:** Don't shock until you can see the eyes of the animatronic. Sometimes an animatronic will rush at you but never fully appear. This trick can waste your battery—don't fall for it! Wait until the animatronic fully de-cloaks to shock. Failure to shock will result in a jump scare and loss.
- **Haywire:** If you see an animatronic go haywire, its eyes might be glowing, its movements might be erratic, and colored bands may appear across your screen. When this happens, look down as fast as possible and wait for it to stop. You may need to react faster to some animatronics than others. Do not shock an animatronic that's gone haywire!

REMEMBER TO SHOCK AN ANIMATRONIC UNTIL ITS HEALTH BAR IS DEPLETED. IT'S OFTEN NOT ENOUGH TO SHOCK IT ONCE!

WINNING . . . AND LOSING

Winning animatronic encounters have many benefits . . .

- **XP:** XP is granted at the end of each encounter, but you get significantly more by winning. Rewards are granted with each level up.
- **Buffs:** You may get buffs for winning, which give you an advantage in your next encounter.
- **Endoskeletons, CPUs, Mods, and Plush Suits:** Defeating animatronics will sometimes help you obtain their components.
- **Unlock Slots:** You might unlock slots in the workshop to help you upgrade animatronics.
- **Parts:** Parts are needed to repair, assemble, and upgrade your animatronics. Mods can open up new abilities for your animatronics.
- **Faz-Coins:** Faz-Coins can be used to purchase helpful items from the store, including lures.
- **Remnant:** You can gain Remnant, which can make encounters easier and make your own animatronics stronger.

Losing an encounter leaves you with less power, and doesn't net you any rewards other than a little XP.

THE STORE

PURCHASABLE WITH PARTS

You can use the parts collected from encounters to buy helpful devices . . .

- **Transponder:** Reveals the identity of an item on the map.
- **Salvage Scanner:** Boosts your animatronics' salvaging efficiency.
- **EMF Meter:** Increases the quality of collected Remnant.

PURCHASABLE WITH FAZ-COINS

You can purchase Faz-Coins to spend on . . .

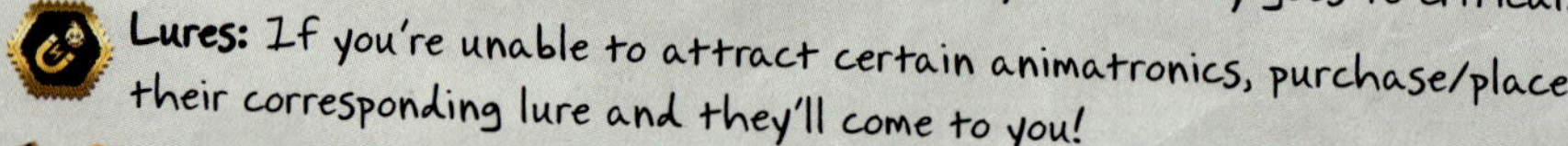

- **Extra Battery:** Automatically activates if your battery goes to critical.
- **Lures:** If you're unable to attract certain animatronics, purchase/place their corresponding lure and they'll come to you!

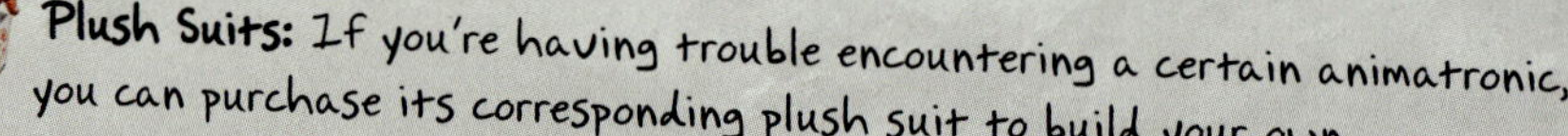

- **Plush Suits:** If you're having trouble encountering a certain animatronic, you can purchase its corresponding plush suit to build your own.

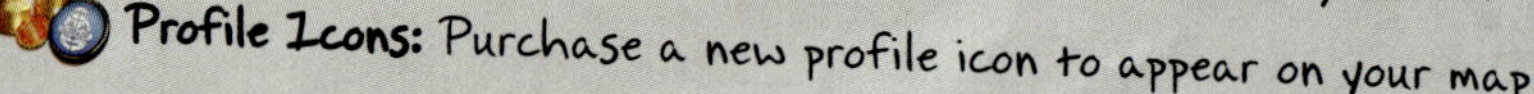

- **Profile Icons:** Purchase a new profile icon to appear on your map.

REMNANT

Remnant plays a special role in the game. Collecting a lot of it can help you reach Remnant Milestones, which provide helpful benefits, such as increasing the amount of time animatronics are vulnerable. Remnant can be obtained by winning encounters or by collecting it between encounters. Between encounters, use your flashlight to draw Remnant in, or you can tap to collect it.

When collecting Remnant, there are two types of Remnant to consider:

- **Bright Remnant:** Small, glowing orbs will appear in various colors. The orbs increase your Remnant count differently depending on their color.
- **Shadowy Remnant:** These dark orbs often appear circling Bright Remnant. Collecting too many of them will crowd your screen in shadow until you are attacked by RWQFSFASXC (Shadow Bonnie). Catch him in your flashlight to defeat him. Doing so will reward you with more Remnant.

BE CAREFUL, RWQFSFASXC CAN BE TOUGH TO BEAT.

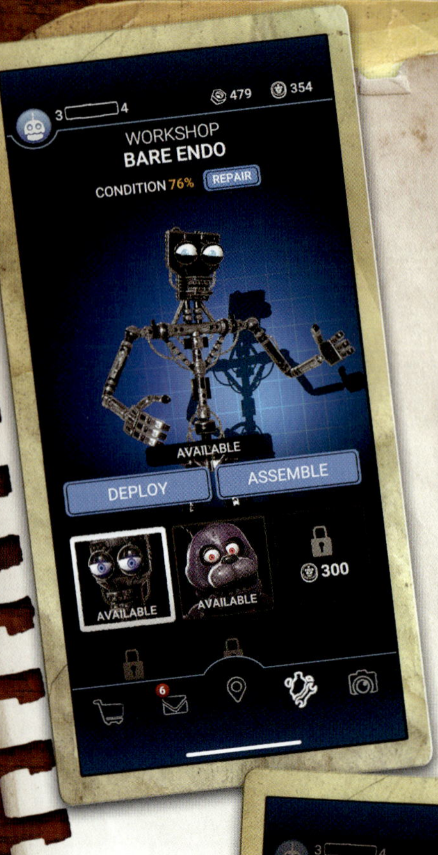

Workshop

This is where the magic happens. Here you can put the parts and components you received from animatronic encounters to good use.

- **Deploy/Send:** Send an animatronic to attack someone on your friend list. If your animatronic jump-scares your friend, you'll receive Parts. Your animatronic will likely need repairs when it returns.
- **Deploy/Salvage:** Send an animatronic to scavenge for Parts. Your animatronic will likely need repairs when it returns.
- **Recall:** Return a deployed animatronic to the Workshop.
- **Assemble:** Build an animatronic using Remnant and various components.
- **Repair:** After being deployed, an animatronic's condition will likely decrease. You can use Parts to repair it.

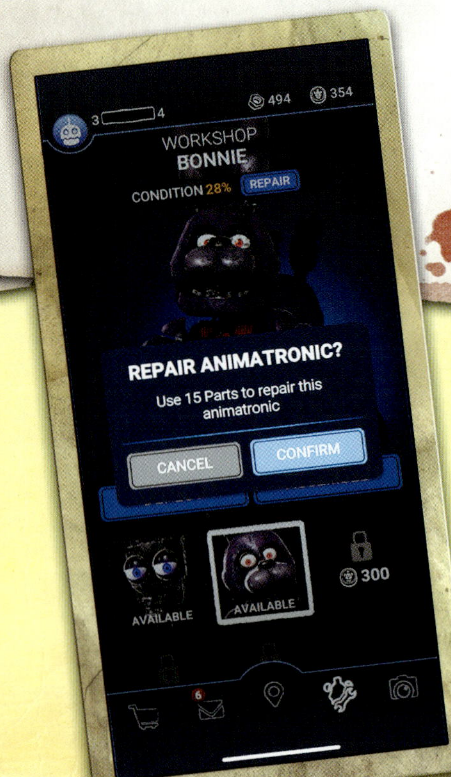

IT'S ALIVE!

Assembling a functioning animatronic isn't quite as complicated as one might think. All you need is . . .

- **Endoskeleton:** Similar to a skeleton, every animatronic needs an endoskeleton frame. You can acquire more endoskeletons by leveling up.

- **CPU:** Like the brain of an animatronic, the CPU determines the animatronic's behavior patterns and voice synthesizer.

- **Plush Suits:** Plush suits are like skin or clothes. They determine the animatronic's physical appearance on the map and in person.

- **Mods:** Special abilities you can add to an animatronic. Mods can increase an animatronic's static field, rushing speed, etc. You can add up to four mods to each endoskeleton, and each mod is ranked with one to four stars depending on value.

- **Remnant:** Improve your animatronic's salvaging or attacking abilities.

Codes, Glitches, and Secrets

04/18/2021
Staff Advisory: Mail Server
From: Fazbear Entertainment Office of Legal Affairs
To: All Staff

Due to technical complications, our mail server may be directing email to incorrect recipients.

If you receive an email that is not addressed to you, please forward it to the intended recipient and notify the IT department immediately.

As a friendly reminder, reading email that was not intended for your eyes is a violation of Fazbear Entertainment's company policy, and you may be subject to disciplinary action up to and including immediate termination. That policy remains in effect.

Please do not read email that is not your own. Thank you for your cooperation as we resolve this technical complication.

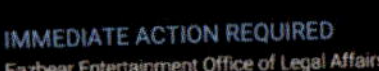

IMMEDIATE ACTION REQUIRED
Fazbear Entertainment Office of Legal Affairs

Dear Ms. Kwemto,

Please immediately cease all work on Fazbear Entertainment properties. Due to unforeseen circumstances, Fazbear Entertainment is ordering a halt to work on all existing contracts, especially in reference to any vintage hardware. We will be in touch regarding our future course of action; please contact our billings department regarding payment for completed work to-date action.

Sincerely,
Kayla Stringer
Associate General Counsel
Fazbear Entertainment

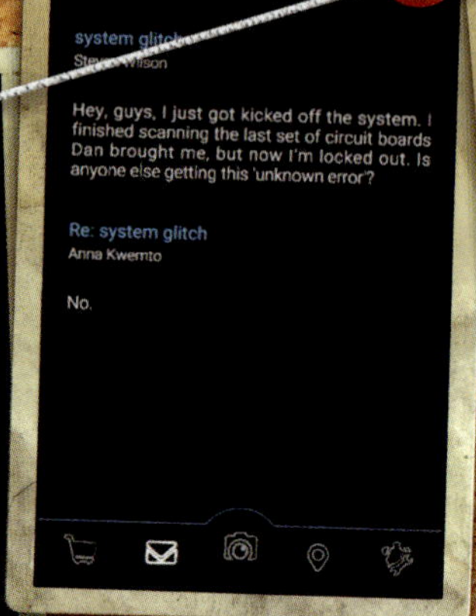

system glitch
Steven Wilson

Hey, guys, I just got kicked off the system. I finished scanning the last set of circuit boards Dan brought me, but now I'm locked out. Is anyone else getting this 'unknown error'?

Re: system glitch
Anna Kwemto

No.

(no subject)
luis.cabrera

Hey, Ness,

I hope you're having a good day! It's no big deal, but I wanted to reach out 'off the radar,' and remind you about the company policy about personal internet usage. Nobody cares if you're online shopping, as long as you get your work done - I promise, I've done my share of last-minute gift-buying! But certain words and phrases trigger red flag reports, so your last order got automatically sent to me; basically anything mentioning 'torture' is going to raise the alarm. So although the *Viking Blood Eagle Twelve-Month Calendar* you ordered is very cool, the searches that got you there did trigger a red flag.

If you have any questions about the policy, let me know. We could even get coffee or something and go over all the words to avoid.

...And now I've raised my own red flag! Good thing I'm the one who gets the notification :-)

-Luis

EMAILS

Besides the store, map, workshop, and AR modes, there's another, less flashy component of *Special Delivery*: your inbox.

Most of the messages in your inbox come from a glitched Fazbear Entertainment account. These might be teasers for new animatronics, helpful tutorials, or notifications that your animatronics have finished salvaging or attacking. But early on, you get an interesting email from the Fazbear Entertainment Office of Legal Affairs. The office advises you that the mail server is malfunctioning, directing messages to the wrong recipients. You can read many of these emails in full on page 364, but three main threads emerge as the most troubling . . .

Shutting Down

Persons Involved:

Anna Kwemto, Kayla Stringer, Steven Wilson

Incident:

Fazbear Entertainment Office of Legal Affairs contacts Anna Kwemto to tell her to cease all work on Fazbear Entertainment properties, especially as it relates to "vintage hardware."

Virus

Persons Involved:

James Campbell, Anna Kwemto, Daniel Rocha, Raha Salib, Steven Wilson

Incident:

One of the Fazbear Entertainment circuit boards that was scanned unleashed a virus in the company's system, including the animatronics. Fazbear Entertainment was unresponsive.

Red Flags

Persons Involved:

Luis Cabrera and nessie97 (Ness)

Incident:

A representative from IT checks in on a coworker whose disturbing searches raised red flags.

(no subject)
luis.cabrera

Hey, Ness,

Just a quick FYI - I know I mentioned trigger words, but the AI is actually a little more sophisticated than that, and of course there are people like me watching the system, too.

So, the word *compliance* by itself isn't going to set off any red flags, but the sentence *how to induce compliance in human subjects*, and *how to induce self-compliance(?)* did actually get my attention. (I think the answer might involve chocolate chip cookies? Always works on me.)

I also thought it was strange that these were immediately followed by searches that couldn't possibly have any relevant answers for you. Did you search for 'help' by itself?

Anyway, my offer still stands if you want to go over the company policy. I'm free any day after work - we could grab dinner or coffee if you want. In the meantime you might want to do some of your more... interesting research at home.

-Luis

EMAILS

NESS AND TAPE GIRL

- The secret "merge" ending of *Help Wanted* seemed to indicate that Tape Girl met a similar fate—Glitchtrap found a way out of the game through her. And since the Reluctant Follower mask and secret audio cropped up in *Curse of Dreadbear*, fans quickly connected Tape Girl with Vanny.
- But with the release of *Special Delivery*, fans seemingly found another breadcrumb: The names "Vanny" and "Ness" could conceivably form a whole . . . "Vanessa."
- If Ness, Vanny, and Tape Girl are all one and the same, many pieces fall into place.
    - Ness's searches of "help" and "how to induce self-compliance" seem to indicate that Ness is fighting the digital consciousness transference.
    - Ness's experience with programming and QA testing also explains how she ended up in yet another job in a related field.
    - Her interest in IT and security via Luis would explain how she was able to slip the circuit board containing the Glitchtrap virus into the company's possession as well.

THE VIRUS

- *Help Wanted* introduced players to the Glitchtrap virus, and it was similarly uploaded to the Freddy Fazbear Virtual Experience via scanning old animatronic circuit boards.
- The cease-work order from the Fazbear Entertainment Office of Legal Affairs seems to indicate that the company at some point becomes aware of the problem and tries to put a stop to it. That leaves one question . . . just who is running the company?

REMNANT

Remnant has been referenced many times in the *FNAF* canon, but those who solely play the games may be only loosely familiar with it.

- Canonically, Remnant first popped up in *Sister Location*. The HRY223 blueprint for "SCUP" (found in *Pizzeria Simulator*) revealed that the Scooping Machine was actually built to inject Remnant, not animatronic endoskeletons, as was initially believed.
- Remnant was further expanded on in *The Fourth Closet* novel, where William Afton is shown combining the Remnant from the five original animatronics into one.
- The Fazbear Frights series further expanded on the concept, showing more scientists studying the properties of the material, and explaining it as . . .

"In nonscientific terms, it's like the metal is haunted. It's more complicated than that, of course, but it's similar to the way that water conducts electricity. Remnant is the mixing of the tangible with the intangible, of memory with the present. The people and things that are lost—it makes them almost real again."

- The Aftons seem to believe that Remnant is the key to power and eternal life, and they want as much of it as they can get.

Remnant in Special Delivery

- You've probably realized by now that one of the major goals in *Special Delivery* is to obtain Remnant, as much as you can. You find it in the animatronics you defeat, or scavenge it from the world around you. And the directive to obtain Remnant only appears after the virus takes over the Fazbear Funtime Service system.
- There are two kinds of Remnant—bright and shadowy—and when they spawn, the room is filled with ethereal whispering. If Remnant is a conductor of emotion, it's possible that bright Remnant forms from positive emotions, while shadowy Remnant is formed from negative ones.
- Why does RWQFSFASXC appear when you collect too much shadowy Remnant?
    - ◊ It's unclear. It's possible that RWQFSFASXC doesn't want you collecting this power . . . or it's possible that RWQFSFASXC wants to kill you to create more. Either way, seeing this character return in this capacity, many years after it first appeared in *FNAF2*, is sure to get fans talking.

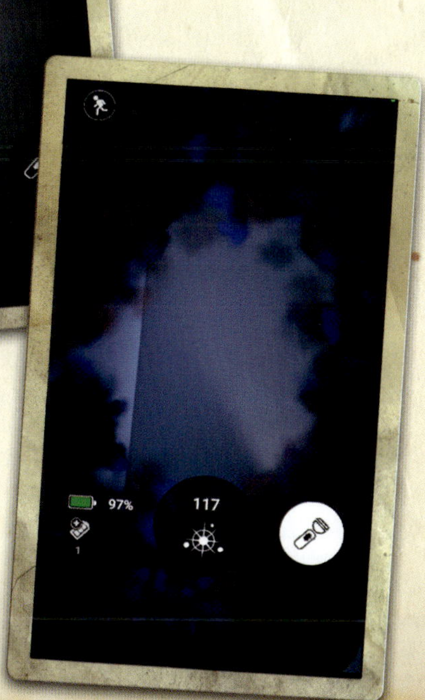

Chapter 11

SECURITY BREACH

Whoo-aa! A whole afternoon at Freddy Fazbear's Mega Pizzaplex! Awesome stage shows, wicked rides, arcade games, popcorn, and pizza. Yummy! What starts as a day to remember for one wide-eyed schoolkid, Gregory, turns into a freakish nightmare he'll want to forget.

Locked inside the Pizzaplex after hours, Gregory must stay safe until morning, avoiding the attention of security guard Vanessa who knows he's sneaking around somewhere. Vanessa is not the only presence Gregory has to worry about, however. Malfunctioning animatronic attractions have joined the hunt. If they catch up with Gregory, it's . . . well, it's GAME OVER!

With the whole place otherwise empty, Gregory pads silently around the Pizzaplex, where you can almost smell the soda-soaked carpets and popcorn-meets-hot dog funk. This is no place for a kid after dark, even under the neon lights' cheery glow. Mercifully, Gregory has found himself an animatronic ally in the form of Freddy Fazbear. Here the fun really starts.

Wire-strewn backstage areas, box-filled basements, and sewers reveal the darker side to the Pizzaplex that cannot be unseen. This unlikely robo-partnership with Freddy gives Gregory access to main attractions, too, but mysterious nighttime protocols make for a wild ride . . .

The Freddy Scoop

FREDDY FAZBEAR

During a spectacular stage show, "frontman" Freddy Fazbear collapses in front of the crowded arena! In some kind of system shock, Freddy later reboots in his Rockstar Row Green Room. Freddy is only too happy to help Gregory, and fast becomes the ultimate personal assistant. And if you were wondering who Gregory is, keep reading . . .

GREGORY

Gregory, a lost kid seeking a place to hide, has stowed himself inside Freddy's belly compartment. From the moment he springs out, Gregory keeps it moving, thinking smart. One of the biggest advantages of being a kid is that you're small. You're usually fast, too. Combine these traits with resourcefulness and youthful optimism, and you stand a chance. Of course, there are some scary circumstances when the only thing to do is RUN. Being a hero of the not-so-super variety, though, means that Gregory easily runs out of steam. His stamina bar indicates when it's time for a rest.

It would be too easy, though, for Gregory to rely on Freddy too much. There are limitations. Like, Freddy needs to recharge his batteries every once in a while, encouraging Gregory to go it alone. Owing to Freddy's bulk, he cannot sneak into smaller spaces like his pal. Freddy mostly advises via Faz-Watch and can be summoned to Gregory's side when possible.

WELCOME TO THE PIZZAPLEX!

It's important to know that one thing, a lot of the time, leads to another in the Pizzaplex. A Complimentary Entry Pass only gets Gregory so far. A malfunctioning machine involves a modest little work-around quest, reminding him of low-level danger from security patrols.

Some acquisitions are strictly temporary, and soon replaced. The security badge is needed many times to grant access, but its status requires upgrading several times. Some items trigger an event the moment Gregory has them in his grasp. Anything not neatly wrapped or tucked in a bag can spell trouble! That "what now?!" sinking sensation of dread becomes familiar fast.

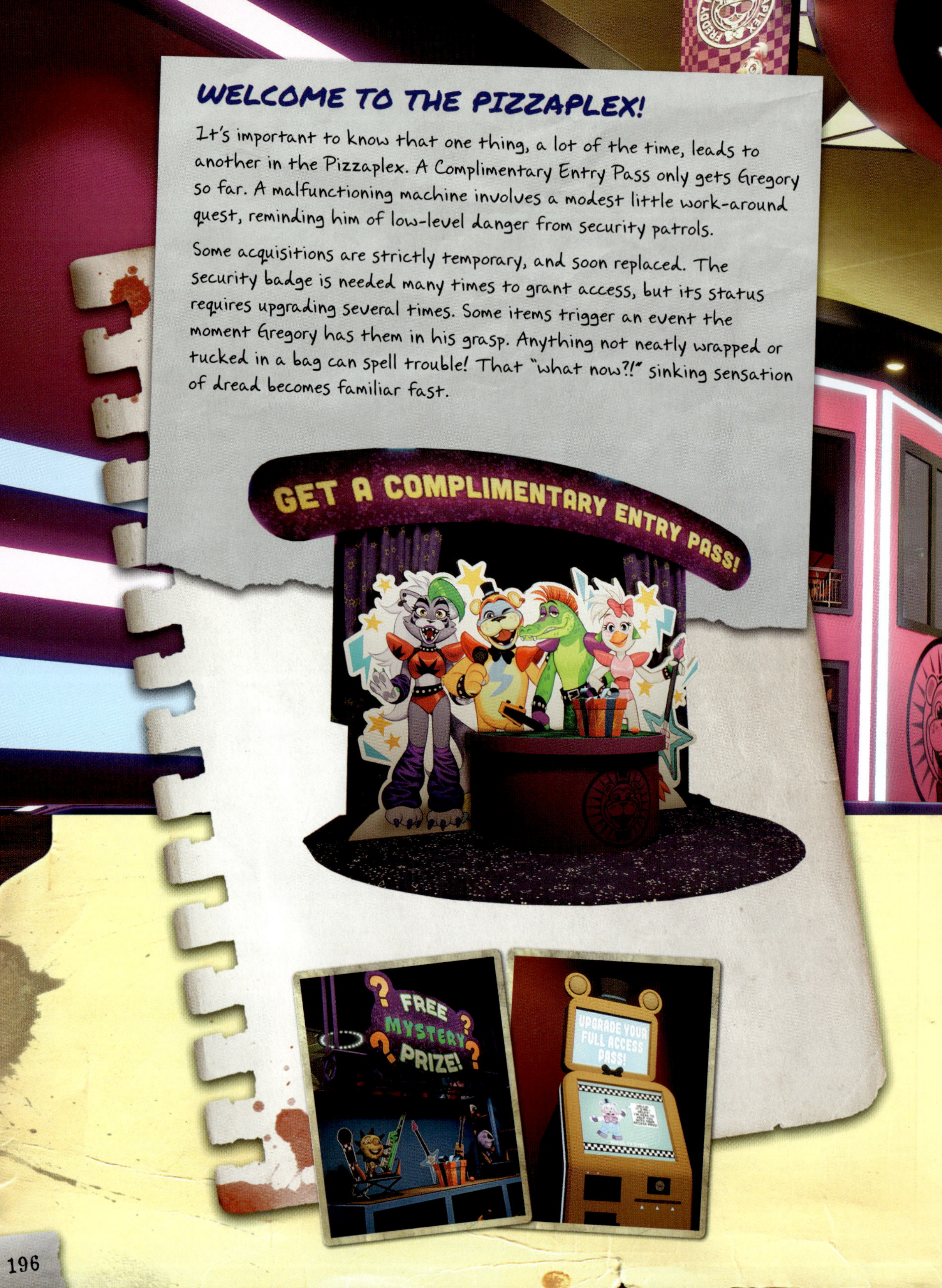

12:00 A.M.

Glamrock Freddy takes time out to recharge, which leaves Gregory to find his way into the Pizzaplex. This lobby entrance is jaw-dropping. The whole place feels like stepping into a 1980s mall.

Gregory plots his own route through this swanky, wide-open space, calculating many risks. Freddy makes it clear where Gregory should go, but there are so many more areas where Gregory could go to claim rewards. He can watch and wait for low-risk opportunities from his place in the shadows or check the security-cam feed on his Faz-Watch. The tension slowly builds . . .

SUPERSTAR DAYCARE PICK-UP

DAYCARE PASS REQUIRED FOR ENTRY

Even when Gregory follows simple instructions to his next destination, the path ahead is hardly ever straight. Main entrances are all gated and locked, leaving Gregory searching for other ways around. Once inside, things may not work as expected, but clues can be found.

The Pizzaplex lobby is a training ground for Gregory, before the hunting party turns up the heat. It gets him used to thinking about all the up and down, front and back of the place—how not to get spotted in larger spaces, and how to navigate through tighter, claustrophobic ones.

In no time at all, Gregory and Freddy have stirred the hornet's nest. Pizzaplex security bots are activated, scooting swiftly around polished floors, armed with . . . flashlights? They might appear harmless, but should Gregory be caught, they raise the alarm, and that is very bad.

The chase is on, and to cap it all off, there's the first spooky sighting of a dancing rabbit lady.

Jettisoned into a ball pit at the Superstar Daycare, Gregory is suddenly locked inside a primary-colored prison with the most eccentric roommate—the Daycare Attendant. No amount of joyful "music" can make this place anything less than disquieting. There's something eerie about a soft-play area with no visitors. Gregory must keep moving to avoid getting caught, and plan his escape.

Initially, the room is brightly lit so that Gregory can get his bearings, but he will soon be stranded in the pitch-blackness. Gregory absolutely needs a plan of action to make clean work of the confusing task lying ahead.

Gregory triggers a power failure immediately upon collecting the Security Badge, which is waiting for him at the reception desk. With the lights gone, the only way out of daycare is by restoring power to five generators. Gregory is wise to plot their whereabouts in advance, to avoid marching blindly into the clutches of Moon, the attendant's nighttime alter ego.

A flashlight is found near the counter to pierce the darkness. Without orientation, however, Gregory is sentenced to always stumbling back into Moon's gleeful clutches . . .

1:00 A.M.

Still haunted by his sighting of "dancing rabbit lady," but with Freddy confidently picking up the pace, Gregory is emboldened to make his choice of where to go next. There are two areas, just a short elevator ride down, accessed from the atrium: Loading Dock and Prize Counter.

Both available routes introduce a vent-crawling entity, Mini Music Man, as Gregory squeezes into the air ducts toward the Loading Dock or Prize Counter.

The Loading Dock route takes Gregory to places that regular Pizzaplex customers never get to see, including the Fizzy Faz syrup vats (where Chica is on the march) and the Kitchen Office (where Gregory must prepare some life-saving pizza for a hangry Chica, who is trying to bang the door down). After Gregory has gratified the Glamrock glutton, he draws closer to being indestructible. But then, just when the kid thinks he's cleared the way, the security level is raised.

If you don't go with the alternate Loading Dock route, an army of Mop Bots present problems for Gregory in the Superstarcade. Roxy is hunting close by, but the darkness and many machines make it easy to keep out of sight with the self-obsessed animatronic.

With conventional exits blocked off, Gregory slides into the Pizzaplex vents where he is chased by Mini Music Man until he drops into the Prize Counter Security Office. There, a Security Level 2 badge is offered but taking it is a trap, which triggers a lockdown, summoning Monty and Roxy. Gregory must master flicking between security cam feeds, shutting doors briefly to preserve their power. Keeping things calm really is key to locking the bad guys out. When the lockdown ends, Monty and Roxy slouch disgruntledly toward the Prize Counter.

Natural hide-and-seek skills are enough to see Gregory make his escape via the Prize Counter elevator, as long as he keeps checking corners, marine style. Within the Prize Counter area, a huge glass-domed feature allows Gregory to spy on Roxy without her knowing. She's not smart enough to use such tactics herself, which is sooo helpful.

After surviving the trials of the Loading Dock or Prize Counter, just as he sees himself as quite the escape artist, Gregory is finally rounded up by Vanessa, the security guard, but now he's in command of hiding spots, Faz-Cam feeds, and well-timed roadie runs to safety. Mysteriously, at some point during this encounter, Gregory is left unconscious. Maybe he was feeling tired . . .

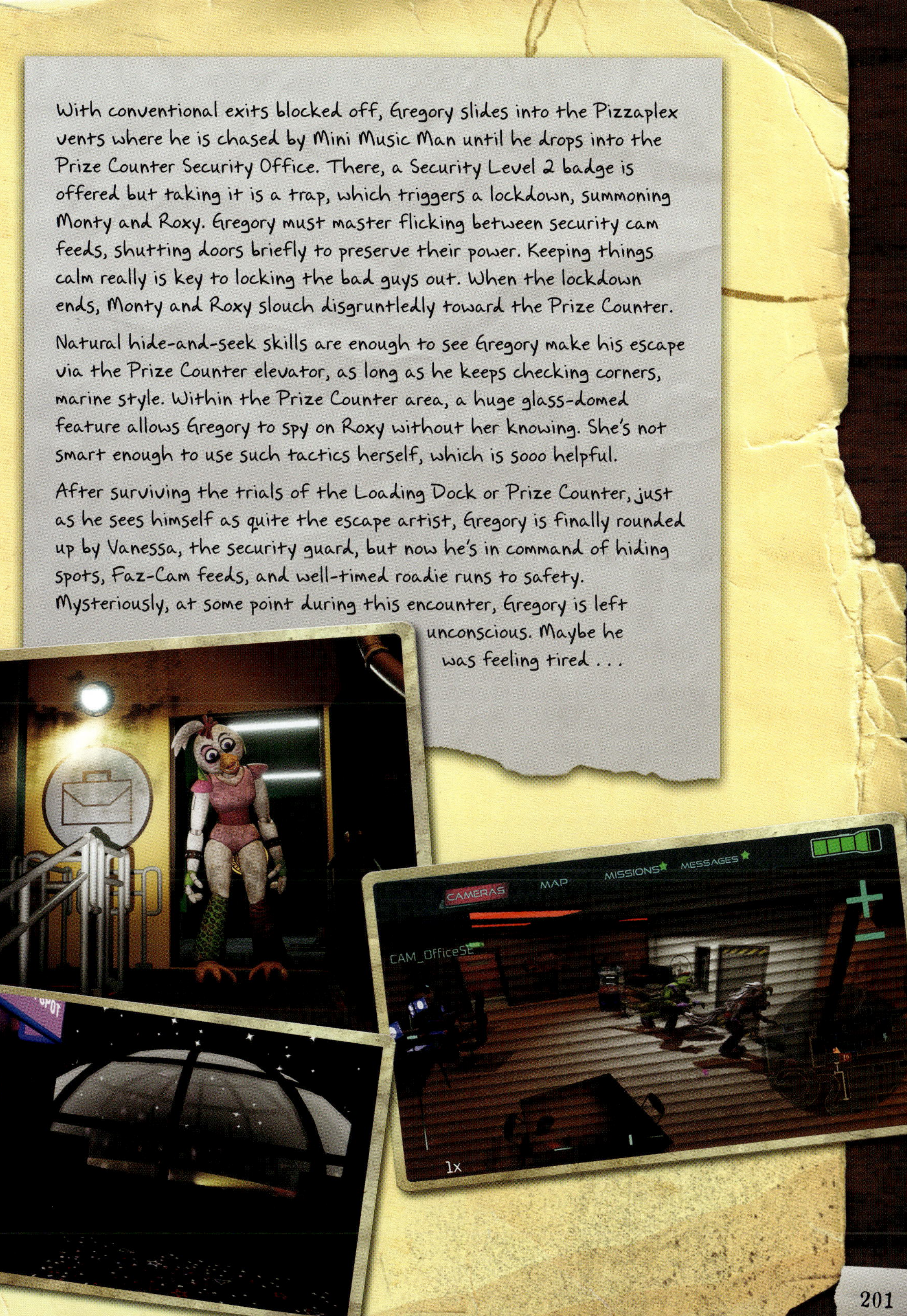

Locked in Lost and Found, Gregory is told that the only way out is in the company of his parents, or the police. Vanessa's scowling face fills the office monitors. This is bad enough, but things take an even darker turn when the distorted visage of Vanny (aka "dancing rabbit lady") replaces Vanessa. Luckily this is soon fixed with a simple screwdriver, used to pry open an air vent to escape!

With Vanny's disembodied voice whispering in his ears, Gregory takes flight to the Atrium elevator. It's here where Freddy regains contact but is heard struggling to maintain it, due to "something" jamming his comms. Gregory is directed to the Roxy Raceway, but S.T.A.F.F. Bots are out in force.

After dodging the S.T.A.F.F. Bots, jumping over a pile of boxes, and now finally reunited with Freddy, Gregory sees his powerful animatronic guardian lying helpless on the floor. Freddy needs access to Parts and Service, but before that he enters Rest Mode while Gregory heads off to the Glamrockers' inner sanctum backstage.

The area beneath the main stage has plenty to explore, but the corridors have plenty of bothersome security bots whizzing up and down, too, ready to alert Roxy to Gregory's presence. Locating a Backstage Pass in the Rehearsal Room grants access to Stage Controls: Staff Only Quest.

Another trap is triggered in the Stage Controls room, right after Gregory acquires his Security Level 3 badge, and, somehow, Gregory has fixed Freddy's problematic signal. No time to party, though! Monty and Roxy hammer on the doors, and Vanny races Freddy to an area beneath the floor. Opening and closing five sets of doors before Monty and Roxy drain them of power completely allows Freddy to reach Gregory. If you catch Monty or Roxy banging on a specific door, you can press the button next to that specific door and shock them to halt them from draining your power for a bit.

The guys return to the Atrium, and put into practice everything Gregory has learned since the night began—until they reach the elevator that will take them to Parts and Service.

Just then, Gregory remembers the "moon thing" from Superstar Daycare. Right on cue, Moon is spied taunting the friends from the edge of the platform . . . almost certainly waiting for them below. Gregory, terrified by Moon's taunts, makes a run for the Recharge Station as instructed by Freddy. The door hisses shut. Outside, Moon drags Freddy's lifeless body away. It's about to get worse.

3:00 A.M.

Shortly into the fifth hour of this mess, Gregory faces another dilemma in the form of Endos—the internal parts of animatronics, who attack when you're not looking.

Just one Endo is tricky to deal with when you're still balancing flashlight power, stamina, and general navigation skills. Consider, then, the task of outmaneuvering multiple Endos! Gregory needs to be in full control of his current capabilities, all while walking backward. Also, he needs to know what's behind him while moving backward, in case of more Endos. Gregory has to keep the Endos in view if he wants to stall their movement, but there are Endos in all sorts of locations and hallways, so he has to balance his view between stalling the ones behind him and stalling any ahead so he doesn't get attacked.

Gregory's first mission in Parts and Service is to reach the Warehouse Security Office and get the Security Level 4 badge. But the office is sectioned off behind movable walls in a mazelike network of tunnels, with Endos ready to be activated.

Inside the Security Office are a bunch of inactive Endos, literally just hanging. As soon as the badge is snatched, the Endos activate and start targeting Gregory. The punch line to the Warehouse setup is that Gregory can quite easily make headway into the maze, without too much caution, as long as he keeps moving.

Gregory next finds Freddy in Parts and Service, and the animatronic is sorely in need of repair. Like, badly in need of a head on his shoulders.

Gregory must reconnect color-coded wires to fix Freddy. Before he starts the procedure, a nearby console shows some other possibilities for Freddy, much further down the line. Power, Claws, Voice Box, and Ocular enhancements are listed. Gregory learns from the wall diagrams that Chica, Roxy, and Monty have all benefited from such upgrades. There's no need for any of this just now, though. Freddy, back on his feet and feeling much better, has more survival tips for Gregory. He's sure gonna need them . . .

Next stop, Chica's Green Room in Rockstar Row! Gregory hopes to bag a Party Pass, with the long-term plan of gaining access to either the Fazer Blast or Monty Golf attractions where he can fetch the Fazerblaster or Faz-Cam, respectively, to help halt bothersome bots.

No sooner is the Party Pass in Gregory's pocket than the scary "moon thing" miasma descends. Gregory's only hope is to find a Recharge Station, which, luckily, is highlighted right there on the Faz-Watch map.

4:00 A.M.

Gregory has survived countless scares while solving a few mysteries. He's used to searching high and low for duffel bags and prize boxes, has a knack for side-stepping S.T.A.F.F. Bots, and is unfazed if he accidentally raises any alarms. Gregory's Pizzaplex survival skills might have plateaued; however, there is still a mountain to climb before reaching the peak.

Gregory's next couple hours will be defined by his choice of whether to use his Party Pass for Monty Golf or Fazer Blast.

If he goes for Gator Golf, it's all about reaching the back office, which has some important items to plunder. These include an upgraded Security Badge, Faz-Cam, and a ticket for the Mazercise attraction on Level 3. For now, the Faz-Cam is the biggest win, since it can stun groups of S.T.A.F.F. Bots and animatronics. But not Monty—because he wears shades!

Using a Mazercise Ticket to unlock it, Gregory must solve a very involved puzzle that shifts walls in a room, letting him access a vent path to the Monty's Gator Golf catwalks area. But once . . . inside, Monty is waiting to pounce. It's a boss battle! Gregory hits plastic cannonballs into the "Hurricane Hole-in-One" bucket while Monty tries to destroy the cannons. But Gregory wins and Monty falls into a pit, shattering. Gregory descends and helps himself to Monty's Claws.

If Gregory chooses the Fazer Blast route to get to Monty, he will discover Rule Number One: "No running, climbing, jumping, hitting, kicking, pushing, shoving. No shooting Fazerblasters close to players' eyes." Tonight, Fazer Blast is empty anyway. Victory earns Gregory a golden Fazerblaster, which briefly stuns its victims (except Monty). Gregory also can grab the Bonnie Bowl Unlimited Pass from a gift box and upgrade his Security Badge in one of the back office rooms. He takes a long detour to swipe a box of Monty's Mystery Mix from Bonnie Bowl's office—it will help defeat Chica!

Together with Freddy, Gregory uses his new security clearance to take the elevator down to the Kitchen where Chica was previously seen, munching freshly made pizza. Gregory spots a trash compactor, and places the Monty Mystery Mix inside. Chica takes the bait and is instantly crushed! The result, apart from being not too pretty, is that Chica's Beak is yanked from its owner. Her voice box is detached, and you can recover it in the dump area.

Whether Gregory chooses Monty's Gator Golf or Fazer Blast first, the opportunity to return and finish both jobs is irresistible. But he has to remain after 6:00 a.m. and get a second Party Pass to do so. Rewards for doing so are extremely worthwhile, as they should be—this is the final countdown.

In possession of Monty's Claws or Chica's Beak, Gregory hurries back to the upgrade station in Parts and Service. The color-coded wiring sequences are much harder than they were last time, but . . . upgraded Freddy is marvelous!

As dawn approaches, Gregory is considerably better armed and dangerous. Freddy has received literally game-changing upgrades. With Chica's voice box, he can stun animatronics. Monty's Claws slice clean through chains and access all those areas marked NO MONTY. Each of these items has its advantages and can allow you access to various parts of the Pizzaplex previously blocked off. Now, where might that rascal Roxy have gone . . . ?

5:00 A.M.

Faced with a locked gate at the entrance to Roxy's Raceway, Gregory can use Chica's Voice or Monty's Claws to work his way inside. It depends on the choice he made at 4:00 a.m., to target Monty or Chica. The one he chose to ignore is still roaming free. Noooo!

The obvious thing to do at a raceway is find something to race with. But the only available go-kart is missing a head for its driver! A lengthy search leads to a broken S.T.A.F.F. Bot, whose head looks about right for the job. So Gregory heads off to a repair station at the West Arcade.

He swings by the garages beneath Roxy's Raceway, where he finds a Dance Pass. After flashing this to the Party Bot at the entrance to the West Arcade, Gregory makes his way to the West Arcade Security Office. Unfortunately, the power goes out.

Gregory attempts to reboot the West Arcade, but he is pursued by either Chica or Monty. He has to flip breaker switches but faces animatronic enemies at every turn. The final switch, in the Maintenance Hall, summons the magnificent DJ Music Man. He gives chase, hurling arcade machines at Gregory as our unlikely hero flees as fast as he can, testing his stamina to the limit. Pumped, Gregory returns to the Security Office to repair the robot head, and avail himself of the Level 7 Security badge. Now, where were we? Yes, Roxy!

Roxy's attempt to jump-scare the go-kart equipped with the S.T.A.F.F. Bot head spectacularly backfires. The tiny but superheavy vehicle spirals out of control, strikes Roxy square in the face, and pins her to the floor.

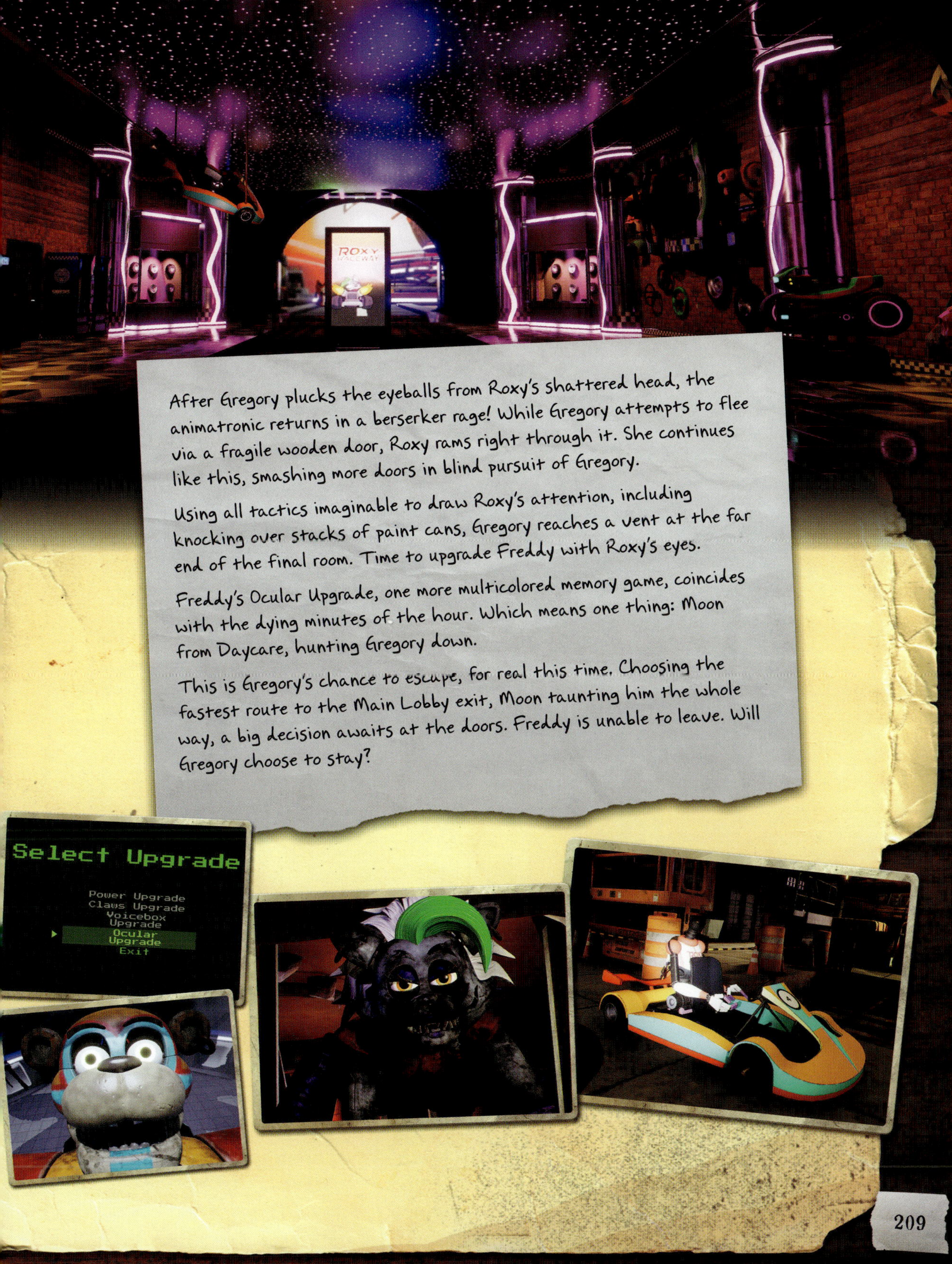

After Gregory plucks the eyeballs from Roxy's shattered head, the animatronic returns in a berserker rage! While Gregory attempts to flee via a fragile wooden door, Roxy rams right through it. She continues like this, smashing more doors in blind pursuit of Gregory.

Using all tactics imaginable to draw Roxy's attention, including knocking over stacks of paint cans, Gregory reaches a vent at the far end of the final room. Time to upgrade Freddy with Roxy's eyes.

Freddy's Ocular Upgrade, one more multicolored memory game, coincides with the dying minutes of the hour. Which means one thing: Moon from Daycare, hunting Gregory down.

This is Gregory's chance to escape, for real this time. Choosing the fastest route to the Main Lobby exit, Moon taunting him the whole way, a big decision awaits at the doors. Freddy is unable to leave. Will Gregory choose to stay?

6:00 A.M.

Outside, Gregory can be free of this nightmare. Or . . . he can stay! And—with Freddy—fight to bring an end to these, um, quite frankly terrible goings-on when the lights go down.

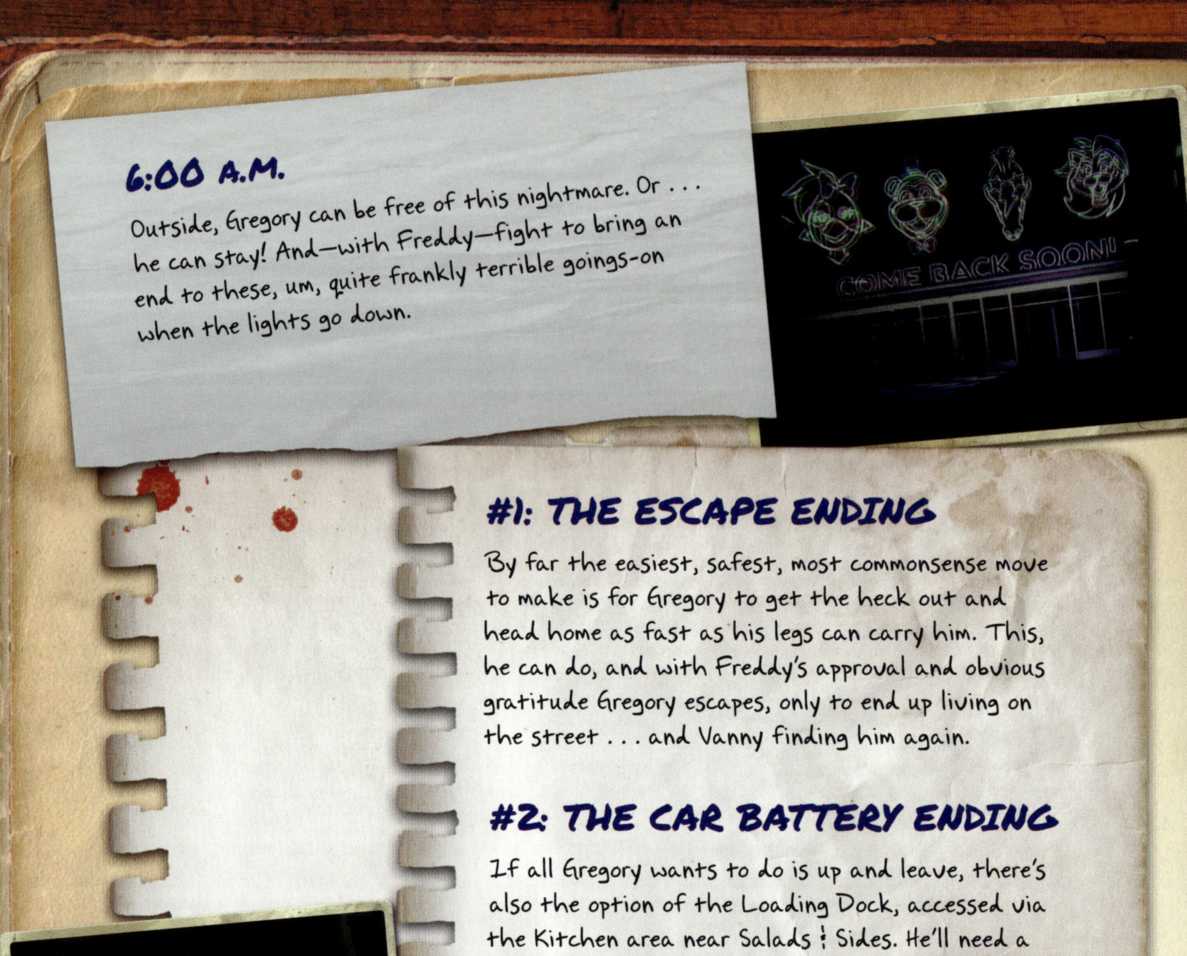

#1: THE ESCAPE ENDING

By far the easiest, safest, most commonsense move to make is for Gregory to get the heck out and head home as fast as his legs can carry him. This, he can do, and with Freddy's approval and obvious gratitude Gregory escapes, only to end up living on the street . . . and Vanny finding him again.

#2: THE CAR BATTERY ENDING

If all Gregory wants to do is up and leave, there's also the option of the Loading Dock, accessed via the Kitchen area near Salads & Sides. He'll need a Level 6 security clearance to take advantage of this, though the effort required to escape from here is worth it . . .

Main Entrance or Loading Dock, Gregory can quit. But, they call that . . . erm, quitting.

#3: VANNY ENDING

Of all the encounters Gregory faces, the specter of Vanny might forever haunt him were he to flee without some kind of closure. But was Gregory enough of a sleuth to sniff out Vanny's secret hideout back in Fazer Blast? In case Gregory pursued Monty and not Chica earlier, he'll need to explore quite a bit more for this.

Choosing to stay at the Pizzaplex is not only brave but the absolute best thing to do if Gregory wants to try everything. He also receives a shiny new Party Pass, granting access to any missed attractions.

Gregory has an additional choice alongside staying and leaving: "Vanny." In case Gregory's nerves are not already fried enough, this doesn't bode well for Freddy, and leads to a hare-raising chase to Vanny's hideout before Vanny and Roxy catch you.

#4: PRINCESS QUEST ENDING

Exploring. It's awesome. You should definitely try it. In true 1980s style, Gregory discovers three playable arcade cabinets called *Princess Quest I, II, and III* in the Pizzaplex.

The first two are kinda hidden away, but Gregory may have found them. To play the final cabinet, Gregory simply chooses to pursue Vanny at whichever exit he chooses, where he is then rushed to the entrance that goes from under Fazer Blast to Vanny's secret hideaway above. Inside is the *Princess Quest III* machine. The ending of *Princess Quest* leads to a scenario where Gregory finds a discarded Vanny mask and bowtie before reaching Vanessa and exiting the Pizzaplex together.

#5: VIP ENDING

Once Gregory realizes that animatronic avoidance is a mere trifle, the Pizzaplex is a fun place to be. No, truly! In fact, Gregory can even take time out to smell the fake flowers and point his handy Faz-Cam at random (or is it?) stuff left lying around. You need 39 gift box items that aren't upgrades or equipment to gain access.

There are also four character cutouts—Bonnie, Chica, Freddy, and Foxy—to enshrine as instant photos before the Golden Moon plush can be unlocked. Then, Gregory can enter a hidden door behind the Captain Foxy's Pirate Adventure poster in the Fazbear Theater where you can find the Golden Moon plush and a pipe leading to the Balloon Boy arcade minigame. Gregory needs to move fast, though, to reach the VIP exit at the Prize Counter before getting himself caught.

#6: BURN IT ALL DOWN ENDING

For this ending, you have to use both Monty's and Chica's abilities and get to the elevator shaft hidden in Roxy's Raceway.

Taking this elevator leads to the charred remnants of Freddy Fazbear's Pizza Place from *Five Nights at Freddy's Pizzeria Simulator*. Once there, Gregory encounters The Blob, a grotesque combination of cables and pieces of other animatronics. Gregory eventually ends up in a secret office where he faces off with Burntrap. Defeat it, and this ending is yours.

Gameplay and Strategy

GOOD TO KNOW!

Freddy often highlights the essentials, but Gregory is always on the lookout for anything conspicuous that might offer an advantage or secret reveal. Every location has something fun to interact with, or another part of the puzzle to trigger before leaving. You'd like to think that Gregory gets used to everything he touches having consequences.

- **Do touch:** One of Gregory's top skills is his meddling hands. Forget every time you've been told "DO NOT TOUCH," because prying and poking stuff is highly recommended around the Pizzaplex. Abandoned duffel bags and prize boxes contain many key items, plus some cool collectibles.
- **Make some noise:** There are also noisemakers dotted around the venue such as old paint cans. Knocking these over creates a distraction.
- **Sneaky!:** Sneaking, by crouching, is often the wisest strategy for Gregory, which reduces noise and lowers his profile. He is, however, much slower while being stealthy. In order to move quickly while remaining completely unseen, Gregory sticks to the creepy corners and haunting shadows.
- **Hide-and-hope-they-don't-seek:** Not everything that Gregory needs is carried on his person. He soon learns to identify hiding spots, such as laundry carts, photo booths, and strollers. There are stacks of things that help create distractions: piles of paint cans being used for refurb or colorful playground toys.
- **Constant vigilance:** Gregory doesn't trust Vanessa, the security guard. He learns to scan every wide-open area for signs of light and movement in his peripheral vision. It makes the habit of checking security-cam feeds that much more important.

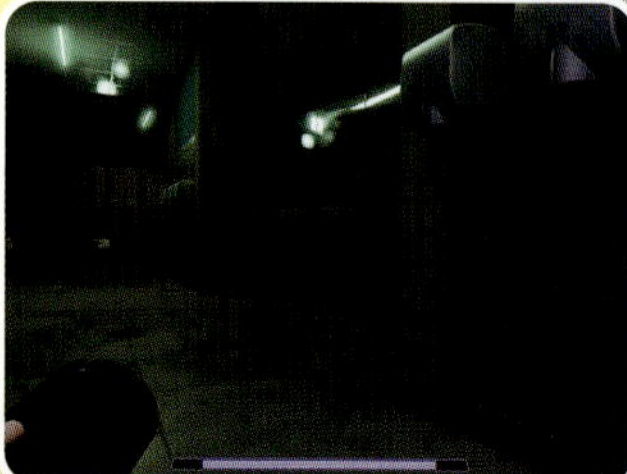

USEFUL ITEMS

- **Flashlight:** The most illuminating and essential item offered to Gregory just after midnight is the flashlight. He learns about flashlight management—fear of the dark vs. battery life. Flashlight upgrades can be found, but only by those brave and industrious enough to seek them out. Flashlight charging stations are also located throughout the areas.

- **Faz-Watch:** Gregory learns fast how to survive, with the Faz-Watch as the centerpiece of all the items he needs. This Freddy souvenir connects the duo online and stores all intel discovered: emails from angry parents, staff memos, and more. It monitors security cams, provides a map, and keeps track of the latest missions. With the Faz-Watch, Gregory has a chance to think before he acts.

- **Freddy Photo Pass:** A Freddy Photo Pass is complimentary if you know where to look. It literally opens doors for Gregory, but higher levels of security require upgrades.

- **Party Pass:** A Party Pass gives access to new areas of the Pizzaplex. This definition of Party, though, is not in any dictionary we know.

- **Fizzy Faz:** There are four flavors to collect. Each flavor represents a member of the Glamrock Band, and each one energizes Gregory with a stamina boost.

ANIMATRONICS

GLAMROCK FREDDY

This animatronic gets fried during a concert and he ends up becoming an ally to Gregory. Freddy's secret stomach area (usually reserved for piñatas and "oversized birthday cakes") keeps Gregory shielded from most Pizzaplex patrols. Part tour guide, part bodyguard, all buddy. The kind and charismatic animatronic undergoes some major upgrades before the night is through. And, you know, they're hardly what you would call "off-the-shelf"!

Freddy was the only animatronic to get fried during the concert. His Glamrock bandmates Chica, Roxanne "Roxy" Wolf, and Montgomery "Monty" Gator are all still primed to round up intruders and . . . who knows what they will do upon capturing them.

GLAMROCK CHICA

Chica roams the Pizzaplex, attracted by loud noises. She is the first major encounter that forces Gregory to use his stealthy smarts; she'll give chase if not extra, extra careful. It turns out Chica is one ravenous animatronic, but fortunately she loves pizza! Chica's beak can be torn from her shattered face and used to upgrade Freddy's voice box.

GLAMROCK MONTY

Montgomery "Monty" Gator hangs out at Gator Golf but can also be found walking around the empty Pizzaplex in his cool shades. He serves up an early major scare, which is a hair-raisin' test of how useful Gregory is at running. Monty's Claws make a great Freddy update and allow him to break gates and gain access to secret areas.

GLAMROCK ROXY

Roxanne "Roxy" Wolf can be found—and should be avoided—in the Pizzaplex East Arcade and Roxy's Raceway, using her speed to chase Gregory. Her eyeballs provide an ocular upgrade for Freddy, though this barely stops the wolf animatronic. The chase is still on, and she pursues Gregory furiously, even though she can't see!

ENDO

These are the skeletal insides of animatronics, with a particularly alarming habit: they only move to attack when their target's not looking their way. Whatever you do, don't turn your back on them!

DJ MUSIC MAN

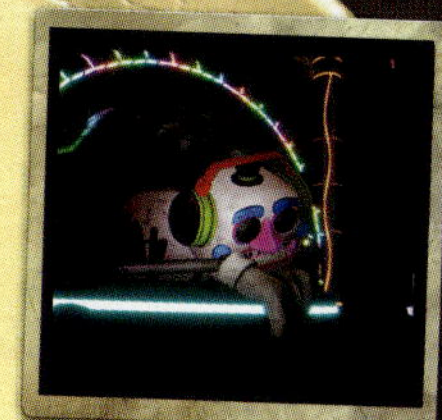

He's in the pipes! And once DJ Music Man gives chase, there is no going back. Something about a giant, beat-up, grimacing animatronic makes you never want to turn around and face the music. It's the kind of thing that any sensible young human instinctively runs away from.

VANNY

The freakishly cheerful "dancing rabbit lady" is also known as Vanny. Her glowing red eyes are never a welcome sight in the darkness of the Pizzaplex. She likes to laugh gleefully as she chases Gregory and unfortunately, she cannot be stunned by the Fazerblaster or Faz-Cam, which makes her a constant threat.

DAYCARE ATTENDANT

Superstar Daycare is the first, though by no means last, sighting of the terrifying two-faced Attendant. When the lights are on, it is Sun—mocking enemies in garishly bright attire. In the darkness, it prowls in mournful hues as Moon. Whenever Pizzaplex lights power down, Moon resumes the hunt. It's one of the hardest-working animatronics around for sure.

> To make Sun/Moon more appealing to the trusting little ones, the Pizzaplex publicity department has started marketing Sunnydrop Energizing Candy! and Moondrop Sleepy-Time Candy! Sun/Moon is the infant-friendly face of the place, with imagery festooned on so many walls. What's not to trust?

THE ENTITY AKA M.X.E.S.

Appearing in *RUIN*, the Entity is a glitchy rabbit that won't leave Cassie alone! It can lock her out of the AR, but worse—it can alert animatronics to Cassie's location, which is much more immediately deadly.

MIMIC

Like its name suggests, the Mimic copies what others do—and does a pretty convincing impression of Gregory's voice in RUIN. It actually looks like an Endo (the inside parts of an animatronic)—but this is no Endo! It is an experimental AI creation, and is therefore much more dangerous.

S.T.A.F.F. BOTS

Some staff never sleep—and the Pizzaplex S.T.A.F.F. Bots are here all night. They carry out menial jobs, such as security and janitorial tasks. Oh, and they'll also alert the animatronics if they spot you!

MINIGAMES

BALLOON WORLD

A secret arcade machine that can be discovered by entering through a hidden door behind the Captain Foxy's Pirate Adventure poster in Fazbear Theater. Balloon Boy must avoid obstacles and keep his balloons from popping. The gameplay exists in day or night mode. By day, the player can wear a fetching party hat. By night, they must avoid bats. You might notice a purple glitching effect in this game. Touch it quickly to return to normal, collect the glitches to get a secret "good night" message, or don't touch them at all to ensure Eclipse doesn't end the game.

CHICA'S FEEDING FRENZY

This game can only be accessed in the *RUIN* update. To reach it, climb through the crawl space in the women's bathroom, near the Cupcake Shoppe. The player plays as Chica, battling against enemy waves. Completing wave 20 will give you a prize. But don't get too excited—the only one who will appreciate the prize is Chica herself.

MONTY'S GATOR GOLF

Found—unsurprisingly—in Monty's Gator Golf, this arcade game offers nine holes of Fazbear-themed—you guessed it—golf. Holes 2, 3, 4, and 6 are based on moments from other *FNAF* games, while holes 1, 5, 7, and 9 have a *Security Breach*-specific theme. Hole 8 features Balloon Boy and Nightmare Balloon Boy! In *Security Breach* there are 9 holes, but in RUIN, the back 9 are available on the cabinet there.

PRINCESS QUEST I

This game already appeared in *FNAF: Help Wanted*, but only in the mobile port. Here it is available as an arcade game. Find it in the Glamrock Beauty Salon, in a supply room of course! Guide the princess player through a series of puzzles in the castle and cemetery until she faces Glitchtrap, a purple rabbit creature.

PRINCESS QUEST II

A new sequel to *Princess Quest I*, this game can be found where Gregory raced like never before to flee DJ Music Man, in the shady extremities of the West Arcade, aka Fazcade. In this iteration, the princess has a sword of light with which to battle her enemies.

PRINCESS QUEST III

A second new sequel, this game is hard to find. You must first win a game of Fazer Blast and receive a Fazerblaster, then access Vanny's secret room. The gameplay is set in a re-creation of the main hub room from *Help Wanted*, and the *Corn Maze* minigame from *Curse of Dreadbear*. The princess player must find the Vanny mask and a Glitchtrap plush, then trade them in for a purple key. Completing this game is the only way to access ending #4.

RUIN

RUIN is free additional downloadable content for Security Breach—a whole new story set in the same location, after the events of the main game. The Pizzaplex lies derelict after an earthquake—and somewhere inside it, Gregory is trapped . . .

CASSIE

Cassie is a huge fan of the Fazbear franchise—her father was a maintenance worker for Fazbear Entertainment. She met Gregory at her birthday party, which her friends didn't show up to, and they became best friends. Cassie's nervous, but she pushes through it as she tries to find and rescue Gregory. But is this all a trap?

USEFUL TOOLS

- **Flashlight:** An essential accessory for exploring any derelict entertainment complex! Cassie didn't bring one with her, but she finds one in the hand of a security bot slumped in a booth in the lobby.
- **Roxy-Talky:** This allows Cassie to communicate with Gregory, and he offers her guidance. Gregory talks to her using his Glamrock Freddy-Talky.
- **Faz Wrench:** This allows Cassie to complete the conduit puzzles that crop up regularly. In all these, the wires can be charged up but will start to go down when the wrench is removed. The trick is to get the power in every wire into the blue zone at once, switching the Faz-Wrench between the wires.
- **Security Mask:** It's a mask that resembles Vanny's, and it brings Cassie into the AR world, where she can make repairs to security nodes, operate special AR cameras, and walk through spaces that were previously obstructed! It's all good! Well, except it leaves Cassie vulnerable to attacks from the Entity, a digital foe that infects AR. Whenever Cassie wears the Security Mask for too long, the Entity moves gradually toward her and, if he reaches her, summons an animatronic to attack. This means Cassie must work quickly when doing puzzles in AR. The mask also allows her to communicate with "HELPI" and see collectibles that aren't visible in the real world.

WALKTHROUGH

♦ Entrance

Cassie makes her way into the Pizzaplex through a broken window, then drops into the mall and down a ladder to the lobby. A gateway leads to a darker area, and Cassie needs to light it up by getting the flashlight from the security bot.

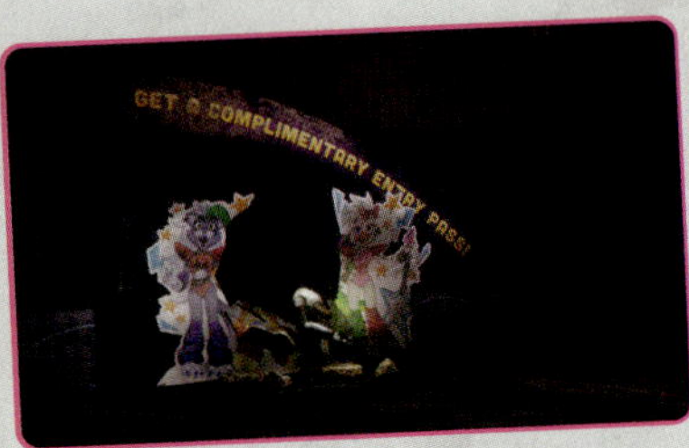

Cassie makes her way upstairs, where she hears Gregory's voice, pleading for help. When she tracks down the source of the noise, it's actually a discarded Roxy-Talky, which Gregory speaks through, telling Cassie he's been captured and is in the sinkhole underneath Roxy Raceway.

Cassie heads off to help and makes it to the Kitchen, which is full of disgusting, rotting food. She runs into Chica, who jump-scares her but then deactivates. Cassie picks up the Faz-Wrench—"Just like my dad's"—from a toolbox. She reaches a pipe, and when she looks into it, Monty Gator attacks . . .

♦ Monty's Gator Golf

After running from Monty, Cassie finds herself in the derelict golf course. She runs into Map Bot, who gives her the Security Mask. Wearing it, Cassie enters Artificial Reality (AR), guided by HELPI, the mask's AI. As Cassie proceeds, she finds a Fazbear Technician 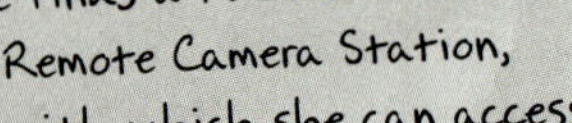 Remote Camera Station, 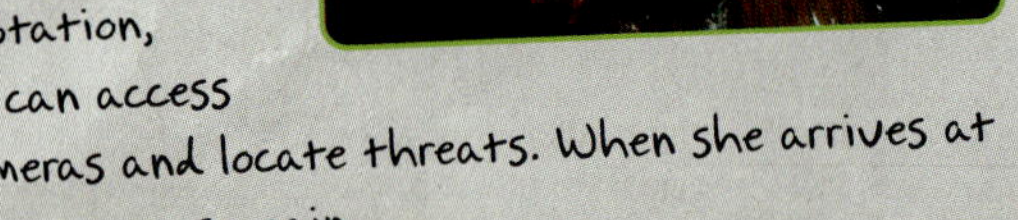 with which she can access the security cameras and locate threats. When she arrives at the fence, Monty appears again.

Cassie follows Monty, and Gregory tells her she has to shut down all security measures. Cassie attempts to do this, but she ends up triggering the first appearance of the Entity . . .

The Entity will summon Monty if he reaches Cassie, so she removes the mask whenever possible while going through these locations, completing puzzles and avoiding calamity along the way. Eventually she destroys the Monty cutout in AR to create a path in the real world, which means Cassie can escape into Daycare . . .

Daycare

Gregory informs Cassie she needs to head for the Daycare Theater. First, she needs to go through the playpen, which she can reach by going past the arcade machines, up the boxes, and through some playpen areas. As she proceeds through the soft play area, Moon grabs her—but the flashlight scares him away.

After using the mask to get through a blockage, Cassie meets Sun, who wants her to use the Faz-Wrench to reboot him and tells her to turn the generators on to activate the lights. After this, he doesn't trouble Cassie, but she must watch out for the Entity, who will summon Glamrock Endo if he catches her here.

Cassie completes the task and reboots Moon, turning him into Eclipse, who guides Cassie out of the playpen.

Cassie can now reach the theater, but the gate is closed, so she needs to use the mask. This will trigger the Endoskeletons in this area, and Cassie has to watch them to stop them from moving. However, they can't see her when she has the mask on. But if she collides with them, they will still attack her.

When she gets inside the theater, she has to complete another Camera Station quarantine puzzle—after that, a jumbo Endoskeleton comes crashing through the theater screen in AR, but don't be scared! Cassie can go over to it, climb up the boxes to its mouth, and go inside. Cassie is terrified, but she takes off the Security Mask and realizes she's in a vent. The vent collapses and she lands back in Monty's Gator Golf, riding a gondola.

Catwalk

The gondola track needs to be shifted by activating another mother node in the AR. Cassie shoots and targets and chooses various paths until she gets to a pipe with a glitchy portal in it. This leads to a room where the Entity appears—but HELPI and Gregory put up a barrier to stop him.

Maintenance Room

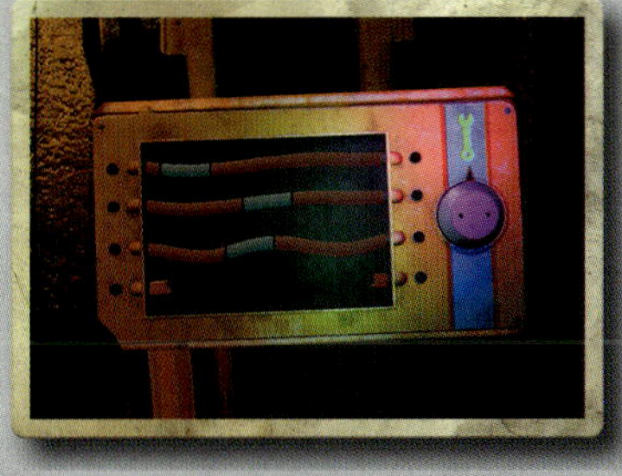

Before she can reach the Maintenance Room, Cassie has to complete another puzzle before she can ride the gondola out of here. Then she takes the stairs up to the Maintenance Room.

Cassie sees Chica traveling on a conveyor belt and climbs up some boxes to get onto it herself! By going into AR, she can pass through the gate at the end—but then the Entity uses an inhibitor to remove her ability to use AR!

Chica's Bakery

As Cassie moves on, she'll see a red door that leads to the Chica's Feeding Frenzy arcade cabinet. The reward for completing this game is Chica's voice box—though this is optional. There's another pathway to the right, and as soon as Cassie goes through this, Chica will return, and the other path will no longer be available.

After escaping Chica, Cassie heads past some counters, where the inhibitor is. Disabling this allows Cassie to use the Security Mask again—but the Entity is very active around here, so Cassie should keep it off as much as possible.

Into the Server Room, which can be accessed by wearing the Security Mask that will be stuck to her head, Cassie walks to find a camera station where she must complete a camera anomaly puzzle. In the next room, the Entity can hurt Cassie—despite what HELPI told her. She needs to quickly find another camera station if she wants to escape. Phew!

Glamrock Salon

Roxy is at the salon, and when she hears the voice of the boy who took her eyes on the Roxy-Talky she goes to find him, locking the doors behind her. To unlock them, Cassie needs to use the mask.

Walking on, the now harmless Chica appears. Cassie can restore her voice box if she has it. Passing through the flooded passage where Monty Gator lurks, Cassie is safe while she's on a floating platform, so she should jump between them when Monty is the farthest away.

Cassie gets out of the water just before it's electrified—but Monty is caught in it . . .

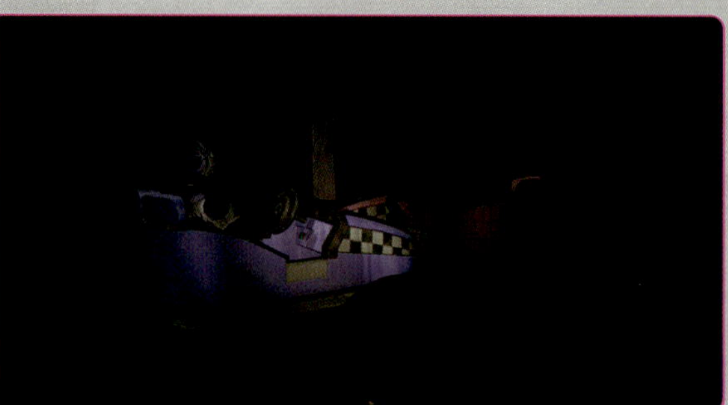

Roxy Raceway

After failing to hail Gregory, Cassie heads into Roxy's Raceway and encounters a Faz-Wrench conduit puzzle. Roxy is here, but she can't see, so Cassie can move past her if she's quiet. There are a few invisible boundaries that force a jump-scare by Roxy if you traverse in any manner before luring her away with the Intercom. The ideal is just to use the Intercom to bring Roxy to where she needs to be. However, Cassie needs to use Roxy to break down doors. She can go to the camera station and use CAM Ø5 and the intercom to send Roxy toward the door.

In the next area, a go-kart drives itself at Cassie, so she needs to run to her right. Then Roxy pops up, demanding her eyes back. Cassie gets away but learns from Gregory that the sinkhole under the raceway can't be accessed without going to Bonnie Bowl and Fazer Blast . . .

Bonnie Bowl

Cassie walks through the Roxy Raceway office, opens a hatch to drop down into a sewer area, then ends up in an office before finally reaching the staff area of Bonnie Bowl. Cassie needs to use the Security Mask to make her invisible to the Mini Music Men dotted around. The mask is disabled as Cassie enters a storage room for arcade cabinets, so she must go right and disable an inhibitor.

On the bowling alleys is another camera station from where Cassie can draw the Mini Music Men away. After deactivating several inhibitors in Bonnie Bowl, going through Bonnie's Green Room, she can enter AR and go through an open vent.

Fazer Blast

Moving through a weird vortex, Cassie finds herself in an office and can make her way to Fazer Blast. She goes down the vents and enters AR to go through a portal to the laser tag maze. Again, Cassie can't take off the mask, but the inhibitor is in the next tunnel, so Cassie can take off her mask again.

Crawling through the hole in the junk, Cassie finds Freddy—but his head is missing. He chases Cassie, who must run as fast as she can, as long as her stamina doesn't reach the bottom!

Cassie winds up in a room with an inhibitor, which she must approach quietly before the headless Freddy jump-scares her. She can operate the inhibitor and put on her mask, causing Freddy to vanish. Cassie proceeds to a vent where she must run to escape a Lil' Music Man before she can return to Roxy's Raceway. With the Security Mask on, Cassie can approach Roxy, and it turns out Roxy remembers her from her birthday party. Cassie deactivates her and can head down . . .

The Sinkhole

Cassie emerges from the elevator into a tunnel before reaching a cave. As she moves toward a lit-up area, her flashlight gets wet and no longer works. She goes inside a building and finds it's full of Fazbear merch. Deeper inside is Candy Cadet, who tells a story—Cassie must collect Faz-Coins to unlock the whole story.

Eventually Cassie comes to a computer room. With the mask on, she uses the old computer console (or "Machine") to deactivate security, and the Entity is sucked inside the M.X.E.S. hardware.

Another Faz-Wrench panel makes a forklift smash through the wall, and Cassie hears Gregory's voice . . . but it's not Gregory! It's the Mimic, who's been copying Gregory's voice. As he looks down on Cassie, Roxy arrives, distracting him long enough for Cassie to escape. The real Gregory speaks over the Roxy-Talkie and guides Cassie as the Mimic chases her.

The elevator takes Cassie out just in time! But there are three possible endings . . .

Endings

You get the **Standard Ending** if you complete the game as instructed on the previous page—Gregory tells Cassie the Mimic tricked her into going there and disabling the security to release it. But he tells Cassie, "We can't risk being followed," and lets the elevator fall with her in it . . . Or does he *cause* it to fall? Is this merciful to save her from the Mimic just outside the elevator door? And what is the significance of "Cassie?" we hear at the end? Is that Roxy, or is that the Mimic? One day, maybe we'll all know!

The **Safe Spot Ending** appears if you followed Gregory's instructions at first, but choosing not to head through the green-glowing passage in the caves. If you turn left and find a cutout of Fredbear, put on the Security Mask to trigger a different ending sequence, where Cassie sees a seemingly happy picture of Gregory and Vanessa.

The **Scooper Ending** is the best one. This requires you to find four hidden cameras in certain camera stations. You need to look out for a black camera on the camera map, then cycle through the cameras to get the feed from the hidden one. Just looking at the hidden camera for long enough will unlock a door.

When you play the final chapter again, a different door from the one you went through before will be open. Go this way until you reach a red button. Press it to set the Scooper against the Mimic!

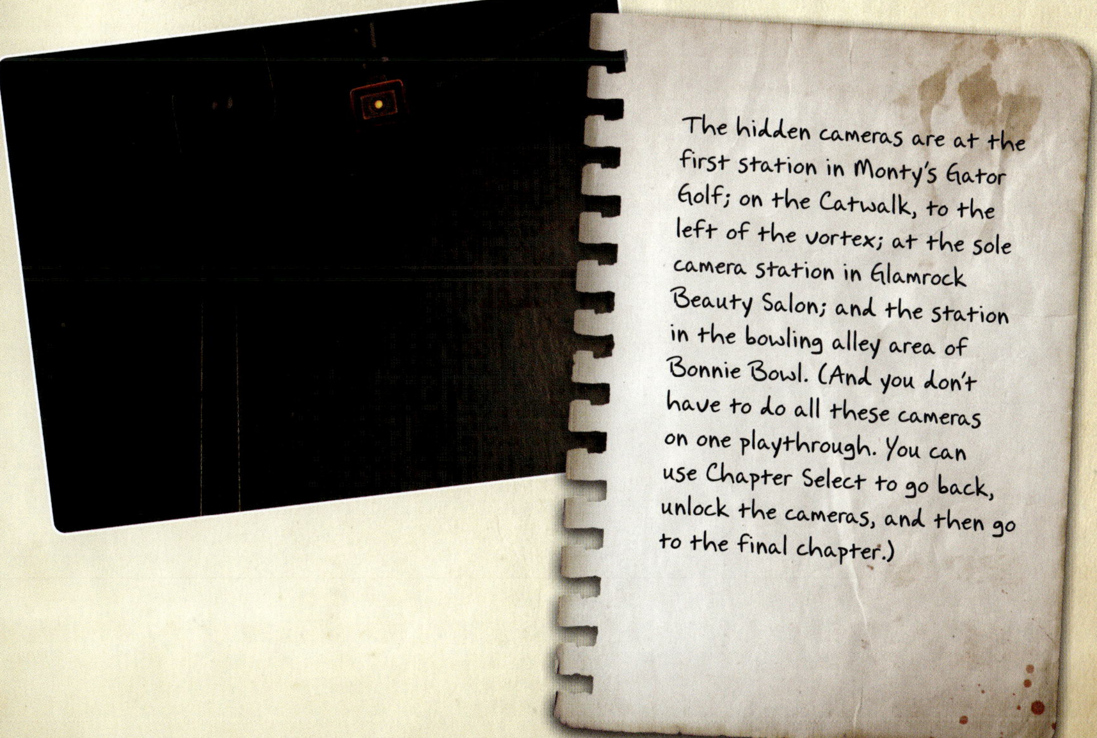

The hidden cameras are at the first station in Monty's Gator Golf; on the Catwalk, to the left of the vortex; at the sole camera station in Glamrock Beauty Salon; and the station in the bowling alley area of Bonnie Bowl. (And you don't have to do all these cameras on one playthrough. You can use Chapter Select to go back, unlock the cameras, and then go to the final chapter.)

Chapter 12

FNAF HELP WANTED 2

Like its predecessor, *Help Wanted*, *Help Wanted 2* is a virtual reality gaming experience, where you get to train in various Fazbear roles and play out scenarios that many a Fazbear employee will have experienced. Hopefully you will get the job!

The game was released in December 2023 on VR platforms, and in spring 2024 as a flat game that can be played without a VR headset. But whether you play with or without VR, you'll still make use of a Vanny VR mask inside the game, so be prepared to wonder exactly what your reality is—virtual reality, augmented reality, 8-bit reality . . . or something else?

So . . . do you have what it takes to make it as a Fazbear employee? Can you manage a pizzeria? How well will you look after customers who aren't feeling quite like themselves? Do you know how to run diagnostics on a collection of animatronic mascots? Are you sharp enough to spot the tiniest clues that will help you discover all sorts of secrets? Great, then let's go!

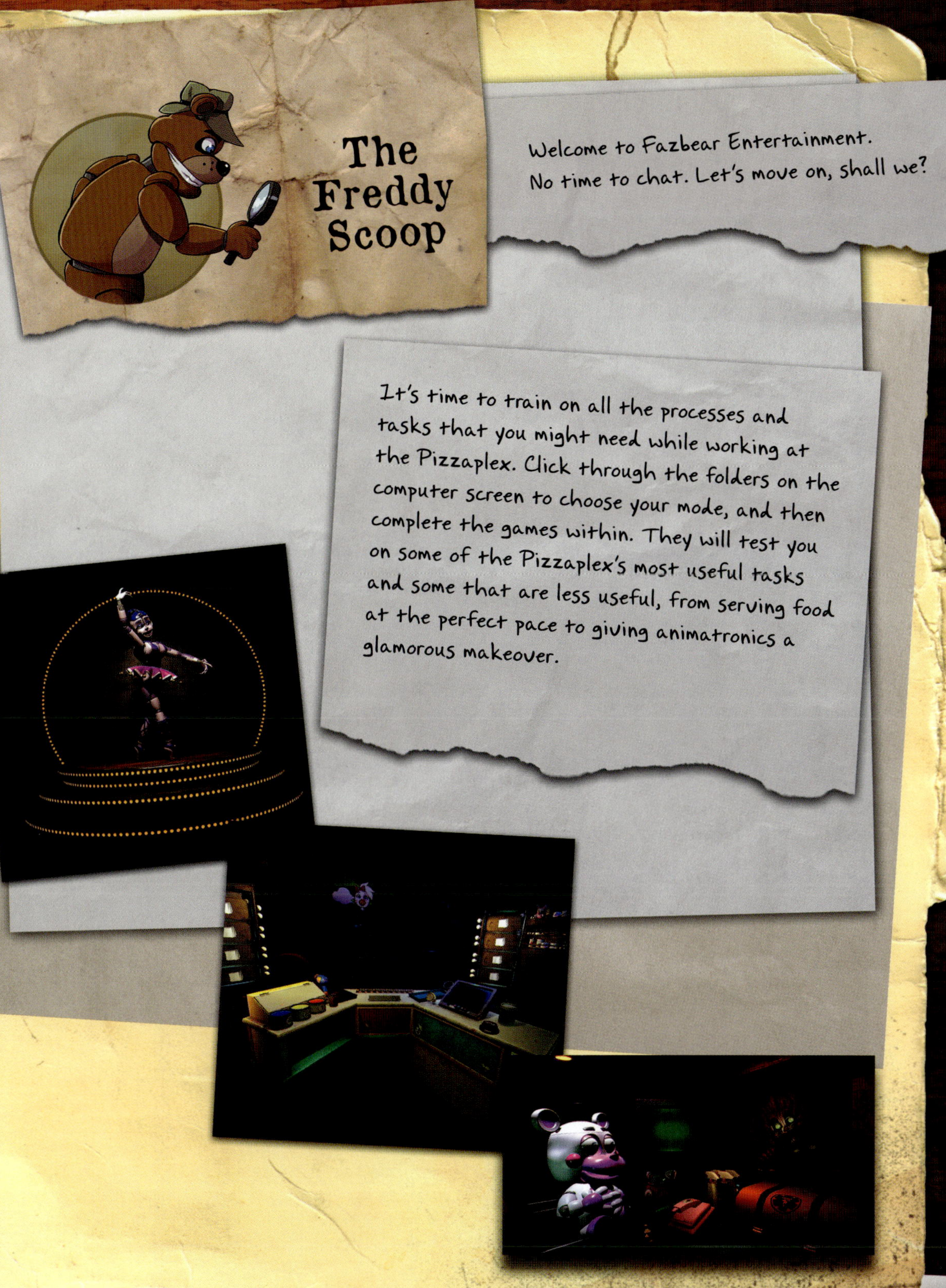

Welcome to Fazbear Entertainment.
No time to chat. Let's move on, shall we?

It's time to train on all the processes and tasks that you might need while working at the Pizzaplex. Click through the folders on the computer screen to choose your mode, and then complete the games within. They will test you on some of the Pizzaplex's most useful tasks and some that are less useful, from serving food at the perfect pace to giving animatronics a glamorous makeover.

Gameplay and Strategy

There are 40 minigames to play in various modes: Staff Only, Food Prep, Ticket Booth, Fazcade, Backstage, and Sister Location. In the second ending, you also play in *Princess Quest* mode.

- Once you complete fifteen games, you receive the Faz-wrench. This will help you unlock additional games.
- The Faz-wrench also allows you to enter a secret room that contains a *Princess Quest IV* arcade game. Once inside, you'll be able to remove the Vanny mask that you may not have even noticed you were wearing.
- Feed enough coins into the change machine next to the Candy Cadet and you will hear two stories. The second one is creepier by far. What could it possibly mean?!
- Collect the FazForce figures—there are six altogether: FazForce Freddy, Mecha Pirate Foxy, Chipset Chica, Bionic Bonnie, and two secret ones (Fredbear and the Puppet). When combined, they take you to the first ending.
- Listen to Mystic Hippo's hints, which leads you to cryptic graffiti around the pizzeria. Solving the clues help when replaying your last game, and show you how to get a plushy—also known as a Memory.
- Collect all the Memory plushies to receive a coin that allows you to play *Princess Quest IV*—which leads to a new in-in-game mode, and a second, secret ending.

ENDING 1

You're back in the Pizzeria, but it is pretty ruined. There's an animatronic charging chamber over there but . . . is that a human hand coming out of it? That question pales into insignificance, however, because you are suddenly attacked by evil S.T.A.F.F. Bots. Is that the end? Nope. You reawaken to find yourself inside a mask. And then through the mask you see . . . Cassie. You TAKE OFF THE MASK and hand it to her, and that's when you realize—this is the same moment at the beginning of *RUIN*, just seen from the other side. Wild!

ENDING 2

Finally, you get to play *Princess Quest IV*—but this game is unlike I, II, or III. After unlocking a certain room in the game, the Princess enters your augmented reality and you GO INTO THE GAME! Not only is this super cool, but you then enter a graveyard where each of the plushies is placed at a tombstone. And then you meet the king, who trades you a Glitchtrap plushy for the Vanny mask. After going up in an elevator (the *Sister Location* elevator to be precise), you find yourself inside a giant crane game, which is being played by a giant Vanny! She takes the plushy, waves, and then leaves you trapped in the game. Bye-bye . . .

UPDATE

A March 2025 update to *Help Wanted 2* leads the player to collect puzzle pieces as they play. Depending on whether you're wearing the Vanny mask or not, the pieces create a picture of what looks like a gift shop with a factory behind it, or of a van. Then, suddenly, you're by the gift shop with the van beside you. Inside the van is a machine with the initials M.X.E.S., who you will remember from *RUIN*. Type the numbers on the mailbox into the machine and M.X.E.S.'s digital form appears before the van drives off.

Animatronics

New

❑ Mystic Hippo

❑ Carnie

❑ Jack-O-Moon

Sister Location

❑ Circus Baby

❑ Ballora

❑ Funtime Freddy + Bon-Bon

❑ Bidybab

❑ Minireena

❑ Bonnet

Pizzeria Simulator

❑ Helpy

❑ Scrap Baby

❑ Lefty

❑ Pigpatch

❑ Funtime Chica

SECURITY BREACH

❏ GLAMROCK FREDDY

❏ GLAMROCK CHICA

❏ SHATTERED CHICA

❏ ROXANNE WOLF

❏ SHATTERED ROXY

❏ SUN

❏ JACK-O-MOON

❏ S.T.A.F.F. BOTS

❏ ENNARD

❏ HEAD CHEF BOT

❏ DJ MUSIC MAN

❏ RUINED DJ MUSIC MAN

❏ ENDO

❏ SHATTERED BONNIE

USEFUL ITEMS

- Faz-coins—For playing games.
- Faz-wrench—For unlocking games, and doors, and who knows what else!
- Vanny mask—On and off, on and off . . .
- FazForce figures—Collect all six!

Lore and Theories

TIMELINE

The state of the Pizzeria helps place the game in the FNAF timeline. It is in a state of disrepair but not yet completely ruined, which tells us that *Help Wanted 2* is set at some point during the timeline of *Security Breach*, but before the start of *RUIN*.

CAROUSEL

During a Ticket Booth game, you repair a spinning carousel. Sun and Moon are on the carousel, but why aren't they in the Daycare? Other carousel details are confusing as well, for example the pumpkin, haybales, and lantern—those are Fall Fest items! Is the carousel a Fall Fest-era attraction? If it is, then how old are Sun and Moon?

SISTER LOCATION

Bet you never expected to be able to explore the *Sister Location* bunker, huh? And even more than that, we bet you can't believe you're getting to see the *Sister Location* animatronics, including Circus Baby! Until now, we've only ever seen her in a minigame. And then she gives you ice cream—without kidnapping anyone. How kind . . .

THE UPDATE

The update scene, showing a van driving off with the M.X.E.S. machine in the back, is a mischievous teaser for the next *FNAF* game, *Secret of the Mimic*. Some fans think that the gift shop and factory behind it might be the workshop of the Mimic's creator, Edwin Murray (as described in the *Tales from the Pizzaplex* story, *The Mimic*). But the fact that the M.X.E.S. machine and digital animatronic also appear in *RUIN* has led to a flurry of theories about how the Mimic might link to *Help Wanted 2*. Most of the theories revolve around similarities between Vanessa and the *Help Wanted 2* player (see the next paragraph for more about the player's identity): how they are the only humans in the Pizzaplex at night, how they are linked to the Vanny mask. Did something similar happen to the *Help Wanted 2* player and Vanessa? Did it have something to do with the Mimic? Is there any connection to the second Candy Cadet story?

WHO ARE YOU?

As if all that speculation wasn't enough, there has been plenty more speculation—this time about who you play as in *Help Wanted 2*. A popular theory points to Cassie's dad. Let's make the case:

- In *RUIN*, Cassie reacts strongly to the Bonnie mask.
- In *RUIN*, when Cassie finds a Faz-wrench, she says her dad used to have one, and that he worked as a Faz-Technician. This fits with the player in *Help Wanted 2*.
- In *RUIN* we learned that Bonnie was Cassie's dad's favorite animatronic. This has spawned many fan theories, including that Cassie's dad was the bully in the Bonnie mask from the *FNAF4* minigame. It would also help understand the scene in *Help Wanted 2* where, in *Princess Quest*, you open a chest to reveal a Bonnie mask, and some words appear: "This looks familiar . . ."

If the player is Cassie's dad, this makes the first ending so much more meaningful—because it shows Cassie's dad passing on the Vanny mask to her, presumably unable to control himself thanks to Glitchtrap/the Mimic.

WHERE'S MONTY?

Monty Gator is conspicuously missing from *Help Wanted 2*. Why? One theory is that it's because the player is Cassie's dad! That's right. Cassie's dad, who loves Bonnie, and presumably thinks (or *knows*) that Monty destroyed Glamrock Bonnie to take his place in the Pizzaplex band, decides not to play any Monty games. Simple as that.

WHAT MAKES YOU SO SPECIAL?

You'll hear this question several times throughout the game, asked by Mystic Hippo, Moon, and Circus Baby. So come on then, what *does* make you so special?

Chapter 13

CHICA'S SECRET PARTY

SCOTT CAWTHON'S MINIGAME GUIDE

Chica's throwing a party! At this party, there are plenty of guests to feed sweet cupcakes and some very *unwanted* guests that crashed the party.

Chica's Secret Party was very nearly a secret game, as it was only available online for a short time—three days to be precise—on scottgames.com back in 2016. Information and tips can still be found on fan wiki websites about the elusive secret party, so check them out if you want to know more!

CHICA

Chica moves through her secret party, hopping and jumping through levels, collecting all the pink cupcakes she can scoop up. Throughout the levels, there are babies demanding yummy cupcakes. Chica brings the babies the cupcakes she's collected, turning the crying babies into happy babies. The more babies she appeases powers up her life force, allowing her to speed up when needed for special levels. The question is, can Chica accomplish all of the levels without being caught by the mysterious shadow figures?

THE CRYING BABIES

The Secret Party levels are filled with upset babies, whom Chica must feed the cupcakes to in order to accomplish her tasks. In most of the levels, the babies are happy with just one cupcake. Chica discovers that occasionally the babies need more than one cupcake to stop their tantrums and sometimes she needs to be superfast to accomplish her tasks.

THE SHADOW FIGURES

In a stealthy game twist, there are two shadow figures sneaking through the party as well. Chica needs to follow one of the shadow figures to discover who the person is behind the shadow. When she finds herself toe-to-toe with a shadow figure, her best bet is to run in the opposite direction and hide. Beware: It's very important to *not* follow the *wrong* shadow figure—or else!

THE HOUSE

The secret party takes place in a house that is a maze of adventurous goals with 10 crafty levels to complete in order to win the game. There are two bedrooms (and a secret room!), a bathroom, a kitchen and dining area, a living room, a home office, a garage, a basement, and an attic. All with a unique undertaking that Chica must tackle in order to beat the levels, and ultimately, say goodnight to her guests.

THE LEVELS

The room levels are sporadically laid out throughout the three-story house. Interestingly, Fredbear appears walking through the hallways. Chica may find it useful to see what he has to say; however, when he decides to talk to her is somewhat of a mystery. Chica may discover interesting secret tips and tools throughout the party to help her fulfill her goals.

THE DARK BASEMENT

Not only is the basement dark and creepy, but also a pipe has broken and the basement is filling up with water! There are three crying babies that need to be fed cupcakes and saved, each one strategically hidden within the dark basement. Once you feed a baby, the little one stops crying and floats happily onto the rising water and safely out of the basement window. However, Chica must save the babies within a three-minute time limit!

Once Chica completes this level, the doorbell to the front door rings. When Chica opens the door, a package is left on the doorstep. Inside the package is a secret tool—a block of cheese!

Most interestingly is that once Chica completes a level, Fredbear is ready to talk. He shares just how much dogs love pizza!

THE KITCHEN AND DINING AREA

Three babies are crying and sprawled across the kitchen and dining area. There are cupcakes hidden within the kitchen cupboards. The challenge is a very sneaky dog, wanting to jump and gobble up the cupcakes once Chica opens a cupboard. In order to distract the sneaky dog, Chica must grab a pizza cooking in the oven to entice the hungry hound away from the cupcakes, giving Chica enough time to feed the needy babies. The sneaky mutt eats quickly and Chica can only grab another pizza after 30 seconds. Chica may or may not need a power-up in order to feed these babies.

THE LIVING ROOM

The impatient babies were more than a little distraught and knocked over things in the Living Room. A circuit has blown and the lamps are flashing off and on. Each time the lights flash back on, the babies have moved into a different spot, leaving Chica confused. Once you step into the living room, the timer flashes to 1:30 and begins a countdown, and (yikes!) one of the Shadow Figures just might catch Chica when she's not looking. Chica must find the hidden cupcakes and catch the babies in the right place when the lights flash on in order to feed them before the timer runs out—or before she's caught off guard!

MASTER BEDROOM

When Chica looks out the master bedroom window, she mysteriously sees Bonnie walking back and forth in the backyard. In the bedroom, there are two crying babies. One is on top of the bed and another is in the closet—with cupcakes nowhere to be seen! As Chica approaches the bed, she notices some pink frosting on the floor. Moving closer to inspect, a golden, fuzzy hand snaps out, nearly catching Chica by the leg! Chica hops out of the way just in time. Chica needs to figure out how to get the guarded cupcakes from under the bed without getting snatched up.

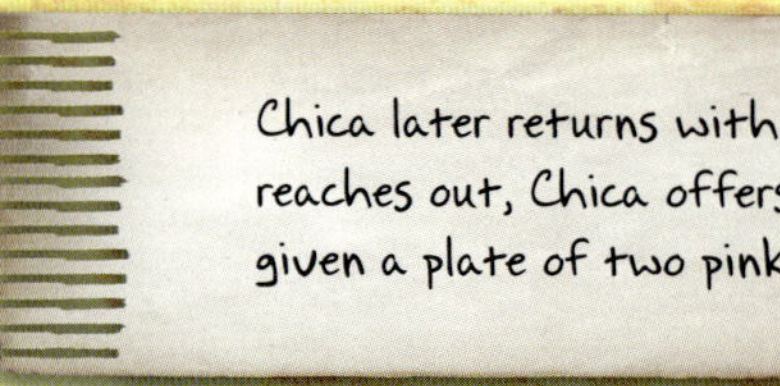

Chica later returns with a tiny, black hat. Once the hand reaches out, Chica offers the black hat, and in return she is given a plate of two pink cupcakes.

KID'S BEDROOM

Chica moves into the kid's room filled with scattered toys and wall posters of Freddy Fazbear. There's one crying baby in the middle of the bedroom, but once again, the elusive cupcakes are missing! Chica decides to pick up the toys and move them into a toy box. Her cleanliness pays off. Once all the toys are picked up, a drawer opens with a cupcake inside for the hungry baby!

THE SECRET ROOM

Unbeknownst to Chica, the secret room can only be unlocked after you have cleared the two bedroom levels. The secret room has an interesting and useful, secret tool—one that can help her finish the game!—an essential golden key. It's here that you'll also catch a glimpse of a box that longtime fans will be familiar with, as well as a peek inside (which won't be spoiled here) to those creative enough to find their way to it.

HOME OFFICE

The home office is quite small with only two, crying babies, and a strange Gray Man sitting at the desk. The obstacle is finding the undisclosed cupcakes. Chica looks around but doesn't see them. Aha! That is until she discovers a locked mini safe. Chica must discover the four-digit code in order to get to the cupcakes. The Gray Man doesn't seem to want to chat so Chica leaves to find the four-digit code.

Later on, Chica retrieves the four-digit code and opens the safe, quickly feeding the babies. Finally, the Gray Man decides to speak, giving a hint about something scary under a bed!

THE BATHROOM

In the bathroom, Chica is tasked with capturing a floating cupcake in the bathtub to appease the wailing baby sitting on the floor. Chica must take out all the floating duck toys in order to drain the water from the tub so she can grab the cupcake to feed the impatient baby. *Surprise*—there is something else that is very significant at the bottom of the tub!

THE GARAGE

The dreary garage is filled with boxes, old bikes, rusty tools, and a broken-down car. There are four crying babies and cupcakes waiting for Chica. However, there's a problem: scurrying rats are trying to steal the cupcakes! Chica needs the secret tool of cheese in order to distract the scurrying rats from stealing the cupcakes. With the rats distracted by the cheese, Chica can accomplish the task of collecting the cupcakes and feeding the bellowing babies.

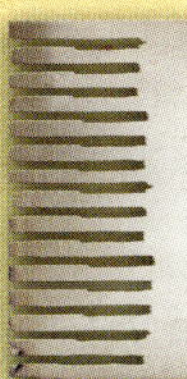

After the babies are appeased, an old static radio flickers on and starts repeating a series of numbers. Chica needs to remember these numbers for something important.

THE ATTIC

Chica realizes she needs the golden key in order to enter the final level. The attic is the grand finale, with 10 hidden, hungry babies and 20 cupcakes in a mass of storage boxes and old trunks. One cupcake is not enough for each baby and the additional challenge is that the boxes and trunks will move and shift like a moving maze. Chica has a difficult time finding where she's been or where she is going, all the while trying to beat the three minute clock! Watch out for those shadow figures; they pop up at the most unfortunate of times. Hopefully, Chica saved a power-up—or two—for this level in order to finish under three minutes.

THE FINISH!

Cha-cha-cha! Chica wins the game by feeding all the babies with sweet cupcakes. Her secret party is over and she's pacified all her guests and managed to elude the shadow figures, who have thankfully vanished just as stealthily as they appeared. Suddenly, music blasts through the house and confetti showers around her. All her uninvited guests—Fredbear, Gray Man, Bonnie, and Golden Freddy—move through the halls dancing. Chica decides to join the dance train throughout the house. After all, the party doesn't have to end!

Chapter 14

SECRET OF THE MIMIC

In *Secret of the Mimic*, you play as Arnold, an employee at Fazbear Entertainment who must retrieve the Mimic schematics from Murray's Costume Manor. The manor is currently closed, and any deliveries and work inquiries must be brought to the client and deliveries entrance around the side of the building. After venturing through various playground equipment and statues themed after Edwin's creations, you make your way through a gap in the fence and enter the lobby.

A clip of Edwin discussing his creations plays, and a door opens where you can view the Welcome Show. There is a problem with the show, and you must reset the Rocktapus animatronic to get to the storage area of the facility. The power is not on, but there is a generator outside of the Security Office. Revving that generator up results in the door to the security office opening.

After hitting the flashing button on the communication device in the Security Office, the Dispatch tells you the basic details of the mission. You are here to retrieve the schematics to the Mimic technology that Edwin developed. As an incentive, working really hard could result in you getting a $25 gift card, so why not get going and just grab the schematics and bring home that prize? Around you in the Security Office are multiple machines—a H.E.L.P.E.R. computer on the main desk, an Inventory Bin with its computer, and a Data Diver Upgrade station.

What would Arnold encounter on this adventure? It certainly seems dangerous! Is the voice on the other side of the line friendly, or are you being used for nefarious purposes? For now, Arnold must take one step at a time to upgrade his Data Diver to access more and more of the facility, and perhaps later in his stay, he will be able to make some pretty major decisions as he avoids costumed animatronics, repairs various parts of the facility, and solves puzzles along the way.

TIPS

Some helpful pointers for this game: get efficient at starting power generators, keep a mechanical rat in hand and ready to throw, use noisemaker distractions, and always know your surroundings!

DATA DIVER UPGRADE STATIONS

Your Data Diver has various permission levels that allow you to access parts of the MCM Facility, and each Data Diver Upgrade Station increments your permission level to the next level up. There are six levels—could there be another? Each Data Diver upgrade requires a puzzle to be solved, and each subsequent upgrade involves a bit more complexity.

POWER CONDUIT PUZZLES

In order to restore power to certain areas of the MCM Facility, you must find Power Conduit Puzzles and repair them so power flows from one corner to the other. You must complete the circuit, and sometimes search the area for missing pieces that have been dislodged from the puzzle. Once you have a complete route from start to finish, you can turn the flow all the way up to see the power gradually go from beginning to end, ultimately powering the area of interest.

DOOR CODES

Some of the more significant rooms in the game require a 4-digit or 5-digit door code. Get your puzzle-solving hats on—some of these require great effort to figure out the answer.

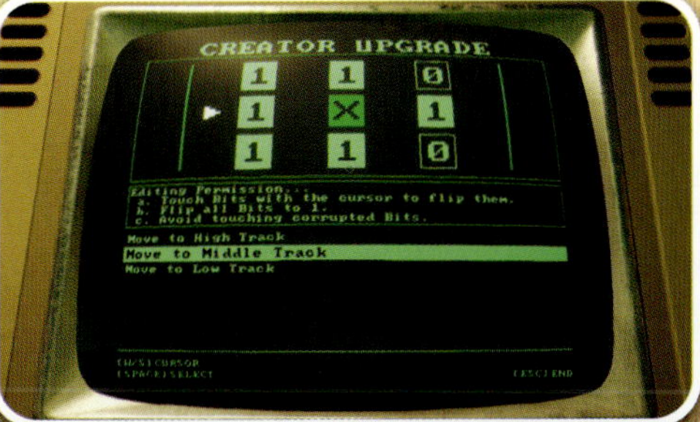

Gameplay and Strategy

Carnival Games

Can you set high scores on all of the Carnival Games? Not all of the games are confined to one area—let's see how your aim is shooting targets from within a Springlock suit!

Collectibles

There are 25 collectibles that you can find in Gift Boxes. What significance could those have? You may also find various Film Reels along the way that you can watch. What story will be uncovered?

Audio Clips and Text Logs

Standalone audio players and audio players embedded in some office walls allow for you to hear various aspects of the story at Murray's Costume Manor. There are also Mail kiosks from which you can download messages via your Data Diver, and you can view them from any H.E.L.P.E.R. computer in the MCM Facility.

What Is Hidden

There are many layers of gameplay, and various endings that you can uncover. Will you choose to escape after completing the mission, or could there be more to do? You decide in the end, and fortunately the game can be replayed if you don't feel that your trip was all that it could have been! Even the most common computer terminal in the game could lead to a major shift in Arnold's journey. Explore well, and explore wisely!

USEFUL ITEMS

- **Windup Rat:** Cute, but also useful to distract things that might be hunting you.

- **Gift Box:** Collectibles are there to be collected.

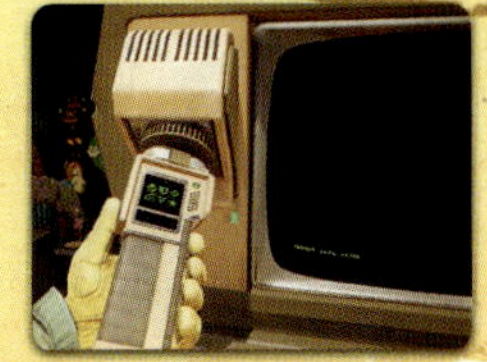

- **Data Diver:** Needed to access Edwin's computer and various areas of the game with different permission levels.

- **Crank:** This can be found on Jackie's box. Taking it will help you, but it will also activate Jackie, who has a non-zero chance of chasing you. There are other generic cranks in the game that can be used to pull back sliding doors or pull up gateway doors.

ANIMATRONICS

ELEPHANT

This freaky fellow is somewhat familiar. Oh, that's right, we spied him in RUIN. Now he's here, and most probably spying on you!

JACKIE

This clown-faced menace is ripped from its box, but that doesn't stop it from being agile enough to clamber through the vents and across the walls and ceilings of the warehouse. Those orange eyes. Terrifying.

DOLLIE

This nurse is an animatronic rather than a suit. What's in her backpack??

BIG TOP

This animatronic collects tickets for the Big Top Showroom and scans for visitors to his area who are without tickets, even if they've already given him one to enter.

MYCELIUM MAN

Mycelium Man looks cute and harmless, but if you look into its eyes and realize they are glowing . . . run!

WHITE TIGER

Keep an eye on him whenever possible, and run toward illuminated areas. He can chase and attack you very quickly if you try to flee from him in darkness.

SHARPAY

Woof! Have we met this dog before? Perhaps in the *Tales from the Pizzaplex* Epilogues?

HEDGEHOG HUDGIE

This suit is displayed in the Costume Gallery Hall. How welcoming will the Mimic find it?

MR. HIPPO

Mr. Hippo is back in *Secret of the Mimic*, but here he's back with the Mediocre Melodies, playing the violin.

HAPPY FROG

She was a not-so-happy frog in *Ultimate Custom Night*, before popping up in *Security Breach* and *Help Wanted 2*. Now we see her where she first started, part of the Mediocre Melodies.

MR. HELPFUL

An early form of Helpy. You can use your Data Diver to retrieve varying messages based on permission level from these audio kiosks.

MR. ALLIGATOR?

We never knew there was a banjo-playing alligator in the Mediocre Melodies. Makes you wonder what happened to him . . .

EDWIN MURRAY

♦ **Disappeared**

Many fans are eager to learn more about the mysterious Edwin Murray, and some are hopeful that Secret of the Mimic will shed light on the question of where Edwin disappeared to.

♦ **David Murray**

The tragic story of Edwin's son David is described in *The Mimic*, in the Pizzaplex stories. It's nice to see some of David's childish drawings on the walls of his father's office. Fans think they might catch a glimpse of the Murrays' living quarters, which are somewhere in the warehouse.

MURRAY'S COSTUME MANOR

In the *Help Wanted 2* update, collectable puzzle pieces formed a picture of a mask and gift shop with a factory behind it. The letterbox outside had a triangular logo and the number 4625. We now know that the logo is for MCM—Murray's Costume Manor—which implies that the factory in the picture is the warehouse we explore in *Secret of the Mimic*. Edwin also says in an audio clip that he built to set the frequency to 4625.

M.X.E.S.

Edwin's Surveillance Room computer, short for Mechanical X-form Experimental Storage. The computer hosts an executable named CRADLE.EXE, which can only be run with executive permissions on the Data Diver. Fiona suggested Edwin build the CRADLE program to protect people from his creation, which has become dangerous.

FALL FEST

This mysterious festival is only hinted at in the games and books, but we know it took place as early as 1970. Some fans are certain we will see some Fall Fest characters among the animatronics in the warehouse.

PIZZAPLEX THEORIES

♦ **Springlock Surprise?**

In the *Tales from the Pizzaplex* story *The Mimic*, pink and yellow jesters are mentioned. In the epilogues, there's even a springlock suit of this character, which is the suit that finally kills the Mimic. In *Secret of the Mimic*, we see a cardboard cutout of a yellow jester. Does this suggest there will be a springlock suit to find within the warehouse?

> If we do find a springlock suit, it will be the first time we get to see an in-game model of a working springlock suit!

♦ **Timeline of the TALES**

There's a tiny, creepy, and definitely not 'armless detail in *Secret of the Mimic*: behind an elephant suit that is piled in a corner, a human arm pokes out. This arm appears to be wearing the same uniform as you—the player. Since you are a Fazbear employee, does this mean the arm belongs to another Fazbear employee? Perhaps it was a member of one of the teams sent in to Edwin's warehouse in the story *The Mimic*. Two teams were sent in, and both were killed. Could that arm be one of theirs? It's possible that this morbid detail helps to determine when *Secret of the Mimic* takes place—which would be sometime after the events of *The Mimic* story.

MEDIOCRE MELODIES

Is this the earliest iteration of the animatronic entertainers? Clearly, they were created long before Freddy Fazbear's Pizza existed, so what was their original purpose? In fact, were they even commissioned by Fazbear—or was Edwin designing them for something completely different?

The way the Mediocre Melodies are positioned, it's possible Edwin designed them as an attraction for a theme park ride.

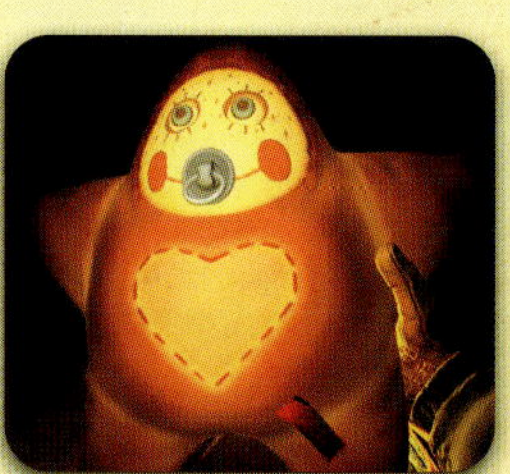

> There has been some speculation that Nedd Bear from the Mediocre Melodies was based on Freddy, but perhaps it's the other way around?

WHO ARE YOU?

You are are an overworked Fazbear employee named Arnold. Nicknamed Arnie, you just finished an absurdly long shift at work, and now you're being sent to Murray's Costume Manor to retrieve the schematics for the Mimic, which the dispatch says belongs to Fazbear Entertainment. Others had also been sent, but they did not make it through.

AGONY

It could be that this incident with the Mimic and the Fazbear employees was actually the earliest tragedy in the history of the Fazbear company? It comes before the Bite of '83, Charlie's death, and the missing children. Is this where it all began?

FAZBEAR ENTERTAINMENT'S BIGGEST SECRET?

Exploring Edwin's workshop has left us with more questions than answers! How much of what we see inside the warehouse was designed by Edwin? Look at the Mediocre Melodies and the Music Man prototype. There's also an early version of HELPI (H.E.L.P.E.R.) and a strangely familiar alligator animatronic. There's even a postal worker bot that looks a little like the *Security Breach* Pizzaplex S.T.A.F.F. Bots. Seeing so many things that later appear in Fazbear attractions begs the question—what are they doing in Edwin's warehouse all the way back in 1979?

Don't stop questioning!

- Were all these things of Edwin's own design, and his intellectual property?
- Just what, exactly, did Fazbear Entertainment retrieve from Edwin's abandoned warehouse?
- Is it possible they came away with a lot more than just their *own* property?
- How much can we actually trust Fazbear Entertainment?

Chapter 15
THE BOOKS

Following the overwhelming success of the video game series, *FNAF* creator Scott Cawthon worked to expand the lore and tell a bigger story through the eyes of a teenager affected by the events that took place at Freddy Fazbear's Pizza. *The Silver Eyes*, *The Twisted Ones*, and *The Fourth Closet*, all written by Scott Cawthon and Kira Breed-Wrisley, are a trilogy of novels set in the *FNAF* universe. The story follows Charlie, the daughter of Henry, founder of Fredbear's Family Diner and the engineer behind the original animatronics. Graphic novel adaptations were later released, which featured new insights and visual representations of the ideas first showcased in the novels.

Since the first book went into print, debates have raged among fans about how the books tie into the games, but one thing isn't in question: the books introduced many elements that later appeared in the game, from minor technology up to the name of the universe's central villain, William Afton.

FIVE NIGHTS AT FREDDY'S: SURVIVAL LOGBOOK

Released shortly after *Freddy Fazbear's Pizzeria Simulator*, the *Five Nights at Freddy's: Survival Logbook* offered a chance for *FNAF* fans to put themselves in the shoes of a new night guard at Freddy Fazbear's Pizza and reflect on their first week on the job. The book is divided into five sections, representing a guard's first five nights on the job, and is filled with interactive quizzes, activities, and "incident reports" to fill out. There are also a few secrets hiding in those pages that can help solve the many mysteries in *Freddy Fazbear's Pizzeria Simulator*!

Five Nights at Freddy's
THE SILVER EYES
SCOTT CAWTHON
Minersville
Lund
VALLEY
THE SILVER EYES
Ten years after the horrific murders at Freddy Fazbear's Pizza, the people of Hurricane, Utah, have mostly moved on. But Charlie and her childhood friends, who were directly affected by those events, can never forget. The old gang is thrown together again for a memorial service marking the anniversary of the children who were murdered—including their friend, Michael Brooks.
To face their tragic past, the group decides to visit the old pizza place one last time . . . When they arrive at the long-abandoned location, however, they're surprised to discover that the restaurant and its animatronics are very much intact. Little has changed for Freddy and his friends, and many of its nightmares have remained.
HI.
LET'S EAT!!!
. . . CHICA . . .
. . . AND FREDDY.

Insights from the Graphic Novel

The graphic novel is filled with fascinating visuals, many of which are firsts for the canon. For example, this is our first time seeing William Afton, who's previously only been glimpsed inside the Springtrap suit, or as his notorious purple sprite. His nasty scars from an accident with the springlock suit are shown as well. Through Charlie's flashbacks we also get our first image of Henry, as well as the dark moment when he ended his life. This is also our first time seeing Fredbear's Family Diner, the origins of the Freddy's franchise, up close.

THE TWISTED ONES

The second book in the series takes place one year later and opens on Charlie, who is now in her freshman year of college in the neighboring town of New Harmony. Studying robotics like her father before her, Charlie has found herself connected to her past more than ever. After a tornado tears through Hurricane, a body is discovered, and it bears injuries that resemble those from a springlock suit. Police chief Clay Burke reaches out to Charlie for help in solving the murder, but on their hunt for the killer, they unearth more sinister monsters long forgotten. And these monsters won't stop until they have what they want: Charlie.

DON'T TRUST YOUR EYES

Insights from the Graphic Novel

The Twisted Ones introduced tons of fascinating new technology to the canon, from illusion discs to wearable earpieces that help people interact with animatronics. One of the best parts of the graphic novel is seeing all this technology come to life. But perhaps the most terrifying parts come from seeing how the illusion discs turn a normal animatronic into its twisted counterpart.

One of the more gruesome moments in the graphic novel comes from the close-ups of the newly born Springtrap, Afton's body fused to the animatronic.

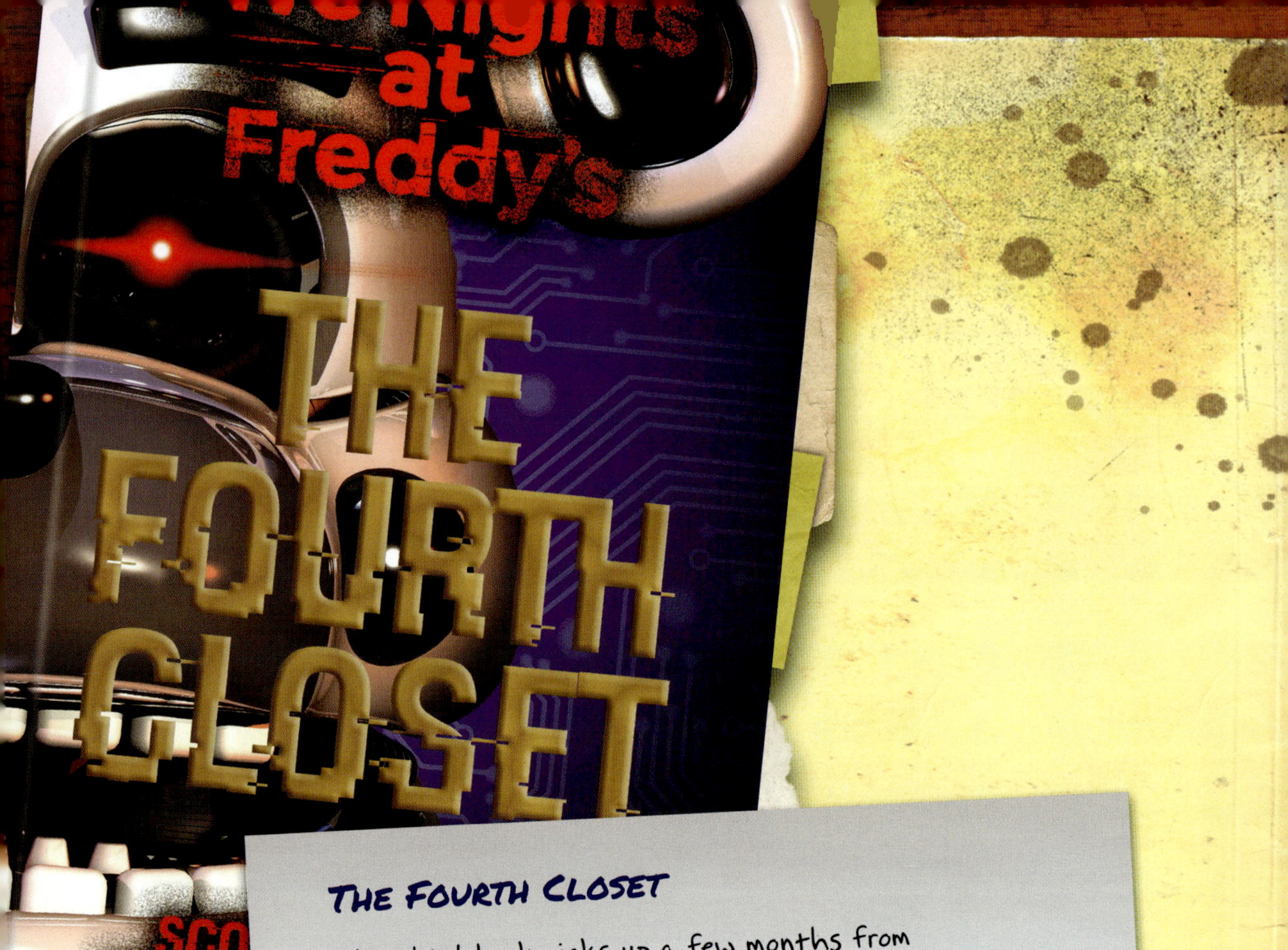

The Fourth Closet

The third book picks up a few months from where *The Twisted Ones* left off, and John can't seem to shake the feeling that something is wrong with Charlie. Too bad John seems to be the only one actually interested in investigating the mysterious circumstances of Charlie's supposed death and miraculous reappearance. While the whole gang wants to forget about Freddy's, a new animatronic pizzeria opens in town. With it comes a string of new kidnappings and new nightmares. John, Jessica, Marla, and Carlton join forces to figure out what's going on and try to stop more children from going missing. But the real mystery is what happened to Charlie . . . and the legacy her father's creations left behind.

Insights from the Graphic Novel

The Fourth Closet puts all the pieces of the novel series together—from Remnant to the illusion discs to Charlie's childhood trauma. In an interesting first, the interior of an active Circus Baby's Pizza is shown in detail here. The scenes in Afton's laboratory give fans an interesting glimpse at the specific process behind using Remnant, and an idea of how Molten Freddy came to be. Also of note is a peek at the ghosts of the missing children.

Character Profiles

CHARLIE: Grew up in Hurricane, but left ten years earlier to live with her aunt Jen, who taught her to be fiercely independent and self-sufficient. Charlie becomes increasingly determined to find answers to the mysteries of her haunted past, clinging to the few childhood memories that have stuck with her.

JOHN: Charlie's childhood friend and crush, John is a writer and a keen observer of the world around him. He cares deeply for Charlie, always offering her support no matter how difficult or dangerous the situation.

JESSICA: One of Charlie's best friends, a sophisticated young woman with a love of fashion only surpassed by her love of forensics. Jessica frequently finds herself taking on the role of leader and strategist in the group.

CARLTON: A childhood friend of Charlie's who likes to goof around. His comedic nature helps to hide how the troubling events of his childhood affected him.

MARLA: Another childhood friend, a determined and strong-willed young woman training to be a nurse. Marla is extremely loyal to those she loves.

JASON: Marla's younger half brother, who sometimes fights to be taken seriously.

LAMAR: Smart and hardworking, Lamar is often the voice of reason among his friends.

AUNT JEN: Stepped in as Charlie's guardian after Henry's death. She taught Charlie to be ready for the harshness of the world, but believes painful memories are best forgotten.

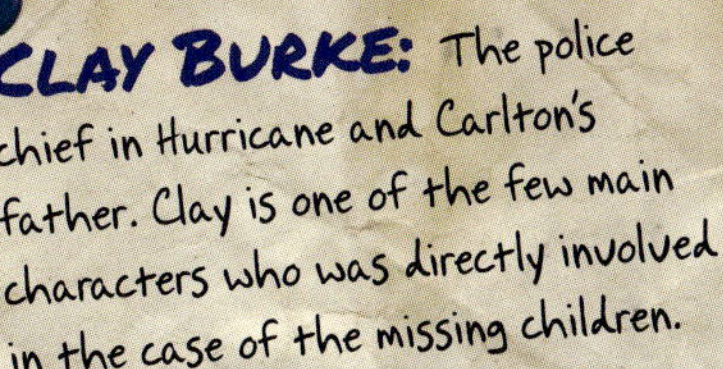

CLAY BURKE: The police chief in Hurricane and Carlton's father. Clay is one of the few main characters who was directly involved in the case of the missing children.

"You know, I wasn't the chief back then. I was still a detective, and I was working on those disappearances. To this day, it was the worst thing I've ever had to see."
—from *The Silver Eyes*

WILLIAM AFTON: Business partner to Charlie's late father, Afton was also one of the prime suspects in the missing children case from ten years ago. Though he was never officially charged, he left town quickly and his current whereabouts are unknown.

"Before him stood someone who had spent so much of his life fighting like a cornered rat that he had taken on the mantle of bitter sadism as an integral part of himself. He would strike out against others and revel in their pain, feeling righteously that the world owed him his cruel pleasures."
—from *The Silver Eyes*

HENRY: The founder of Fredbear's Family Diner, Charlie's father was an engineer with a childlike sense of imagination. He personally built all the animatronics at the restaurant. Charlie remembers him as a good man, but he took many dark secrets to his grave.

THE MISSING CHILDREN: Ten years prior to the events of the first novel, five children from Hurricane went missing—Susie; Cassidy; Fritz; an unnamed boy; and Michael Brooks, Charlie's childhood friend. Their disappearance is tied to Freddy Fazbear's Pizza, but their bodies have never been found, nor has their kidnapper been caught.

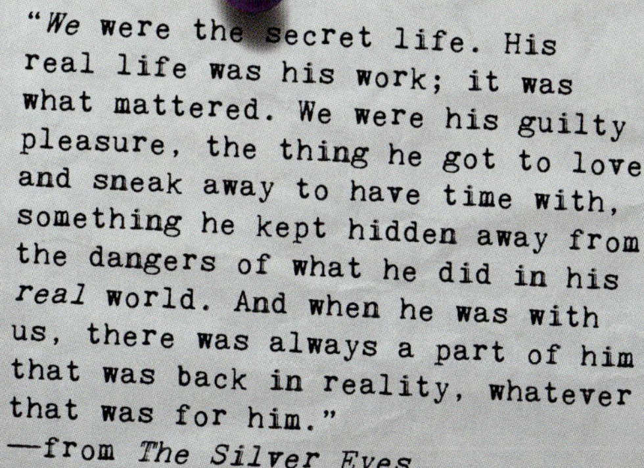

"*We* were the secret life. His real life was his work; it was what mattered. We were his guilty pleasure, the thing he got to love and sneak away to have time with, something he kept hidden away from the dangers of what he did in his *real* world. And when he was with us, there was always a part of him that was back in reality, whatever that was for him."
—from *The Silver Eyes*

Connections Between the Books and Games

While the books are set in a separate continuity from the games, they are considered canon. Many concepts first introduced in the novels later took hold in the games, while concepts introduced in the games were sometimes expanded on in the novels.

TECHNOLOGY: Several pieces of technology cross over between the books and games. Springlock suits in particular feature heavily in both. We saw the idea of making someone or someplace invisible to an animatronic in both *FNAF3* and *The Fourth Closet*. The illusion discs in *The Twisted Ones* may have a place in the games as well, one possibility being the nightmare animatronics in *FNAF4*.

THE MISSING CHILDREN: While many fans have been quick to point out that Henry, William Afton, Charlie (Charlotte), and Elizabeth are all characters from the games and books, fans have also noted that two of the original victims in the books (Susie and Fritz) match the names etched on the tombstones in *Pizzeria Simulator*. One of the missing children in *The Fourth Closet* goes unnamed, though it is noted that he wears a striped shirt.

REMNANT: Remnant was initially mentioned in two of the hidden schematics in *Pizzeria Simulator*, but it wasn't until *The Fourth Closet* that this concept was seen in action. In Afton's lab, we see the superheating and injection of Remnant into an animatronic, and we see the spirits of the children haunting the animatronic. It seems Candy Cadet's secret stories of "five becoming one" were borne out after all.

THE CREATORS: The books offer a closer peek at Henry and William Afton, how their partnership flourished early on, and how their view of the animatronics evolved over time. Thoughtful fans might want to give these sections a closer look to determine how they impact the story of the games as well.

Chapter 16

INTERACTIVE NOVELS

Interactive novels—what a cool idea! It's just perfect for the FNAF world because it replicates the feeling of a video game by allowing you—the reader—to control the main character, and play the game . . . in a book!

FNAF: The Week Before is the first in the interactive novel series. Written by Scott Cawthon and E.C. Myers, this book was released in September 2024, but it is set way earlier—back in the heyday of Freddy Fazbear's Pizzeria, a week before the events of *FNAF1*. *FNAF: Return to the Pit* is the second interactive novel, written by Cawthon and Adrienne Kress. It was published in December 2024, and while the story begins in recent years, the character travels back in time before *FNAF2*, and way before *FNAF1*.

The third interactive novel, *FNAF: Escape the Pizzaplex*, was written by Cawthon and Lindsay Ely and published in April 2025. It takes place in Freddy Fazbear's Mega Pizzaplex, sometime before the game *Security Breach*. And let's not forget *FNAF: VIP* by Cawthon and E.C. Myers, which was the first interactive novel to be written (August 2024). It isn't considered Book #1 in the series though, but is instead designated Interactive Novel #0.

Confused? Read on. (Though it's likely that reading on will only add to your confusion. Still, it's all part of the Freddy fun!)

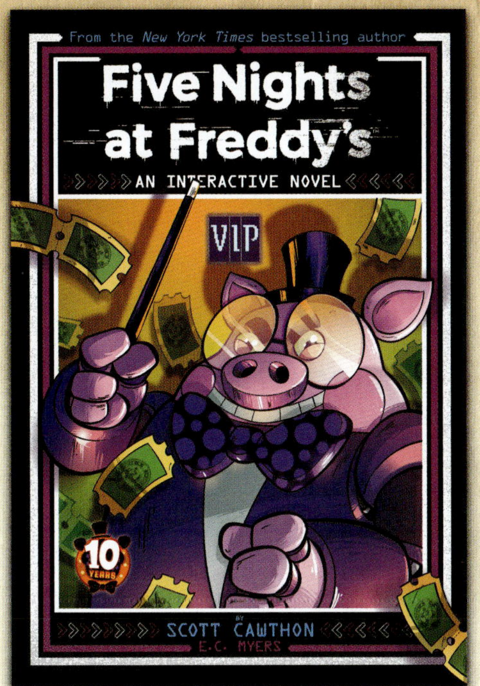
From the New York Times bestselling author
Five Nights at Freddy's
AN INTERACTIVE NOVEL
VIP
10 YEARS
SCOTT CAWTHON
E.C. MYERS

From the New York Times bestselling author
Five Nights at Freddy's
AN INTERACTIVE NOVEL
THE WEEK BEFORE
SCOTT CAWTHON
E.C. MYERS

From the New York Times bestselling author
Five Nights at Freddy's
AN INTERACTIVE NOVEL
RETURN TO THE PIT
SCOTT CAWTHON
ADRIENNE KRESS

From the New York Times bestselling author
Five Nights at Freddy's
AN INTERACTIVE NOVEL
ESCAPE THE PIZZAPLEX
SCOTT CAWTHON
LYNDSAY ELY

VIP

Interactive Novel #0—*FNAF: VIP*—was a special 10th anniversary eBook, released in August 2024. It was intended to pave the way for Interactive Novel #1, *The Week Before*. In November 2024, *VIP* was released in print for the first time, as a free addition to the *FNAF Interactive Novel Box Set*.

VIP puts you in the shoes of Devon, who mysteriously receives a VIP pass to the Pizzaplex. There, he meets an animatronic pig named VIP (which stands for Very Informative Pig) who will accompany him and his little brother Ike for the day. Unfortunately, VIP is more clingy and creepy than informative, and when he locks Ike away, Devon must follow VIP's rules to get him back.

THE GAMES

If he ever wants to see his little brother again, Devon must score 1,000 points by the end of the day. How? By playing games at the Pizzaplex, of course! And it's up to you, intrepid reader, to help Devon play the games successfully so he can rack up enough points to save Ike from a very piggy fate.

MEET DEVON: Devon is a 12-year-old boy who is excited to explore the Pizzaplex as a VIP, but less excited about having to bring his brother Ike along.

POINTS POINTERS

Scoring 1,000 points to rescue Ike is tricky, but definitely doable. You'll need to get the maximum 300 points at Fazer Blast, Monty's Maze, and Roxy's Raceway, and then head over to the Fazcade or Rockstar Row for the final 100 points.

EXTRA, EXTRA!

Rescuing Ike is good. Devon's mom will be happy, for sure! But if you can rack up 100,000 points, you'll get the chance to stop VIP for good. Which, we think you'll agree, is even better! 100,000 sounds like a lot, but it's possible. First, head to the Atrium, then put on the Max Occupancy Experience (MOE) headset, which takes the form of Freddy's head. This restarts the game and makes any points you earn worth ten times more. But that's not all—if you go back to the MOE headset *again*, all points will be worth a hundred times more.

LET'S PLAY

Devon visits these Pizzaplex attractions on his quest for points:

- Fazer Blast
- Monty's Maze
- Roxy Raceway
- Fazcade
- Rockstar Row

POTENTIALLY USEFUL ITEMS

- VIP Pass: All-you-can-eat special pass with a Very Informative Pig
- Faz-Token: All you need to play!
- Bonnie Bites: Monty is not a fan.
- Balloon: A floating distraction.
- Security badge: For a career in the security business.
- Max Occupancy Experience headset: Experience the Pizzaplex with multiplied points!
- Tortilla chips: Make lots of crumbs.
- Roxy's autograph: For Ike.

EARLY DAYS OF THE PIZZAPLEX

This novel is set in the early days of the Pizzaplex, before it has all the attractions we see in *Security Breach* and *Tales of the Pizzaplex*. Superstar Daycare has not been built, and Monty's Gator Golf does not yet exist—it is currently an attraction named Monty's Maze. One other notable difference: the early Glamrock lineup includes Bonnie!

SECRETS OF THE PIG

VIP tells Devon that he's sent VIP passes to children who live close to the Pizzaplex but haven't visited for a while. This implies that he may have had, or will have in the future, other potential victims.

MISSING KIDS

While VIP doesn't appear elsewhere in the FNAF world, his penchant for kidnapping kids rings a lot of bells. In one unfortunate ending, Devon finds himself in a storage room deep in the Pizzaplex, where he discovers the bodies of VIP's previous victims.

THE WEEK BEFORE

There are five nights to get through (obviously), each with its own task. But every page turn brings new dangers, so choose wisely. There are very few ways to make it out alive, as the main character Ralph would have been able to testify if only . . . Okay, let's not get ahead of ourselves!

MEET RALPH: Finally, we meet Phone Guy properly. And his name is Ralph. Ralph is a Freddy's security guard who loves his job, is super loyal to Freddy's, and has a young daughter, Coppelia. Lucky Ralph has just one more week to go at this job, which is exciting, huh? He's been given the night shift, so that should mean he'll end his career with five nights of relative quiet. Right?

RANDOM RALPH TRIVIA

- Foxy is his favorite animatronic. Aw.
- He was employee of the month twenty-two times. Go Ralph!
- Ralph had an artichoke and anchovy pizza named after him at Freddy's. It wasn't very popular.

NIGHT 01

Task: Replace the lightbulbs in the men's restroom. Easy peasy.

The obvious first step is to go to the men's restroom. How else could you replace the lightbulbs? But hang on, what's the best way to get there? And what's with the paperclip and the gum wrapper? Someone didn't clean up earlier. Anyway, back to the bathroom, if you got there alive. Foxy's on the prowl, so play it safe. Or don't. It's up to you, after all.

Did you survive? Lucky you—now you can make Coppelia breakfast before school.

2 FIVE NIGHTS AT FREDDY'S

Night 1—12:00 a.m.

The Security Office at Freddy Fazbear's Pizza is practically a second home, you've spent so much of your time here over your career. Probably *too much* time cooped up in a glorified closet, staring at a buzzing, flickering monitor until your eyes dry out. But everyone's gotta make a living—and you have an eleven-year-old daughter, Coppelia, to provide for.

You often feel like the only thing you're good at is protecting others, even at your own expense.

The office is always dark since there aren't any outside windows, but somehow at night it still manages to give you the creeps. You're probably just spooked because you're all alone in the restaurant, aside from Freddy, Bonnie, Chica, and Foxy. Animatronics aren't fantastic conversationalists, but boy, can they sing and dance!

Of course they've also been known to do . . . other things. Rumor is, they've become strangely aggressive lately. But surely those glitches were ironed out or they wouldn't have reopened this place. Not that customers have exactly been flocking back just yet.

After the restaurant closes and everyone is gone, the animatronics enter roaming mode and walk around to prevent their servos from locking up. You hear heavy footsteps echoing out there now. *Clomp. Clomp. Clomp.*

> TURN TO PAGE 3

NIGHT 02

Task: Reattach Bonnie's head. This doesn't sound as simple as lightbulbs, but how bad could it really be?

First, you have to *find* the head. If you're still alive, you'll need Parts and Service to fix Bonnie. And then comes the question of how to fix him. Without him rebooting and snapping your neck as a thank-you.

Did you survive? I knew you would! Enjoy hanging with Coppelia before she goes to school. Try not to show how freaky the past two nights have been.

THE WEEK BEFORE 

You quietly open the stall door and tiptoe to the door. The heavy footsteps are growing more distant. You take a quick look outside the Restroom and see Foxy ambling through the Dining Area on his way back to Pirate Cove.

You wipe a sleeve across your damp brow. *Whew!* That was close. Your fingers ache and twitch from holding the stall door closed. You are going to file a very stern complaint letter to the maintenance staff for leaving a stall door broken until the next shift.

You check your watch. It's just after 4:00 a.m., and you still have a job to do.

> TURN TO PAGE 29

NIGHT 03

Task: Clean up the mess in Party Room 2. Not the best job, but don't complain—it's gonna be the best thing about the whole night!

There's been a break-in. Someone has smashed the window in Party Room 2 and made more than a little mess. Are you going to board up the window or mop up the spill first? Or maybe just jump out the window and run home? It's a life-and-death decision—literally. Next up, when footsteps echo, you'll need to hide or take on Foxy or Chica. If you're still breathing, get cleaning that Party Room. Told you it would be the best job of the night!

Did you survive? Just about. Back home, Coppelia is stressing. Some random woman called and then she didn't sleep well.

NOTES

NIGHT 04

Task: End the animatronic party. A party? And you weren't invited?

Those animatronics sure know how to party, and the Dining Room is getting wrecked. How will you get to the Breaker Room to shut off the power? Straight through the Dining Room, where you might be spotted, or through the twisting labyrinth of vents from the office? If you make it to the Breaker Room in one piece, you still need to figure out how to shut down the power. But don't spend too long deliberating . . .

Did you survive? Somehow. At home Coppelia begs you to quit. But you can't—there's only one more night . . .

NIGHT 05

Task: Survive. Simple enough.

Will you check the cameras to keep track of the four roaming animatronics? Or maybe it's better to hide for the next few hours? Did you bring the water pistol with you? Or maybe you have the flashlight? Will you use them? Will you? Will you? WHAT will you do?

Did you survive? You're not sure. That makes sense.

NIGHT 06

Hang on! You've signed on for overtime? What were you thinking?

Task: A mysterious phone call with someone named Bronwen informs you that the animatronics are planning to leave the restaurant and escape into the real world. That cannot happen. Coppelia lives in the real world. You have to stop them.

First you want to get to the charging panels' generator, which is in the main stage area. Do you check out the cameras first, or just head on over? Or maybe take the vents? And once you make it, there's still some thinking to do. Will you flip the switches up or down? And remember—sssh!

Did you survive? Incredibly, you completed the task by 4:00 a.m.—this has never happened before. Getting home nice and early is a bonus, but a knock at the door means you forgot something. What was it? Oh yes . . . Foxy!

What happens to you and Coppelia depends on what item you chose to give her. Those pesky choices always have consequences, don't they?

GAME OVER

> TO START FROM THE BEGINNING, TURN TO PAGE 2
> TO TRY THIS NIGHT AGAIN, TURN TO PAGE 201

The Game Ending

But wait, there's another ending, the Game Ending. Flicking the switches down brings on Golden Freddy, the phrase "IT'S ME," and death. But this death brings one gift: the ability to play all over again, but this time WITH BRONWEN'S PHONE. Ooooh.

The phone definitely helps you complete your tasks and survive each night, but it also enables you to record your messages—fulfilling your legacy as Phone Guy! It's just a shame because we already know what the True Ending was for Phone Guy . . .

Potentially Useful Items

Lightbulb—You can't change a lightbulb without a new one.

Paperclip—Easy to overlook—but don't!

Chewed gum & gum wrapper—Who doesn't like gum?

Ballpoint pen—Useful for school.

ID Card—Take it, just to be sure.

Flashlight—Shine it in Foxy's freaky eyes.

Freddy head—Can fool some animatronics, but not Foxy . . .

Screwdriver—Only helpful if you're the one who reaches it first!

Coin—If you find one, why not?

Lighter—Not what it seems.

Gold ring—Shiny!

Pink water pistol—Would Coppelia like this more than a gold ring?

Mr. Cupcake—Do kids like cupcakes?

Bronwen's phone (Bonus Item)—Full of data.

Ticket

IT'S ME

This phrase surfaces a lot in the *FNAF* universe, particularly from Golden Freddy. It's creepy, mysterious, and drives fans crazy! In *The Week Before*, Ralph sees "IT'S ME" scribbled on a bathroom door, hears it whispered backstage, and sees it in his mind when staring at Golden Freddy himself. Interestingly, *regular* Freddy says it a couple of times in this book. As do Bronwen, Chica, and even Ralph himself when he's stuffed into an animatronic suit. Many fans think "IT'S ME" were the words of the Crying Child to Michael Afton.

THE BITE OF '87

Many wild rumors swirl around the infamous "Bite of '87," so it's exciting when Ralph talks about it!

Well, at one point Ralph is speaking about Foxy, and he says, "As far as you know, he's never bitten any *kids*. . ." Has Foxy ever bitten an adult?

RETURN TO THE PIT

This interactive novel is based on the first story from the *Fazbear Frights* series, "Into the Pit." It involves the same characters and centers around the same ball-pit-based storyline, but the choose-your-own-path element offers a lot more to learn!

MEET OSWALD:

Oswald is a bored ten-year-old, just starting his summer vacation but without his best friend who has moved away. His dad has a great idea—daily visits to Jeff's Pizza. Who knows what will happen there?

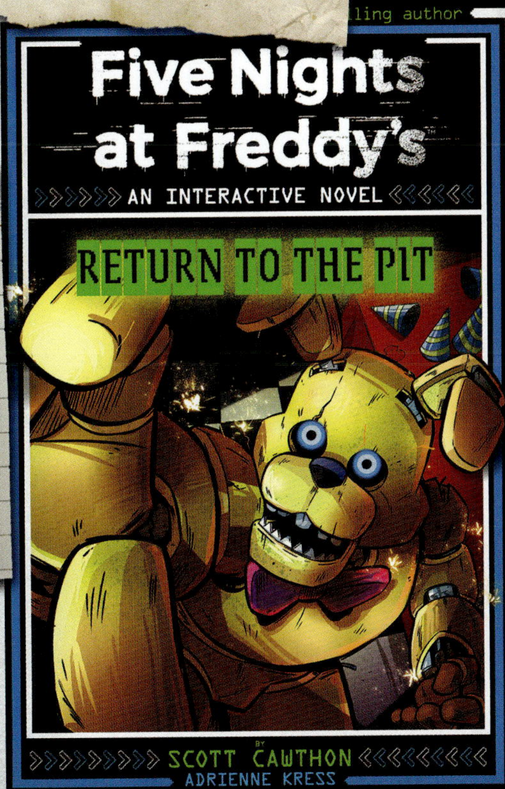

ODD OSWALD TRIVIA

- Oswald likes drawing animal mascot characters. He even draws some of the Freddy's characters, even though he's never seen them before!
- Oswald is a fan of monster movies. I mean, who isn't?

THE WEEK BEFORE

The first choice you need to make is whether you even want to go to Jeff's Pizza at all. If you do, you will visit Jeff's for a week, eating pizza and drinking soda, before deciding whether or not to try out the ball pit. Assuming you, like Oswald, go for it, you'll find yourself back in the Freddy Fazbear's Pizza restaurant of 1985.

DAY 1

Freddy's is fun! And you even meet two potential new friends, Chip and Mike. There's a Yellow Rabbit animatronic in the corner. It's a bit strange. Should you take a closer look? Assuming you choose wisely, you make it back to your dad, and actually get on with him for once.

DAY 2

Back through the ball pit to Freddy's and that Yellow Rabbit is still there. To ignore or not to ignore? That truly is the question. Another question is what you'll choose as a prize after doing well in a game of Skee-Ball (aka Pizzaroller) with your new pals: a Freddy toy, a flashlight, or a pair of yellow bunny ears. Choose wisely.

DAY 3

Back at Freddy's but the Yellow Rabbit is acting differently this time. Eek—it's not a nice rabbit! People flee in terror, but what will you do? You might be tempted to hop back into the ball pit, and I wouldn't blame you. But you may be brave, in which case you could follow that rabbit and find out what it's up to . . .

Assuming you survive for long enough, you will discover the Yellow Rabbit's terrible secret—murdered children in the storage room at the back of the restaurant. Yikes! Now's definitely the time to escape. What took you so long?

Back in the present day, your decisions have a direct impact on your dad. Or should I say your Yellow Dad? Will you run from Yellow Dad, or go home with him?

RETURN TO THE PIT 29

- YOU ARE KIND OF MESMERIZED BY IT, EVEN THOUGH YOU KNOW IT CAN'T BE STARING RIGHT AT YOU. IF YOU DECIDE YOU NEED TO GO OVER AND CHECK IT OUT, TURN TO PAGE 36.
- IF YOU IGNORE THE RABBIT AND TURN BACK TO THE GAME, TURN TO PAGE 21.

DAY 4

The Yellow Rabbit has replaced your dad, but nobody else has noticed! As if that's enough pressure on a ten-year-old, it's your first day of middle school. Good times. At least you make a new friend, Gabrielle. She's a fan of the Greek myths, but which one will she tell you?

Later, it's homework time, but you spot the bunny ears and flashlight in your schoolbag. Which one will you take? Assuming you choose correctly, you are on track to save your dad. But first you need to get out of the house without Yellow Dad spotting you.

You made it back to Jeff's. Nice work! Maybe Dad's still in the ball pit? But maybe Yellow Rabbit is right behind you! Time for fight or flight? But what sort of attack should you use to defeat Yellow Rabbit? If you defeat the bunny, you and Dad can finally head home.

- IF YOU RUN FOR IT, TURN TO PAGE 147.
- IF YOU FREEZE IN PLACE, TURN TO PAGE 148.

ALTERNATE DAY 3 OR 4

Instead of accepting that Mom believes Yellow Dad is Dad, you try to convince her. Makes sense. This path will lead to you running out of the house only to meet a man in a car. If you decide to hop in, you'll discover who he is . . . Chip! All grown up. Will you hunt down Yellow Rabbit together? You meet Chip's team, which includes his daughter, Gabrielle. She seems nice. But unfortunately, the leader of the team is none other than . . . dun-dun-dun . . . Yellow Rabbit in disguise! Maybe you should warn everyone? Or maybe just warn Gabrielle?

POTENTIALLY USEFUL ITEMS

Party hat—It's only a bit of silly fun, isn't it?

Freddy action figure—Who wouldn't want one?

Flashlight—Always useful.

Yellow bunny ears—Probably not very useful.

Half a Faz-Coin—What use is half a coin?!

ALTERNATE DAY 1 AND ENDING

Remember when you first got to 1985 Freddy's? You were so excited to make friends with Chip and Mike, you probably didn't even notice the arcade cabinet *8-Bit Escape*. But it's there. If you manage to collect a full Faz-Coin during a walkthrough of the book, you can come back and play the arcade game next time round. Who knows—you might just save five lives, kill one giant bunny, and enjoy a fantastic summer with your dad.

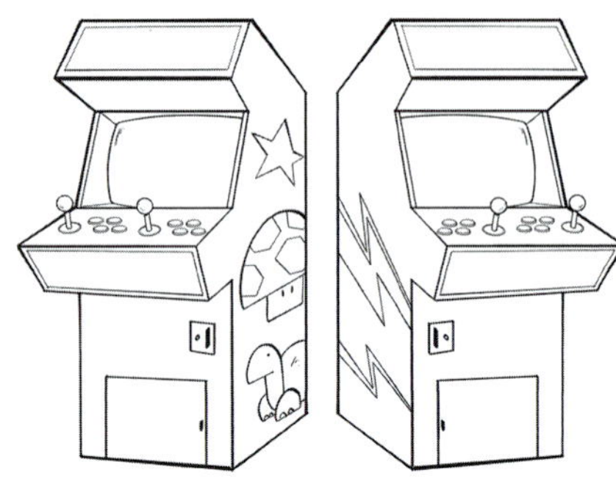
20 FIVE NIGHTS AT FREDDY'S

- THIS IS BEYOND AMAZING. IF YOU THINK YOU ABSOLUTELY NEED TO EXPLORE ALL THIS, TURN TO PAGE 17.
- IT DOESN'T MATTER HOW COOL IT ALL LOOKS, THIS IS ABSOLUTELY FREAKY AND WHO KNOWS WHAT MIGHT HAPPEN IF YOU STEP OUT OF THE BALL PIT. IF YOU NOPE OUT OF THERE AND DIVE BACK INTO THE PIT, TURN TO PAGE 30.

In the *Fazbear Frights* epilogues, an animatronic known as Eleanor wreaks havoc. One of her signature moves is trapping her victims in the ball pit. Sound familiar? To further cement the connection, one of the paths in the book takes Oswald to an alley, where he sees a toy doll with red pigtails, a white face, and a red dress—just like Eleanor. Eleanor also makes an appearance in the *Into the Pit* video game.

Oswald's ball-pit adventure is unique because it has three different FNAF iterations: *Into the Pit*, the original *Fazbear Frights* story and its graphic novel adaptation, *FNAF: Into the Pit*, the video game, and *Return to the Pit*, the interactive novel. It must be a really important story . . .

RETURN TO THE PIT 137

slowly. You jump to your feet. You are so ready to explain and to just get the heck out of there.

In enters the rabbit.

You stumble backward, tripping over your feet. You fall hard onto that cement ground.

The rabbit looms over you and stares down. It raises its hand and ticks its finger back and forth the way you would at a naughty child. Then it opens its mouth wide. And wider. And wider. It unhinges its jaw, revealing rows of razor-sharp teeth. It lunges at you.

GAME OVER
>TO TRY AGAIN TURN TO PAGE 2

ESCAPE THE PIZZAPLEX

What starts as a fun game between friends turns into a five-night fearfest! Gregory invites Cassie to play hide-and-seek with him and Freddy after hours in the Pizzaplex, and Cassie agrees. But the animatronics don't always play nice, and Cassie grows scared. She can never tell if she really has something to fear, or if it's just Gregory playing one of his pranks. But then a new danger surfaces: a Reagent. This bug-eyed bot with a backpack full of toxic chemicals is without a doubt the biggest danger Cassie will face tonight . . .

MEET CASSIE:

Cassie is a friend of Gregory's (the main character in *Security Breach*), and the daughter of a Fazbear technician. In the past, she spent a lot of time in Superstar Daycare while her dad was at work, so she is pretty familiar with the Pizzaplex. She even celebrated her 11th birthday there, though none of her friends showed up—until Roxanne Wolf arrived with Gregory, saving the day. Ever since then, Cassie has idolized Roxy.

COOL CASSIE TRIVIA

- A big fan of Roxy, Cassie likes to wear clothes that match Roxy's colors: purple and green. She even paints her nails to match Roxy's claws!
- Her favorite cake is carrot cake.

NIGHT 01

Gregory's idea of playing hide-and-seek in the deserted Pizzaplex sounds fun. Cassie knows tons of great hiding spots all over the place. But Cassie and Gregory get separated, Cassie can't find Roxy, and Freddy—who is doing the seeking—sounds like he's getting angrier and angrier. Cassie starts to wonder what exactly will Freddy do when he finds her?

NIGHT 02

Night Ø1 didn't go so well, but Cassie joins Gregory in the Pizzaplex after closing time again anyway. This time, it's not Freddy playing hide-and-seek with them but Monty—so let the games begin! Like last night with Freddy, Monty seems . . . different. His eyes look scary and his claws look extra sharp. Gregory swears he knows nothing about it. What in the world is going on? And will Cassie live long enough to find out?

NIGHT 03

After the the last two nights, Cassie doesn't actually want to stay behind at the Pizzaplex. But that choice is taken away when Freddy slams her inside his chest cavity so she can't leave. Eventually, when he lets Cassie out, he tells he that he was protecting her. From what, you might ask? A Reagent, that's what. Yikes! Cassie spends most of Night Ø3 hiding from the Reagent, which is a S.T.A.F.F. Bot that destroys any organic matter in the Pizzaplex overnight. You know, organic matter like pizza crusts and spilled Fizzy Faz. Oh, and also human beings. Double yikes!

NIGHT 04

Grateful to have been rescued from the Reagent, Cassie wakes up the following night in the Pizzaplex—she's been there all day! But where is Gregory? Looking at the security feeds, Cassie sees that the Reagent is occupied cleaning up the Daycare, and then she spots Gregory. He's at the Prize Counter with Freddy, though it looks like they are fighting. Freddy seems to turn on Gregory and Cassie races to help her friend. Will she make it in time to help him?

NIGHT 05

Cassie's been hiding all day, until Roxy comes to apologize for a mean prank she played on Cassie. All is forgiven, and better yet, the Reagent seems to be deactivated—so Cassie breathes a sigh of relief. Until Roxy admits that she's feeling a little . . . off. Uh oh. Has Gregory done something to Roxy's programming? Can Cassie make it to the main computer terminal and fix Roxy's code before it's too late?

POTENTIALLY USEFUL ITEMS

Flashlight—When is a flashlight ever *not* useful?

Bonnie key chain—For stage door access.

Food Service key card—Opens the kitchen doors.

Teethy Chew—In case you get hungry.

Sodaroni—Pepperoni-flavored soda—yum!

Hair clip—Pink and glittery.

A jar of screws and bolts—Quite noisy!

Ice cream scoop—For serving ice cream.

Screwdriver—Handle with care.

Monty's claws—Looking sharp.

Executive Clearance key card—Good for unlocking locked things.

TIMELINE

The fact that there are no human guards at the Pizzaplex suggests that this book takes places sometime after the All Staff Meeting incident mentioned in *Security Breach* when all adult staff were replaced by S.T.A.F.F. Bots—but before Vanessa started as a Pizzaplex security guard.

PIZZAPLEX UPGRADE

Since the events of *Security Breach*, the Pizzaplex has undergone some remodeling. Management has updated the security systems with more keypads and intercoms—you can never be too careful, right?

HIDEY HOLES

In *Security Breach*, we see lots of little hiding spots with sticky notes and signs in them. If you were wondering who made them, we may have our answer: Gregory and Cassie have played many a game of hide-and-seek in these Pizzaplex walls.

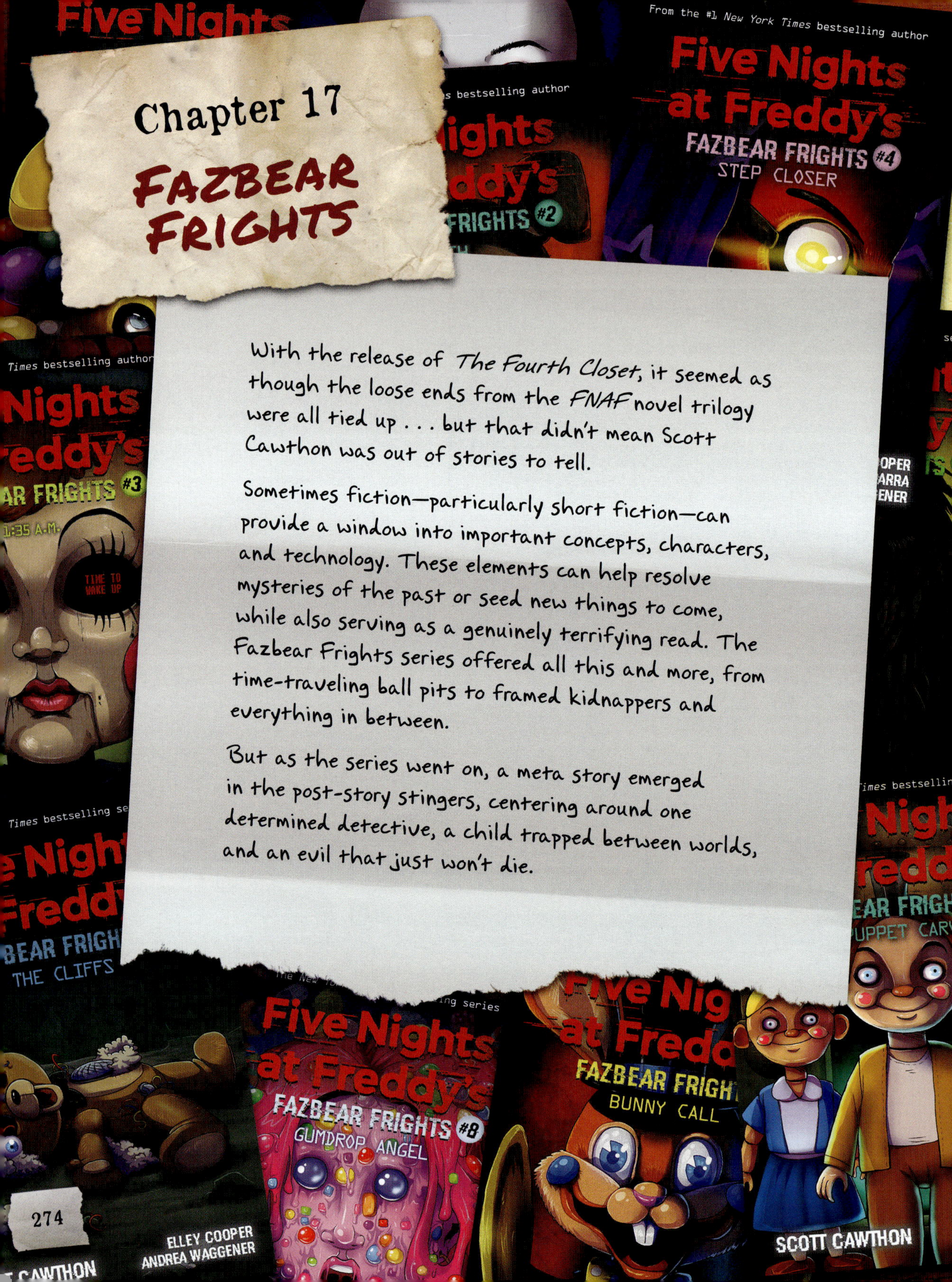

Chapter 17

Fazbear Frights

With the release of *The Fourth Closet*, it seemed as though the loose ends from the *FNAF* novel trilogy were all tied up . . . but that didn't mean Scott Cawthon was out of stories to tell.

Sometimes fiction—particularly short fiction—can provide a window into important concepts, characters, and technology. These elements can help resolve mysteries of the past or seed new things to come, while also serving as a genuinely terrifying read. The Fazbear Frights series offered all this and more, from time-traveling ball pits to framed kidnappers and everything in between.

But as the series went on, a meta story emerged in the post-story stingers, centering around one determined detective, a child trapped between worlds, and an evil that just won't die.

Incident Report • Form 2530973 • *For Official Use Only*

Identities of Involved Persons	Occupation
Oswald	Student
Oswald's Dad	Cashier, Snack Space
Jeff	Owner, Jeff's Pizza
Chip	Student
Mike	Student

Description of Events
Oswald's best friend moved away, and he's having a tough time adjusting, especially as a boring, friendless summer vacation stretches out before him. That all changes when Oswald decides to chuck off his shoes and dive into the old, grody ball pit at Jeff's Pizza. Oswald emerges from the ball pit in Freddy Fazbear's Pizza, circa 1985. There he witnesses something truly horrific . . . and brings something terrible back with him.

Related Elements	Title
Freddy Fazbear's Pizza (remodeled/active): While the Fazbear Frights series features many iterations of Freddy's, this Freddy's is notable for being around in 1985, and for being the site of some of its infamous murders.	Various
Missing Children Incident: During one of his visits to 1985 Freddy's, Oswald follows a yellow rabbit animatronic back into the party room, where he finds six children murdered, still wearing their party hats.	Various
Yellow Rabbit: Oswald sees a man dressed as a yellow rabbit during his visits to 1985 Freddy's, and the rabbit is there when Oswald enters the horrific party room. The rabbit eventually follows him back through the ball pit. Could this be Springtrap, or Spring Bonnie, or something else entirely?	Various
Ball Pit: This isn't the first time something undesirable has been hiding inside a ball pit. In *Pizzeria Simulator*, Molten Freddy sneaks into your pizzeria if you buy the Discounted Ball Pit on Monday.	*Pizzeria Simulator*

New Leads
Time-Traveling Ball Pit: By diving into the pit and staying under for one hundred seconds, Oswald is able to travel back in time. Interestingly, things from the past are also able to switch places with something in the present.

OOPER

Into the Pit: The Game Adaptation

Into the Pit has also been adapted into a video game from Mega Cat Studios, Inc. Originally released to celebrate the 10th anniversary of *Five Nights at Freddy's* in August 2024, the game's 16-bit feel harkens back to the time and place in which *Into the Pit* takes place.

The first night follows the original story relatively closely, with nights four through five expanding the story and giving Oswald tasks like finding his father's belongings in the past.

Into the Pit is not only the first game created from one of the books, it and Sister Location are the only games in the franchise to have exactly five nights.

CHARACTERS

❑ BONNIE

❑ CHICA

❑ CHIP

❑ DAD

❑ DYLAN

❑ FREDDY

❑ MIKE

❑ MOM

❑ MRS. MEECHAM

❑ OSWALD

❑ YELLOW RABBIT

Trophies

There are a lot of Trophies to get to 100% the game!

- **Achievement Not Found:** Get 404 Tickets from arcade machines
- **Arcade Apprentice:** Repair the 10 broken arcade machines in Jeff's Pizza
- **Big Kid/Toddler/Baby:** Trip 5X/10X/100X
- **Chica's Party:** Trigger Chica's Alarm
- **Don't Jinx Yourself/Jinx's Favorite:** Meet your cat, Jinx, in a room 1X/10X
- **Family Fun Night:** Get the three star ending in Creepy or Frightening
- **A Fun Time with Freddy:** Run into Freddy
- **Gimmie Five!:** Collect all 5 of Dad's lost items
- **Good Job, Sport!:** Get the three star ending in Nightmare Mode
- **GOOOAL!:** Kick a plastic ball into the doorframe
- **Hello? Hello? Hello?:** Answer the Phone
- **Hide-n-Seek World Champ:** Successfully hide in every hiding spot while being chased
- **Honk honk!:** Honk Freddy's Nose
- **I Hear You:** Maximize the Noise Meter
- **Impatient:** Skip dialogue 100X
- **Insert Coin to Play:** Play An Arcade Game
- **Into the Pit:** Jump into the Ball Pit
- **It's Me:** Hide in the Golden Freddy Suit
- **Jeff?:** Complete the game with all of Dad's items and the Mysterious/Strange Photo
- **Let there be light!/The Light of '87:** Flick a light switch 10X/87X
- **Looking to the Future:** Unlock all Trophies
- **A Master of Stealth:** Complete the game without getting caught
- **Night Rider:** Beat the game in Nightmare Mode
- **Night Vision:** Beat the game without using the flashlight. (The intro doesn't count.)

- **Not a Gamer:** Complete All Arcade Games
- **Pit-y-Party:** Achieve 1-star ending in either creepy or frightening mode
- **Rock and Roll, Bonnie:** Get caught by Bonnie
- **See Ya Dad:** Leave Dad Behind
- **Social Butterfly:** Interact with NPCs 100X. Can be the same one.
- **Sugar Rush:** Get 10 gumballs out of the machine
- **Terrorformer:** Achieve any ending in Terrifying Mode
- **What Am I?:** When fighting off The Creature, don't not fight back when it attacks you. Let the timer tick down.
- **Who Are They?:** Go into the Party Room after collecting all 5 of Dad's items—gives you the Mysterious/Strange Photo
- **Who You Gonna Call?:** Call 911

THE ENDINGS

- **See Ya, Dad ending:** play the game on any difficulty, leave Dad behind.
- **1-Star Ending:** play the game on normal—don't collect any of Dad's belongings, and survive the Quick Time Events at the end.
- **2-Star Ending:** Collect of of Dad's lost items and the Strange Photo in the Party Room. When attacked by Yellow Rabbit at the end, do not ignore the Quick-Time Event and Yellow Rabbit bite onto your arm.
- **3-Star Ending:** Collect all of Dad's lost items and the picture in the Party Room, repair all the Arcade Cabinets in the present-day pizzeria and play them all once, get all three stickers from the Prize Machine, and play the three secret minigames. You'll have to count the ways to fetch these beautiful minigames.
- **What Am I? Ending:** Fail the quick-time events at the end of Night 5, and see what Oswald becomes!

To Be Beautiful

Incident Report • Form 2530973 • *For Official Use Only*

Identities of Involved Persons	Occupation
Sarah	Student
Abby	Student
Lydia	Student
Mason Blair	Student
Sarah's Mom	Social Worker

Description of Events

If only Sarah were beautiful, her life would be easy: she'd be popular, she'd have cool friends, and she could date her crush. Passing a junkyard on her way home from school, Sarah finds Eleanor, a beautiful animatronic. For saving her, Eleanor says she'll grant Sarah any wish; Sarah wishes to be beautiful. Each night, Eleanor sings to her, and each morning Sarah wakes up a little more beautiful. But is Sarah truly becoming prettier, or is her appearance hiding a monstrous secret?

Related Elements	Title
Illusion Discs: Eleanor gives Sarah a special necklace and tells her to never ever take it off. The end of the story reveals that this pendant seems to function similar to the illusion discs seen elsewhere in the canon.	*The Twisted Ones, The Fourth Closet*
Junkyard Animatronics: Sarah finds Eleanor in a junkyard, where we've seen many animatronics dumped throughout *FNAF* books and games.	*The Fourth Closet, Pizzeria Simulator*

New Leads

Eleanor: She seems to be a new animatronic, albeit with a familiar design. Her description and portrait closely matches that of Circus Baby, and her name, Eleanor, is oddly similar to Afton's daughter's name, Elizabeth.

Incident Report • Form 2530973 • *For Official Use O*

Identities of Involved Persons	Occupation
Millie Fitzsimmons	Student
Dylan	Student
Millie's Grandfather	Retired

Description of Events
It seems like no one wants Millie around. Her parents abandoned her to live with her grandfather in his museum-like house of antiques and oddities. No one at school knows or cares that she exists. Millie spends most of her life romanticizing death, an end to her torment. But when Millie has the chance to get her wish, trapped inside the belly of an animatronic, why isn't she thrilled to die?

Related Elements	Title
Funtime Freddy: The animatronic Millie finds herself trapped in appears to be a Funtime Freddy, based on the description and large storage compartment in its belly.	*Sister Location*
Eaten Alive: Readers of *The Twisted Ones* graphic novel may recognize the similar illustration for this story.	*The Twisted Ones Graphic Novel*

New Leads
The Animatronics' Fate: We've seen several stories in which old animatronics are found in junkyards or abandoned in old pizzeria locations, but this is the first time we've seen an animatronic find its way into the hands of a random collector. It certainly won't be the last time, though.

Fetch

Incident Report • Form 2530973 • *For Official Use Only*

Identities of Involved Persons	Occupation
Greg	Student
Hadi	Student
Cyril	Student
Kimberly Bergstrom	Student
Uncle Dare (Darrin)	Inventor

Description of Events
Greg has become engrossed with the impact that thought and intention can have on random, real-world events. So one night, when he feels drawn to the old, run-down pizzeria in town, he doesn't hesitate before breaking in with his best friends. At the dusty prize counter, Greg finds a robotic dog called Fetch, the ultimate retrieval machine. Greg activates the animatronic but doesn't think much of it . . . until he starts getting strange texts from an unknown sender, and the answers to his darkest wishes.

Related Elements	Title
Freddy Fazbear's Pizza (abandoned): Greg finds Fetch at the prize counter of an abandoned Freddy Fazbear's Pizza. Though the place is dusty, it's largely intact. Cyril researches the location and the franchise on an online forum for people who explore abandoned places.	Various

New Leads
Fetch: This animatronic dog is designed to sync up with your phone in order to retrieve information and other things for you.
Animatronics Interacting with New Tech: From the story, it seems that the pizzeria has been closed for ten years or more. Fetch has been seemingly locked inside the pizzeria for just as long, but he's able to interact with Greg's smartphone. Could this point to the advanced technology of the robotics, or something else?
Random Event Generators (REGs): REGs are machines meant to generate a random response. Scientists designed them to test the power that a person's thought or intention might have over a random outcome. Greg is fascinated by this science, but as Kimberly points out, he's tangling with forces much larger than himself.

Incident Report • Form 2530973 • *For Official Use Only*

Identities of Involved Persons	Occupation
Alec	Student
Hazel	Student

Description of Events
Everything was great for Alec . . . until his spoiled sister, Hazel, came along. When their parents announce that Hazel is getting a birthday party at Freddy Fazbear's Pizza—the kind of party *he's* always wanted—it's the last straw. Alec is determined to ruin his sister's big day at any cost. While scoping out the pizzeria, Alec crosses paths with the "Lonely Freddys," a whole fleet of pint-size animatronics designed to hold conversations with lonely kids. Something about the Lonely Freddys feels creepy, but Alec has bigger priorities, especially when he hears his sister has a shot at winning a prized Yarg Foxy plush.

Related Elements	Title
Freddy Fazbear's Pizza (active): Hazel's birthday party is held at Freddy Fazbear's Pizza.	Various
Remnant: The soul-swapping abilities of the Lonely Freddy animatronics seem to imply some sort of Remnant-capturing technology, though how it works is unknown.	*Pizzeria Simulator, The Fourth Closet, Special Delivery*

New Leads
Lonely Freddy: A series of animatronics deployed at Freddy Fazbear's Pizza locations, designed to keep lonely kids company. In reality, these animatronics seemingly steal the souls of children.
Yarg Foxy: A variation of the Foxy animatronic, and a favorite of Alec and Hazel. The plush toy for Yarg Foxy is rare and can seemingly only be won by catching a prized Yarg Foxy ticket in the Wind Tunnel game.

OUT OF STOCK

530973 • *For Official Use Only*

Identities of Involved Persons	Occupation
Oscar Avila	Student
Raj	Student
Isaac	Student

Description of Events
Oscar and his friends have been eagerly awaiting the release of the hottest new Freddy Fazbear toy, the Plushtrap Chaser. The friends pool their money and head to the store on release day, only to find out that the toy is sold out . . . although, not completely. One Plushtrap Chaser remains, though it looks a little too lifelike, and it's in a mangled box. Oscar is sick of missing out, so he slaps some money on the counter, grabs the toy, and runs. But is Oscar really bringing home the hottest new toy, or is he about to unwrap a nightmare?

Related Elements	Title
Plushtrap: The Plushtrap Chaser follows similar rules to the Plushtrap featured in *FNAF4*, in that it moves in the dark and freezes in the light.	*FNAF4*, *Help Wanted*

New Leads
Plushtrap Chaser: The Plushtrap Chaser is an animatronic toy that moves in the dark and freezes in the light. Oscar notes that Plushtrap is his favorite character from the Freddy Fazbear world, implying that Plushtrap is part of the Freddy Fazbear character canon, something that Fazbear Entertainment is marketing and profiting from, not trying to cover up.
Plushtrap Chaser: While Freddy-themed merchandise is available in the prize counter of Freddy's locations, this is the first time in the canon we've seen Freddy merch in an independent toy store.

1:35 A.M.

Incident Report • Form 2530973 • F

Identities of Involved Persons	Occupation
Delilah	Waitress
Nate	Diner Owner
Harper	Actor

Description of Events
Delilah is a down-on-her-luck waitress, recently divorced and struggling to get by. While browsing a garage sale, she comes across Ella, an elaborate "helper doll" animatronic whose only working function is as an alarm clock. Delilah purchases Ella to help with her chronic lateness at work, and even sets the alarm when she gets home, but it doesn't go off. Thinking the doll is broken, Delilah throws Ella away, but Ella has a job to do, and nothing will stop her from doing it.

Related Elements	Title
Ella: The design of Ella and some of her functions (serve drinks) seem to match the doll Henry created for Charlie in the novel series, though this Ella does seem to have more features and appears to have been mass-produced.	*The Silver Eyes, The Twisted Ones, The Fourth Closet*
Fazbear Entertainment: This is noted as the company that produced Ella, though Delilah says she's never heard of it.	Various

New Leads
Ella: She is an animatronic "helper doll" that can perform an exhaustive list of tasks, such as keep time, serve as an alarm clock, manage appointments, keep track of lists, take photos, read stories, sing songs, serve drinks, test the pH levels in water, and even do personality assessments based on a preprogrammed list of two hundred questions.

ROOM FOR ONE MORE

Incident Report • Form 2530973 • *For Official Use Only*

Identities of Involved Persons	Occupation
Stanley	Night Guard
Melissa	Courthouse Worker

Description of Events

Still reeling from a breakup with his long-term girlfriend, Stanley is feeling lonelier than ever. It doesn't help that Stanley works as the only night guard at an isolated, underground facility. Most nights, Stanley just falls asleep at his desk from sheer boredom. But that all changes when an alarm goes off in one of the vents, and a strange ballerina doll appears on his desk. The doll is whispering that it wants to go home with him . . .

Related Elements	Title
Minireenas: The dolls that made their first appearance in *Sister Location* appear here on Stanley's desk. The dolls speak with him and find a way to go home with Stanley each night.	*Sister Location, Ultimate Custom Night, Help Wanted*
Secretive Underground Facility: Stanley doesn't know the name of his employer, but the deep underground facility, cramped office, and vent monitors seem similar to the setting of *Sister Location*—Circus Baby's Entertainment and Rental.	*Sister Location, Help Wanted*

New Leads

Make Sure Nothing Gets Out: When you play as a *FNAF* security guard, your general mission is to ensure nothing gets into the office. This story seems to follow a thread similar to *Sister Location*, in which the animatronics are looking to escape.

Incident Report • Form 2530973

THE NEW KID

Identities of Involved Persons	
Devon Blaine Marks	**Occupation**
Mick Callahan	Student
Kelsey	Student
Heather	Student
	Student

Description of Events
Devon isn't the most popular kid in school, but he doesn't mind, so long as he can get his crush, Heather, to notice him. That all changes when Kelsey moves to town. The new kid is handsome and popular, and he even catches Heather's eye. Jealous, Devon invites Kelsey to an abandoned pizzeria out in the woods where an old animatronic costume—and revenge—waits.

Related Elements	Title
Golden Freddy Springlock Suit: The old pizzeria contains a Golden Freddy springlock suit that still functions. Kelsey notes that he's heard of more recent mascot costumes that are high-tech, allowing you to speak in the voice of the character. It is later noted that the animatronic does contain a dead body with curly black hair.	*FNAF4*
Freddy Fazbear's Pizza (abandoned): The old pizzeria is a bit moldy but largely intact, with most of its animatronics and furniture still inside.	Various

New Leads
Kelsey: There's something not right about Kelsey. He survives being trapped inside the springlock suit, and seems to entrap multiple kids to similar fates. So who is he . . . and what does he want?

t • Form 2530973 • *For Official Use Only*

Identities of Involved Persons	Occupation
Pete Dinglewood	Student
Chuck Dinglewood	Student

Description of Events
Pete was already having a hard enough time coping with his parents' divorce, but being saddled with his younger brother, Chuck, has made things even worse. While babysitting Chuck at Freddy Fazbear's Pizza, Pete decides to play a prank on his younger brother. He takes him to the out-of-service Pirate Cove stage and activates Foxy. Chuck runs off, but Pete is suddenly entranced by the animatronic, which seems stuck on the same lyric: "You can be a pirate, but first you'll have to lose an eye and an arm! Yarg!" If only Pete knew how true those words would turn out to be . . .

Related Elements	Title
Freddy Fazbear's Pizza (active): This location seems to be fairly active, with the usual out-of-service Pirate Cove.	Various
Foxy: Pete experiences an eerie feeling while watching the animatronic run through its performance, which seems to be due to the curse being placed. Chuck later returns to the animatronic for revenge, but feels nothing.	Various

New Leads
Curse: Pete's actions lead him to fall prey to a nasty curse, one that will stop at nothing to take his eye and arm. This is the first time such a curse has been noted in the canon.

DANCE WITH ME

Incid... ...fficial Use Only

Identities of Involved Persons	Occupation
Kasey	Thief
Jack	Thief
AJ	Thief

Description of Events
Since her mom's boyfriend kicked her out, Kasey has had to fight to survive. When she discovered that stealing could get her much further, much faster than minimum wage, Kasey fell in with Jack and AJ, with whom she now steals for a living. But one night, Kasey steals from a family outside Circus Baby's Pizza World. The score isn't much, but it includes an interesting set of novelty glasses that show an animatronic ballerina dancing, slowly getting closer and closer . . .

Related Elements	Title
Ballora: Ballora seems to appear only when the novelty glasses are worn, but some of Kasey's later interactions demonstrate that Ballora is physically present, regardless of whether the glasses are worn.	*Sister Location, Ultimate Custom Night*
Circus Baby's Pizza World: Kasey robs a family as they're leaving the pizzeria. The children can be overheard talking about some of the notable animatronics, including Circus Baby and Ballora.	*Sister Location, Help Wanted*

New Leads
Novelty Glasses: A pair of cardboard glasses with flimsy plastic lenses. A small slip of paper that comes with the glasses reads, "Put on the glasses, and Ballora will dance for you." When worn, the glasses make Kasey dizzy, and she's able to see Ballora dancing in the distance. No one else can see the animatronic, except Kasey and the girl she stole the glasses from.

Incident Report • Form 25309

For Official Use Only

Identities of Involved Persons	Occupation
Susie	Child
Samantha	Student
Patricia	Knitter

Description of Events

In a horrific tragedy, Susie was murdered at Freddy Fazbear's Pizza, and her family is still in the throes of grief. Susie has been trying to communicate with her sister for some time now, but no matter how hard she tries, Samantha isn't getting her messages. Susie's time with her family is almost up, but she's determined to show her mom and sister that she loves them, one last time.

Related Elements	Title
Missing Children Incident: The story explains that Susie was taken at Freddy Fazbear's Pizza, and her body was never recovered.	Various
Chica: Susie is shown here to be possessing the Chica animatronic.	Various

New Leads

Susie: She is noted as one of the missing children in both *The Fourth Closet* and on a tombstone in the secret ending of *Pizzeria Simulator*, but this is the first time fans have gotten to see a story dedicated to her and the aftermath of her disappearance.

Bunny Call

Incident Report • Form 2530973 • *For Official Use Only*

Identities of Involved Persons	
Bob Mackenzie	**Occupation**
Wanda Mackenzie	Unknown
Tyler Mackenzie	Unknown
Aaron Mackenzie	Student
Cindy Mackenzie	Student
	Child

Description of Events
Bob is an overworked, underappreciated dad who wishes he could catch a break. His family has dragged him to a summer vacation at Camp Etenia, which seems guaranteed to be the opposite of the restful break he so desperately needs. After a lengthy car ride and fraught check-in, Bob is told about the "Bunny Call," a traditional camp prank he can play on his family. Eager for some revenge, Bob quickly signs up, but he might later regret inviting the creepy Ralpho rabbit into their cabin . . .

Related Elements	Title
Survive 'Til 6:00 a.m.: Ralpho may be a new animatronic, but the desperate defense Bob mounts until 6:00 a.m. will feel familiar to longtime *FNAF* players.	Various

New Leads
Ralpho: A massive rabbit suit worn by staff at Camp Etenia for conducting "Bunny Calls"—terrible prank wake-up calls with crashing symbols, loud screaming, and head spinning—that take place between 5:00 a.m. and 6:00 a.m.
How'd That Get Here?: A summer camp is certainly one of the more out-of-the-way places to find an animatronic, and it should be noted that no one in the story mentions Ralpho being affiliated with Fazbear Entertainment. The character's origins thus remain a mystery.

t • Form 2530973 • *For Official Use Only*

Identities of Involved Persons	Occupation
Matt	Game Developer
Jason	Call Center Representative
Gene	Unemployed

Description of Events
Matt is a game developer working on a new VR game for the popular *FNAF* series called *Springtrap's Revenge*. Matt redirects all the anger of his divorce and general dissatisfaction with life into the game, a maze in which players must avoid Springtrap. But when Matt hops in to quickly playtest the game, he's frustrated by the difficulty of the Springtrap AI. In a fit of rage, Matt programs the AI to torture itself to the point of corruption.

Related Elements	Title
***FNAF* (game):** The game series of *FNAF* was mentioned in the introductory sequence of *Help Wanted*. Though Fazbear Entertainment initially claimed to be suing the developer, it was later revealed via Tape Girl that they were working with him.	*Help Wanted*
Springtrap/Glitchtrap: While it's unclear if the Springtrap seen here is related to Glitchtrap, many similar elements are present. This Springtrap is born of corrupted programming that makes its way into the real world by merging with a game developer.	*Help Wanted, The Curse of Dreadbear*

New Leads
Another VR Company?: Matt works for a VR game developer that was clearly in partnership with the indie developer of the in-world version of *FNAF*. So, what relationship—if any—does Matt's company have to Jeremiah's company from "The Prankster" or Tape Girl's company from *Help Wanted*?

Incident Report • Form 2530973 • *For Official Use Only*

Identities of Involved Persons	Occupation
Arthur Blythe	Priest
The Patient	Unknown
Mia Fremont	Nurse
Nurse Ackerman	Head Nurse
Nurse Colton	Nurse
Nurse Thomas	Nurse

Description of Events
Father Blythe is called to Room 1280 of Heracles Hospital to visit a patient in a dire state. The patient is horrifically burned, his organs exposed in places, and he is largely unable to communicate. The nurses who tend to him have noted that there are two distinct electromagnetic signals in his brain. They take this to mean that there are two souls inside him, tormenting each other—it's the definition of evil. Father Blythe feels the nurses are biased against the man due to his gruesome appearance, so he sets out to help him. But the best-laid plans often have unintended consequences.

Related Elements	Title
The Stitchwraith: While several Fazbear Frights stories tie in to the series' larger meta story, "The Man in Room 1280" leads directly into the meta story—and the return of Afton.	Stitchwraith Stingers
William Afton: The events of the story seem to indicate that the man in Room 1280 is William Afton. This is backed up by the man's injuries (matching the ending of *Pizzeria Simulator*), the fact that he seems to be unkillable, the supernatural events that surround him, and the events of the stingers that follow the story.	Various

New Leads
Shadow Child: Throughout the story, various characters report seeing a little boy with curly black hair and a feral smile wearing an alligator mask. The boy is believed by many to be a ghost and possesses some supernatural powers.

BLACKBIRD

Incident Report • Form 2530973 • *For Official Use Only*

Identities of Involved Persons	Occupation
Nole Markman	College Student
Sam O'Neil	College Student
Amber	College Student
Christine Wilbur	College Student

Description of Events
Nole and Sam are working on a short horror film for their filmography class when they decide to make a monster movie about a creepy animatronic-inspired creature called the Blackbird. They decide the Blackbird will punish guilty people, forcing them to admit to their past transgressions. But in talking about the Blackbird, Nole admits to having done some bullying in high school, which upsets Sam, who was himself the target of bullying. Nole doesn't see what the big deal is, but the Blackbird does.

Related Elements	Title
Freddy Fazbear's Pizza (past): Nole and Sam talk about how the characters at Freddy's used to freak them out as children.	Various

New Leads
The Blackbird: Nole is haunted by the Blackbird until he atones for the bullying he did. But when the haunting is over, Nole notes that Sam and the costume's location were accounted for during that time period, so what exactly was pursuing Nole?

The Real Jake

Incident Report • Form 2530973 • *For Official Use Only*

Identities of Involved Persons	Occupation
Jake	Student
Evan	Soldier
Margie	Caretaker
Michael	Unknown

Description of Events
Nine-year-old Jake is growing weaker by the day, losing his battle with a rare brain tumor. His father, Evan, is with the military, stationed overseas, but he's left Jake in the care of Margie. Each night, Margie and Evan use a walkie-talkie to make it sound like a secret friend lives in the cupboard by Jake's bed. This friend, "Simon," asks Jake to pretend he isn't sick, and asks what his day was like—all the things he would've done if he had no limitations. When Jake is well enough, the idea is that he'll get out of bed, open the cabinet, and find a doll, the perfect replica of "The Real Jake"—one with baseball game tickets and grass stains on his knees, mementos of all the things he would've done. But will such a day ever arrive for Jake?

Related Elements	Title
Michael: Some fans have called attention to the use of the name "Michael" for Jake's uncle, particularly around the fact that he's wealthy and is said to act "robotic." Could this be a reference to Michael Afton?	*Sister Location*

New Leads
The Real Jake Doll: The idea of a powerful spirit inhabiting something other than an animatronic is somewhat new for the canon.
The Stitchwraith: This story is highly significant to the meta story being told in the stingers, and the true identity of the Stitchwraith (see page 310).

HIDE-AND-SEEK

Incident Report • Form 2530973 • *For Official Use Only*

Identities of Involved Persons	Occupation
Toby	Student/Worker, Freddy Fazbear's Pizza and Games
Connor	Unknown
Tabitha	Student
Dan	Manager, Freddy Fazbear's Pizza and Games

Description of Events
Toby is sick of being in constant competition with Connor, his perfect older brother. Not only did Connor once work the same job as Toby at Freddy Fazbear's Pizza and Games, he also holds the high score on every game in the pizzeria. Fortunately, that is about to change: the pizzeria is installing a new game, called Hide-and-Seek. Toby is determined to get the high score and show his brother who's really the best, no matter the cost.

Related Elements	Title
Freddy Fazbear's Pizza and Games (active): Though named slightly different from other Freddy's locations, this restaurant and arcade seems to function the same.	Various
RWQFSFASXC (Shadow Bonnie): After destroying the game in a fit of anger, Shadow Bonnie attaches itself to Toby. Toby is able to see the animatronic behind him when he looks in the mirror, though no one else can.	*FNAF2, FNAF3, Ultimate Custom Night, Special Delivery*

New Leads
Hide-and-Seek Game: A new game/attraction that's set up in its own room. A Shadow Bonnie cutout travels on a track and is able to hide in one of three locations at each stop (the stops are painted to look like various parts of a town, including a police station, pizzeria, etc.). Players have three tries in three minutes to guess where Shadow Bonnie is hiding.

Incident Report • Form 2530973 • *For Official Use Only*

Identities of Involved Persons	Occupation
Robert Stanton	Graphic Designer
Tyler Stanton	Child
Jess	Copy Editor

Description of Events
Ever since his wife died in childbirth, Robert has been struggling to survive. Putting aside his insurmountable grief, Robert has devoted his life to raising their son, Tyler, a two-year-old ball of energy. Robert never stops worrying about his son and if he's doing a good enough job raising him, but some burden is lifted when his son picks out a new Tag-Along Freddy toy at the store. The toy purports to watch your child and send you live updates via a wristwatch that comes with the toy. Robert sees it as a win-win: Tyler gets a new playmate, and Robert gets some peace of mind. But when Tyler vanishes, Robert wonders if the toy was really "a kid's and parents' best pal" or something far more sinister.

Related Elements	Title
Fredbear Plush/Monitor: Fans will recall a similar, albeit different Fredbear plush that monitored another child—the bite victim from *FNAF4*.	*FNAF4*, *Sister Location*
Merch: This is the second instance of a mass-produced toy being available outside of a Freddy's location (the first being the Plushtrap Chaser).	"Out of Stock"

New Leads
Tag-Along Freddy: A Freddy Fazbear plush toy that monitors children and sends a live update to a matching Tag-Along Time Wristwatch. The updates can get quite specific, even noting activities like finger painting, nap times, and meals.

THE BREAKING WHEEL

Incident Report • Form 2530973 • *For Official Use Only*

Identities of Involved Persons	Occupation
Reed	Student
Julius	Student
Shelly Girard	Student
Pickle Girard	Student
Ory Girard	Student

Description of Events
Reed is tired of being bullied by Julius, a jock who's always had it in for Reed. While Reed is struggling through their robotics class with his action-figure-size endoskeleton, Julius has managed to create what he calls an "exosuit"—a life-size exoskeleton that can make him stronger and faster. After class one day, while wearing the suit, Julius threatens Reed yet again. But then Julius's exosuit malfunctions, and Reed locks the bully inside it. Reed sees this as Julius's just rewards and leaves him in the classroom, thinking he'll let him out in the morning. But is the exosuit really broken? Or is it just responding to a different set of commands?

Related Elements	Title
Robotics Class: Several Fazbear Frights short stories take place in classrooms, including some specifically dedicated to robotics. In these settings, animatronics provide an interesting avenue to study the field.	"Together Forever"

New Leads
Exosuit: For his class project, Julius creates an "exosuit"—a metal exoskeleton that a person can strap into and use to lift heavy objects, run faster, etc. It's pointed out in class that Julian's project uses the same frequency as Pickle's robot, making it follow any input from Pickle's remote.
IR and RF Remotes: Remotes that can control robots from afar. IR (infrared) remotes have a shorter range, and must be pointed directly at a receiver to transmit. RF (radio frequency) remotes have a much longer range, with a signal that can penetrate doors, windows, walls, etc. Pickle's remote uses an extender to further the range of his remote.

He Told Me Everything

Incident Report • Form 2530973 • *For Official Use Only*

Identities of Involved Persons	Occupation
Chris Watson	Student
Dr. Little	High School Teacher

Description of Events
Chris is anxious to start high school, wanting to leave behind his working-class family and immature friends to make a better life for himself as a scientist. But the first step to becoming a scientist is acing Dr. Little's freshman science class and joining the exclusive Science Club, reserved for only the best and brightest. On the first day of class, Dr. Little announces the annual lock-in experiment, which is worth 500 points of extra credit and is all but required for those looking to join the Science Club. The lock-in seems like a life-changing experience, and Chris is all too eager to get in on the action.

Related Elements	Title
Biology-Altering Substances: The Fazbear Frights series contains several references to mystery substances, such as Faz-Goo, the Gumdrop Nose, and Sea Bonnies. These items, all produced by Fazbear Entertainment, seem to alter the biology of the people they come into contact with.	"Gumdrop Angel," "Sea Bonnies"

New Leads
Freddy Fazbear Mad Scientist Kit: A mass-produced "toy" science kit containing Faz-Goo. Interestingly, Dr. Little assures the class it is "most definitely not a toy, and if you treat it as one, it will be at your own peril."
Faz-Goo: A gooey pink substance seemingly capable of cloning when provided with DNA (such as a tooth) and a supply of living red blood cells. Organs seemed to be sucked out of the host's body until all that remains of the host is goo.
Dr. Little: He seems to know what the Faz-Goo does, and encourages its use among his students, so is he part of some larger conspiracy?

GUMDROP ANGEL

Incident Report • Form 2530973 • *For Official Use Only*

Identities of Involved Persons	Occupation
Angel	Student
Ophelia	Student
Dominic	Assistant Manager, Freddy Fazbear's Pizza

Description of Events
Angel is one month away from graduation, and it can't come fast enough. Ever since her mom married her new stepdad, Angel's life has been taken over by Ophelia, her spoiled younger stepsister. At Freddy Fazbear's Pizza, during Ophelia's extravagant birthday party, Ophelia is gifted with a Birthday Gummy, a life-size molded gummy treat. Angel is both mesmerized and disturbed by the gummy, especially after it starts to move on its own . . .

Related Elements	Title
Freddy Fazbear's Pizza (active): Ophelia has an extravagant birthday party at Freddy Fazbear's Pizza.	Various
Biology-Altering Substances: As noted, several Fazbear Frights stories are focused around biology-altering substances, including the Gumdrop Nose, Faz-Goo, and Sea Bonnies.	"He Told Me Everything," "Sea Bonnies"

New Leads
Birthday Gummy: A living gummy candy unlike any other. The treat is created when a person consumes the Gumdrop Nose, which changes the consumer's DNA into a gummy substance. Freddy Fazbear's Pizza offers them as a grand finale treat at birthday parties.
Complicit Fazbear Entertainment Employee: Dominic is noted to be the assistant manager at Freddy Fazbear's Pizza, and he seems to be fully aware of what's happening to Angel. While most Freddy's employees are unaware of the nefarious things that often happen at the pizzeria, Dominic seems fully complicit, if remorseful.

Sergio's Lucky Day

Incident Report • Form 2530973 • *For Official Use Only*

Identities of Involved Persons	Occupation
Sergio	Project Manager, Architectural Firm
Dale	Senior Manager, Architectural Firm
Sophia Manchester	Unknown

Description of Events

Sergio is feeling pretty out of luck. The new promotion he received is too much work for too little pay, his SUV dies on the way home from the job, and he's stuck trudging through downtown in the rain looking for a phone . . . which is when he finds Lucky Boy. Lucky Boy is a small figurine who wants to make big changes in Sergio's life. But the more Sergio listens to Lucky Boy, the more he realizes he needs to take a more hands-on approach to happiness . . . even if it means taking a hacksaw to his life.

Related Elements	Title
Balloon Boy: The Lucky Boy figurine bears resemblance to Balloon Boy and similar animatronics and even laughs in the same manner.	Various
Illusion Discs?: Sergio becomes more entranced by Lucky Boy—and more detached from reality—as the story goes on, even altering his body by himself. It's unclear if Lucky Boy contains some form of illusion technology, as seen in "To Be Beautiful," but others notice Sergio's at-home plastic surgery only after he leaves Lucky Boy in the hall.	*The Twisted Ones*, *The Fourth Closet*, "To Be Beautiful"

New Leads

Lucky Boy: A small electronic figurine, bearing some resemblance to Balloon Boy, except the sign in his hand reads I'M A LUCKY BOY. Sergio finds the toy on the street. Lucky Boy gives Sergio vague advice on how he can change his life for the better, mainly by following his desires, no matter the consequences.

WHAT WE FOUND

530973 • *For Official Use Only*

Identities of Involved Persons	Occupation
Hudson	Security Guard
Barry	Military
Duane	Military

Description of Events
Hudson is grateful when he scores a well-paying job as a security guard at the Fazbear's Fright Horror Attraction in town. But that's about the beginning and end of Hudson's good fortune. Hudson is burdened with a dark past that seems to poison everything he touches in the present, a dark past he'll be forced to confront during his midnight shifts at Fazbear's Fright.

Related Elements	Title
Fazbear's Fright Horror Attraction: A haunted house of sorts, set up to look like an old Freddy Fazbear's Pizza. Real artifacts from the restaurant's history are being brought in to make the attraction feel authentic.	*FNAF3, Help Wanted*
Springtrap: Hudson faces off with Springtrap throughout the night, even noticing that there is a dead body within the animatronic.	*FNAF3, Help Wanted*

New Leads
Hudson: Is Hudson the night guard from *FNAF3*? In general, the events of the story seem to follow the events of *FNAF3* almost to the letter, right down to the ending. Hudson also experiences hallucinations throughout the night while dealing with Springtrap.

Incident Report • Form 2530973 • *For Official Use Only*

Identities of Involved Persons	Occupation
Jack	Owner, Pizza Playground
Porter	Handyman, Inventor
Sage Brantley	Custodian, Writer
Edwin	Cook
Angie	Waitress
Becky	Homemaker
Tyson	Student

Description of Events
Jack is a franchisee of the floundering Pizza Playground, an animatronic pizzeria. He employs Porter as handyman and animatronic technician, Sage as custodian, Edwin as cook, and Angie as waitress. Off the clock, Porter has invented a new machine, the Puppet Carver, that can carve low-cost animatronics for the restaurant out of a simple block of wood, but he hasn't quite worked out all the kinks yet. When a demonstration of the machine fails, Jack fires the staff in a fit of anger, determined to declare bankruptcy. Later that night, Jack hears a ticking coming from inside the machine. He enters the machine, trying to find a way to turn it off, and nearly dies when the machine turns on. But after his near-death experience, he feels like a changed man.

Related Elements	Title
Mediocre Melodies: Pigpatch, or an animatronic much like him (a pig strumming a banjo) appears in Pizza Playground.	*Pizzeria Simulator*

New Leads
New Animatronics: Baron von Bear and an unknown bird animatronic are described in the story, and the bear is even recognized by one of the restaurant's young patrons.
Pizza Playground: An animatronic pizzeria franchise. It is unclear whether this franchise is related to Fazbear Entertainment or if it's a competitor.
The Puppet Carver: Peppered throughout the story are excerpts from Sage's novel, about a wooden puppet's journey to becoming human.

JUMP FOR TICKETS

Incident Report • Form 2530973 • *For Official Use Only*

Identities of Involved Persons	Occupation
Colton	Student
Aidan	Student
Mike	Mechanic
Mr. Harrison	Shop Teacher
Colton's Mom	Nurse

Description of Events
Colton's mom doesn't make enough money to afford the newest gaming console, so Colton decides to earn the console himself by winning tickets at Freddy Fazbear's Pizza. The highest ticket-generating game in the arcade is the Ticket Pulverizer, but the game is rigged to favor little kids. Colton does some research into the game and makes a plan to break into Freddy's after hours to "fix" the Ticket Pulverizer for good.

Related Elements	Title
Freddy Fazbear's Pizza (active): This Freddy's location is an active hub for kids and teens.	Various
Arcade Games: References to other animatronics appear in some of the arcade games mentioned, such as "BB's Ball Drop" and "Dee Dee's Fishing Hole." Dee Dee's game might be a reference to her fishing hole in *FNAF World*.	*FNAF2, FNAF World, Ultimate Custom Night*

New Leads
Coils the Birthday Clown: A clown animatronic with a gaping grin, googly eyes, spiral limbs, and a lanky body dressed in lemon-and-lime-colored stripes. It doesn't speak, but you can hear its jingly bells as it draws near. The animatronic seems to be sentient or to have some sort of child-monitoring capabilities, based on its actions in the story.
Ticket Pulverizer: An arcade game consisting of a sealed, transparent booth where players must jump as hard as they can within the time limit to generate tickets. Players may keep the tickets they catch. The game typically costs four tokens, but one visit is free on birthdays. The voice actor for Coils the Birthday Clown recorded a message that starts the game.

Incident Report • Form 2530973 • *For Official Use Only*

Identities of Involved Persons	Occupation
Payton Thompson	Student
Marley	Student
Abigail	Student
Mrs. Crutchfield	Home Economics Teacher
Payton's Mom	Unknown
Ms. Bryant	Freddy's Factory Manager

Description of Events
Payton has recently befriended Marley, one of the pretty, popular girls in school. Marley can be a bit rebellious, and during a trip to the Freddy Fazbear's Pizza Kit Factory, she urges Payton to break away from the tour group. While separated from the group, Marley seemingly falls into a vat of boiling pizza sauce and doesn't return. Payton is afraid to get in trouble, so she doesn't tell anyone what happened. But her guilt might just eat her alive.

Related Elements	Title
Freddy Fazbear's Pizza (past): Freddy Fazbear's Pizza is referenced as being nostalgic, though active locations aren't mentioned.	Various

New Leads
Freddy Fazbear's Pizza Kits: A popular kit of customizable components for kids to make their own single-serve Freddy Fazbear's pizzas.
Freddy Fazbear's Pizza Kit Factory: The factory where pizza kit components are made and shipped to stores and Freddy's locations. Kids can also tour the facility and make their own pizza kits.

Friendly Face

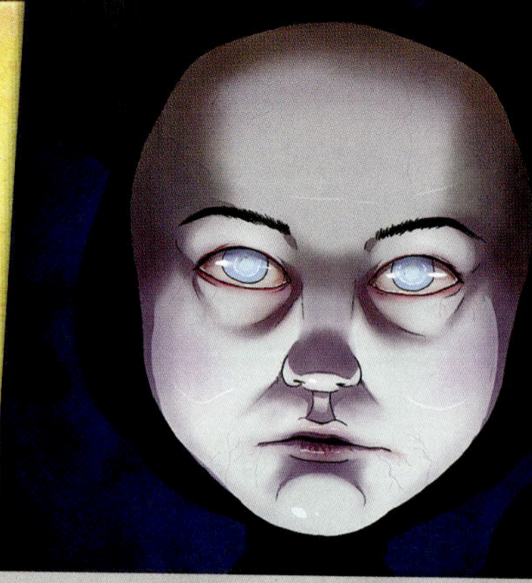

Incident Report • Form 2530973 • *For Official Use Only*

Identities of Involved Persons	Occupation
Edward	Student
Jack Weston	Student
Faraday	Cat
Edward's Mom	Unknown

Description of Events
Edward is a careless young man whose mind always seems to be somewhere else. He and his best friend, Jack, adopt a kitten they name Faraday, who quickly becomes the center of their world. But this happiness is shattered one afternoon when Faraday races out into a busy street, and Jack runs after him without thinking. Both of Edward's best friends are killed in the resulting accident. Drowning in grief, Edward sees a commercial for a new product — Fazbear Friendly Faces, and believes it could be the key to coping with the tragedy.

Related Elements	Title
Fazbear Entertainment: Fazbear Entertainment is mentioned in the commercial for Fazbear Friendly Faces. This seems to be the first time the company is seen marketing something mass-produced, outside of a toy, to an older demographic.	Various

New Leads
Fazbear Friendly Faces: An innovative new product from Fazbear Entertainment that uses a pet's DNA to craft an identical face, which is then integrated onto an animatronic body to create a loyal pet that will follow the consumer around forever.

Incident Report • Form 2530973 • *For Official Use Only*

Identities of Involved Persons	Occupation
Mott	Student
Rory	Student
Fritz	Goldfish
Dr. T (Ron Tabor)	Pediatrician

Description of Events
Mott's younger brother, Rory, wins a package of brand-new Sea Bonnies from the Freddy Fazbear's Pizza prize counter. Ever the dutiful big brother, Mott helps Rory set up the colony of disturbing creatures, but things quickly take a strange turn. The Sea Bonnies first attack Rory's goldfish, Fritz, and then they seemingly become the fish. Worried for his brother's safety, Mott flushes the Sea Bonnies down the toilet . . . but far from ending the nightmare, it seems Mott has simply given the monsters a bigger home.

Related Elements	Title
Freddy Fazbear's Pizza (active): Rory frequents Freddy Fazbear's Pizza, where Mott often babysits him.	Various
Biology-Altering Substances: As noted, several Fazbear Frights stories are focused around biology-altering substances, including the Gumdrop Nose, Faz-Goo, and Sea Bonnies.	"He Told Me Everything," "Gumdrop Angel"
Fritz: Rory's goldfish is named "Fritz," which matches one of the names of the missing children seen on a tombstone of the secret ending of *Pizzeria Simulator* and *The Fourth Closet* novel. They seem unrelated.	*Pizzeria Simulator, The Fourth Closet*

New Leads
Astounding Live Sea Bonnies: A prize at the Freddy Fazbear's Pizza prize counter that allows users to grow and nurture their own healthy colony of happy Sea Bonnies. Sea Bonnies are purplish-blue creatures genetically engineered to look like a cross between sea monkeys and rabbits, guaranteed to live for three years. The prize package contains two packets of Sea Bonnie live eggs, one packet of Sea Bonnie water purification powder, and one packet of Sea Bonnie super-duper growth food.

Incident Report • Form 2530973 • *For Official Use Only*

Identities of Involved Persons	Occupation
Jessica	Student
Brittany	Student
Mindy	Student
Cindy	Student
Mr. Thornton	Robotics Teacher

Description of Events
Sophomore best friends Jessica and Brittany are annoyed when eighth-grade gifted students Cindy and Mindy are invited to join their robotics class. The class is starting up a new assignment—reprogramming old animatronics—and Jessica and Brittany are assigned to Rosie Porkchop, a massive springlock animatronic. As Jessica delves deeper into the assignment, she comes up with a genius plan to put the eighth graders in their place.

Related Elements	Title
Springlock Animatronics: As the girls read Rosie's operating manual, we learn that Rosie is a springlock suit, capable of being switched into a human interface or "suit" mode.	Various
Animatronic Mechanisms: In working on the assignment, we come across several animatronic mechanisms we've heard of before (such as servos), as well as the problems that can plague different aspects of the machinery.	*The Twisted Ones, Help Wanted, Sister Location*
Robotics Class: Several Fazbear Frights short stories take place in classrooms, including some specifically dedicated to robotics. In these settings, animatronics provide an interesting avenue to study the field.	"The Breaking Wheel"

New Leads
Animatronic Remains: At the start of the assignment, Mr. Thornton wheels out a cartful of old animatronics: endoskeletons, aliens, dogs, cats, as well as a cow, horse, orangutan, black panther, flamingo, and pig.
Rosie Porkchop: Rosie is the only life-size animatronic on Mr. Thornton's cart, a massive pig dressed in a frilly dark pink waitress uniform. The pig animatronic is said to be old, with worn felt that can't fully hide its endoskeleton. Rosie is later revealed to be a springlock animatronic, with a tank capable of fitting two people.

Incident Report • Form 2530973 • *For Official Use Only*

Identities of Involved Persons	Occupation
Jeremiah	Game Developer
Hope	Admin, Game Development
Parker	Game Developer
Unnamed Gamemaster	Unknown

Description of Events
Jeremiah, Hope, and Parker work at a small indie game developer that was recently bought out by Fazbear Entertainment. They're developing a Freddy VR game, but company downsizing has delayed the game and forced the three employees to work many late nights. Parker enjoys playing pranks on Jeremiah, some of which cross the line of professionalism. But on Jeremiah's birthday, he's invited to play a sinister game, one that might not be a prank at all.

Related Elements	Title
Secret Tapes: Jeremiah is working for Fazbear Entertainment on a VR game, and his name is misspelled "Jeremy" on his birthday cake. Could he be the "Jeremy" referred to in the secret tapes in *Help Wanted*?	*Help Wanted*
***FNAF* VR:** Matt from "In the Flesh" is also developing a VR game for Fazbear Entertainment.	"In the Flesh"

New Leads
Unnamed Gamemaster: This character's voice is described as sounding deep and electronic, as though it had gone through a filter of some kind.
Meta Story Clues: Some of the puzzle clues, such as "STINGER MOOT" and "EVEN MORE FRIGHTS" may have implications beyond the plot. Careful readers may want to give these scenes a second look.

KIDS AT PLAY

Incident Report • Form 2530973 • *For Official Use Only*

Identities of Involved Persons	Occupation
Joel D'Agostino	Student/Gardener
Steve D'Agostino	Owner, D'Agostino's Nursery and Garden Center
Mrs. D'Agostino	Author of *Knitting Patterns*
Caleb Bell	Student
Chief Montgomery	Police Chief

Description of Events
Joel is set to graduate high school soon, and all he wants is to escape his small town to become a musician and model. His parents are often on his case about working harder, taking life more seriously, and being careful, but Joel finds them uptight and overbearing. One night, Joel is driving recklessly and hits a child. Rather than confront his misdeed, Joel chooses to pretend it never happened. In the days that follow, he is haunted by plastic "Kids at Play" figures, part of a public safety initiative, as he grapples with what to do next.

Related Elements	Title
Fazbear Entertainment: There are a few Freddy's branded things in Joel's world, though a specific Freddy Fazbear's Pizza location isn't mentioned.	Various

New Leads
Kids at Play Figures: These three-foot-tall plastic figures hold a flag that reads KIDS AT PLAY, and are meant to alert drivers to children in the area. The figures seem to be part of a Fazbear Entertainment–sponsored public safety initiative, as Joel finds one in his Fazcrunch cereal box.
Fazbear Fazcrunch Cereal: A Freddy Fazbear–themed cereal that Joel has been eating for a number of years.

FIND PLAYER TWO!

Incident Report • Form 2530973 • *For Official Use Only*

Identities of Involved Persons	Occupation
Aimee	Student
Mary Jo	Student
Emmett Tucker	Unknown
Gretta	Student

Description of Events
Bookish Aimee and outspoken Mary Jo have been best friends since they were small. As eleven-year-olds, they spend most of their time at the local Freddy Fazbear's Pizza, playing in the Hiding Maze, a game that's no longer in active use, but is still playable. One day, a strange man follows the girls into the maze, and Aimee flees the pizzeria. That's the last time she ever sees Mary Jo, but ten years later, Aimee is determined to find out what happened to her friend.

Related Elements	Title
Missing Children Incident: Though Mary Jo's disappearance seems unrelated to the Missing Children Incident, there seems to be a lot of attention on kidnappings at Freddy Fazbear's Pizza locations in the media around this time.	Various
Freddy Fazbear's Pizza (remodeled): This story details the events that preceded the closing of a Freddy's location, and later shows how the building was repurposed.	Various

New Leads
Freddy's Hiding Maze Hide-and-Seek Game: A timed, themed maze game for two players. Player two chooses one of the many cubbyholes throughout the maze to hide in. The cubbyholes are sealed with hatch-like doors. Player one must navigate the rain forest–themed maze to find their companion.
Emmett Tucker: A man arrested for a kidnapping, who was seen by Aimee and Mary Jo at the Freddy Fazbear's Pizza location they frequented.

Incident Report • Form 2530973 • *For Official Use Only*

Identities of Involved Persons	Occupation
Everett Larson	Detective
Jake	N/A
Andrew	N/A
Dr. Phineas Taggart	Scientist
The Agony	N/A
Renelle	Student
Dr. Talbert	Scientist
Eleanor	N/A

Description of Events
Larson: Detective Larson is given the unfortunate task of investigating the "Stitchwraith," a strange case that seems part serial tragedy, part urban legend. A number of strange incidents are tracked in the case file, but all are connected by sightings of animatronics . . . and by a terrifying hooded figure lugging around piles of garbage.
Jake: Years after his death, Jake finds himself possessing an animatronic endoskeleton, which he can control with the help of Andrew, another lost and angry child whose soul is tethered to the animatronic's battery pack. Jake is able to "move on" if he focuses hard enough on a happy memory, but he can't bear the thought of leaving Andrew behind. Plus, Andrew's anger has infected a lot of objects—animatronics, toys, dolls . . . Someone has to destroy them before they hurt someone.

Related Elements	Title
Freddy Fazbear's Pizza: The franchise is mentioned several times, and remnants of the pizzeria (such as a Foxy animatronic) appear.	Various
Missing Children Incident: Larson mentions the "Freddy's murders" and seems aware that William Afton was responsible.	Various
The Fire: The incident shown in *Pizzeria Simulator* and its aftermath are revisited via police evidence . . . It seems that Cassette Man's plan did not work exactly as intended.	*Pizzeria Simulator*
The Puppet: Larson pulls the Puppet from an evidence locker, where evidence from the *Pizzeria Simulator* fire is housed.	Various

Continued on next page (page 1 of 2)

Incident Report • Form 2530973 • *For Official Use Only*

Continued from previous page (page 2 of 2)

Related Elements	Title
William Afton: He makes a terrifying return after the events in "The Man in Room 1280."	"The Man in Room 1280"
Remnant: Experiments on and technology developed around Remnant take center stage in the Stitchwraith story.	Various
Ball Pit: The famous time-traveling ball pit makes a comeback in later stingers.	"Into the Pit"
Eleanor: The animatronic Eleanor makes a reappearance later in the Stitchwraith's story.	"To Be Beautiful"
Witness Reports: Sarah's case is part of the Stitchwraith case file that Larson receives from Chief Monahan.	"To Be Beautiful"
Millie Fitzsimmons: Millie's fate is revealed in the final stinger.	"Count the Ways"
Andrew's Origins: Andrew's spirit possessed the battery pack that powered Fetch.	"Fetch"
REG: Dr. Taggart has an REG and practices visualization and intention-setting, similar to Greg.	"Fetch"
Plushtrap Chaser: The Stitchwraith reclaims the Plushtrap Chaser.	"Out of Stock"
Ella: The Stitchwraith reclaims the Ella doll.	"1:35 A.M."
Step Closer: Larson gains insight into the events of this story, and the Stitchwraith is seen destroying a Foxy animatronic.	"Step Closer"
Blackbird: Larson gains insight into and affects the outcome of this story.	"Blackbird"
Jake: Chronicles the end of Jake's life.	"The Real Jake"
Hide-and-Seek: Larson gains insight into the events of this story.	"Hide-and-Seek"

ANDREW HAS SOMETHING INTERESTING TO SAY ABOUT HIS ANGER, AND THE REASON HE'S TETHERED TO FETCH'S BATTERY PACK: "I DO REMEMBER WANTING TO GET BACK AT SOMEONE WHO HURT ME. I THINK I ATTACHED MYSELF TO HIM. I GOT INTO HIS SOUL, MADE SURE HE COULDN'T MOVE ON WHEN HE SHOULDA DIED.

"I REMEMBER I WANTED HIM TO SUFFER, THE WAY HE MADE ME SUFFER. BUT I DON'T REMEMBER WHAT HE DID. I JUST KNOW I HUNG ON, NO MATTER WHAT THEY DID TO HIM TO TRY AND SAVE HIM. I WANTED HIM TO HURT!"

Stitching It Together

The Real Jake

Takes place three years prior to the stingers.

Jake is the Stitchwraith, focused on cleaning up the "haunted" Remnant-containing objects that are causing chaos.

Fetch

Andrew had possessed Fetch via its battery pack, he seems to have been one of Afton's victims.

The Man in Room 1280

The burned man described in the story is William Afton.

Andrew may be somewhat responsible for Afton's soul remaining tethered to this world, as he insists he couldn't let him go.

Into the Pit

After being stabbed by The Agony, Larson experiences strange visions where he seems to travel through time via a ball pit. He tracks down the ball pit and takes thirty samples, scraped off the balls. When the results come in, they show that the same person has been bleeding in the ball pit over thirty years.

To Be Beautiful

Several elements from this story later return in the Stitchwraith stingers—Eleanor, the heart-shaped pendant, and witness reports of Sarah's story.

Eleanor's pendant is shown to have unique properties, including the ability to change the appearance of the wearer.

Remnant

Dr. Taggart and Dr. Talbert are both scientists studying Remnant and metal as a conductor of powerful emotion.

When the Stitchwraith is initially created, he kills anyone he touches, causing them to wither away and cry black tears.

Chapter 18

TALES FROM THE PIZZAPLEX

The Tales from the Pizzaplex series is another fright-filled extension of the *FNAF* universe, offering eerie, unsettling, and downright horrifying short stories set in and around the world of Freddy Fazbear's Mega Pizzaplex, a dazzling location that was first introduced in the *Security Breach* game. Coauthored by *FNAF* creator Scott Cawthon, and Kelly Parra and Andrea Waggener, this series of eight books follows in the freaky footsteps of the *Fazbear Frights* collection. It delves deeper into the mysteries and horrors that lurk beneath the surface of the Pizzaplex's neon lights and high-tech attractions.

Each book in the series presents three standalone stories which are sometimes interconnected. They explore various characters who encounter the Pizzaplex's cutting-edge animatronics, virtual reality experiences, and seemingly harmless arcade games—only to find themselves trapped in nightmarish situations beyond their control. These frightful tales expand the lore of *FNAF*, introducing new threats, old enemies, twisted fates, intriguing lore, and unexpected connections to many of the franchise's overarching mysteries.

Each book ends with an epilogue, which continues across the books to tell one overarching story. It concerns some gruesome events that happened during the construction of the Pizzaplex. At first, the epilogues might seem only distantly related to the other stories, but after a while, terrifying connections start to form . . .

The *Tales from the Pizzaplex* stories share a general focus on technology-driven horror—which contrasts nicely (or, rather, not-so-nicely) with the shiny, happy vibes of the daytime Pizzaplex. From animatronics learning and thinking for themselves to augmented reality experiences turning sinister, there is plenty to see here.

FRAILTY

LOG ID: Tales from the Pizzaplex #1: *Lally's Game*

Identified Persons	Occupation
Jack	EMT
Dave	EMT
Jessica	Hospital Janitor
Robert	Student
Macy	Nurse
Father Jeremiah	Priest
April	Hospital

Description of Events

Jack, an EMT, and his partner Dave desperately try to revive a teenage boy after a crash, but their efforts fail. Just as they prepare to leave, Jack sees a frail figure hovering over the boy's body, using a knife. When the boy mysteriously returns to life, Jack is left with more questions than answers. The figure, Jessica, is a fourteen-year-old janitor at a hospital who uses a magical silver pendant to heal the sick—and even bring the dead back to life. But with every use, she grows weaker. Struggling with guilt from a bad decision she made in the past, Jessica resists her growing friendship with a boy, Robert, from school. She wants to heal people, but is it so bad to also want to enjoy her own life?

For Further Consideration

Have we come across the pendant before? This pendant has similarities to the heart one from Fazbear Frights stories "To Be Beautiful" and the "Stitchwraith Stingers." Jessica has a nightmare about a robot chasing her and ripping off her limbs. That sounds familiar . . . Is there a connection to Eleanor from "To Be Beautiful"?

LOG ID: Tales from the Pizzaplex #1: *Lally's Game*

Identified Persons	Occupation
Selena	Business Major
Cade	Selena's Fiancé
Janice	Cade's Mother
Lally	Animatronic
Macy	Nurse

Description of Events
Selena and Cade are excited to begin their new life together in Cade's childhood farmhouse, where they'll care for his elderly mother, Janice, before their wedding. But Cade has a childhood trunk that raises Selena's suspicions. When she finds the trunk hidden away and unlocks it, she's shocked by what she uncovers—and Cade's behavior only makes it worse. Selena can't help herself and she delves into Cade's past, learning about a terrifying connection to the Freddy Fazbear's Mega Pizzaplex, an animatronic named Lally, and a disturbing game that has haunted Cade since childhood. Meanwhile, the house seems to get colder as Lally's influence grows . . .

For Further Consideration
We've heard the name "Lally" before—Lally's Lollies was a sponsor in *Freddy Fazbear's Pizzeria Simulator*.

UNDER CONSTRUCTION

LOG ID: Tales from the Pizzaplex #1: *Lally's Game*

Identified Persons	Occupation
Maya	Student
Noelle	Student
Jaxon	Student
Elena	Student
Gran	Maya's Grandmother
Mrs. Carpenter	Teacher

Description of Events

Maya is excited to celebrate her sixteenth birthday with her friends, Noelle and Jaxon, at Freddy Fazbear's Mega Pizzaplex. She wants to visit a unique AR experience called "The World Celebrates You!," which will simulate an epic birthday party, but the sign reads CLOSED, UNDER CONSTRUCTION. Maya sneaks in anyway and enjoys the perfect party. But soon after, strange and tragic events start to unfold. Maya witnesses the sudden illness and death of her loved ones and the spread of a truly bizarre epidemic—and she begins to question if her reality is truly real. With a growing sense of dread, Maya clings to a gold rose pendant her Gran gave her, while the world turns stranger and more terrifying than ever. Will she ever escape the horrors closing in on her?

For Further Consideration

Maya's story seems to echo the storyline of the *Princess Quest* minigame.

An AR booth is mentioned in the later *Tales from the Pizzaplex* story, "Cleithrophobia." Is it the same one Maya visits?

The story mentions some Pizzaplex attractions we haven't heard of before: Urban Legend Role Play Auditorium and Freddy's Fortress. Perhaps we'll revisit them again one day?

LOG ID: Tales from the Pizzaplex #2: *HAPPS*

Identified Persons	Occupation
Steve	Janitor/Game Designer
Brock Edwards	Talent Acquisition
Amanda	Teacher
Victoria	Steve's Wife
Abigail	Child
Avery	Child

Description of Events

Steve, a janitor and aspiring game designer, is offered a high-paying job by Brock Edwards of Fazbear Entertainment to create horror games based on the company's dark past. Steve was going to refuse, but then he meets the beautiful Victoria . . . and the next thing he knows, he's waking up to learn about the memory lapses he's been suffering since a car accident years ago. He doesn't recall his wedding to Victoria and is more than a little surprised to find out they have two children, Abigail and Avery. Now designing games for Edwards, Steve works from the family's secluded cottage, but bizarre events escalate—creatures lurk inside the walls, snakes attack, and a massive spider unleashes hundreds of smaller ones. Eventually, Steve starts to question his new life, his family, and the house itself.

For Further Consideration

There is no mention of the Mega Pizzaplex in this story. Interesting.

The noise Steve hears in the story is reminiscent of the Illusion Discs from the *FNAF* novels and *Fazbear Frights* books. These discs emit a high-pitched sound that only echoes in the subconscious. And it can alter reality. Worth investigating further.

HAPPS

LOG ID: Tales from the Pizzaplex #2: *HAPPS*

Identified Persons	Occupation
Aiden	Student
Jace	Student
Nora	Student
HAPPS	Animatronic

Description of Events
Aiden, a fifteen-year-old loner, finally makes a new friend, Jace, after moving to a new town. He confesses to Jace that sometimes he wishes he was invisible. At Freddy Fazbear's Mega Pizzaplex, they run into some bullies, but Jace suggests they forget about them, and go to Freddy's Fortress—a maze of colorful climbing tubes that winds around the entire Pizzaplex. Enjoying themselves, Aiden and Jace prank a few younger kids, but the fun quickly spirals into a nightmare. After a strange encounter with a malfunctioning robot named HAPPS, the boys find themselves trapped in the maze, with the deranged bot hunting them down. They stumble through the twisted candy-colored tubes, unable to get past the mirrored security barriers, and cut off from the oblivious Pizzaplex visitors below. Aiden panics when he realizes that his wish to be invisible is about to come true, just not the way he'd envisioned. Or . . .

For Further Consideration
We've met other shattered and ruined animatronics in the Pizzaplex before—Glamrock Chica, Glamrock Monty, and Glamrock Roxy. The Fast Freddy attraction appears in several other Tales from the Pizzaplex stories, including "Under Construction" (though it looks like Aiden and Jace are the only characters to have gone in).

B-7

LOG ID: Tales from the Pizzaplex #2: *HAPPS*

Identified Persons	Occupation
Billy	Child
Dan	Office Worker
Vera	Financial Advisor
Dr. Lingstrom	Psychiatrist
Doc	Unlicensed Surgeon
Maliah	Billy's Girlfriend

Description of Events

Billy has always felt different. After a traumatic hospital stay when he was three, he became obsessed with the idea of being an animatronic. The older Billy gets, the more extreme his behavior becomes. His parents play along at first, but it only gets worse. Billy sneaks into the garage to drink oil at night, and he eventually stops going to school, which he deems unnecessary. Then Billy undergoes painful surgeries to "upgrade" his body with mechanical parts, and everything spirals. The lines between man and machine blur, and Billy is forced to confront the terrifying consequences of what he's done.

For Further Consideration

There is no mention of the Pizzaplex in this story.

The eighth book of the Tales from the Pizzaplex series is titled "B-72" and contains a sequel to this story.

SOMNIPHOBIA

LOG ID: Tales from the Pizzaplex #3: *Somniphobia*

Identified Persons	Occupation
Sam	Student
Raad	Student
Jules	Student
Lydia	Student
Mrs. Barker	Sam's Mother
Moondrop	Animatronic

Description of Events

Sam Barker, an anxious high school senior with a past full of grief, stumbles upon a mysterious object at his friend Raad's birthday party—Moondrop's Dream Sphere. The sphere, a hypnotic tool designed to improve focus and unlock subconscious memories, becomes an unexpected escape for Sam, offering him glimpses into his past and a chance to relive moments with his late father. But Sam grows increasingly obsessed with using the sphere, and it's not long before he struggles to tell the difference between the sphere's world and his own.

For Further Consideration

Moondrop appears to be the name of the "Moon" alter-ego of the Superstar Daycare Attendant from *Security Breach*.

LOG ID: Tales from the Pizzaplex #3: *Somniphobia*

Identified Persons	Occupation
Luca	Student
Maddy	Student
Asher	Student
Nolan	Student
Earl	Fazbear Employee

Description of Events

High school senior Luca carries the trauma of losing his childhood friend, Kenny. Though he is haunted by dreams of failing to save Kenny, Luca's life seems to be getting back on track when he befriends Asher, Maddy, and Nolan. The group heads to Freddy Fazbear's Mega Pizzaplex and they decide to play out a Freddy's-themed scenario in the Urban Legend Role Play Auditorium. Luca is reluctantly persuaded to wear a Springtrap costume, though he is deeply uneasy due to all the ghastly rumors that surround the Freddy's chain. As the game begins, Luca becomes trapped in the nightmarish story, and his fears grow exponentially when the suit malfunctions, piercing his body with its sharp parts. His friends flee from him as part of the game, while Luca grows weaker by the minute. Will he survive the "game" before the suit kills him?

For Further Consideration

Luca suspects that the games in the Urban Legend Role Play Auditorium were created to dispel the rumors of suspicious deaths that surround the Freddy's brand.

Luca is convinced that his Springtrap suit is an original, not just a costume for the Auditorium attraction. What do you think?

Another of the costumes available in the Auditorium is a Golden Freddy suit. Creepy . . .

CLEITHROPHOBIA

LOG ID: Tales from the Pizzaplex #3: *Somniphobia*

Identified Persons	Occupation
Kim	Student
Grady	Fazbear Technician
Ronan	Fazbear Employee and Bodybuilder
Tate	Fazbear Employee

Description of Events
A young visitor to the Pizzaplex, Kim, wonders why her map shows an attraction called Ballora's Fitness & Flex, though no such place seems to exist. Little does she know that a few months earlier, a Fazbear employee, Grady, made his way to that very attraction before the Pizzaplex opened. Designed as a fitness challenge, Ballora's Fitness & Flex is a vertical, tubelike course that narrows toward the bottom. Despite his cleithrophobia (fear of being trapped)—the result of a childhood trauma—Grady decides to test the attraction, to ensure no child will have to face the horror of getting stuck in it. But Grady—alone in the Pizzaplex—gets caught in his own worst nightmare when he gets trapped in the tube. The attraction's animatronic, Ballora, comes to his aid, but she is neither gentle nor caring.

For Further Consideration
When Kim passes the AR booth, she sees "smoke coming out and workers trying to get inside." This reminds us of the end of "Under Construction." Is it possible Maya is still inside? Another "helper" animatronic, HAPPS, is featured in the earlier *Tales from the Pizzaplex* story, "HAPPS." Like Ballora, he, too, was not so helpful.

LOG ID: Tales from the Pizzaplex #4: *Submechanophobia*

Identified Persons	Occupation
Caden	Technician
Roy	Security Guard
Martin	Water Park Owner
Darryl	Student
Yasmine	Student

Description of Events
At age six, Caden lost his parents to the sea, a trauma that left him with submechanophobia, a deep fear of submerged man-made objects. Now nineteen, he takes a job at Freddy's Fantasy Water Park to support his sick grandmother. But the park's eerie underwater attraction, Freddy's Sea Life Mechaquarium pulls the terrified Caden into a chilling mystery. One day, he is repairing malfunctioning animatronics beneath the water when strange things begin to happen. A missing child's shoe, a bizarre bone—and are the animatronics moving on their own? Caden finds himself at the center of a long-buried secret, one that someone—or *something*—will do everything it can to keep buried.

For Further Consideration
This is another *Tales from the Pizzaplex* story named after a phobia. Other stories such as "Somniphobia," "Cleithrophobia," and "Dittophobia" are also in the series. This story is unusual because it has a happy ending. Or does it? While this story doesn't take place in the Mega Pizzaplex, there is a connection. The water park is opened following the success of the Pizzaplex, which is located two towns away.

LOG ID: Tales from the Pizzaplex #4: *Submechanophobia*

Identified Persons	Occupation
Robbie	Student
Dyson	Student
Mr. Renner	School Principal
Zabrina	Student

Description of Events

Sixth-grader Robbie enjoys camping, learning how things work, and spending time at the Mega Pizzaplex. He is a member of his school's Fazbear Fan Club and helped create the role-playing game Animatronic Apocalypse, which is played by the Fan Club. When Jason, the club president, moves, Zabrina is appointed the new president. She dictates a lot of unsettling, weird new rules, that include forgetting about homework to focus on preparing for the apocalypse. Shockingly, the school principal, Mr. Renner, has taken an active and approving role in this. Robbie and his friend Dylan watch in horror as their classmates obey Mr. Renner's orders to eat dirt and stick pins under their fingernails, all to protect them against "toxins." Will Robbie survive long enough to stop all of his friends from succumbing to the madness?

For Further Consideration

Mr. Renner has some similarities to Jessica from "Frailty" (the first *Tales from the Pizzaplex* story), especially bleeding motor oil and leaving scrap metal in his wake. Mr. Renner's obsessive instructions border on mind control. What could be behind these instructions with obvious health-related effects?

BOBBIEDOTS, PART 1

LOG ID: Tales from the Pizzaplex #4: *Submechanophobia*

Identified Persons	Occupation
Abe	Pizzaplex Security Guard
Eva	Pizzaplex Team Leader
Preston	Pizzaplex Employee
Bobbiedots	Holographic Animatronics

Description of Events

Ambitious security guard Abe seizes the chance for a better life when he takes a promotion and sneaks his way into a high-tech apartment at Fazplex Tower. With holographic assistants—Bobbiedots—catering to his every need, it seems like his luck has finally changed. But living in the apartment brings danger: small malfunctions escalate into life-threatening "accidents," and Abe begins to suspect that something is watching him from the shadows. Is the apartment truly empty? Do the Bobbiedots know more than they admit? What's in the hatch in the ceiling? And will Abe survive long enough to find out?

For Further Consideration

This story continues in the first story of the next book, *The Bobbiedots Conclusion*.

We learn a bit more about the Daycare Attendant from *Security Breach*. It seems his Moon persona developed in reaction to continuous blackouts in the theater. Technicians couldn't remove that reaction, so they decided to always leave the lights on instead. Makes sense.

ID: Tales from the Pizzaplex #5: *The Bobbiedots Conclusion*

Identified Persons	Occupation
Toby	Student
Greg	Student
Ellis	Student
Finbarr	Pizzaplex Employee
Crystal	Student
Kenzie	Student

Description of Events

Twelve-year-old Tony is a journalist-in-the-making with a sharp eye for details. He is given a writing assignment, but it quickly spirals into something far more dangerous. On a trip to Freddy Fazbear's Mega Pizzaplex, Tony discovers that a mysterious arcade wiz—who uses the initials GGY—has beaten the scores of other players by millions of points. Tony sees this as the perfect story in the making, but the deeper he digs, the more weird, seemingly unconnected, things he finds. Tony is determined to discover who GGY is, why some of the school counselors have vanished, why his friends are acting strangely, and who has been hacking the code of the Pizzaplex animatronics. But even if Tony figures out all the answers, who says that the mystery will be solved?

For Further Consideration

This story seems to have several connections to the game *Security Breach*:

- The missing counselors could be some of the therapists on the hidden Retro CDs from *Security Breach*.
- Toby's friend is named Greg, and the main character in *Security Breach* is Gregory. Gregory . . . GGY . . . interesting . . .
- In *Security Breach*, the arcade machines show a top scorer named GGY.

The game *FNAF: Help Wanted 2* includes an achievement called "GGY."

THE STORYTELLER

ID: Tales from the Pizzaplex #5: *The Bobbiedots Conclusion*

Identified Persons	Occupation
Mr. Burrows	Fazbear Entertainment Board Chairman
Edwin Murray	Fazbear Entertainment Board Member

Description of Events

Under the leadership of Mr. Burrows, chair of Fazbear Entertainment, the company is about to take a big leap to try to save the Mega Pizzaplex. It isn't making enough money so they are going to use AI to replace some workers. They design The Storyteller—an advanced AI system that connects to every part of the Pizzaplex. It will take the form of a huge tree with multicolor branches. Fazbear board member Edwin Murray sees dangers in this plan that no one else seems to care about. One night, Edwin hides and watches in horror as the AI mechanism is installed inside the tree trunk—it looks like they are plugging in a huge animatronic tiger head! Soon after, the animatronics' personalities begin to change and strange malfunctions spread through the Pizzaplex, Edwin is determined to uncover the truth behind The Storyteller. But little does he know, he is being watched.

For Further Consideration

The tiger head is described as having one green eye and one blue eye—matching the animatronic on the cover of *Tales from the Pizzaplex #7: Tiger Rock*. Is the head that controls The Storyteller Tiger Rock?

Edwin discovers that the AI program running inside The Storyteller is named Mimic1.

LOG ID: Tales from the Pizzaplex #5: *The Bobbiedots Conclusion*

Identified Persons	Occupation
Abe	Pizzaplex Team Leader
Olive	Bobbiedot, gen2
Rose	Bobbiedot, gen2
Gemini	Bobbiedot, gen2
One	Bobbiedot, gen1
Two	Bobbiedot, gen1
Three	Bobbiedot, gen1
Sasha	Social Worker

Description of Events

Following the events of "Bobbiedots, Part 1," Abe finally has the life he's always dreamed of—a great job and a home in the exclusive Fazplex Tower. His apartment even has a team of high-tech holograms, the Bobbiedots, to help him out. But Abe has been hurt several times by strange "accidents" in the apartment, and he suspects they may have been caused by the gen1s. These are the original, physical versions of the Bobbiedots, who were decommissioned and whom Abe suspects live in the crawl space above his ceiling. When Abe meets Sasha, she makes him question everything he knows about the Bobbiedots and the gen1s, and Abe finds himself wondering where the danger really lies.

For Further Consideration

Abe finds a Mr. Hippo animatronic and magnet at the Pizzaplex, which takes us back to the *Security Breach* game, where the same magnet can be used to scramble a machine.

Glamrock Mr. Hippo features in one of the endings of *Security Breach*.

The *Tales from the Pizzaplex* series includes plenty of scary, and sometimes tragic, stories. Only two so far have had a happy ending—"Submechanophobia" and this one.

As a Pizzaplex employee, Abe visits many staff-only areas of the Pizzaplex, many of which (including the Loading Docks, Sewers, and Roxy's Green Room) are locations in *Security Breach*.

NEXIE

LOG ID: Tales from the Pizzaplex #6: *Nexie*

Identified Persons	Occupation
Astrid	Child
Remy	Child
Farfar	Astrid's Grandfather
Warren	Child
Nexie	Animatronic

Description of Events

Astrid is a smart kid but she doesn't fit in at school. She wishes she had a Buddytronic—an animatronic doll that all the kids have—so she could have a friend, and maybe even make real friends of her own. For her ninth birthday, relatives send some money for her to buy a Buddytronic! But at the Pizzaplex, The Storyteller tree is glitching, and instead of building the cute Lexie doll Astrid had designed, it produces an odd-looking, disproportionate version, named Nexie. Teased about Nexie's appearance, and her own, Astrid feels sad. At first, Nexie just wants to be fixed. A new arm, a better face—small changes to make her beautiful. But as Nexie's demands grow, so does Astrid's doubt. The doll whispers insecurities Astrid never had, pushes her to make dangerous choices, and when a classmate is brutally attacked, Astrid realizes too late that she's created something far worse than a friend. But the real horror lies in the answer to this question: What is it that Nexie truly wants?

For Further Consideration

For just a moment, two *Tales from the Pizzaplex* stories collide. As Astrid and Farfar get Nexie at the Pizzaplex, they pass a crowd at the AR attraction watching a "boy in the glass dome." This is the same boy from the story "Tiger Rock," whose name is Kai.

The Storyteller tree is the same one that was created and installed in the earlier story, "The Storyteller."

LOG ID: Tales from the Pizzaplex #6: *Nexie*

Identified Persons	Occupation
Kara	Student
Lola	Student
Francine	Student
Zach	Pizzaplex Employee

Description of Events

Kara is a risk-taker, so she is excited to spend her birthday at the Pizzaplex with her friends, and she can't wait to try out the adventures of the VR booth. But she is disappointed that after lining up for half an hour, the attraction—Coaster City—lasted only five minutes. She convinces a Pizzaplex employee to let her sneak in a second time, activating a "zero" Hypertime setting, which prolongs the experience indefinitely. Kara enters the Waterpark VR and explores a watery world full of slides and pools. It isn't long before she notices a dark-haired girl in the Waterpark with her. And the girl isn't playing nice. No matter how much Kara tries to flee from the girl, or escape the VR altogether, she is horribly unable to.

For Further Consideration

Who is the girl with black hair? Some people think she might be Peggy, Kara's cousin, who slipped into a coma after falling out of a tree as a young child. Kara has always been haunted about not saving her.

Kara sees a music box in the VR.

Using her birthday Day Pass, Kara visits many parts of the Pizzaplex that appear in *Security Breach*, including Fazer Blast, the Fazcade, and Monty's Gator Golf. She also plays laser tag, visits a photo booth, and enjoys a karaoke session with her friends.

LOG ID: Tales from the Pizzaplex #6: *Nexie*

Identified Persons	Occupation
Edwin Murray	Fazbear Entertainment Engineer
David	Edwin's Son
Dominic	Fazbear Employee
Harry	Fazbear Employee
Glen	Fazbear Employee
Mimic	Animatronic

Description of Events

Edwin is a Fazbear engineer, paid to create animatronics for the company. Raising his young son David on his own, Edwin creates a special robot to entertain David while Edwin works. He builds a partial endoskeleton (head, torso, and arms) and programs it to learn through mimicking. David and Mimic get along, and Mimic learns a lot from watching David. One day, tragically, David is hit by a van and killed. Devastated, Edwin mourns, until one day Mimic repeats an action that reminds Edwin too much of his son. Edwin beats the robot savagely, damaging it. Months later, Edwin has gone missing, so Fazbear sends a team to the factory. Dominic, Harry, and Glen discover endoskeletons and animatronic costumes, including Freddy, Chica, and Bonnie, but quickly realize that they are not the first team to have been sent here. A tape recording from the previous team explains they were just about to start work on an endoskeleton that has no legs. Dominic and his team are about to find out exactly what happened to the last team . . . and exactly who—or what—was responsible . . .

For Further Consideration

It is rumored that this story takes place in 1979, making it the earliest story in the *Tales from the Pizzaplex* chronology.

The story suggests that Edwin created the endoskeletons for Freddy Fazbear and most of the other "main" animatronics.

This story precedes another *Tales from the Pizzaplex* tale, "The Storyteller," which carries on Edwin's story when he returns from his disappearance.

It also leads up to the events of the game *FNAF: Secret of the Mimic*.

LOG ID: Tales from the Pizzaplex #7: *Tiger Rock*

Identified Persons	Occupation
Kai	Student
Todd	Student
Asher	Student
Tiger Rock	Animatronic

Description of Events

Kai heads to the Pizzaplex with his friends, Todd and Asher. They want to try a new attraction, The Storyteller tree, but are disappointed to find it closed. Instead, Kai tries out an AR simulation of the Pizzaplex set ten years in the future. What begins as a fun experience soon turns sinister when Kai meets Tiger Rock, a mysterious white tiger animatronic with one green eye and one blue. Tiger Rock grips Kai's arm tightly, and Kai races to escape from him. Eventually, Kai leaves the simulation—or does he? Strange things keep happening and Kai sees various forms of Tiger Rock at home and at school. Eventually, he realizes that he doesn't quite recognize the reality he is seeing, which means he's still in the AR! He manages to force himself awake, but will he ever be truly safe?

For Further Consideration

Many things about Tiger Rock relate to the Mimic1 program, which was invented by Edwin in the previous story, "The Mimic" (in *Tales from the Pizzaplex #6*). Consider that Edwin's son, David, who was used to train Mimic at first, had a stuffed toy called Tiger . . .

Awakening from his AR experience, Kai spots a girl, her grandfather, and a funny-looking doll in the crowds passing by. They are Astrid, her farfar, and Nexie from the story "Nexie."

Could it be . . . that the reason The Storyteller tree is shut down is because two Fazbear employees were found dead inside? (Refer to "The Storyteller" to find out more.)

THE MONTY WITHIN

LOG ID: Tales from the Pizzaplex #7: *Tiger Rock*

Identified Persons	Occupation
Kane	Student
Archer	Student
Sienna	Student
Orville Elephant	Animatronic
Bonnie	Animatronic
Glamrock Chica	Animatronic
Montgomery Gator	Animatronic

Description of Events

High school senior Kane takes his younger brother Archer to the Pizzaplex. They decide to play a new game, Fazcade Tag-Team, in which they have a virtual food fight against another team somewhere else in the Pizzaplex. Kane chooses his animatronic character, Orville Elephant, and gets partnered with Monty Gator, who is synced up to Kane's brain. Kane notices that Monty is watching and learning from his tactics in the virtual food fight, and they win easily. The next day, Kane goes back to play again but when he tries to find out more about Monty in the game, it short-circuits, so he goes home. But all is not as it was before. Kane begins to suspect that his brain is still synced with Monty, and he has to repeatedly stop himself from carrying out Monty's disturbing actions. Will Kane ever be himself again?

For Further Consideration

We first met Orville Elephant in the game *Freddy Fazbear's Pizzeria Simulator.*

Monty repeats many of his catchphrases throughout the story, such as "Run, run, run!," "Rock and roll!," and "Party time!" He says the same things in the game *Security Breach*, which is also set in the Pizzaplex.

LOG ID: Tales from the Pizzaplex #7: *Tiger Rock*

Identified Persons	Occupation
Danny	Student
Daisy	Student
Aaron	Student
Bobby	Student

Description of Events
Fifteen-year-old Danny has a crush on Daisy, the only girl in school with a tattoo. His brother Bobby suggests Danny buy Daisy a Christmas present, so he looks around at the Pizzaplex. He notices a wrapping booth that perfectly wraps presents. Next to it is a booth that paints tattoos with precision. Danny wants to impress Daisy so he steals some of the tiny bots from the booth, slipping them into his pocket. Back home, the bots are gone. Danny starts talking to Daisy and casually mentions that he'd like a heart tattoo. Suddenly he feels a pain on his side and later discovers that the tiny bots are inside his body, and they carved a heart tattoo into his skin when he requested it. Falling in love, Danny realizes he will do anything for Daisy, including designing tattoos that she requests. But each tattoo takes more of a toll on Danny, which begs the question: How far will Danny go to get the girl?

For Further Consideration
Freddy and Roxy Wolf wear Santa hats.
This story is the first mention of Santa's Giftplex. It's a Christmas gift shop selling plushies, candies, and other Fazbear merch.

B7-2

LOG ID: Tales from the Pizzaplex #8: *B7-2*

Identified Persons	Occupation
Billy	Patient
Gloria	Nurse
Dr. Herrera	Doctor
Angie	Physical Therapist
Dr. Lingstrom	Psychiatrist
Clark	Billy's Friend
Peter	Billy's Friend
Grandma	Billy's Grandmother
Frank	Author

Description of Events

Billy awakens in the hospital, fully aware of how he got there (trying to destroy his mostly mechanical body in a trash compactor) and surprised to have survived. His human body has been patched up to some extent, though he will need prosthetics for some limbs. It won't be an easy road to recovery. To make matters worse, Billy starts seeing B-7, the "animatronic" part of himself, and hears it whispering to him. He goes to live with his grandmother, who has rejected technology and uses a simple rotary phone. Over time, they grow closer and Billy finds new purpose in helping his grandmother and writing—though he finds the ringing of his grandmother's phone at 9:03 p.m. every day a little disturbing. One night, the phone doesn't ring and Billy goes into his grandma's room, where he sees something completely unexpected.

For Further Consideration

This is the second two-part story from *Tales from the Pizzaplex*. The first was "Bobbiedots."

There is no mention of the Mega Pizzaplex in this story.

ALONE TOGETHER

LOG ID: Tales from the Pizzaplex #8: *B7-2*

Identified Persons	Occupation
Travis	Student
Mr. Hutchins	Travis's Father
Travis's Grandmother	Retired
Mr. Middlefield	Teacher
Marissa	Student
Sunman	Animatronic
Glamrock Freddy	Animatronic

Description of Events
Young Travis has become used to being alone. He finds it hard to make new friends and so he imagines that he is surrounded by a bubble, protecting him from other people. One day in woodshop, the teacher announces a new project: building something unique. Travis decides to build his own version of a Mechanical Turk (a device with a mechanical figure that moves), based on the animatronic Sun, or Sunman. As he and his father build the device, Travis begins feeling weird. He has a near-constant feeling of déjà vu and starts having visions of the Mechanical Turk. He also meets a new girl at school who behaves strangely around him. Eventually, his grandmother suggests Travis is being haunted. He decides to investigate who might be haunting him, and so begins an investigation that leads him to all the hidden spaces at school. Finally, he finds what he's looking for—but the revelation changes everything.

For Further Consideration
This story shares some similarities with the stories "Coming Home" and "Find Player Two!" from the *Fazbear Frights* series. Marissa is gifted with the ability to see ghosts.

DITTOPHOBIA

ID: Tales from the Pizzaplex #8: *B7-2*

Identified Persons	Occupation
Rory	Child
Wade	Student
Nightmare Foxy	Animatronic
Nightmare Bonnie	Animatronic
Nightmare Chica	Animatronic
Nightmare Freddy	Animatronic

Description of Events

Rory wakes up in the middle of the night, frozen in fear as monsters creep into his room. A rotting fox, a decaying chicken, a twisted bunny—all with razor-sharp teeth—close in on his bed. Just as he tries to escape, a mutilated bear lunges at him. Then he wakes up. Just a nightmare. Right? Rory wanders around the house, hearing the patter of the shower and the hum of the fridge. He eats, walks around more, then goes to bed. Strangely, this happens again and again until one morning he realizes he is a teenager. Out of whatever slumber he's been in, he explores the house and realizes nothing is what it seems. What has been going on for the last ten years? Where are his parents? Who has been feeding him? What are the abandoned buildings connected to his house? Is it his house? As Rory explores further, he starts to wonder if he actually wants to know the answers to these questions . . .

For Further Consideration

The house in this story looks very similar to the house in *FNAF4*. Does this offer an insight into the main character of *FNAF4* and what he's experienced?

The house also features on a map in *Sister Location*, where it is called *Obsv. 2*.

As Rory explores the tunnel leading away from the house, he reaches Circus Baby's Entertainment and Rental, a facility owned by Fazbear Entertainment, which is the primary location of *Sister Location*.

EPILOGUES

At the end of each *Tales from the Pizzaplex* book is an epilogue. Most of the epilogues have no connections to the Pizzaplex tales themselves, though they tell an overarching story that connects in parts, most notably with stories that mention the Mimic and The Storyteller tree.

Gil leads a team of construction workers at the Freddy Fazbear's Mega Pizzaplex construction site. His crew is actually working in the old pizzeria, breaking down the retired endoskeletons. They find an out-of-place endoskeleton and Gil tinkers with it, boots it up, and tasks it with dismantling all the other endoskeletons—by tearing them limb from limb. The endo does as instructed, but then turns on the human builders. Uh-oh . . .

Sometime later, high school senior Lucia and her friends decide to explore the construction site and break into the old pizzeria, even though someone had blocked the entrance with cement. They discover the carnage that used to be Gil's construction crew and try to leave, but quickly realize that they are not alone. Metallic sounds and flickering lights abound as Lucia's friends are killed, one by one. The mysterious attacker seems to be changing into various animatronic costumes. In an old Fazbear operator's manual, Lucia discovers that the entity chasing them is an adjustable endoskeleton designed to fit into various suits. It is known as a Mimic Model 1 or 2.

Lucia and her last surviving friend, Kelly, try to trick the Mimic by forcing it to enter a springlock jester suit. Kelly doesn't make it but Lucia does, trapping the Mimic in the springlock suit and then powering it down. Filled with relief, but sadly alone, Lucia escapes from the pizzeria.

The epilogues stirred up a lot of chatter and many theories about the Mimic. Combined with the stories "The Mimic" and "The Storyteller," a lot of new backstory was provided in the Tales from the Pizzaplex series. Here are a few observations, connections, and fan theories.

ORIGINS—WHAT WE KNOW

- The Mimic was created by Edwin Murray as a companion for his son, and Edwin programmed it to mimic behavior. When Edwin attacked the companion bot following his son's death, the Mimic learned violence.
- Fazbear Entertainment got hold of the Mimic programming and eventually produced a line of Mimic endos to assist in animatronic performances, since they could wear any costume.
- It seems as though the Mimic witnessed something it shouldn't have (possibly a hide-and-seek-like situation involving Spring Bonnie luring children), and the bots were decommissioned.
- Years later, the Pizzaplex is built and the Mimic is installed in the Storyteller's Tree, which is connected to all the systems in the complex.

WHITE TIGERS!

Young David Murray had a white tiger toy. In "The Storyteller," Edwin (David's dad) is horrified when he sees what the machine at the center of the Storyteller's Tree looks like—a white tiger animatronic head with one green eye and one blue. Later, it is revealed that the Storyteller's Tree runs on the program Mimic1. Not long after we meet the animatronic in "Tiger Rock," it is a white tiger with one blue eye, one green eye.

IN RUIN

The Mimic makes an appearance in the *Security Breach* update *RUIN*. It imitates Gregory to lure Cassie, though she manages to escape. In the Scooper Ending of *RUIN*, the Mimic battles the Scooper—and loses.

ORANGE EYES

In *RUIN*, the Mimic's eyes glow orange—does this mean it has a connection with HELPI?

CREEPY CAMEO

You can spot the Mimic as one of the endoskeletons in the Animatronic Gallery in *Help Wanted 2*.

TAKE NOTE

The Mimic's endoskeleton has an activation switch on the back of its neck.

THREE IN ONE

Some theories suggest that the Mimic, Glitchtrap, and Burntrap are all the same! There are many reasons for this, including the fact that Glitchtrap has mimicked other peoples' voices, and that it hands over a white tiger doll in *Help Wanted 2* (suggesting a connecting to David, the son of Mimic creator, Edwin Murray), and that Burntrap's purple eyes match the Mimic's.

READY OR NOT, HERE I COME

The Mimic's behavior in the epilogues suggest that it has learned some behavior from once observing a version of the game hide-and-seek, which is why it lures people by hiding. This also makes sense when you think about "Tiger Rock," in which the animatronic tries to trap Kai.

THE SAME NAMES?

Remember Jace and Aiden from the story "HAPPS"? Well, isn't it interesting that two of Lucia's (now dead) friends were called *Adrian* and Jayce?

THE GRAPHIC NOVEL

The first *Tales from the Pizzaplex* graphic novel was released following the first eight books in the series. It includes three of the Pizzaplex stories: "Under Construction," "HAPPS," and "Cleithrophobia." The front cover shows the animatronic Ballora—a fan favorite! In *Tales from the Pizzaplex*, she appears as a "helpful" bot that works in the never-opened (for a very good reason) Pizzaplex attraction called Ballora's Fitness & Flex.

UNDER CONSTRUCTION

This is the first time fans will get to see the full majesty of Freddy Fazbear's Mega Pizzaplex, with its soaring Atrium and dazzling attractions. The AR dome appears for the first time, too. It helps visualize how the AR works, and also it enables us to picture the haunting scene where Kai becomes trapped in the dome—even though we won't be seeing that story in this volume. We also finally see the famous Pizzaplex roller coaster, which Maya and her friends ride around the upper reaches of the Atrium.

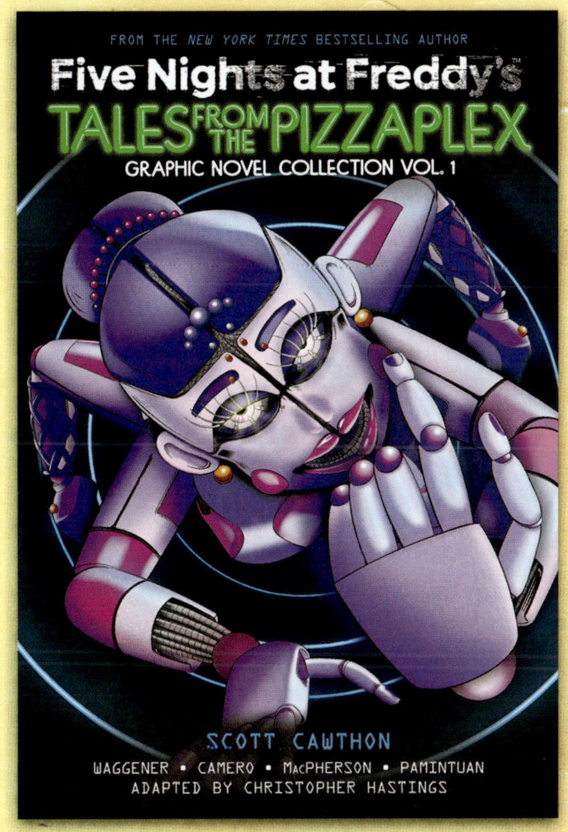

HAPPS

Until now, we've only seen damaged HAPPS, from the front cover of *Tales from the Pizzaplex #2: HAPPS*. In the graphic novel, we meet pristine HAPPS, who's actually quite cute! Okay, maybe just cuter than damaged, destructive HAPPS. The scale of the Freddy's Fortress tube maze is cool to see, and the artwork really helps envision it as a labyrinthine attraction.

CLEITHROPHOBIA

The early pages of this story show us the Pizzaplex as we've never seen it before: during its construction. As Grady walks around the unfinished complex, it feels like we're getting a behind-the-scenes view. Nobody who has ever gone to the Pizzaplex has ever seen Ballora's Fitness & Flex. The graphic novel brings this eerie attraction to life, and the story artwork lives up to the blood-filled horror of the gory story.

Chapter 19

Fazbear Entertainment Archives

Over the years, Fazbear Entertainment and its associated enterprises have accumulated an archive of documents as winding and varied as the company itself. From recipes to soap opera scripts, blueprints and schematics to training tape transcripts, pore over this treasure trove of documents straight from the source!

Pirate Plunderbar

Ingredients:

- 12 tbsp unsalted butter
- 16 oz mini marshmallows
- 1/2 teaspoon cinnamon
- 1/2 teaspoon salt
- 1/4 teaspoon vanilla extract
- 8 cups toasted rice cereal
- 8 oz semisweet chocolate chips

Directions:

1. Melt butter over medium heat in a large pot, then add marshmallows. Stir until fully melted.
2. Add cinnamon, salt, and vanilla extract and stir until evenly mixed.
3. Remove from heat and add rice cereal. Stir until roughly even.
4. Line a 9-by-13-in. pan with parchment or wax paper. Empty marshmallow-rice mixture into the pan and shape so the surface is even. Do not compress the mixture too hard.
5. Once cool, slice into rectangular bars and remove from pan.
6. In a medium pot, melt the chocolate chips.
7. Once melted, cover marshmallow-rice bars. Place in the refrigerator for 30 minutes, until chocolate hardens.

NEW

A TREASURE TROVE OF TASTE!

PIRATE

PLUNDERBAR

FAZBEAR ENTERTAINMENT RECIPES

Fazbear's Twisted Pizza

Ingredients:

- Two 1-lb. loaves Fazbear Entertainment Brand Frozen Bread (roll) Dough
- Tomato sauce
- Shredded mozzarella cheese
- Mini pepperonis
- Parmesan cheese
- Italian seasoning
- Flour

Directions:

1. Thaw the bread dough and roll it onto flour-covered boards. Shape into half-inch thick rectangles.
2. Spread the pizza sauce lightly on one rectangle, then sprinkle with the mozzarella cheese and pepperonis. Place the second dough rectangle on top of the first one and press it together before slicing into one-inch wide strips.
3. Twist these strips, sprinkle with Parmesan cheese and Italian seasoning (optional), and place them onto a baking sheet.
4. Bake at 400 degrees for 15 to 20 minutes, or until the sticks are golden brown. Plate with extra tomato sauce for dipping.

*KIDS, ASK A PARENT TO HELP YOU!

Chica's Golden Cupcake Pizzas

Ingredients:

- 1 can (8 oz) Fazbear Entertainment Brand Triangle Dinner Rolls
- Pizza sauce
- Mini pepperonis
- Shredded mozzarella cheese
- Italian sausage, precooked

Directions:

1. Spray a cupcake pan with cooking spray. Separate the eight triangle dinner rolls and press each one into a cup.
2. In a separate bowl, mix about a half cup of pizza sauce with mini pepperonis, shredded mozzarella cheese, and precooked Italian sausage. Spoon the mixture into each cup, then top with additional mozzarella cheese.
3. Bake at 350 degrees for 16 to 18 minutes or until the edges are lightly browned.

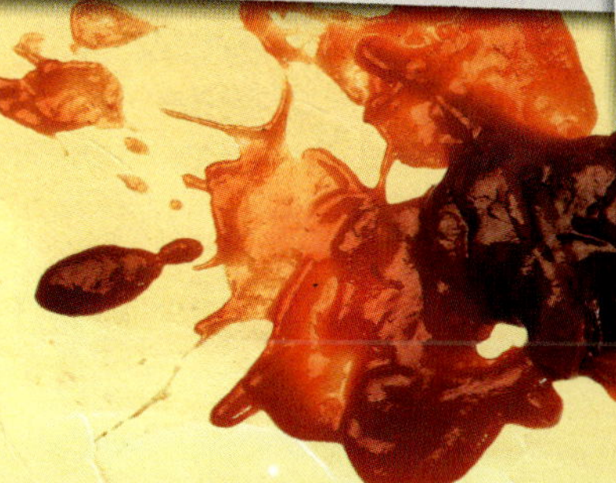

FNAF PHONE GUY TRANSCRIPTS

Night 01: Hello, hello? Hello? Uh, I wanted to record a message for you to help you get settled in on your first night. Um, I actually worked in that office before you. I'm finishing up my last week now, as a matter of fact. So, I know it can be a bit overwhelming, but I'm here to tell you there's nothing to worry about. Uh, you'll do fine. So, let's just focus on getting you through your first week. Okay? Uh, let's see, first there's an introductory greeting from the company that I'm supposed to read. Uh, it-it's kind of a legal thing, you know. Um, "Welcome to Freddy Fazbear's Pizza. A magical place for kids and grown-ups alike, where fantasy and fun come to life. Fazbear Entertainment is not responsible for damage to property or person. Upon discovering that damage or death has occurred, a missing person report will be filed within 90 days, or as soon as property and premises have been thoroughly cleaned and bleached, and the carpets have been replaced." Blah blah blah, now that might sound bad, I know, but there's really nothing to worry about. Uh, the animatronic characters here do get a bit quirky at night, but do I blame them? No. If I were forced to sing those same stupid songs for twenty years and I never got a bath? I'd probably be a bit irritable at night, too. So, remember, these characters hold a special place in the hearts of children and we need to show them a little respect, right? Okay. So, just be aware, the characters do tend to wander a bit. Uh, they're left in some kind of free roaming mode at night. Uh, something about their servos locking up if they get turned off for too long. Uh, they used to be allowed to walk around during the day, too. But then there was the Bite of '87. Yeah. I-it's amazing that the human body can live without the frontal lobe, you know? Uh, now concerning your safety, the only real risk to you as a night watchman here, if any, is the fact that these characters, uh, if they happen to see you after hours, probably won't recognize you as a person. They'll p-they'll most likely see you as a metal endoskeleton without its costume on. Now since that's against the rules here at Freddy Fazbear's Pizza, they'll probably try to . . . forcefully stuff you inside a Freddy Fazbear suit. Um, now, that wouldn't be so bad if the suits themselves weren't filled with crossbeams, wires, and animatronic devices, especially around the facial area. So, you could imagine how having your head forcefully pressed inside one of those could cause a bit of discomfort . . . and death. Uh, the only parts of you that would likely see the light of day again would be your eyeballs and teeth when they pop out the front of the mask, heh.

Y-yeah, they don't tell you these things when you sign up. But hey, first day should be a breeze. I'll chat with you tomorrow. Uh, check those cameras, and remember to close the doors only if absolutely necessary. Gotta conserve power. All right, good night.

Night 02: Uh, Hello? Hello? Uh, well, if you're hearing this and you made it to day two, uh, congrats! I-I-I won't talk quite as long this time since Freddy and his friends tend to become more active as the week progresses. Uh, it might be a good idea to peek at those cameras while I talk just to make sure everyone's in their proper place, you know. Uh, interestingly enough, Freddy himself doesn't come offstage very often. I heard he becomes a lot more active in the dark, though, so, hey, I guess that's one more reason not to run out of power, right? I-I also want to emphasize the importance of using your door lights. Uh, there are blind spots in your camera views, and those blind spots happen to be right outside of your doors. So if-if you can't find something, or someone, on your cameras, uh, be sure to check the door lights. Uh, you might only have a few seconds to react . . . Uh, not that you would be in any danger, of course. Uh, I'm not implying that. Uh, also, uh check on the curtain in Pirate Cove from time to time. The character in there seems unique in that he becomes more active if the cameras remain off for long periods of time. I guess he doesn't like being watched. I don't know. Uh, anyway, I'm sure you have everything under control! Uh, talk to you soon.

Night 03: Hello, hello? Hey you're doing great! Uh, most people don't last this long. I mean, you know, they usually move on to other things by now. Uh, I'm not implying that they died. Th-th-that's not what I meant. Uh, anyway I-I better not take up too much of your time. Uh, things start getting real tonight. Uh, yeah-hey, listen, I-I had an idea: if you happen to get caught and want to avoid getting stuffed into a Freddy suit, uh, try playing dead. You know, go limp. Then there's a chance that, uh, maybe they'll think that you're an empty costume instead. Then again if they think you're an empty costume, they might try to . . . stuff a metal skeleton into you. I wonder how that would work. Yeah, never mind, scratch that. It's best just not to get caught. Um . . . O-okay, I'll leave you to it. Uh, see you on the flip side.

Night 04: Hello, hello? Hey! Hey, wow, day four. I knew you could do it. Uh, hey, listen, I may not be around to send you a message tomorrow. *banging* It's-it's been a bad night here for me. Um, I-I'm kinda glad that I recorded my messages for you *clears throat* uh, when I did. Uh, hey, do me a favor. *banging* Maybe sometime, uh, you could check inside those suits, uh, in the back room? *banging* I'm gonna try to hold out until someone checks. Maybe it won't be so bad. *banging* Uh, I-I-I-I always wondered what was in all those empty heads back there. *Torreador March plays*. You know . . . *moan* oh, no— *animatronic scream* *static*

FNAF 2 PHONE GUY TRANSCRIPTS

Night 01: Uh, hello? Hello, hello? Uh, hello and welcome to your new summer job at the new and improved Freddy Fazbear's Pizza. Uh, I'm here to talk you through some of the things you can expect to see during your first week here and to help you get started down this new and exciting career path. Uh, now, I want you to forget anything you may have heard about the old location, you know. Uh, some people still have a somewhat negative impression of the company. Uh, that old restaurant was kind of left to rot for quite a while, but I want to reassure you, Fazbear Entertainment is committed to family fun and, above all, safety. They've spent a small fortune on these new animatronics, uh, facial recognition, advanced mobility, they even let them walk around during the day. Isn't that neat? *clears throat* But most importantly, they're all tied into some kind of criminal database so they can detect a predator a mile away. Heck, we should be paying them to guard you. Uh, now that being said, no new system is without its . . . kinks. Uh, you're only the second guard to work at that location. Uh, the first guy finished his week, but complained about . . . conditions. Uh, we switched him over to the day shift, so hey, lucky you, right? Uh mainly he expressed concern that certain characters seemed to move around at night and even attempted to get into his office. Now, from what we know, that should be impossible. Uh, that restaurant should be the safest place on earth. So while our engineers don't really have an explanation for this, the working theory is that . . . the robots were never given a proper "night mode." So when it gets quiet, they think they're in the wrong room, so then they go try to find where the people are, and in this case, that's your office. So, our temporary solution is this: there's a music box over by the prize counter, and it's rigged to be wound up remotely. So just, every once in a while, switch over to the prize counter video feed and wind it up for a few seconds. It doesn't seem to affect all of the animatronics, but it does affect . . . one of them. *clears throat* Uh, and as for the rest of them, we have an even easier solution. You see, there may be a minor glitch in the system, something about robots seeing you as an endoskeleton without its costume on, and wanting to stuff you in a suit, so hey, we've given you an empty Freddy Fazbear head. Problem solved! You can put it on anytime and leave it on for as long as you want. Eventually anything that wandered in will wander back out. Uh, something else worth mentioning is kind of the quirky modern design of the building. You may have noticed there are no doors for you to close, heh. Uh, but hey, you have a light! And even though your flashlight can run out of power, the building cannot. So, don't worry about the place going dark. Well, I think that's it. Uh, you should be golden. Uh, check the lights, put on the Freddy head if you need to, uh, keep the music box wound up, piece of cake. Have a good night, and I'll talk to you tomorrow.

Night 02: Uh, hello, hello? Uh, see, I told you your first night wouldn't be a problem. You're a natural! Uh, by now I'm sure you've noticed the older models sitting in the back room. Uh, those are from the previous location, and we just use them for parts now. The idea at first was to repair them . . . uh, they even started retrofitting them with some of the newer technology, but they were just so ugly, you know? And the smell . . . uh, uh, so the company decided to just go in a whole new direction and make them super kid-friendly. Uh, those older ones shouldn't be able to walk around, but if they do, the whole Freddy head trick should work on them, too, so, whatever.

Uh, heh . . . I love those old characters. Uh, did you ever see Foxy the pirate? Oh wait, Foxy . . . oh yeah, Foxy! Uh, hey, listen, uh, that one was always a bit twitchy, uh, I'm not sure the Freddy head trick will work on Foxy, uh. If for some reason he activates during the night and you see him standing at the far end of the hall, uh, just flash your light at him from time to time. Those older models would always get disoriented with bright lights. It would cause a system restart, or something. Uh, come to think of it, you might want to try that on any room where something undesirable might be. It might hold them in place for a few seconds. That glitch might've carried over to the newer models, too. One more thing—don't forget the music box. I'll be honest, I never liked that puppet thing. It's always . . . thinking, and it can go anywhere . . . uh, I don't think a Freddy mask will fool it, so just don't forget the music box. Um, anyway, I'm sure it won't be a problem. Uh, have a good night, and I'll talk to you tomorrow.

Night 03: Uh, hello, hello! See? I told ya you wouldn't have any problems! Did, uh, did Foxy ever appear in the hallway? Probably not. I was just curious. Like I said, he was always my favorite. They tried to remake Foxy, ya know? Uh, they thought the first one was too scary, so they redesigned him to be more kid-friendly and put him in Kid's Cove. To keep the toddlers entertained, you know . . . But kids these days just can't keep their hands to themselves. The staff literally had to put Foxy back together at the end of every shift. So eventually they stopped trying and left him as some kind of "take apart and put back together" attraction. Now he's just a mess of parts. I think the employees refer to him as just "The Mangle." Uh, oh, hey, before I go, uh, I wanted to ease your mind about any rumors you might have heard lately. Uh, you know how these local stories come and go and seldom mean anything. I can personally assure you that, whatever is going on out there, and however tragic it may be, has nothing to do with our establishment. It's just all rumor and speculation . . . People trying to make a buck, you know . . . Uh, our guard during the day has reported nothing unusual. And he's on watch from opening till close. Okay, well anyway, hang in there and I'll talk with you tomorrow.

Night 04: Hello, hello? Uh, hey there, night four! I told you you'd get the hang of it! Okay, so uh, just to update you, uh, there's been somewhat of an investigation going on. Uh, we may end up having to close for a few days . . . I don't know. Uh, I want to emphasize, though, that it's really just a precaution. Uh, Fazbear Entertainment denies any wrongdoing. These things happen sometimes. Um . . . it'll all get sorted out in a few days. Just keep an eye on things, and I'll keep you posted. Uh, just as a side note, though, try to avoid eye contact with any of the animatronics tonight if you can. Uh, someone may have tampered with their facial recognition systems—we're not sure. But the characters have been acting very unusual, almost aggressive toward the staff. They interact with the kids just fine, but when they encounter an adult, they just . . . stare. Uh, anyways, hang tight. It'll all pass. Good night!

Night 05: Hello, hello? Hey, good job, night five! Um, hey, uh, keep a close eye on things tonight, okay? Uh, from what I understand, the building is on *lockdown*, uh, no one is allowed in or out, y'know, especially concerning any . . . *previous employees*. Um, when we get it all sorted out, we may move you to the day shift. A position just became . . . available. Uh, we don't have a replacement for your shift yet, but we're working on it. Uh, we're going to try to contact the original restaurant owner. Uh, I think the name of the place was . . . "Fredbear's Family Diner" or something like that. It's been closed for years, though, I doubt we'll be able to track anybody down. Uh, so just get through one more night! Uh, hang in there! Good night!

Night 06: Hello, hello, uh, what on earth are you doing there? Uh didn't you get the memo? Uh, the place is closed down, a-at least for a while. Someone used one of the suits. We had a spare in the back, a yellow one, someone used it . . . now none of them are acting right. Listen, j-just finish your shift, it's safer than trying to leave in the middle of the night. Uh, we have one more event scheduled for tomorrow, a-a birthday. You'll be on day shift. Wear your uniform, stay close to the animatronics, and make sure they don't hurt anyone, okay? Uh, for now just make it through the night, uh, when the place eventually opens again, I'll probably take the night shift myself. Okay, good night and good luck.

FNAF3 Phone Guy/Phone Dude Transcripts

Night 01:

Phone Dude: Hey, hey! Glad you came back for another night! I promise it'll be a lot more interesting this time. We found some- some great new relics over the weekend. And we're out tracking down a new lead, right now. So, uh, lemme just update you real quick, then you can get to work. Like, the attraction opens in, like, a week, so we had to make sure everything works, and nothing catches on fire! Uh, when the place opens, people will come in at the opposite end of the building and work their way toward you, then past you and out the exit. Uh, yeah. You've officially become a part of the attraction. Uh, you'll be starring as . . . the security guard! So not only will you be monitoring the people on the camera as they pass through, y'know, to make sure no one steals anything or makes out in the corner, but you'll also be a part of the show. It'll make it feel really authentic, I think. Uh, now let me tell you about what's new. We found another set of drawings, always nice, and a Foxy head! Which we think could be authentic . . . then again it might just be another crappy cosplay, and we found a desk fan, very old-school metal, though, so watch the fingers. Uh-heh, uh, right now the place is basically just, you know, flashing lights and spooky props. Uh, I honestly thought we'd have more by now, uh, if we don't have something really cool by next week, then we may have to suit you up in a furry suit and make you walk around saying, "Boo" . . . he-he, uh, but, you know, like I said, we're trying to track down a good lead right now. Uh, some guy who helped design one of the buildings says there was, like, an extra room that got boarded up or, uh, something like that. So, we're gonna take a peek and see what we can find. Uh, for now just get comfortable with the new setup, um . . . You can check the security cameras over to your right with a click of that blue button. Uh, you can toggle between the hall cams and the vent cams . . . Uh, then over to your far left, uh, you can flip up your maintenance panel. Y'know, use this to reboot any systems that may go offline. Heh. So, in trying to make the place feel vintage we may have overdone it a bit, he-he . . . Some of this equipment is barely functional. Yeah, I wasn't joking about the fire. Tha-tha-that's a real risk. Uh, the most important thing you want to watch for is the ventilation. Look, this place will give you the spooks, man, and if you let that ventilation go offline, then you'll start seeing some crazy stuff, man. Keep that air a flowin'. Okay, keep an eye on things, and we'll try to have something new for ya tomorrow night.

Night 02:

Phone Dude: Hey, man. Okay, I have some awesome news for you! First of all, we found some vintage audio training cassettes! Dude, these are, like, *prehistoric!* I think they were, like, training tapes for, like, other employees or something like that. So, I thought we could, like, have them playing, like, over the speakers as people walk through the attraction. Dude, that makes this feel legit, man. But I have an even better surprise for you, and you're not gonna believe this. We found one. A *real* one. Uh-oh-uh, gotta go man. Uh, well-well, look, i-it's in there somewhere, I'm-I'm sure you'll see it. Okay, I'll leave you with some of this great audio that I found! Talk to you later, man!

Phone Guy: Uh, hello! Hello, hello! Uh, welcome to your new career as a performer/entertainer for Freddy Fazbear's Pizza. Uh, these tapes will provide you with much needed information on how to handle/climb into/climb out of mascot costumes. Right now, we have two specially designed suits that double as both animatronic and suit. So please pay close attention while learning how to operate these suits, as accidents/injuries/death/irreparable and grotesque maiming can occur. First, we'll discuss how to operate the mascots when they are in animatronic form. For ease of operation, the animatronics are set to turn and walk toward sound machines they hear, which is an easy and hands-free approach to making sure the animatronics stay where the children are for maximum entertainment/crowd-pleasing value. To change the animatronics to suit mode, insert and turn firmly the hand crank provided by the manufacturer. Turning the crank will recoil and compress the animatronic parts around the sides of the suit, providing room to climb inside. Please make sure the springlocks are fastened tight to ensure the animatronic devices remain fixed. We will cover this in more detail in tomorrow's session. Remember to smile; you are the face of Freddy Fazbear's Pizza.

Night 03:

Phone Guy: Uh, hello, hello. Uh, for today's lesson, we will be continuing our training on proper suit-handling techniques. When using an animatronic as a suit, please ensure that the animatronic parts are tightly compressed and fastened by the springlocks located around the inside of the suit. It may take a few moments to position your head and torso between these parts in a manner where you can move and speak. Try not to nudge or press against any of the springlocks inside the suit. Do not touch the springlocks at any time. Do not breathe on the springlocks, as moisture may loosen them and cause them to break loose. In the case that the springlocks come loose while you are wearing the suit, please try to maneuver away from populated areas before bleeding out, as to not ruin the customers' experience. As always, if there is ever an emergency, please go to the designated safe room. Every location is built with one extra room that is not included in the digital map layouts programmed in the animatronics or the security system. This room is hidden to customers, invisible to animatronics, and is always off-camera. As always, remember to smile; you are the face of Freddy Fazbear's Pizza.

Night 04:

Phone Guy: Uh, hello? Hello, hello! Uh, there's been a slight change of company policy concerning use of the suits. Um, *don't*. After learning of an unfortunate incident at the sister location, involving multiple and simultaneous springlock failures, the company has deemed the suits temporarily unfit for employees. Safety is top priority at Freddy Fazbear's Pizza, which is why the classic suits are being retired to an appropriate location, while being looked at by our technician. Until replacements arrive, you'll be expected to wear the temporary costumes provided to you. Keep in mind that they were found on very short notice, so questions about appropriateness/relevance should be deflected. I repeat, the classic suits are not to be touched, activated, or worn. That being said, we are free of liability, do as you wish. As always, remember to smile; you are the face of Freddy Fazbear's Pizza.

Night 05:

Phone Guy: Hello? Hello? Um, this is just a reminder of company policy concerning the safe room. The safe room is reserved for equipment and/or other property not being currently used and as a backup safety location for employees only. This is not a break room, and should not be considered a place for employees to hide and/or congregate, and under no circumstance should a customer ever be taken into this room and out of the main show area. Management has also been made aware that the Spring Bonnie animatronic has been noticeably moved. We would like to remind employees that this costume is not safe to wear under any circumstances. Thank you and remember to smile; you are the face of Freddy Fazbear's Pizza.

Nightmare:

Phone Guy: Uh, hello? Hello? Uh, this is just to inform all employees that due to budget restrictions, the previously mentioned safe rooms are being sealed at most locations, including this one. Work crews will be here most of the day today, constructing a false wall over the old door face. Nothing is being taken out beforehand, so if you've left anything inside, then it's your own fault. Management also requests that this room not be mentioned to family, friends, or insurance representatives. Thanks again, and remember to smile; you are the face of Freddy Fazbear's Pizza.

Sister Location: The Immortal and the Restless Scripts

The Immortal and the Restless [Episode 1]

Narrator: Another day, another dramatic entry in the lives of Vlad and his distressed mistress! Where will they go? What will they do? All of that and more . . . happening now!

Vlad: Clara, I tell you, the baby isn't mine!

Clara: Count, I tell you that it is! You're the only vampire I've ever loved! And the baby turns his bottles into powdered milk.

Vlad: That doesn't mean anything.

Clara: He sleeps on the ceiling fan!

Vlad: Upright, or upside down?

Clara: What does it matter? You *need* to be part of your son's life!

Vlad: I'm an old man, Clara! I can't be a father!

Clara: Well, then, at least pay your child support, you deadbeat!

Narrator: Will Vlad and his distressed mistress find common ground? Tune in next time!

The Immortal and the Restless [Episode 2]

Narrator: As the sun sets, so also does another chapter in the saga of love lost between Vlad and his distressed mistress. Can they be reconciled? Can their love rise again? That and more . . . happening now!

Vlad: Clara, the baby isn't mine!

Clara: It is, Vlad! They had trouble catching him in the nursery today!

Vlad: So what? Lots of kids get hyper and run around and stuff.

Clara: They had to knock him out of the air with a broom!

Vlad: I have to go.

Clara: They're going to dock your paychecks.

Vlad: They can't do that! I'm a vampire, I don't get paychecks!

Clara: You work the graveyard shift at the Fry Me Taco. Don't lie to me!

Narrator: Oh, the humanity! When will the heartbreak end? When will these two ships passing in the night rekindle their long-lost love? Tune in tomorrow to find out.

The Immortal and the Restless [Episode 3]

Narrator: As the moon rises, so also rises the tension between sworn lovers.

Vlad: Clara, it's not my baby.

Clara: Vlad, you suck.

Vlad: Wait, was that a vampire joke? That was so lame, Clara, like I've never heard that a million times.

Clara: Okay, well how's this: I'm taking the car!

Vlad: The joke's on you! It's a rental.

Clara: Well, the joke's on you. I set the thermostat to ninety before I left.

Vlad: Good, I like it warm.

Clara: Good! Because I also set the house on fire!

Narrator: How will it all end? The passion! The tension! The intrigue! Tune in tomorrow for the exciting conclusion.

The Immortal and the Restless [Episode 4]

Narrator: As the trees sway in the wind, so also do emotions sway between star-crossed lovers!

Vlad: You burned down my house?!

Clara: You call that a house? It was like a morgue in there.

Vlad: I may be undead, but you're heartless.

Clara: You need to see your son!

Vlad: The baby isn't mine!

Clara: He ate the cat!

Vlad: Sounds like something he got from your side of the family!

Clara: Well, how's this? I'm keeping the diamond ring.

Vlad: The joke's on you! I found it in a kid's meal!

Clara: You bought a kid's meal? Oh, Vlad!

Vlad: Clara!

Narrator: As the hair on the back of the cat stands up straight, so also does the love between Vlad and Clara stand up against all obstacles. But what about the baby? What about the back child support? Stay tuned next season for those answers, and more.

To be continued . . .

Sister Location Animatronic Blueprints
C
B
D
Name: Circus Baby
Height: 7.2 ft
Weight: 585 lbs
A: Air Hose Attachment
B: Internal Ice Cream Dispenser
C: Song Databank
D: Emergency Stop
Afton Robotics, LLC
A
B
C
D
Name: Ballora
Height: 6.2 ft
Weight: 347 lbs
A: Audio Activation Sensor
B: Deter & Misdirect
Remote Activation
see: Circus Baby dir07
C: Balance/ Stability
D: Collision Sensor

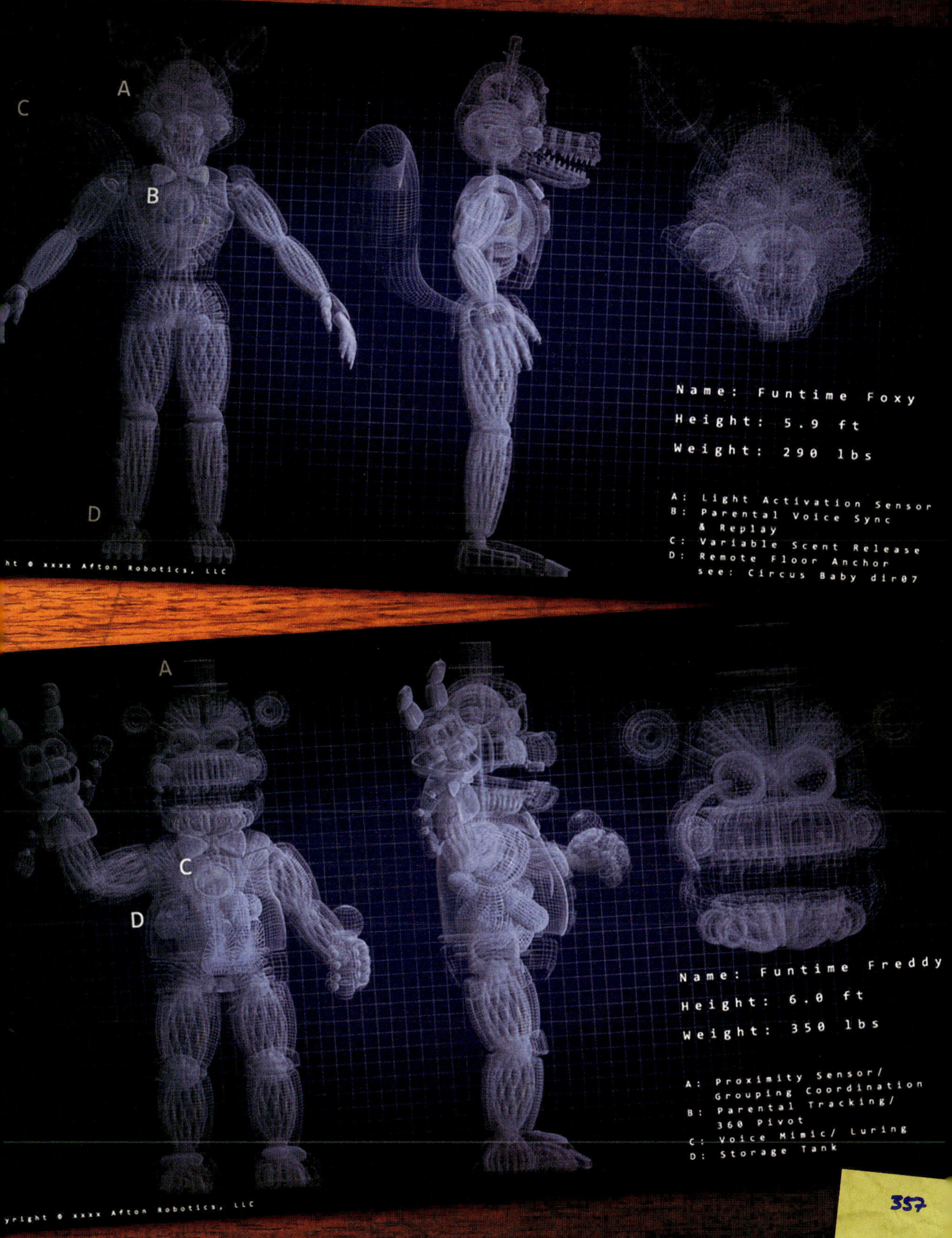
A
C
B
D
ht © xxxx Afton Robotics, LLC
Name: Funtime Foxy
Height: 5.9 ft
Weight: 290 lbs
A: Light Activation Sensor
B: Parental Voice Sync
& Replay
C: Variable Scent Release
D: Remote Floor Anchor
see: Circus Baby dir07
A
C
D
Name: Funtime Freddy
Height: 6.0 ft
Weight: 350 lbs
A: Proximity Sensor/
Grouping Coordination
B: Parental Tracking/
360 Pivot
C: Voice Mimic/ Luring
D: Storage Tank
yright © xxxx Afton Robotics, LLC
357

Pizzeria Simulator Blueprints

L.ure E.ncapsulate F.use T.ransport & E.xtract

A: Navigational Sensors

B: False Sensory Output

NOTES: Bracelet code 93401233. Emit for security receiver frequency FZ554.

C: "Dream Wand"/ Soother

NOTES: Use lullaby index 01. Upon suit-seal, provide steady voltage throughout. Behavior upon suit-seal not guaranteed.

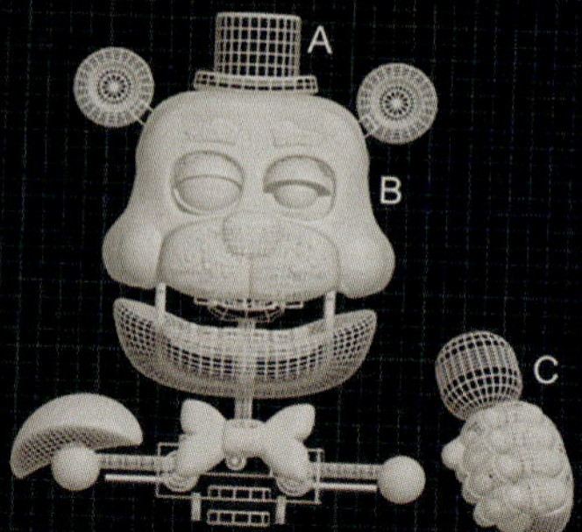

Fazbear Entertainment, Inc

Facial Recognition File 0072

Security Tags Active:

001 "Funtime Freddy"
002 "Funtime Foxy"
003 "Ballora"

Priority One

With the most amount of remnant collectively in its structure, this amalgamation of Afton's constructs is a necessary element of Paragraph 4.

R.emote A.ctivated S.imulated C.

A: Navigational Sensors

B: Heat Uplink / Sensor Override

NOTES: Must remain connected to central server at all times or risk duplicate signature. Variable Alpha to remain at 98.6.

C: Individual Emitter

NOTES: Must remain connected to central server at all times or risk inaccurate represented population. Audio controlled by central server.

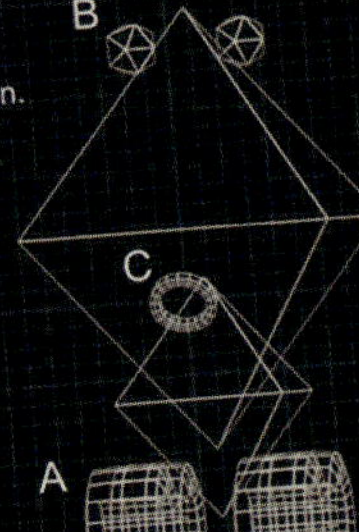

Fazbear Entertainment, Inc

S.calable C.reation of U.lterior P.resence

A: Excavating Arm

B: Remnant Injector

NOTES: Leave trace line amount on interior. Over-usage/ Over-exposure negates effect.

C: Arm Base and Balance

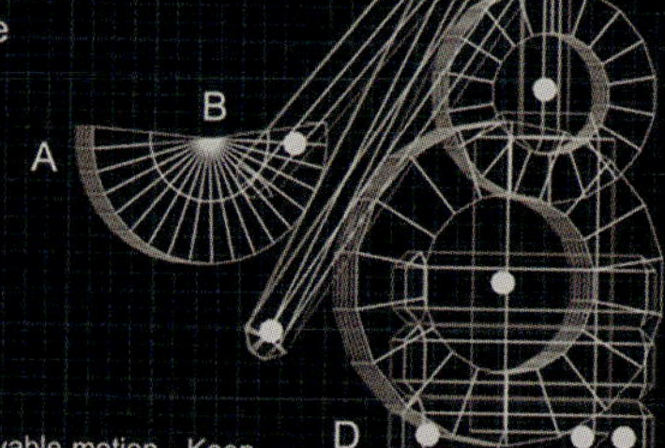

D: Remnant Reservoir

NOTES: When heated, no observable motion. Keep in heated tank at sustained temperature. Substance should be malleable, but not more.

There is a possibility that overheating might neutralize the effects permanently.

Afton Robotics, LLC

Help Wanted: Full Legal Disclaimer

Welcome to the Fazbear quality assurance team. Before we can officially congratulate you on your fabulous lifetime career choice, you must first agree to this simple waiver. Our lawyers have come up with a way to save you time by bypassing all the legal terms, and pages and pages of law-related verbiage by creating this simple in-game app. The important points have been condensed to a single page. Consider precious moments of your life saved.

The auto-scroll feature was designed to protect you from potential repetitive stress injuries. It's just another way that Fazbear Entertainment cares for its employees. You should also take care not to overexert your eyes while looking at such small text on a highly contrasting document screen. Therefore, it is recommended that you rest your eyes while accepting these terms. Please close them now, for safety purposes. Are they closed? Good. If you agree to the terms presented, you may press the button in front of you to confirm. Or, if you would like to further reduce the risk of repetitive stress injury, you may allow the ACCEPT "button" to remain untouched for ten seconds. The ten-second mark will let us know that you intend to press the ACCEPT "button" but are a health-conscious individual.

Help Wanted Tape Transcripts

Tape One:
Hello? Can you hear me? Don't exit this room, okay? This isn't a mistake. This *room* isn't a mistake. I had to hide these logs away from the core gameplay files, in a place that only a beta tester would look and in a place where the files could be protected. I just really, really hope that the next development team finds this before the game is released to the public. This game has some kind of malicious code in it that we haven't been able to fully contain or even understand for that matter. We're over budget and out of time. But that's not the reason that we're shutting down. Listen, I have to keep this short so the file size will be small enough to fly under the radar. There are more. They may not be in order.

Tape Two:
I saw it for the first time today. There was a character, I couldn't make out who it was, standing at the end of the hall. I thought it was just bugged out, so I made a note of it and kept playing. But then it was looking in the window . . . and not like Chica or Bonnie would. It was like it was actually looking in the window, seeing what I was doing.

Tape Three:
I heard a pretty heated conversation this morning between Dale, our manager, and someone else on the line. It really feels like this project is in trouble, in no small part because of the lawsuit, I'm sure. There has to be a lawsuit. There's no way there isn't. It happened in this building just a few doors down from me. I think it's made worse by the fact that Jeremy tried to tell us something was wrong. But as a dev team, we all just saw it as a challenge to find what the problem was and fix it. Who could have known that—I have to go.

Tape Four:
Have you ever heard of a guillotine paper slicer? It sounds made up, but it's an actual piece of office equipment. I didn't even know we had one in the supply room. I guess they're more common at businesses that do a lot of graphic design work. I remember seeing one when I was still in school, and even then, I knew how dangerous it looked. I was always afraid of losing a finger. That seems so silly now. Jeremy used to do design work. I guess that's how he knew it was there.

Tape Five:
The drawers have been emptied out. Someone was here. I don't think it was spring cleaning, either. No. There was plastic on the floor. Someone was definitely here during the night—it had to have been the client. I mean, they sent us that stuff in the first place with no explanation, told us to scan it, said it would expedite the process so we wouldn't need to program any pathfinding ourselves. It was a budget thing, I guess. It was just junk—circuit boards and things like that. Looked pretty old. Somehow, though, there was usable code on some of it. It seemed to take hold by itself. Things started changing. But then he started appearing . . . At least that's what Jeremy said.

Tape Six:
I came in early that morning. No one else was there. At least, that's what I thought. The supply room was lit. I didn't even notice Jeremy standing in the testing room as I walked past. The supply room was so bright, glowing from all the way down the hall.

Tape Seven:
Jeremy complained of nightmares when he came in this morning. He wasn't talking about it like someone telling a friend about his dreams, though. He was pale. Looked like he hadn't eaten in days. He spent an hour talking in Dale's office, but it didn't look like he was given much sympathy. When he came out, he went directly back to the testing room. He doesn't even jump anymore—nothing scares him. He just stands there like he's talking to someone. Sometimes he rocks from side to side. We were told to leave him alone. I knew I was in line to do the testing next. They'd been prepping me for it. I guess they knew that Jeremy would need to be replaced soon.

Tape Eight:

You can always tell when a company is getting ready to fire someone. They start giving out written warnings for silly things, making sure to build a paper trail and make a case for a firing. Things that normally no one would care about suddenly become grave offenses, all worthy of being written and documented. I guess it works two ways, because it also encourages a person to quit rather than be scrutinized so heavily. I think Jeremy was too far gone to consider that option, though. The thing about it is, that I don't think they were going to fire him because of anything he was doing wrong. They just *knew* he'd seen something. They *needed* to discredit him.

Tape Nine:

There was something that looked like a Halloween mask laying on the floor. I didn't understand. Ink must have spilled. It was only then that I heard a shuffle from the testing room and realized Jeremy must be there. I went back and peered in the window. I couldn't see his face. He had the visor covering his head. He had ink spilled on himself as well. The front of his shirt looked black in the dark room. He turned his head in my direction, but I don't think he *knew* I was there.

Tape Ten:

I was told I had three days to finish Jeremy's work, but I know it's just passing the time. They don't really expect me to do anything. It's just to keep up appearances until the buyout is complete. We have to *look* like we have things under control. There's another potential development studio that wants to pick up from here, but who knows what kind of lies they're being fed to convince them to do it. Against my better judgment, I'm going to do my best to see what's here, make notes of it, and try to isolate where this thing is hiding. At least then the next person that tests this will have a chance of getting rid of it.

Tape Eleven:

Today was my last day of beta testing and the anomaly that I've been seeing is nowhere to be found. But after inspecting some of the files, it seems that it's attached itself to these logs. *My logs*. That *can't* be an accident. So now I have to make a choice. Do I leave these logs here for you to find, or do I try to purge this thing myself by destroying the logs? I've chosen the latter.

Tape Twelve:

I can't delete them. By creating a protected area to store these logs apart from the game, I effectively gave this thing a safe place to hide itself. It's *in* here now. I may not be able to delete it, but I might be able to do something else now that it's attached itself. I have an idea.

Tape Thirteen:
They lied to us. They lied to all of us. They told us that the whole point of this VR game was to undo the bad PR done by a rogue indie game developer, who supposedly made up a bunch of crazy stories that tarnished the brand. But that's not true at all. In their haste to develop this VR game and clear their name, they sent us some things I don't think they intended us to see, such as a hard drive containing emails between Fazbear Entertainment and a certain indie developer. Fazbear Entertainment *hired* the game developer. Those indie games were designed to conceal and make light of what happened. This isn't just an attempt to rebrand—it's an elaborate cover-up, a campaign to discredit everything.

Tape Fourteen:
I ran a fragmentation program on the area of memory that was storing these logs for you. I effectively broke the files into pieces and broke the anomaly along with it. That means that you won't have my warnings to guide you. But hopefully, it also means that this anomaly—this virus, or whatever it is—will remain broken and unable to do more damage.

Tape Fifteen:
Hello. You don't know me. I'd created a series of logs for you documenting the troubled development of this VR game that you're now testing, in hopes that you, whoever you are, and whatever team you are with, will abandon development. Now I fear that those logs are being used as a trojan horse. If you're unable to abandon development, hide all traces of these logs that I've created. I fear that finding them and reassembling them will also reassemble the very thing I've tried so desperately to destroy.

Tape Sixteen:
There is a way to kill it. It wants to escape. To escape through someone. Someone plugged into this game. That's *you* now. You have to let it begin the process of leaving through you, then use the disconnect switch that I've embedded by the main stage. Let it approach you. Let it begin to merge with you. Play the music and flip the switch. That will cause a hard restart of the game and flush the memory, effectively killing it . . . I hope. I don't know when it will come for you.

SPECIAL DELIVERY EMAILS

Staff Advisory: Mail Server

From: Fazbear Entertainment Office of Legal Affairs

Due to technical complications, our mail server may be directing email to incorrect recipients.

If you receive an email that is not addressed to you, please forward it to the intended recipient and notify the IT department immediately.

As a friendly reminder, reading an email that was not intended for your eyes is a violation of Fazbear Entertainment's company policy, and you may be subject to disciplinary action up to and including immediate termination. That policy remains in effect.

Please do not read an email that is not your own. Thank you for your cooperation as we resolve this technical complication.

11/28/2019
(no subject)
From: luis.cabrera
To: nessie97

Hey, Ness,

I hope you're having a good day! It's no big deal, but I wanted to reach out "off the radar," and remind you about the company policy about personal internet usage. Nobody cares if you're online shopping, as long as you get your work done—I promise—I've done my share of last-minute gift-buying! But certain words and phrases trigger red flag reports, so your last order got automatically sent to me: basically anything mentioning "torture" is going to raise the alarm. So although the *Viking Blood Eagle Twelve-Month Calendar* you ordered is very cool, the searches that got you there did trigger a red flag.

If you have any questions about the policy, let me know. We could even get coffee or something and go over all the words to avoid.

. . . And now I've raised my own red flag! Good thing I'm the one who gets the notification :-)

-Luis

11/28/2019
Re: (no subject)
From: Mark Cho

These things are creeping me out.

Re: (no subject)
From: Raha Salib

Seriously. We don't have room for them, I don't know why Anna agreed to take this job.

Re: (no subject)

From: Mark Cho

$$$$$

Re: (no subject)
From: Raha Salib

More like $

Re: (no subject)
From: Mark Cho

lol

11/29/2019
Can I use power tools?
From: Daniel Rocha
To: Anna Kwemto

Hey, Anna,

The casings on the animatronics are really hard to get off. Can you approve me to use the power drill?

Best,
Dan

Re: Can I use power tools?
From: Anna Kwemto
To: Daniel Rocha

No.

Re: Can I use power tools?
From: Daniel Rocha
To: Anna Kwemto

Please? I'm serious, I can't get the casing off without it.

Re: Can I use power tools?
From: Anna Kwemto
To: Daniel Rocha

Raha is the only one certified. Quit asking.

11/29/2019
Come drill for me?
From: Daniel Rocha
To: Raha Salib

Need to get the circuit boards out. Anna says you're the only one who can use the power drill.

Re: Come drill for me?
From: Raha Salib
To: Daniel Rocha

15 min.

11/30/2019
System glitch
From: Steven Wilson

Hey, guys, I just got kicked off the system. I finished scanning the last set of circuit boards Dan brought me, but now I'm locked out. Is anyone else getting this "unknown error"?

Re: System glitch
From: Anna Kwemto

No.

12/01/2019
IMMEDIATE ACTION REQUIRED
From: Fazbear Entertainment Office of Legal Affairs
To: Anna Kwemto

Dear Ms. Kwemto,

Please immediately cease all work on Fazbear Entertainment properties. Due to unforeseen circumstances, Fazbear Entertainment is ordering a halt to work on all existing contracts, especially in reference to any vintage hardware. We will be in touch regarding our future course of action; please contact our billing department regarding payment for completed work-to-date action.

Sincerely,

Kayla Stringer

Associate General Counsel

Fazbear Entertainment

12/01/2019
Fwd: IMMEDIATE ACTION REQUIRED
From: Anna Kwemto

Fazbear just ordered us to stop working. It sounds like they're halting work with all their contractors, not just us. They said they'll be in touch about "our future course of action."

Re: Fwd: IMMEDIATE ACTION REQUIRED
From: Steven Wilson

Anna, are we still getting paid for this?

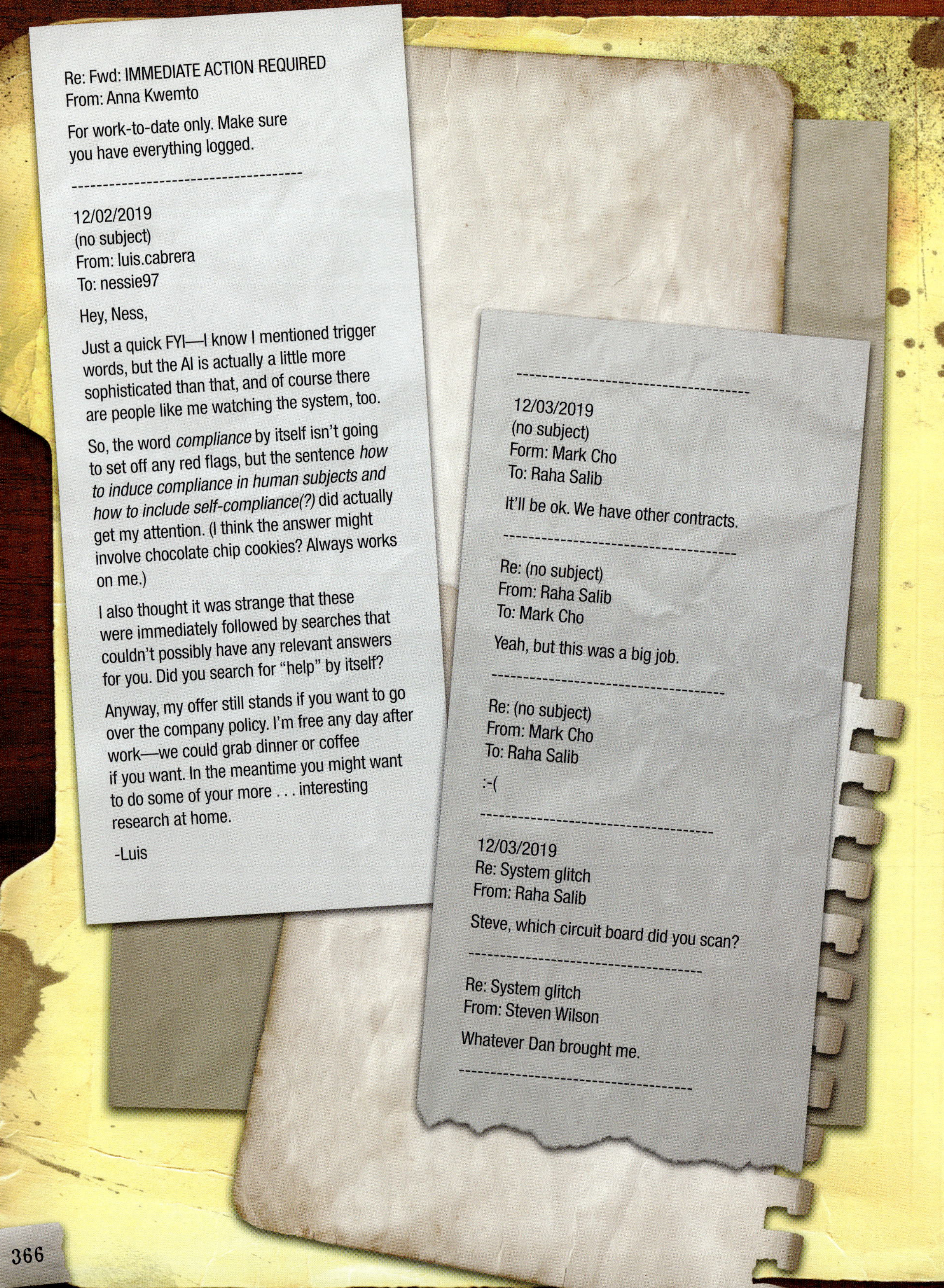

Re: Fwd: IMMEDIATE ACTION REQUIRED
From: Anna Kwemto

For work-to-date only. Make sure you have everything logged.

12/02/2019
(no subject)
From: luis.cabrera
To: nessie97

Hey, Ness,

Just a quick FYI—I know I mentioned trigger words, but the AI is actually a little more sophisticated than that, and of course there are people like me watching the system, too.

So, the word *compliance* by itself isn't going to set off any red flags, but the sentence *how to induce compliance in human subjects and how to include self-compliance(?)* did actually get my attention. (I think the answer might involve chocolate chip cookies? Always works on me.)

I also thought it was strange that these were immediately followed by searches that couldn't possibly have any relevant answers for you. Did you search for "help" by itself?

Anyway, my offer still stands if you want to go over the company policy. I'm free any day after work—we could grab dinner or coffee if you want. In the meantime you might want to do some of your more . . . interesting research at home.

-Luis

12/03/2019
(no subject)
Form: Mark Cho
To: Raha Salib

It'll be ok. We have other contracts.

Re: (no subject)
From: Raha Salib
To: Mark Cho

Yeah, but this was a big job.

Re: (no subject)
From: Mark Cho
To: Raha Salib

:-(

12/03/2019
Re: System glitch
From: Raha Salib

Steve, which circuit board did you scan?

Re: System glitch
From: Steven Wilson

Whatever Dan brought me.

12/04/2019
(no subject)
From: luis.cabrera
To: nessie97

Hey, Ness,

I wanted to see if you're doing ok. I appreciate your taking my advice about red flag search terms, if I thought I'd have to file an incident report on you, I think I'd just have to quit instead. So, my student loans thank you!

I do have to keep checking online activity periodically after getting a red flag report, and I was a little worried maybe something is going on with you? One day you're researching flowers and the migration patterns of bees (fascinating, right?) and the next day you type in "How far can a human being be cut in half before losing consciousness."

I figured, maybe you're writing a screenplay or something? But it was a little startling to see it written out. I hope you know I'm always here if you need me.

-Luis

12/05/2019
Virus detected
From: Daniel Rocha

Turns out that wasn't just a glitch, we released a virus when we scanned that last circuit board. It's spreading really fast, we're going to need all hands on deck.

12/06/2019
(no subject)
From: luis.cabrera
To: nessie97

Hey, Ness,

I hope things are good! I saw you ordered three "lifelike, human male rubber masks" and I was dying to ask what they're for—was my screenplay guess right? Are you making a movie, or putting together some kind of performance?

Everything's the same as usual with me—but I guess you know that, you see me every day at work! Maybe one day soon we can get that coffee.

-Luis

12/07/2019
URGENT: Virus caused by FE circuit board upload
To: James Campbell
From: Steven Wilson

Hey, Jim,

We have a virus spreading through our system, and we've traced it back to one of the circuit board scans we performed for Fazbear Entertainment. Are you aware of this issue? Can you send any guidance?

Best,

Steve

12/08/2019
(no subject)
To: nessie97
From: luis.cabrera

Hey, Ness,

It was really great talking to you today. I think that might be the first time we've actually had an in-person conversation, lol. It's weird, I feel like I know you so well, but I guess you don't know so much about me. We're just going to have to fix that!

I had no idea you were into IT stuff. I always think my job sounds so boring, but you were so interested it made me start thinking, hey, maybe IT is cool after all. Or maybe you're just a good listener. Anyway, it was nice to have some in-person time. Maybe we can do it again soon. I still owe you that coffee I keep saying we should get.

-Luis

12/09/2019
(no subject)
To: nessie97
From: luis.cabrera

Hey, Ness,

Is everything OK? I came by your desk to say hi today and I don't think you even heard me. You had your face so close to the screen, that can't be good for your eyes (I know, I know, I sound like somebody's grandma). I waited for a second to see if you would turn around, but it was like you were in another world. It must be useful to be able to shut out the world and focus like that, I wish I could do it. I thought you were on a conference call at first because I heard voices.

Ness, if you ever want to talk about anything, I'm always here for you. I thought your hair looked nice today, the rainbow streaks brightened up the office—and the office is always in desperate need of some brightening!

-Luis

12/10/2019

URGENT: Virus

To: James Campbell, Anna Kwemto

From: Steven Wilson

Hi, Jim,

Just checking in. I emailed you earlier this week about a virus caused by one of your circuit boards, which is currently spreading throughout our systems and causing serious problems. Please contact me ASAP. Thanks.

Best,

Steve.

12/17/2019
Might need more time
To: Compliance Team
From: Nora (R&D)

Okay, we got the new one up and running, like you guys wanted. Gotta say, though . . . the facial recognition upgrades aren't taking the exact effect we expected. We've got our best looking at it, now.

I would suggest getting an extension, if possible. Would hate for these to go out before they're ready.

Thanks, Nora

P.S. Still waiting to hear back about the other ones. Did anyone even see that request?

Re: Might need more time

To: Nora (R&D)

From: Tristan (Compliance Team)

That's a no-go on an extension. You mentioned the other day in the sync meeting that your guys found a work-around, right?

Just go with that and hit the original dates.

Tristan

Oh and I saw the earlier request, nothing I can say about them yet. (You know how it is . . .)

1/17/2020
Still can't reproduce the issue
From: Charles (QA)
To: Nora (R&D)

We've tried everything we can think of here to reproduce the issue you were seeing with the new toy model, but can't seem to get it to happen here.

Are you sure about the eyes changing color before the behavioral matrix went haywire?

CD

1/17/2020
Re: Still can't reproduce the issue
From: Nora (R&D)
To: Charles (QA)

It was only the once, and only one of the guys reported it. I've caught him sleeping on the job twice this week, too, so he's probably just imagining things.

Honestly, what's the worst that could happen?

Just note it in the log as "Cannot Reproduce" and move on to the rest, or we're never going to meet the new deadline.

Nora

1/31/2020
Not cool
From: Tristan (Compliance Team)
To: Nora (R&D)

Nora,

I heard about you trying to go over my head to my boss about the Toy Freddy issue. While I appreciate you are trying to do what you feel is your job, defining compliance and safety standards is my department, not yours.

Our product analysts have determined that the Toy Freddy issue is negligible. We'll just slap a note at the bottom of the outgoing customer outreach mails—it's not like any of the users even read those, and we'll be covered legally.

Tristan

P.S. Next time you feel like going over my head, come talk to me, or you'll force me to bring this up with Human Resources. Sorry to be the bad guy about this, but you're really not leaving me with any other choice.

2/04/2020
Re: Not cool
From: Nora (R&D)
To: Tristan (Compliance Team)

Fine. But I want it noted in writing what my department reported.

Toy Freddy is *not* safe to go out to the public. The interference happening with the upgraded facial recognition suite risks rendering *all* the safety functions on the users' handsets useless.

Nora

2/12/2020
Couple of weird customer reports
From: Isolde (Customer Service)
To: Tristan (Compliance Team)

Hey, Tristan,

We've been getting some weird reports here in Customer Service that I don't really know how to respond to.

A handful of our more hardcore users of the service have been reporting service calls from an animatronic that isn't appearing anywhere in our database. Some kind of vintage Bonnie model. A couple of people have mentioned a really bad smell from it as well.

Is it possible some old secondhand model somehow made it into the deployment rotation?

Izzy

3/03/2020
New Multarticulus Model Delays
From: Tristan (Compliance Team)
To: Nora (R&D)

Nora,

I've been looking over those reports on the motility tests for the new model, and I gotta say I'm a little disturbed by the lack of progress. The original was purportedly able to move along the ceiling, and from what I'm seeing here, we're having issues getting our rebuilds to even move on level ground properly.

What kind of shop are you guys running down there? The marketing guys are lighting fires under me to promise we'll hit the launch date for this, and what I'm seeing is not filling me with confidence.

Tristan

3/05/2020

Re: New Multarticulus Model Delays
From: Nora (R&D)
To: Tristan (Compliance Team)

First, tell the marketing people to go jump off a bridge. They just have to write some fancy copy while we're down here trying to make their crazy promises work in reality on unrealistic budgets and completely insane timelines. We're doing the best we can.

Second, there's a *huge* difference between a new model based on the same bipedal chassis and one based on a . . . whatever you want to call this thing. A quadruped? A spider? A tripod? The locomotion is *completely* different, which means the power needs are different, the hydraulic calibrations have to be completely redone, and the CPU has to be switched out for a newer one with a faster baud rate. And then on top of all that, we have to put together this "Controlled Disassembly" feature? The marketing people are crazy.

Third, GET OFF MY BACK!!! I *warned* management that reproducing the more exotic endoskeletons would be a problem, and they decided to go ahead and put them on the schedule anyway. They're just going to have to live with the limitations of, you know, *basic physics.*

Nora

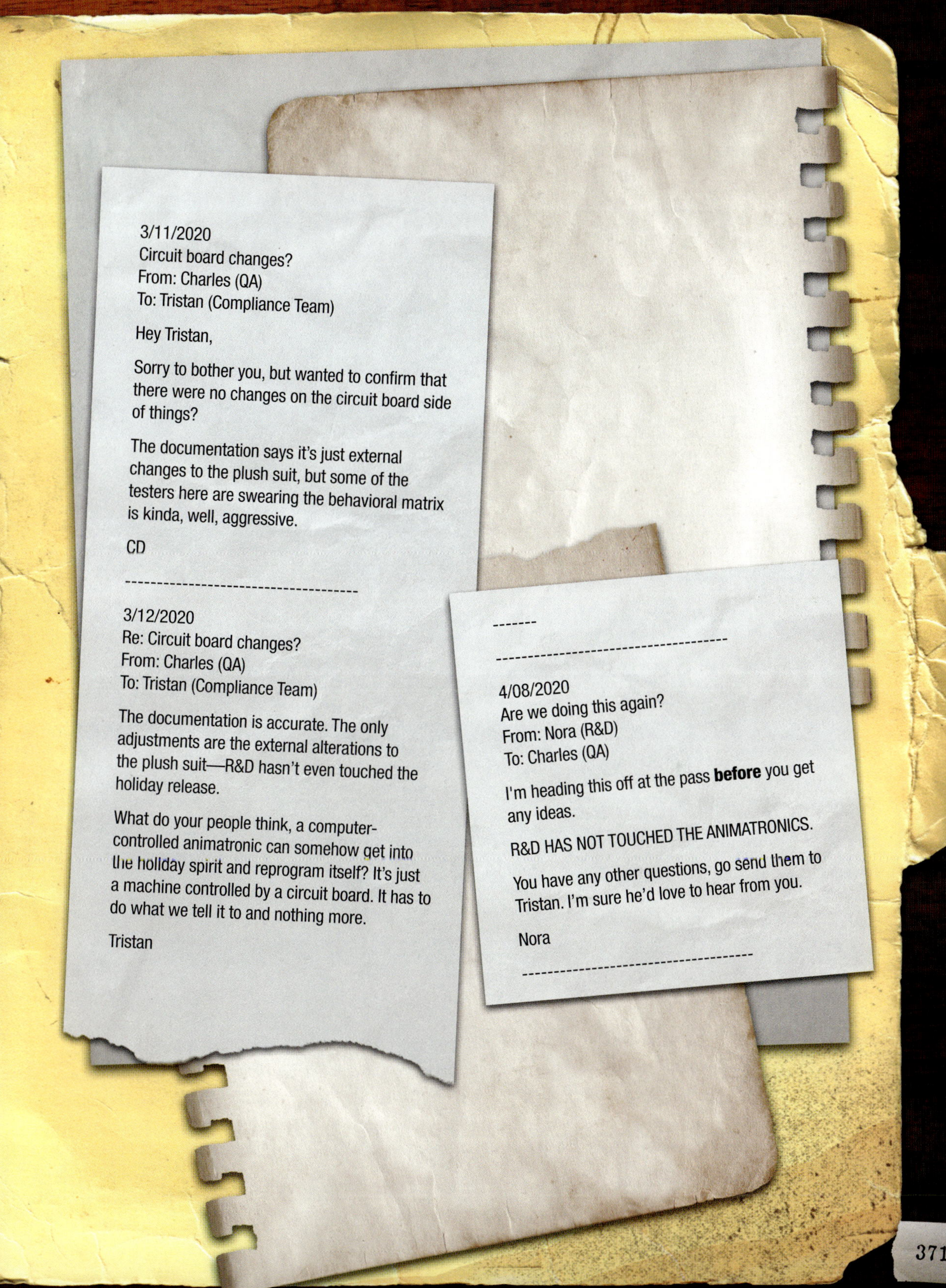
3/11/2020
Circuit board changes?
From: Charles (QA)
To: Tristan (Compliance Team)

Hey Tristan,

Sorry to bother you, but wanted to confirm that there were no changes on the circuit board side of things?

The documentation says it's just external changes to the plush suit, but some of the testers here are swearing the behavioral matrix is kinda, well, aggressive.

CD

3/12/2020
Re: Circuit board changes?
From: Charles (QA)
To: Tristan (Compliance Team)

The documentation is accurate. The only adjustments are the external alterations to the plush suit—R&D hasn't even touched the holiday release.

What do your people think, a computer-controlled animatronic can somehow get into the holiday spirit and reprogram itself? It's just a machine controlled by a circuit board. It has to do what we tell it to and nothing more.

Tristan

4/08/2020
Are we doing this again?
From: Nora (R&D)
To: Charles (QA)

I'm heading this off at the pass **before** you get any ideas.

R&D HAS NOT TOUCHED THE ANIMATRONICS.

You have any other questions, go send them to Tristan. I'm sure he'd love to hear from you.

Nora

Chapter 20

ANIMATRONICS INVENTORY

Withered, twisted, rockstar, mediocre, shadow, nightmare, phantom . . . is your head spinning yet? *FNAF*'s roster of animatronics has grown beyond 150+ since the series first reached gamers. The original five animatronics were reimagined through countless lenses all while entirely new animatronics were released. Explore a curated list of the animatronics from the games, stories, and books here, from the main attractions to the smallest side character.

8-BIT BABY: An arcade-themed animatronic, with a design similar to Circus Baby's minigame in *Sister Location*. 8-Bit Baby is manufactured and delivered by Fazbear Funtime Service.

Appearances: *Sister Location, Special Delivery*

ARCTIC BALLORA: A winter skin used to customize the Ballora plush suit in *Special Delivery*.

Appearances: *Special Delivery*

THE BABY CRAWLERS: Baby-like animatronics that are made of metal and have plastic, clown-painted faces.

Appearances: *The Fourth Closet*

BALLOON BOY (BB): A humanoid animatronic that wears a red-and-blue-striped shirt and a propeller beanie. He carries a balloon as well as a sign that reads BALLOONS! He often calls out "Hello?" and "Hi!" and sometimes giggles. In several games, Balloon Boy doesn't kill you, but he does disable your defenses, which can leave you completely helpless.

Appearances: *FNAF2, FNAF3, Ultimate Custom Night, Help Wanted, Curse of Dreadbear, Special Delivery, The Twisted Ones, Freddy Fazbear's Pizzeria Simulator* (minigame), *Help Wanted 2, VIP*

BALLORA: A sound-activated ballerina animatronic with painted white skin, rosy cheeks, blue hair, and a purple tutu. She occupies Ballora Gallery in *Sister Location*, and sings a creepy song on Night 02 if you listen closely. Ballora is often accompanied by minireenas (see page 387), and has several unique capabilities mentioned in her blueprint (see page 352).

Appearances: *Sister Location, Ultimate Custom Night, Help Wanted 2, Special Delivery,* "Dance with Me," "Cleithrophobia," "Room for One More," "Somniphobia," "Step Closer," "Dittophobia," "1:35 a.m." (as Nurse Ballora)

BIDYBABS: Small, baby doll–like animatronics that typically perform alongside Circus Baby. They appear in the Circus Gallery in *Sister Location*; players must fend them off once in the secret compartment and again in the Private Room.

Appearances: *Sister Location, Ultimate Custom Night, Help Wanted, Help Wanted 2*

BLACK HEART BONNIE: A holiday-themed animatronic skin for the Bonnie plush suit in *Special Delivery*.

Appearances: *Special Delivery*

BLACK ICE FREDDY FROSTBEAR: A winter-themed animatronic skin for the Freddy Frostbear plush suit in *Special Delivery*.

Appearances: *Special Delivery*

BLIZZARD BALLOON BOY: A winter-themed animatronic skin for the Balloon Boy plush suit in *Special Delivery*.

Appearances: *Special Delivery*

THE BLOB: An amalgamation of various animatronics, made up of wire tentacles, animatronic parts, and glowing red eyes. Not much is known about the Blob, but it may have its origins in Ennard. It has the face of Funtime Freddy, but clearly also has parts from Chica, Bonnie, Mangle, Circus Baby, and the Puppet. Avoid its tentacles during the Burn it All Down Ending of *Security Breach*.

Appearances: *Security Breach*

THE BOBBIEDOTS: Three assistants who control the tech and security of an apartment in Fazplex Tower. First Generation are physical, while Second Generation are holograms. The Bobbiedots seem helpful but they also like to be in control. Gemini (also known as One) is responsible for entertainment systems. Olive (also known as Two) deals with news from the outside world. Rose (also known as Three) is in charge of healthy living.

Appearances: "Bobbiedots, Part 1," "Bobbiedots, Part 2"

BON-BON (BONNIE HAND PUPPET): An animatronic hand puppet with a Bonnie design that typically appears on the right arm of Funtime Freddy. He seems to have a calming effect on the Funtime Freddy animatronic. Bon-Bon has a female counterpart named Bonnet.

Appearances: *Sister Location, Ultimate Custom Night, Help Wanted*

BONNET: A pink animatronic hand puppet with a Bonnie design, seemingly built to go with Funtime Freddy. Bonnet first appears in the Private Room in *Sister Location*, but in *Help Wanted*, she appears alongside Funtime Freddy and Bonnet's male counterpart, Bon-Bon. Bonnet is one of the hidden/secret animatronics in *Ultimate Custom Night*.

Appearances: *Sister Location, Ultimate Custom Night, Help Wanted*

BONNIE: A bluish-purple animatronic rabbit with a red bow tie, plays guitar in the animatronic band. Typically approaches from the left, but it should be noted that Bonnie doesn't seem to abide by the laws of physics.

Appearances: *FNAF, FNAF2* (minigame/hallucinations), *FNAF3* (minigame), *FNAF4* (minigame), *Ultimate Custom Night, Help Wanted, Curse of Dreadbear, Special Delivery, The Silver Eyes, The Twisted Ones, The Fourth Closet*, "The New Kid," "Hide-and-Seek," "Sea Bonnies," "Find Player Two!," Stitchwraith Stingers, *Security Breach, FNAF* (movie), *Into the Pit* (game), *The Week Before, Secret of the Mimic*

BOULDER TOY BONNIE: A forest-themed animatronic skin for the Toy Bonnie plush suit in *Special Delivery*.

Appearances: *Special Delivery*

BROILER BABY: A heat wave-themed animatronic skin for the Circus Baby plush suit in *Special Delivery*.

Appearances: *Special Delivery*

BROW BOY: A humanoid animatronic who resembles Balloon Boy but has a purple-and-black-striped shirt, a prominent unibrow, enlarged fists, and wears an orange propeller with a black stem.

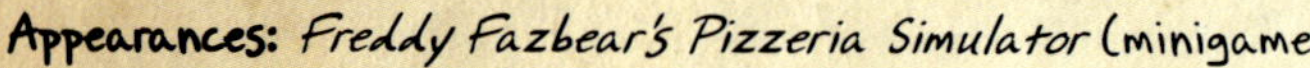

Appearances: *Freddy Fazbear's Pizzeria Simulator* (minigame)

CANDY CADET: A robot animatronic that will tell the player stories if play tested. Candy Cadet tells three stories, each about five things merging into one. He will tell pieces of another story as you provide coins to him in *RUIN*.

Appearances: *Pizzeria Simulator, Ultimate Custom Night* (deactivated), *RUIN, Help Wanted 2*

CAPTAIN FOXY: A fox animatronic dressed in a pirate coat and hat, with a model nearly identical to Foxy. Captain Foxy presides over Captain Foxy's Pirate Adventure (Pirate Ride), a classic dark ride in *Curse of Dreadbear.*

Appearances: *Curse of Dreadbear*

CATRINA TOY CHICA: A holiday-themed animatronic skin for the Toy Chica plush suit in *Special Delivery.*

Appearances: *Special Delivery*

CHARLIE: (Spoilers) A highly complex humanoid animatronic crafted by Henry, the original inventor of the animatronics, to fill the void left by the murder of his beloved daughter, Charlotte. It's stated that Charlie is actually four animatronics—each built to allow Charlie to grow up. Her "youngest" incarnation was the Ella doll, while her "oldest" was unfinished, completed by William Afton, and ultimately possessed by Elizabeth Afton.

Appearances: *The Silver Eyes, The Twisted Ones, The Fourth Closet*

CHICA: A yellow animatronic chicken who wears a bib that says LET'S EAT! Chica carries a plate with an anthropomorphic pink cupcake that seems to have a life of its own. Chica can often be found in the Kitchen in various games, and generally approaches players from the right. Chica was confirmed to be possessed by Susie in the story "Coming Home."

Appearances: *FNAF, FNAF2* (minigame/hallucinations), *FNAF3* (minigame), *FNAF4* (minigame), *Ultimate Custom Night, Help Wanted, Curse of Dreadbear, Special Delivery, The Silver Eyes, The Twisted Ones, The Fourth Closet,* "Coming Home," "The New Kid," "What We Found," "Pizza Kit," "Sea Bonnies," "Find Player Two!" *FNAF* (movie), *Into the Pit* (game), *Secret of the Mimic*

CHOCOLATE BONNIE:

A holiday-themed animatronic skin for the Bonnie plush suit in *Special Delivery.*

Appearances: *Special Delivery*

CIRCUS BABY (BABY): A humanoid animatronic and the mascot of Circus Baby's Pizza World. Circus Baby is possessed by the spirit of Elizabeth Afton, William Afton's daughter, who was snatched by the animatronic after being told to stay away from her. After the possession, Circus Baby's eyes turned green. Circus Baby assists in her father's plans, particularly in *The Fourth Closet.* In *Sister Location,* she orchestrates the escape of the animatronics from Circus Baby's Entertainment and Rental.

Appearances: *Sister Location, Ultimate Custom Night, Help Wanted, Special Delivery, The Fourth Closet,* "Dance with Me," *Security Breach, Pizzeria Simulator, Help Wanted 2*

CLOWN SPRINGTRAP: A circus-themed animatronic skin for the Springtrap plush suit in *Special Delivery*.

Appearances: *Special Delivery*

COILS THE BIRTHDAY CLOWN: A clown animatronic with a lanky body and coiled arms, dressed in a lemon-and-lime striped costume with bells. The animatronic seems to have some sort of awareness or safety features, since it tries to rescue Colton in "Jump for Tickets."

Appearances: "Jump for Tickets"

THE CURSE: An Aztec-themed animatronic skin for the Springtrap plush suit in *Special Delivery*.

Appearances: *Special Delivery*

DEE DEE: A humanoid animatronic with a similar design to BB and JJ. She complicates *Ultimate Custom Night* by triggering a whole new set of animatronics at random. She also seems to have her own arcade game (Dee Dee's Fishing Hole), as seen in "Jump for Tickets."

Appearances: *Ultimate Custom Night*, "Jump for Tickets" (referenced)

DELILAH THE MERMAID: Delilah is a mermaid animatronic in the Sea Life Mechaquarium at Freddy's Fantasy Water Park. Like the other animatronics at the water park, she is old and rundown with chips to her paintwork, exposed wiring, and faded hair.

Appearances: "Submechanophobia"

DOLLIE: This nurse is an animatronic rather than a suit. What's in her backpack??

Appearances: *Secret of the Mimic*

DREADBEAR (FRANKEN FREDDY): An animatronic Frankensteined with stitching and neck bolts in the likeness of Freddy Fazbear. His feet have three toes (matching the toy animatronics), while his hands have five fingers (matching the nightmare animatronics). Dreadbear appears as part of a research and development game, where players must program his brain.

Appearances: *Curse of Dreadbear*, *Help Wanted 2*

EASTER BONNIE: A holiday-themed animatronic skin for the Bonnie plush suit in *Special Delivery*.

Appearances: *Special Delivery*

EGG BABY: An animatronic featuring a data archive. It's key to unlocking some of the secrets in *Pizzeria Simulator*.

Appearances: *Pizzeria Simulator, Ultimate Custom Night*

EL CHIP: A beaver animatronic that wears a sombrero and plays a mandolin. El Chip is purchasable as an animatronic in *Pizzeria Simulator*, but appears in *Ultimate Custom Night* as the mascot for a restaurant, El Chip's Fiesta Buffet. In *Help Wanted*, he has his own branded tortilla chips.

Appearances: *Pizzeria Simulator, Ultimate Custom Night, Help Wanted* (referenced), Security Breach

ELEANOR: A humanoid animatronic resembling Circus Baby, found deactivated in a junkyard. Eleanor possesses a special heart-shaped pendant that seemingly allows her to change form at will, whether her own form or that of another.

Appearances: "1:35 A.M.," "To Be Beautiful," Stitchwraith Stingers, *Into the Pit* (minigame)

ELECTROBAB:

An electrified variation of the Bidybab, capable of draining power. Appears in the Private Room in *Sister Location*.

Appearances: *Sister Location*

ELEPHANT: This freaky fellow is somewhat familiar. Oh, that's right, we spied him in RUIN. Now he's here, and most probably spying on you!

Appearances: *RUIN, Secret of the Mimic*

ELLA: (Spoilers) A highly complex humanoid animatronic, the youngest incarnation meant to house Charlie's consciousness. After Charlie "grew out" of Ella's size, Henry reprogrammed her as a plaything for Charlie. She occupied a closet, and would exit it on a track to serve tea. It seems the doll was later mass-produced by Fazbear Entertainment as a "helper" doll with a variety of functions. The doll in "1:35 A.M." is later confirmed to contain Remnant.

Appearances: *The Silver Eyes, The Twisted Ones, The Fourth Closet*, "1:35 A.M.," Stitchwraith Stingers

ENDO-01 (BARE ENDO): A simple animatronic endoskeleton that appears rarely in *FNAF* and *Help Wanted*. In *Special Delivery*, Endo-Ø1 is referred to as "Bare Endo" and can be customized with different plush suits and CPUs.

Appearances: *FNAF, Help Wanted, Special Delivery*

ENDO-02: A sturdier animatronic endoskeleton, judging by its articulated joints, bulkier framing, and more complex electronics.

Appearances: *FNAF2, Help Wanted*

ENNARD: A terrifying amalgamation formed from the "scooped" *Sister Location* animatronics (Ballora, Bon-Bon, Circus Baby, Funtime Foxy, Funtime Freddy). Ennard does not wear a typical plush suit, instead entering the body of Michael Afton. After abandoning Michael, Ennard was mainly controlled by Circus Baby. When the other animatronics kicked Baby out, Ennard was split into Scrap Baby and Molten Freddy.

Appearances: *Sister Location, Ultimate Custom Night, Help Wanted*

FETCH: A dog animatronic programmed to sync up with the user's phone and retrieve whatever the user needs. The animatronic was the "Top Prize" at an abandoned Freddy Fazbear's Pizza location. It's noted that the animatronic looks as though it was created before smartphone technology.

Appearances: "Fetch," Stitchwraith Stingers

FIREWORK FREDDY: A holiday-themed animatronic skin for the Freddy Fazbear plush suit in *Special Delivery*.

Appearances: *Special Delivery*

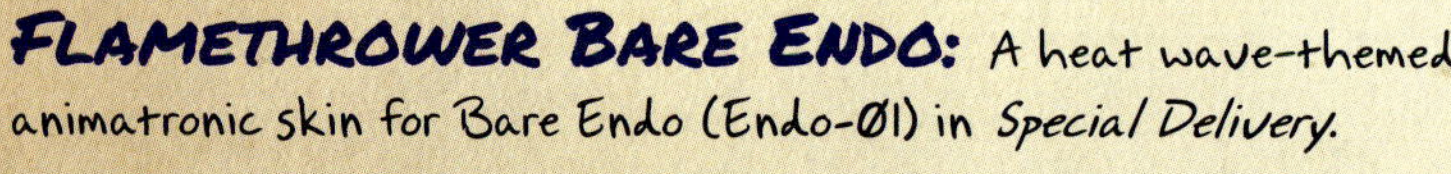

FLAMETHROWER BARE ENDO: A heat wave-themed animatronic skin for Bare Endo (Endo-Ø1) in *Special Delivery*.

Appearances: *Special Delivery*

FLAMING SPRINGTRAP: A heat wave-themed animatronic skin for the Springtrap plush suit in *Special Delivery*.

Appearances: *Special Delivery*

FOXY: An animatronic pirate fox with an eye patch over his right eye and a hook for his right hand. Foxy is housed on his own stage, Pirate Cove, separate from the other animatronics. The stage notes that Foxy is out of order, and his plush suit is damaged in places. He operates differently from the other animatronics, advancing in phases before attacking.

Appearances: *FNAF*, *FNAF2* (minigame), *FNAF3* (minigame), *FNAF4* (minigame), *Ultimate Custom Night*, *Help Wanted*, *Curse of Dreadbear*, *Special Delivery*, *The Silver Eyes*, *The Twisted Ones*, *The Fourth Closet*, "Lonely Freddy," "Step Closer," "The New Kid," "What We Found," "Sea Bonnies," Stitchwraith Stingers, *FNAF* (movie), *The Week Before*, *Secret of the Mimic*, *Into the Pit* (game)

FRANK THE DIVER: Frank is an animatronic that wears a brown, vintage scuba suit. It is a one of the features of the Sea Life Mechaquarium attraction at Freddy's Fantasy Water Park. It appears as though Frank can take the diving suit off at times, because Caden, the water park's tank cleaner, has reason to suspect that someone *else* may be wearing the diving suit for more sinister purposes.

Appearances: *"Submechanophobia"*

FREDBEAR: A yellow bear springlock animatronic with a purple bow tie and top hat, the first known animatronic Henry made, and the mascot of Fredbear's Family Diner. Fredbear is mentioned or shown in 8-bit from across several games, but only appears physically in *Ultimately Custom Night*. In *The Silver Eyes*, Henry is known to have worn the Fredbear suit.

Appearances: *FNAF2* (mention), *FNAF3* (minigame), *FNAF4* (plush, minigame), *Ultimate Custom Night*, *The Silver Eyes* (mention), "The New Kid"

FREDDLES: Small nightmare animatronics similar in design to Nightmare Freddy. Freddles sometimes hang off Nightmare Freddy, and other times sprout from the bed behind you in *FNAF4*. They flee from your flashlight, similar to plush animatronics.

Appearances: *FNAF4*, *Ultimate Custom Night*, *Curse of Dreadbear*, *Help Wanted VR*

FREDDY FAZBEAR: A light brown bear animatronic with a black bow tie and top hat, singer in the animatronic band, and the mascot of Freddy Fazbear's Pizza. When his face is enhanced, it reveals a handprint on his right eye and another across his lower jaw. His eyes change color from brown to blue when he appears outside the office door.

Appearances: *FNAF*, *FNAF2* (minigame/hallucinations), *FNAF3* (minigame), *FNAF4* (minigame), *Ultimate Custom Night*, *Help Wanted*, *Curse of Dreadbear*, *Special Delivery*, *The Silver Eyes*, *The Twisted Ones*, *The Fourth Closet*, "Into the Pit," "To Be Beautiful," "Lonely Freddy," "Out of Stock," "The New Kid," "Step Closer," "Blackbird," "Hide-and-Seek," "The Cliffs," "He Told Me Everything," "Gumdrop Angel," "What We Found," "Jump for Tickets," "Pizza Kit," "Friendly Face," "Sea Bonnies," "The Prankster," "Kids at Play," "Find Player Two!" *FNAF* (movie), *Into the Pit* (game), *The Week Before*, *Secret of the Mimic*

FROST PLUSHTRAP: A winter-themed animatronic skin for the Plushtrap plush suit in *Special Delivery*.

Appearances: *Special Delivery*

FUNTIME CHICA: A funtime animatronic with Chica's design. Funtime Chica debuted later than the other funtime animatronics; she first appears in *Pizzeria Simulator*. Funtime Chica loves to pose for the camera—she distracts the player with some of her poses in *Ultimate Custom Night*.

Appearances: *Pizzeria Simulator*, *Ultimate Custom Night*, *Help Wanted 2*

FUNTIME FOXY: A funtime animatronic with Foxy's design. Funtime Foxy is motion activated and lives in the Funtime Auditorium. The animatronic has several unique capabilities, as seen in its blueprint (see page 353).

Appearances: *Sister Location*, *Ultimate Custom Night*, *Help Wanted*, *The Fourth Closet*, *FNAF World*, *Help Wanted*

FUNTIME FREDDY: A funtime animatronic with Freddy Fazbear's design. Funtime Freddy contains a special arm that can be removed and replaced with a hand puppet animatronic like Bon-Bon or Bonnet. He has several other special features noted in his blueprint (see page 353), including a massive storage tank, as seen in "Count the Ways."

Appearances: *Sister Location*, *Ultimate Custom Night*, *Help Wanted*, *The Fourth Closet*, "Count the Ways," *Help Wanted 2*, *Special Delivery*

GLAMROCK BONNIE: Apparently, there was a Glamrock Bonnie in the Pizzaplex band, though—as it was later discovered—the animatronic was damaged and replaced by Monty. For a while, no one was quite sure where Glamrock Bonnie was—though it definitely wasn't at the deserted Bonnie Bowl! During the events of *RUIN*, Bonnie finally shows up, its Glamrock costume tattered beyond repair.

Appearances: *RUIN, Help Wanted 2*

GLAMROCK CHICA: Based on the original Chica from Freddy Fazbear's Pizza, Glamrock Chica wears pink makeup—including lipstick on her beak—and metallic green earrings, but no LET'S EAT! bib. She plays guitar in the Pizzaplex band and also fronts the Mazercise attraction, until her systems get corrupted. This animatronic is fitted with an unusual voice box that can stun other animatronics, or even open certain locked doors.

Appearances: *Security Breach, RUIN, Help Wanted 2*, "Under Construction," "Somniphobia" (poster), "Animatronic Apocalypse" (in-game character), "The Storyteller," "Bobbiedots, Part 2," "The Monty Within," "Bleeding Heart" (action figure)

GLAMROCK FREDDY: Built as the main mascot for Freddy Fazbear's Mega Pizzaplex, Glamrock Freddy has a brand-new '80s vibe. He has blue glamrock-inspired makeup, shoulder pads, and leg warmers, and he leads a band of Glamrock animatronics that entertains Pizzaplex visitors. Unlike older Freddy designs, this one can walk where it likes without relying on tracks, needs regular recharging, and cannot leave the Pizzaplex. He also has a large chest cavity that can conceal a birthday cake or piñata—or a human boy should one get lost in the Pizzaplex after hours.

Appearances: *Security Breach, RUIN, Help Wanted 2*, "Lally's Game" (photo), "Under Construction" (hologram), "Somniphobia," "Animatronic Apocalypse" (poster), "Bobbiedots, Part 1" (statue), "GGY," "The Storyteller," "Tiger Rock," "The Monty Within," "Bleeding Heart," "Alone Together," interactive novels

GLAMROCK MR. HIPPO: Glamrock Mr. Hippo plays the triangle in the Pizzaplex band, though he later takes over Monty's role as bassist. The hippo animatronic is glammed up with a star painted around one eye, and a cool flower on his chest.

Appearances: *Security Breach*

GLITCHTRAP (THE ANOMALY): A virus replicating within *The Freddy Fazbear Virtual Experience* game. The virus appears as a man inside a Spring Bonnie animatronic, starting out as green glitching code with purple eyes, and slowly becoming more solid. Glitchtrap seems capable of digital consciousness transference.

Appearances: *Help Wanted*, *Help Wanted 2*, *Curse of Dreadbear*, *Special Delivery*, "In the Flesh," "The Prankster"

GOLDEN FREDDY: A yellow bear animatronic that appears to be nonfunctioning. Golden Freddy appears at random in the office and causes the game to crash. Though it holds some resemblance to the Fredbear animatronic, its true origins are unknown.

Appearances: *FNAF*, *FNAF2*, *FNAF3*, *Ultimate Custom Night*, *Special Delivery*, *Into the Pit* (game)

GRIMM FOXY: A flaming animatronic that uses Foxy's design, but replaces his hook with a scythe.

Appearances: *Curse of Dreadbear*, *Security Breach*

HAPPS: This square-shaped cleaner bot is a Helpful Automated Pipe Protection Server (also known as HAPPS), who keeps an eye on the tube-maze Pizzaplex attraction, Freddy's Fortress. It rolls along on tread wheels, keeping the maze clean with its disinfectant dispenser, and using its calm, reassuring voice to help kids who get lost.

Appearances: "HAPPS"

HANDUNIT/TUTORIAL UNIT: A monitor at various Fazbear Entertainment locations that's designed to help guide workers through their nightly duties.

Appearances: *Sister Location*, *Pizzeria Simulator*, *Help Wanted*, *Curse of Dreadbear*, *Special Delivery*

HANK THE HAMMER: Hank the Hammer is the hammerhead shark at the water park.

Appearances: "Submechanophobia"

HAPPY FROG: A frog animatronic, part of the Mediocre Melodies. It's unconfirmed, but a child in the *FNAF3 Happiest Day* minigame appears to be wearing a Happy Frog mask. In *Ultimate Custom Night*, she climbs around in the overhead duct system, making her way toward the hoses that drop into your office. Use the lure to hold her in place, but she is immune to the effects of the heater.

Appearances: *Pizzeria Simulator, Ultimate Custom Night*

HEARTSICK BABY: A holiday-themed animatronic skin for the Circus Baby plush suit in *Special Delivery*.

Appearances: *Special Delivery*

HIGHSCORE TOY CHICA: An arcade-themed animatronic skin for the Toy Chica plush suit in *Special Delivery*.

Appearances: *Special Delivery*

JACKIE: This clown-faced menace is ripped from its box, but that doesn't stop it from being agile enough to clamber through the vents and across the walls and ceilings of the warehouse. Those orange eyes. Terrifying.

Appearances: *Secret of the Mimic*

JACK-O-BONNIE: A nightmare animatronic designed after Nightmare Bonnie, with a jack-o'-lantern twist.

Appearances: *FNAF4* (Halloween DLC), *Curse of Dreadbear, Special Delivery*

JACK-O-CHICA: A nightmare animatronic designed after Nightmare Chica, with a jack-o'-lantern twist.

Appearances: *FNAF4* (Halloween DLC), *Ultimate Custom Night, Curse of Dreadbear*

JJ (BALLOON GIRL): A humanoid animatronic similar to Balloon Boy, but with a different color scheme.

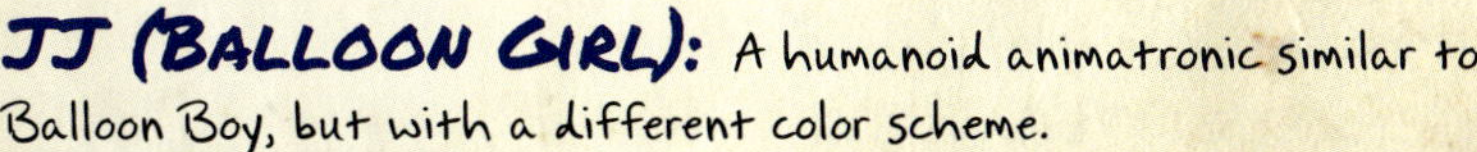

Appearances: *FNAF2, Ultimate Custom Night. FNAF World, Freddy Fazbear's Pizzeria Simulator* (minigame)

LALLY

A child-size animatronic, Lally was originally built to befriend lonely children. He featured in a Pizzaplex attraction named Lally's Game, where he played a pretend game of hide-and-seek. When the attraction was destroyed during renovations, Lally went missing.

Appearances: "Lally's Game"

LEFTY (L.E.F.T.E.): A rockstar animatronic with a bear design and microphone similar to Freddy, though his left eye seems to be broken. Lefty gets his name from an acronym—Lure Encapsulate Fuse Transport Extract—and has several special features according to his blueprint. Lefty is later shown to have the Puppet inside him.

Appearances: *Pizzeria Simulator, Ultimate Custom Night, Help Wanted 2*

LIBERTY CHICA: A holiday-themed animatronic skin for the Chica plush suit in *Special Delivery*.

Appearances: *Special Delivery*

LITTLE JOE: A humanoid figure that appears hanging from the wall in Circus Control. It's unconfirmed if Little Joe is a functioning animatronic, but he does appear in the Lally's Lollies advertisement in *Pizzeria Simulator*.

Appearances: *Sister Location, Pizzeria Simulator*

LOLBIT: A Funtime, fox-themed animatronic with purple, orange, and white coloring.

Appearances: *Sister Location, Ultimate Custom Night, Help Wanted*

LONELY FREDDY: A series of smaller Freddy animatronics dispatched to various Freddy Fazbear's Pizza locations. The animatronics use patented technology to befriend misfit children and ultimately swap bodies.

Appearances: "Lonely Freddy"

LUCKY BOY: A small, ten-inch figurine roughly matching the design of Balloon Boy. Instead of a sign saying BALLOONS!, Lucky Boy's sign says I'M A LUCKY BOY (and IT'S YOUR LUCKY DAY in some images). Lucky Boy can speak and give advice. He's found on the street, near a dumpster.

Appearances: "Sergio's Lucky Day"

MAC THE MUSCLE: The largest of the three shark animatronics in the Sea Life Mechaquarium at Freddy's Fantasy Water Park, is named Mac the Muscle. Tank cleaner Caden feels uneasy when Mac gets too close.

Appearances: "Submechanophobia"

MAGICIAN: A humanoid figure that appears on the dashboard in Circus Control. It's unconfirmed if Magician is just a toy or a functioning animatronic.

Appearances: *Sister Location*

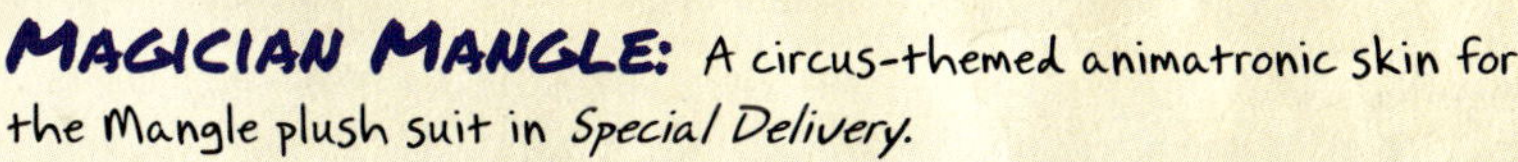

MAGICIAN MANGLE: A circus-themed animatronic skin for the Mangle plush suit in *Special Delivery*.

Appearances: *Special Delivery*

MANGLE: He was previously a Foxy animatronic, but now she's an amalgamation of various animatronics—part of a "take apart, put back together" attraction in Kid's Cove. Mangle features in his own game, *Build-A-Mangle*, in *Curse of Dreadbear*, in which players can create their own Mangle from various animatronic parts.

Appearances: *FNAF2, FNAF3, FNAF4, Ultimate Custom Night, Help Wanted, Help Wanted 2, Curse of Dreadbear, Special Delivery, The Fourth Closet, Security Breach*

MARCO AND POLO THE SERPENTS: This pair of mechanical serpent animatronics can be found at Freddy's Fantasy Water Park. They swim in the waterpark's main attraction, Freddy's Sea Life Mechaquarium. Park employee Roy names them Marco (the purple one) and Polo (the pink one) because they are known for hiding within the Mechaquarium.

Appearances: "Submechanophobia"

MELTED CHOCOLATE BONNIE: A holiday-themed animatronic skin for the Bonnie plush suit in *Special Delivery*.

Appearances: *Special Delivery*

THE MIMIC: The Mimic is an unusual animatronic, which often imitates others by entering different suits. Seen without such a disguise, it looks like a primitive, unusually tall endoskeleton, put together from a haphazard mix of wires, gears, and other machinery. Its face was built around two large doll's eyes, and later sculpted and altered to look more "real." Originally, the Mimic was created without legs, as a companion bot for a young boy named David Murray, whose father, Edwin, worked for Fazbear Entertainment. Programmed to copy the actions of those it sees, the Mimic soon learned more disturbing behavior after it witnessed anguish and violence.

Appearances: *Security Breach, RUIN, Help Wanted 2, Tales from the Pizzaplex* series Epilogues, "The Storyteller," "GGY" (referenced), "Nexie," "The Mimic," "Tiger Rock," *Secret of the Mimic*

MINIREENAS: Small, puppetlike dolls with tutus and white face masks. Minireenas typically accompany Ballora, and are stored with her in the Ballora Gallery. They're capable of speech and of organizing to achieve their goals, as seen in "Room for One More."

Appearances: *Sister Location, Ultimate Custom Night, Help Wanted, Help Wanted 2, Special Delivery*, "Room for One More"

MOLTEN FREDDY: A crumbling amalgamation of animatronics (Ballora, Bon-Bon, Funtime Foxy, Funtime Freddy) formed after Circus Baby was ejected from Ennard. Eyeballs from the various animatronics can be seen poking out at random.

Appearances: *Pizzeria Simulator, Ultimate Custom Night*

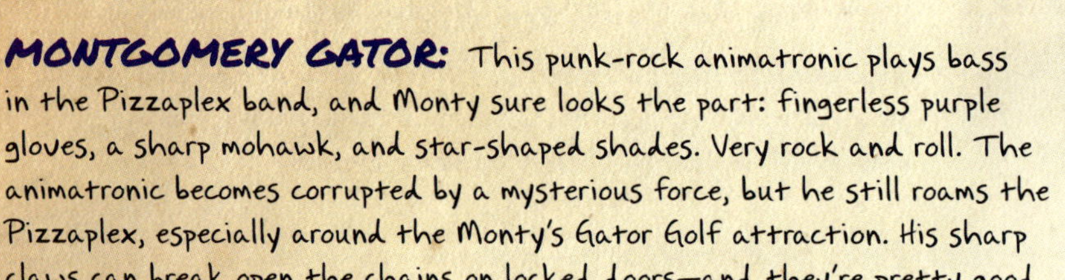

MONTGOMERY GATOR: This punk-rock animatronic plays bass in the Pizzaplex band, and Monty sure looks the part: fingerless purple gloves, a sharp mohawk, and star-shaped shades. Very rock and roll. The animatronic becomes corrupted by a mysterious force, but he still roams the Pizzaplex, especially around the Monty's Gator Golf attraction. His sharp claws can break open the chains on locked doors—and they're pretty good at picking the strings on the bass guitar, too!

Appearances: *Security Breach, RUIN, Help Wanted 2*, "Under Construction," "Somniphobia" (poster), "GGY," "The Storyteller," "Bobbiedots, Part 2" (hologram), "The Monty Within," "Bleeding Heart" (action figure), *Secret of the Mimic, VIP, Escape the Pizzaplex*

MR. ALLIGATOR: We never knew there was a banjo-playing alligator in the Mediocre Melodies. Makes you wonder what happened to him . . .

Appearances: *Secret of the Mimic*

MR. CUPCAKE: An anthropomorphic cupcake animatronic, usually accompanied by Chica. He has pink frosting, two large yellow eyes, and a yellow-striped birthday candle.

Appearances: *FNAF, FNAF2, FNAF3, Sister Location, Ultimate Custom Night, Help Wanted, Help Wanted 2, Special Delivery, Security Breach, Secret of the Mimic, FNAF* (movie)

MR. HAPPY FROG: This member of the Mediocre Melodies might have been in the original lineup, but he didn't make it much further. He seems happy playing the xylophone, though!

Appearances: *Secret of the Mimic*

MR. HIPPO: A hippo animatronic, part of the Mediocre Melodies. Mr. Hippo is quite long-winded; he loves to talk about his good friend, Orville Elephant. It's unconfirmed, but a child in the *FNAF3 Happiest Day* minigame appears to be wearing a Mr. Hippo mask.

Appearances: *Pizzeria Simulator, Ultimate Custom Night, Security Breach*

MUSIC MAN: A sound-sensitive animatronic that appears to be a spider in the same family as the funtime animatronics. Music Man will smash his cymbals together when agitated and will attack in *Ultimate Custom Night* if the excess volume does not cease quickly enough.

Appearances: *Pizzeria Simulator, Ultimate Custom Night*

NEDD BEAR: A bear animatronic, part of the Mediocre Melodies. In *Pizzeria Simulator*, he has an electrical power source box that is needed to activate him.

Appearances: *Pizzeria Simulator, Ultimate Custom Night, Security Breach*

NEXIE: A doll-like customized animatronic, Nexie didn't come out quite as her owner planned. Astrid wanted a cute Buddytronic like her friends had, but due to a glitch in the Pizzaplex's systems, the companion doll was produced with an asymmetrical face and disproportionate body. Nexie started out as an attentive companion, though she becomes rather obsessed with her looks.

Appearances: "Nexie," "Tiger Rock"

NIGHTMARE: A nightmare animatronic with swapped Fredbear coloring (black fur, yellow bow tie/top hat).

Appearances: *FNAF4, Ultimate Custom Night, Help Wanted.*

NIGHTMARE BALLOON BOY (NIGHTMARE BB):
A nightmare animatronic with a Balloon Boy design; he's notably missing his balloon and sign, and possesses fingers. He pauses in the light, per his minigame *Fun with Balloon Boy.*

Appearances: *FNAF4* (Halloween DLC), *Ultimate Custom Night, Help Wanted, Curse of Dreadbear, Security Breach*

NIGHTMARE BONNIE: A nightmare animatronic with a Bonnie design.

Appearances: *FNAF4, Ultimate Custom Night, Help Wanted, Curse of Dreadbear*

NIGHTMARE CHICA:
A nightmare animatronic with a Chica design. Notably, Chica's cupcake can enter the bedroom and attack players there.

Appearances: *FNAF4, Ultimate Custom Night, Help Wanted, Curse of Dreadbear*

NIGHTMARE ENDO: A bare endoskeleton outfitted for the nightmare animatronics.

Appearances: *Help Wanted*

NIGHTMARE FOXY: A nightmare animatronic with a Foxy design, notably missing his eye patch. In lieu of the Pirate Cove stage, Nightmare Foxy cycles through various poses via the bedroom closet.

Appearances: *FNAF4*, *Ultimate Custom Night*, *Curse of Dreadbear*

NIGHTMARE FREDBEAR: A nightmare animatronic with a Fredbear design; notably has a large slit across his stomach and bloodstained teeth. You can hear his now-infamous laughter as he approaches.

Appearances: *FNAF4*, *Ultimate Custom Night*, *Help Wanted*, *Security Breach*

NIGHTMARE FREDDY: A nightmare animatronic with a Freddy Fazbear design; three miniature animatronics, called "Freddles," are attached to his body. Prolonged exposure to a flashlight's light will get rid of the Freddles.

Appearances: *FNAF4*, *Ultimate Custom Night*, *Curse of Dreadbear*

NIGHTMARE MANGLE: A nightmare animatronic with a Mangle design; notably possesses a bulkier endoskeleton with three legs.

Appearances: *FNAF4* (Halloween DLC), *Ultimate Custom Night*

NIGHTMARIONNE: A nightmare animatronic with a Puppet design. The Puppet's music box plays while Nightmarionne is active, but there is nothing mechanical (such as keeping the box wound) that can prevent its attack.

Appearances: *FNAF 4* (Halloween DLC), *Ultimate Custom Night*, *Help Wanted*, *RUIN*

OLD MAN CONSEQUENCES: An 8-bit sprite who sits fishing at a pond and urges players to rest and avoid digging too deep.

Appearances: *Ultimate Custom Night, Into the Pit* (game), *Security Breach, Help Wanted 2*

ORVILLE ELEPHANT: An elephant magician animatronic, part of the Mediocre Melodies. Orville is good friends with Mr. Hippo. It's unconfirmed, but a child in the *FNAF3 Happiest Day* minigame appears to be wearing an Orville Elephant mask.

Appearances: *Pizzeria Simulator, Ultimate Custom Night*

PHANTOM BALLOON BOY: A phantom animatronic, hallucinated with a Balloon Boy design; notably missing his balloon and sign.

Appearances: *FNAF3, Ultimate Custom Night, Help Wanted*

PHANTOM CHICA: A phantom animatronic, hallucinated with a Chica design. Phantom Chica does not carry a cupcake.

Appearances: *FNAF3, Ultimate Custom Night*

PHANTOM FOXY: A phantom animatronic, hallucinated with a Foxy design.

Appearances: *FNAF3, Help Wanted*

PHANTOM FREDDY: A phantom animatronic, hallucinated with a Freddy design.

Appearances: *FNAF3, Ultimate Custom Night, Help Wanted*

PHANTOM MANGLE: A phantom animatronic, hallucinated with a Mangle design.

Appearances: *FNAF3, Ultimate Custom Night, Help Wanted*

PHANTOM PUPPET: A phantom animatronic, hallucinated with a Puppet design.

Appearances: *FNAF3*

PHONE GUY: A former night guard at Freddy Fazbear's Pizza, responsible for training the new night guard. His lessons can be heard via the answering machine and can sometimes be a challenging distraction for players.

Appearances: *FNAF*, *FNAF2*, *FNAF3*, *Ultimate Custom Night*, *Help Wanted*, *The Week Before*, *Into the Pit*

PIGPATCH: A pig animatronic that plays the banjo, part of the Mediocre Melodies. It's unconfirmed, but a child in the *FNAF3 Happiest Day* minigame appears to be wearing a Pigpatch mask.

Appearances: *Pizzeria Simulator*, *Ultimate Custom Night*, "The Puppet Carver," *FNAF World*, *Help Wanted 2*

PLUSHBABIES: Small plush doll animatronics, made with Circus Baby's design. The classic PlushBaby comes in red, yellow, and blue dress colors. There's also a variation that's modeled after Scrap Baby. A third variation, the Plushkin, dons a BB, Chica, Foxy, or Freddy mask. Much like other plush animatronics, they flee from light.

Appearances: *Help Wanted*, *Help Wanted 2*, *Curse of Dreadbear*, *RUIN*

PLUSHTRAP: A smaller plush animatronic, made with Springtrap's design. Like other plush animatronics, it flees or freezes in light. A variation of Plushtrap, called the Plushtrap Chaser, was mass-produced and distributed by Fazbear Entertainment.

Appearances: *FNAF4*, *Ultimate Custom Night*, *Help Wanted*, *Special Delivery*, "Out of Stock," *Security Breach*

THE PUPPET (THE MARIONETTE): A puppet animatronic with a lanky black body, white stripes on his arms and legs, and a white face with painted cheeks and lips. The Puppet usually stays inside its gift box so long as its music box is wound. Henry's daughter, Charlotte, is confirmed to possess the Puppet. After her death, she helped William Afton's murder victims find new life—and a chance for revenge—in possessing the other animatronics.

Appearances: *FNAF2, FNAF3, Pizzeria Simulator, Ultimate Custom Night, Help Wanted, Help Wanted 2, Security Breach*

RADIOACTIVE FOXY: A wasteland-themed animatronic skin for the Foxy plush suit in *Special Delivery*.

Appearances: *Special Delivery*

FREDDY'S FUN FACT

The music box song, "My Grandfather's Clock," is about a clock that worked for ninety years, responding to a man's joys and sorrows, until it rang an alarm on his deathbed and stopped working when he died.

RALPHO: A rabbit mascot costume, or possibly animatronic, owned by Camp Etenia. Ralpho conducts "bunny calls" as a prank to unsuspecting campers between the hours of 5:00 a.m. and 6:00 a.m. Reportedly, he bursts into the cabin screaming, crashing his cymbals, and spinning his head.

Appearances: "Bunny Call"

RINGMASTER FOXY: A circus-themed animatronic skin for the Foxy plush suit in *Special Delivery*.

Appearances: *Special Delivery*

ROCKSTAR BONNIE: A rockstar animatronic with a Bonnie design.

Appearances: *Pizzeria Simulator, Ultimate Custom Night*

ROCKSTAR CHICA: A rockstar animatronic with a Chica design. Rockstar Chica is the only incarnation of Chica to not have a cupcake. Instead she holds maracas, and her bib reads LET'S ROCK!

Appearances: *Pizzeria Simulator, Ultimate Custom Night*

ROCKSTAR FOXY: A rockstar animatronic with a Foxy design. Rockstar Foxy has a peg leg, plays the accordion, and has a companion parrot that sits on his left shoulder.

Appearances: *Pizzeria Simulator, Ultimate Custom Night, Security Breach, Help Wanted 2*

ROCKSTAR FREDDY: A rockstar animatronic with a Freddy design.

Appearances: *Pizzeria Simulator, Ultimate Custom Night, Security Breach, Help Wanted 2*

ROXANNE WOLF: Roxanne "Roxy" Wolf is a wolf animatronic who makes her first proper *FNAF* appearance in *Security Breach*, as a keytar-playing member of the Glamrock Animatronics band, entertaining visitors at the Pizzaplex. After being corrupted, she becomes cruel and sadistic, roaming the dark arcades of the Pizzaplex. Roxy hosts the Roxy's Raceway attraction, and appears to be very self-centered. She becomes unable to look in the mirror, however, after losing her eyes. In *RUIN*, Roxy becomes uncorrupted once more and forms an alliance with Cassie.

Appearances: *Security Breach, RUIN, Help Wanted 2*, "Somniphobia," "Animatronic Apocalypse" (in-game character), "Bobbiedots, Part 1," "The Storyteller," "Bobbiedots, Part 2" (poster), "The Monty Within," "Bleeding Heart," *VIP, Escape the Pizzaplex*

RWQFSFASXC (SHADOW BONNIE): A shadow version of Toy Bonnie. Similar to Golden Freddy, doesn't appear to follow normal laws of physics, appearing and disappearing at will, phasing through various minigames in *FNAF3*, etc. In *Special Delivery*, Shadow Bonnie appears when the player collects too much dark Remnant.

Appearances: *FNAF2, FNAF3* (minigame), *Ultimate Custom Night, Curse of Dreadbear* (Easter egg), *Special Delivery, Security Breach, Fazbear Frights: Blackbird*

SCORCHING CHICA: A heat wave-themed animatronic skin for the Chica plush suit in *Special Delivery*.

Appearances: *Special Delivery*

SCRAP BABY: A humanoid animatronic, re-formed in the likeness of Circus Baby after she was ejected from Ennard.

Appearances: *Pizzeria Simulator, Ultimate Custom Night, Help Wanted 2, Security Breach*

SCRAPTRAP: A tattered springlock animatronic, a more worn version of Springtrap. Scraptrap sports a severed forearm, no ears, and some rotting, human-looking parts beneath his fur.

Appearances: *Pizzeria Simulator, Ultimate Custom Night*

SECURITY PUPPET: A puppet animatronic with security functions. Play-testing the Security Puppet in *Pizzeria Simulator* takes players to a minigame with lore implications for the Puppet.

Appearances: *Pizzeria Simulator, Ultimate Custom Night*

SERPENT MANGLE: An Aztec-themed animatronic skin for the Mangle plush suit in *Special Delivery*.

Appearances: *Special Delivery*

SHADOW FREDDY: A shadow bear animatronic. Similar to RWQFSFASXC, Shadow Freddy moves mysteriously, seemingly appearing/disappearing at random. Shadow Freddy also appears in 8-bit form in several minigames, guiding players through all the night-end minigames in *FNAF3*.

Appearances: *FNAF2, FNAF3, Pizzeria Simulator*

IMAGE NOT FOUND

SHADOW MANGLE (BLACKLIGHT MANGLE): A shadow animatronic that looks similar to Mangle, but with different colored eyes. Attacks alongside Mangle in the blacklight level of *Vent Repair: Mangle*.

Appearances: *Help Wanted*

SHAMROCK FREDDY: A holiday-themed animatronic skin for the Freddy Fazbear plush suit in *Special Delivery*.

Appearances: *Special Delivery*

SPRING BONNIE: A yellow rabbit springlock animatronic, one of the first created by Henry. Spring Bonnie was often worn by William Afton, who prided himself on effortlessly performing in the suit. He used the costume to gain the trust of, and ultimately murder, numerous children.

Appearances: *FNAF3* (minigame), *FNAF4* (minigame), *Pizzeria Simulator*, *Ultimate Custom Night* (Easter egg), *The Silver Eyes*, *Into the Pit* (game), *Secret of the Mimic*

SPRINGTRAP: A tarnished Spring Bonnie springlock animatronic, fused with the corpse of William Afton, who continues to possess the animatronic.

Appearances: *FNAF3*, *Sister Location* (secret ending), *Ultimate Custom Night*, *Help Wanted*, *Curse of Dreadbear*, *Special Delivery*, *The Silver Eyes*, *The Twisted Ones*, *The Fourth Closet*, "In the Flesh," Stitchwraith Stingers

STANLEY: A white unicorn animatronic created by Henry for Charlie. Stanley travels on a track around Charlie's room.

Appearances: *The Silver Eyes*, *The Twisted Ones*, *The Fourth Closet*

STITCHWRAITH: An animatronic created by Dr. Phineas Taggart in his studies of emotion. It was formed from an endoskeleton, the doll from "The Real Jake," and the battery pack from the Fetch animatronic.

Appearances: Stitchwraith Stingers

SUN/MOON: This jester-like animatronic has a split personality. By day (or under artificial lighting), it is known as Sun, and it works as the Daycare Attendant at Superstar Daycare in the Mega Pizzaplex. Its bright, yellow colors and sun-themed clothing reflect its cheerful personality—helpful, keen to tidy up, and always ready to have fun with the kids under its care. However, if the lights go out, the animatronic turns into Moon, a much darker version. Moon also likes to clean up messes, but in a much more disturbing way, and it also likes to taunt and chase its prey through the dark Pizzaplex.

Appearances: *Security Breach*, *Help Wanted 2*, "Somniphobia," *RUIN*, *Secret of the Mimic*

SWAMP BALLOON BOY: A forest-themed animatronic skin for the Balloon Boy plush suit in *Special Delivery*.

Appearances: *Special Delivery*

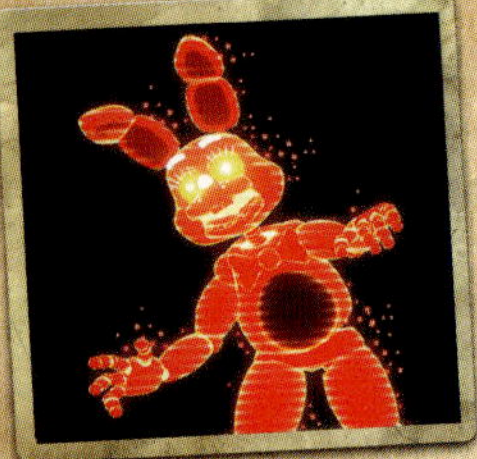

SYSTEM ERROR TOY BONNIE: An arcade-themed animatronic skin for the Toy Bonnie plush suit in *Special Delivery*.

Appearances: *Special Delivery*

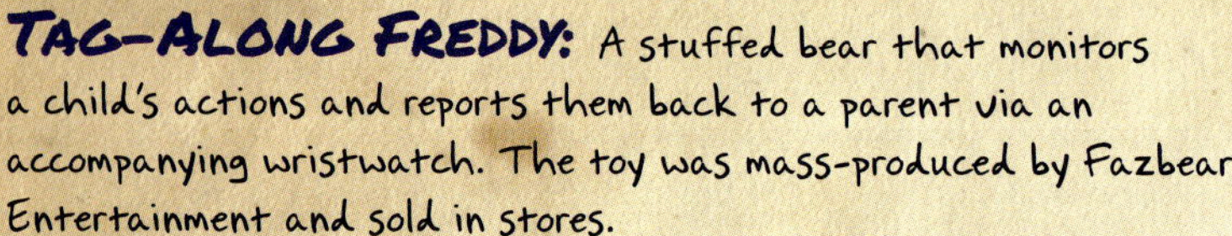

TAG-ALONG FREDDY: A stuffed bear that monitors a child's actions and reports them back to a parent via an accompanying wristwatch. The toy was mass-produced by Fazbear Entertainment and sold in stores.

Appearances: "The Cliffs"

THEODORE: A small purple rabbit animatronic created by Henry for Charlie. It could wave, tilt its head, and repeat a recording from Henry saying, "I love you, Charlie." Charlie later takes Theodore apart for her robotics project.

Appearances: *The Silver Eyes, The Twisted Ones, The Fourth Closet*

TIGER ROCK: Tiger Rock is a white tiger animatronic with black stripes, silver teeth, one green eye, and one blue eye. It accompanies Kai within his AR booth, eventually hunting him.

Appearances: "The Storyteller" (mention of head), "Tiger Rock"

TOXIC SPRINGTRAP: A wasteland-themed animatronic skin for the Springtrap plush suit in *Special Delivery*.

Appearances: *Special Delivery*

TOY BONNIE: A toy animatronic with a Bonnie design, featuring glossy green eyes and buck teeth.

Appearances: *FNAF2, FNAF3, FNAF4* (minigame), *Ultimate Custom Night, Help Wanted, Special Delivery, Security Breach, Help Wanted 2*

TOY CHICA: A toy animatronic with a Chica design; her bib reads LET'S PARTY! After leaving the Show Stage in *FNAF2*, her eyes and bill are missing. Toy Chica stars in *Toy Chica: The High School Years* in *Ultimate Custom Night*, where she romantically pursues various animatronics.

Appearances: *FNAF2*, *FNAF3*, *FNAF4* (minigame), *Ultimate Custom Night*, *Help Wanted*, *Special Delivery*, *Security Breach*, *Help Wanted 2*

TOY FREDDY: A toy animatronic with a Freddy design. In *Ultimate Custom Night*, he plays his own version of *FNAF*, *Five Nights with Mr. Hugs*.

Appearances: *FNAF2*, *FNAF3*, *FNAF4* (minigame), *Ultimate Custom Night*, *Help Wanted*, *Special Delivery*, *Security Breach*, *Help Wanted 2*

TRASH AND THE GANG: The cheapest series of "animatronics" to purchase in *Pizzeria Simulator*, this set is made up of Bucket Bob, Mr. Can-Do, Mr. Hugs, No. 1 Crate, and Pan Stan. In *Pizzeria Simulator*, Pan Stan can be seen sitting when a salvage animatronic entered the pizzeria through other means. In *Ultimate Custom Night*, Mr. Hugs plays a *FNAF*-like game with Toy Freddy.

Appearances: *Pizzeria Simulator*, *Ultimate Custom Night*, *Into the Pit*, *Help Wanted 2*, *Secret of the Mimic*

TWISTED BONNIE: A twisted animatronic with Bonnie's design; illusion disc technology makes him appear biological, with boils, spikes, and multiple rows of teeth.

Appearances: *The Twisted Ones*

TWISTED CHICA: A twisted animatronic with Chica's design; illusion disc technology makes her appear biological, with warts and a second mouth in her stomach. Although Twisted Chica was never seen in the book series, her existence is implied, and she appears in other media.

Appearances: *The Twisted Ones* (implied)

TWISTED FOXY: A twisted animatronic with Foxy's design; illusion disc technology makes him appear biological, with rotting flesh, barnacle-like growths, and too many teeth.

Appearances: *The Twisted Ones*

TWISTED FREDDY: A twisted animatronic with Freddy's design; illusion disc technology makes him appear biological, with lengthy talons and bubbling blisters eating his face.

Appearances: *The Twisted Ones*

TWISTED WOLF: A twisted animatronic of a gray wolf. A long mane runs over its back, turning into spikes when illusion disc technology is activated. Though Twisted Wolf debuted without a name, there is speculation that it could be a twisted version of Roxanne Wolf.

Appearances: *Pizzeria Simulator* (Easter egg), *Ultimate Custom Night* (Easter egg), *The Twisted Ones*

VR TOY FREDDY: An arcade-themed animatronic skin for the Toy Freddy plush suit in *Special Delivery*.

Appearances: *Special Delivery*

WITHERED BONNIE: A withered animatronic with a Bonnie design, notably missing his face.

Appearances: *FNAF2*, *Ultimate Custom Night*, *Help Wanted*, *Help Wanted 2*

WITHERED CHICA: A withered animatronic with a Chica design, notably missing her arms and cupcake. Her design—less rounded frame, all-yellow legs, and three toes—also differs substantially from *FNAF*'s Chica.

Appearances: *FNAF2*, *Ultimate Custom Night*, *Help Wanted*

WITHERED FOXY: A withered animatronic with a Foxy design.

Appearances: *FNAF2*, *Help Wanted*

WITHERED FREDDY: A withered animatronic with a Freddy design.

Appearances: *FNAF2, Help Wanted*

WITHERED GOLDEN FREDDY: A withered animatronic with a Golden Freddy design.

Appearances: *FNAF2, Ultimate Custom Night*

WOODLAND TOY FREDDY: A forest-themed animatronic skin for the Toy Freddy plush suit in *Special Delivery*.

Appearances: *Special Delivery*

XOR (SHADOW DEE DEE): A shadow animatronic of Dee Dee, who appears to complicate your night in *Ultimate Custom Night*, and is also a regular visitor of 5Ø/2Ø mode.

Appearances: *Ultimate Custom Night*

YARG FOXY: A pirate-themed animatronic with a Foxy design. This animatronic appears to really sell the pirate theme with a hook, peg leg, and eye patch.

Appearances: "Lonely Freddy"

YENNDO: A burly endoskeleton capable of supporting the funtime animatronics.

Appearances: *Sister Location*

ZEUS THE SEA DRAGON: The largest animatronic in the Sea Life Mechaquarium at Freddy's Fantasy Water Park, Zeus is a green reptilian sea dragon, with metal spikes along its back and tail. It has wings, claws, and sharp teeth, though many of them are broken, and its body is rusted and almost falling apart after years of neglect. Zeus is the main attraction of the Mechaquarium, and it is also the animatronic who is most helpful to the tank cleaner, Caden, as he unravels a decades-old mystery that begins when he finds a child's shoe inside Zeus's mouth!

Appearances: "Submechanophobia"